BASINS OF SILVER

The Story of Silverton, Colorado's Las Animas Mining District

By Eric Twitty

WESTERN REFLECTIONS PUBLISHING COMPANY®

Lake City, CO

ISBN 978-1-932738-83-4

Library of Congress Control Number: 2007936892

Cover and book design: Laurie Goralka Design
Cover photo: Laurie Casselberry
Cover inset photo: The Silver Lake mine, one of Silverton's most famous and productive. Courtesy: San Juan County Historical Society
Back cover photo: Some of the most important dignitaries at the Silver Lake Mine — the cook and his staff — pose in front of mine workers in this mid-1890s photograph. Source: Denver Public Library, Western History Collection, X 60864.

First Edition

Printed in the United States

Western Reflections Publishing Company®
P.O. Box 1149, 951 N. Highway 149
Lake City, CO 81235
1-800-993-4490
publisher@westernreflectionspublishing.com
www.westernreflectionspublishing.com

DEDICATION

This book is dedicated to Amy, who grew tired of hearing about mines, mines, and more mines. Thanks for graciously giving me the time to write.

ACKNOWLEDGEMENTS

I wish to thank Jon Horn, expert in Native American studies and early electrical technology, for reading the manuscript and saving me from embarrassing myself. I also express gratitude to miner and Silverton historian Zeke Zanoni for offering important comments. The entire book as I envisioned it would not be possible without the cooperation of Kristie Arrington, Bureau of Land Management archaeologist, and the Bureau of Land Management in general. The BLM allowed me to use archaeological information that was key in conveying the true histories of the people and mines of the Las Animas Mining District. Thanks also to Bob Sorgenfrei, archivist at the Colorado School of Mines, for providing endless material, and to Beth Zecca, image expert at the School of Mines, for scanning images.

TABLE OF CONTENTS

AUTHOR ERIC TWITTY became interested in mining history at the early age of seven. Since that time he has documented and assessed the important mines and mining districts for more than a decade. He is owner of Mountain States Historical in Boulder, Colorado, which is a firm specializing in mining sites and history. Twitty also wrote *Blown to Bits in the Mine – A History of Mining and Explosives in the United States* and *Riches to Rust – A Guide to Mining in the Old West*, both of which are published by Western Reflections Publishing Co. Twitty earned his master's degree in American History, with an emphasis in mining, and started his mining consulting business soon thereafter.

CHAPTER 1

Introduction

IRONICALLY, THE LAS ANIMAS MINING DISTRICT'S long and lustful affair with silver began not among the San Juan Mountains, nor with silver, but instead amid the placer gold fields hundreds of miles to the northeast. In 1858, two parties of prospectors discovered placer gold on the plains east of the Rocky Mountains at the site of today's Denver, and the find incited the famed Pikes Peak Gold Rush. By 1859, wealth seekers penetrated the Front Range mountains and busily extracted the precious metal throughout today's Boulder, Gilpin, and Clear Creek Counties. Each new strike enticed prospectors deeper into the mountains, where they crossed over ranges and valleys and found additional deposits in South Park, the upper Blue River drainage at today's Breckenridge, and California Gulch near Leadville. Through 1859 and 1860, the various discoveries drew many more prospectors than there was gold, forcing the overflow population to either optimistically wander or seek employment from organized placer companies.

One prospector named Charles Baker was among the overflow population. The exact year when Baker arrived in the mountains remains unknown, although he was apparently tardy for most of the rushes. After investigating several centers of placer mining only to find the best ground claimed, he joined the rush to California Gulch

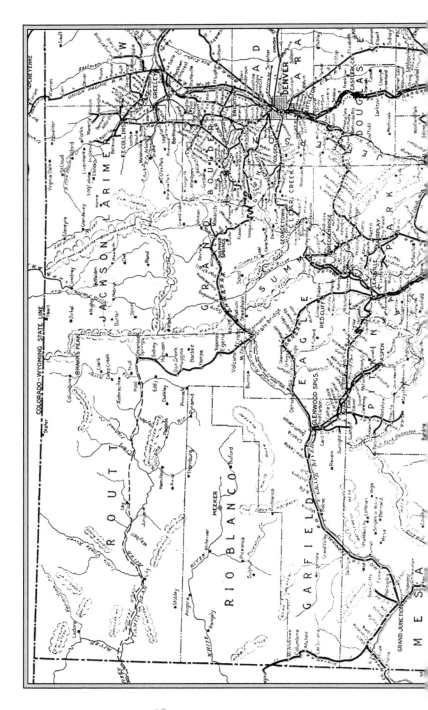

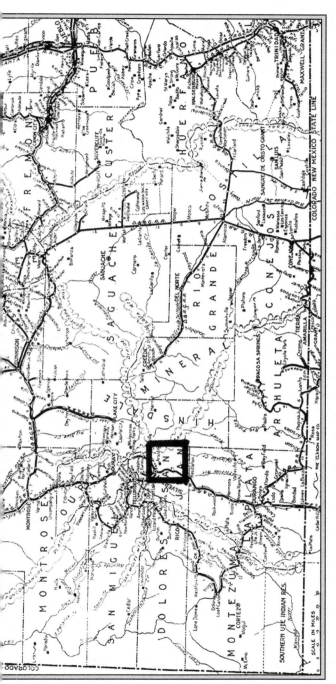

The heavy black square in the lower right portion of this 1911 map of Colorado illustrates where the Las Animas Mining District and Silverton are located. Source: Engineering & Mining Journal 1/7/11, p52.

above present-day Leadville and found the same set of conditions. Still retaining hope, but in need of money, in 1860 Baker joined a crew of miners working in the gulch for S.B. Kellogg & Company.[1]

Familiar with the geographic distribution of gold fields in Colorado as they were known at that time, Baker speculated that California Gulch was merely a point on a lengthy mineral belt that continued southwest into uncharted lands. Baker convinced Kellogg to fund an expedition intended to prove his hypothesis, and to be the first to open new placer deposits and profit from the discoveries. During the summer, the Baker party crossed west into the Gunnison Basin and descended the Gunnison River, sampling gravel along the way. Repeated failures to find even traces of gold proved to the party that the basin was bereft of riches, leaving them with the choice of either turning north or veering southwest toward the San Juan Mountains. Probably intent on proving the mineral belt hypothesis, the party decided on the southwesterly course and sought a negotiable port of entry into the mountains, which it found along the Lake Fork of the Gunnison River. When the Baker party arrived at Lake San Cristobal, a fantastic mountain-locked body of snowmelt, members felt some vindication when they finally found placer gold. While testing clearly demonstrated the presence of the metal, the find was uneconomical and soured some of the party's members, who turned back. The gold, however, was enough to tantalize Baker and six or seven other prospectors into further exploration, and they crossed west over Cinnamon Pass into the Animas River drainage. As the summer passed its zenith, Baker and partners discovered what they thought were bonanza deposits at the mouths of Cunningham and Arrastra Gulches, and near the later townsite of Eureka, probably named after the initial placer strike. When word of the discoveries trickled through the established gold fields to the east, groups of daring prospectors packed their belongings and began the dangerous journey to join the Baker party.

In keeping with gold rush behavior, these early prospectors limited their investigations to placer gold and inadvertently overlooked dozens of rich silver and gold veins in bedrock waiting for discovery and almost within sight around them. It was the hardrock ore in these veins, won only through sheer determination and ingenuity, and not the placer gold, that later made the region legendary among the greater mining industry. Known as the Las Animas Mining District by the 1870s, the region laid claim to many firsts in the San Juan Mountains and Colorado, and served as a cradle for engineering and mining practices that revolutionized the mining industry. The district was the scene of the first two mineral rushes in the San Juan Mountains, and featured the first hardrock mine and ore treatment mill. In 1873, the first aerial tramway in the San Juans, also one of the first in Colorado, was built; and by the late 1890s, the district claimed some of the longest tramways in Colorado. Mining engineers credit one of the district's companies with developing the practice of mining and milling low-grade ore in economies of scale during the first half of the 1890s. This deviated from the convention of emphasizing medium- and high-grade material. This production strategy ultimately saved Colorado's ebbing mining industry at the end of the decade when metals prices were low and high-grade material was largely exhausted. During the 1890s, the district featured one of the most advanced electrical grids for its time and one of the largest Alternating Current power plants in the West. One of the highest and most profitable mines in the United States lay on North Star Peak. One of the nation's largest and most advanced was in Silver Lake Basin, and miners bored one of the most extensive mazes of underground workings beneath much of the district during the 1930s and 1940s. For at least a century, the Las Animas Mining District continued to impress engineers, metallurgists, investors, and the mineworkers who were the foundation of its awesome industry.

The development of a successful mining industry in the Las Animas District was no easy feat. The topography was among the most rugged that the West had to offer and the climate was second in harshness only to Alaska. Winters were so severe that contact with the outside world was tenuous at best, despite rail service; and a period of monsoon storms often compressed the already short summers. Yet, the region drew the cast of characters necessary for mining. Individual reasons why they came are many, although several common factors are apparent, such as the potential for wealth, a lust for adventure, and the need for employment. But these common factors offer only a partial explanation as to why anyone would attempt life in the remote and hostile environment of the Las Animas Mining District. They also were there for the intrigue and mystique of the San Juan Mountains, where heavy industry collided with the wilderness.

Between the years 2000 and 2002, I documented and assessed the historic significance of most of the principal mine and mill sites in the Las Animas District for the Bureau of Land Management. During the project, I became aware of just how important the district was and felt compelled to convey the region's overdue story. Much has already been published on mining in the San Juan Mountains and some books have even discussed several of the mines in the Las Animas District. No book, however, has discussed the district and its exciting past, from its beginning with Charles Baker to the decline of mining in the 1950s.

Because little has been written on the district's full history, most of this book is based on original research undertaken in two different arenas. The first consists of archival sources upon which historians traditionally rely. The second is information gathered from my archaeological studies in the district, which proved as informative as archival research. When people think of archaeological investigations, they often imagine the weathered archaeologist cautiously excavating buried material with brushes and dustpans. While this is not inaccurate, archaeological research actually takes in much more. Historically, mines typically had surface plants that consisted of buildings, structures such as ore bins and trestles, and topographical alterations and features such as roads and waste rock dumps. When a mining company abandoned its property, the company or creditors almost always removed the buildings, structures, and machinery because of their value, while leaving telltale evidence in the form of archaeological features and artifacts. By acting as a detective, the archaeologist can use this evidence to interpret aspects of the mining operation, and, hence, aspects of the site's history not conveyed by archival sources. Archaeological features such as foundations, building footprints, and structural remnants can reveal exactly what buildings and machines were present, how they were arranged, and the years when the facilities were installed and removed. By analyzing artifacts such as broken bottles, empty food cans, and miscellaneous domestic items cast off as trash by the former occupants, the researcher can also secret out many conclusions regarding the inhabitants.

This is where archaeological research is as important as traditional archival research. While most archival sources tend to be sound, the documenters of the past recorded facts and details they thought were important at the time, leaving many fascinating topics of life on the mining frontier poorly chronicled. Archaeological evidence can fill information gaps inherent in incomplete archival sources, depicting more fully the history of a mining operation, the greater area, and the people involved. For example, by studying the assemblage of features and artifacts for a townsite, the archaeologist may be able to define the distribution of businesses, socioeconomic classes, women, families, and the modes of employment of the residents. Material evidence also can reveal much about aspects of life that were poorly documented in the past because they were either taboo or mundane, including diet, health, the consumption of alcohol, and drug use.

Further, a combination of lore and incomplete-to-inaccurate popular publications gave rise to a variety of exaggerated and, sometimes, completely false stereotypes regarding the inhabitants of the mining frontier. Archaeological evidence offers the potential to dispel such myths. For example, careful studies of material evidence amid many of Colorado's historic townsites reveal that miners did not subsist on canned beans and liquor. Instead, most people preferred fresh foods, and those forced by circumstance to eat preserved foods consumed a variety of items similar in proportion to today's diets. Also like today's culture, most individuals drank only moderate quantities of alcohol, while only a few inhabitants drank to excess. Another myth suggests that the mining frontier was a man's world, that women were present primarily as prostitutes, and that nearly every mining camp had a red light district. According to archaeological studies throughout Colorado, women were, in fact, ubiquitous across the mining frontier and kept home in the most unlikely and remote locations. Nearly every town had a small population of women and families, few if any prostitutes, and many women ran or participated in local businesses.

As can be inferred, archaeological research was an important source of information for a complete history of the Las Animas Mining District. Since 2000, historic preservation interests, including the Bureau of Land Management, have funded a number of projects involving the district's mines, mills, and settlements. The fruits of these efforts are the basis for this book, which is made possible in part through the cooperation and support of Bureau of Land Management archaeologist Kristie Arrington.

If you are reading this book, chances are good that you have either been to the Silverton area, are very interested in its fascinating historical sites, or are planning to visit them. Anyone who has been to the area repeated times over the last twenty years will verify that the rich legacy left by the mining industry is literally disappearing. While natural decay is a principal reason, so is human impact. Old building materials and pieces of machinery are a favorite target for removal. The uneducated also pick up small items such as iron objects, purple glass, and miscellaneous things as souvenirs to remember their trips. Through such actions, the Las Animas Mining District has literally walked off or been carried away piece by piece. The most egregious, however, is bottle- and coin collecting. Semi-professional collectors armed with metal detectors and shovels have excavated many privy pits, plowed through the debris of collapsed buildings, and even destroyed structures in their search for treasure. This has not only greatly accelerated the decay of the district's important legacy, but also has caused damage that can never be repaired. As a professional historian and archaeologist intimate with the Las Animas District, I can assure you that the treasure is gone, few if any bottles remain, and the miners of yesteryear were more cautious with their coins and items of value than we are today. We all bear the responsibility to preserve the legacy of the Las Animas District for the future out of respect for the past.

CHAPTER 2

A Gold Rush
in a Land of Silver

WHEN THE BAKER PARTY ARRIVED on Cinnamon Pass in June of 1860, the six members could not help but survey the landscape around them and marvel at the seemingly endless array of peaks and valleys that were the San Juans. Behind them to the east was the valley from where they came, and in front, to the west, was a deep drainage separating them from lofty mountains. The party descended from the pass into the drainage, and followed it south then west where it opened into the upper reaches of the Animas River Valley. Taking stock of the area, the party then traveled down the river to a broad, open area where additional drainages converged from nearly all directions. Here, the members decided to pitch camp and begin their search for wealth at a spot where few, if any, prospectors had ever been. Understanding that a systematic effort was best to find gold, the party allotted specific drainages to its members, who would later compare findings in camp. W.H. Cunningham decided to return to the first deep gulch near camp that extended south, a man named Mason prospected the only gulch to its west, Baker assumed the Animas River, and others fanned out into the various drainages extending north.[2]

Over the course of several months, the expedition evolved into one of both prospecting and general exploration of the unknown region, and the members were able to piece together its general geography. At camp, the party apparently erected several crude cabins and subsisted on a combination of provisions and game. Prospecting, however, commanded their attention and, because placer gold tended to lie amid stream gravel, the party members spent most of their time in the lower reaches of the drainages.

Prospecting for placer gold was an arduous, labor-intensive project that involved much more than merely shoveling gravel into a gold pan. Because gold was heavy, stream action sifted it downward into the deep portions of gravel deposits, but gold-bearing gravel usually offered enough fine material near the surface to suggest to the prospector that more may lie at depth. Finding gravel that offered fine gold required the excavation of countless pits in cobble-laden ground and the reduction of samples with a pan. Because most gravel was barren of gold, the prospector could invest days and weeks with no guarantee of even a hint of the metal. If a prospector was fortunate enough to encounter fine gold, he refrained from celebration until he proved that the metal was present in economic quantities. This meant digging in rebellious ground until he struck bedrock where the gold collected, which could have been more than ten feet down. Once the prospector confirmed gold, he set up a sluice, an open-ended trough with riffles, and then shoveled in the metalliferous gravel. A water current running through the sluice washed off the light gravel and left the hard-won gold. Where lumber or water were in short supply, some prospectors used a device known as a cradle or rocker, which was a portable wooden box with a short, slanted trough studded with riffles. One prospector rocked the box with a lever and another poured in water; the action caused the gold to settle against the riffles while the light gravel rolled and washed off.

The Baker party labored through July and probably into August, when several of the members finally encountered gold-bearing gravel. Cunningham found gold near the mouth of his allotted drainage, which the party recognized as Cunningham Gulch; Mason found even better samples in his drainage, which was called Mason Gulch; and someone else, probably Baker, had luck on the south side of the Animas above and east of Cunningham Gulch. Success at last, or so the party thought. During August, the members converged on the discoveries and pursued the deeper deposits that seemed to hold value. Had they taken the time, however, to track the horizontal extent of the gold-bearing gravel, the prospectors may have felt a pang of doubt.

Regardless, they began mining with pans and possibly sluices in gravel that was relatively shallow. The party of six labored through September and, as the aspen trees began to turn, realized that the season's end was near. In need of supplies, and in an attempt to popularize the find, Baker decided to exit the San Juans and make contact with the outside world. In October, he followed the Animas River south out of the mountains, roughly paralleling its route since the actual river canyon was impenetrable, and made first contact at the New Mexican trading outpost of Abiquiu. After relaying his story, he turned east and trekked to settlements on the Rio Grande River, where he not only acquired the requisite goods, but also found a ready audience. After heavily promoting the placer discoveries, Baker assembled a party of up to 150 prospectors and other individuals willing to try their luck in what Baker referred to as Baker's Park.[3]

By mid-October, Baker's original party welcomed Baker back into the Animas River Valley and was impressed, if not astonished, to see the 150 member entourage. By this time, the temperatures had grown cold, the aspens dropped their golden leaves, and the weather was questionable and unpredictable. Perhaps Baker neglected to inform the 150 prospectors that their timeframe for exploring the Animas drainage would be very narrow, and that all would have to leave before deep snows stranded them. Still, the participants of the small rush had just enough time to examine the placer fields for themselves, stake claims, and begin mining. In response to the new competition and out of certainty that the following year would see a major rush, Baker's party claimed their collection of cabins and surrounding land as Baker's Park. As winter set in during November, the entire assemblage of prospectors decided their season was truly over and descended south out of the mountains.[4]

When they approached the piedmont area, the men broke into several groups. Wanting more than the discoveries in the Animas River Valley, Baker and several others wrapped northwest around the San Juans to the Dolores River area for additional prospecting.

*The principal places of activity in 1860.
Source: Author.*

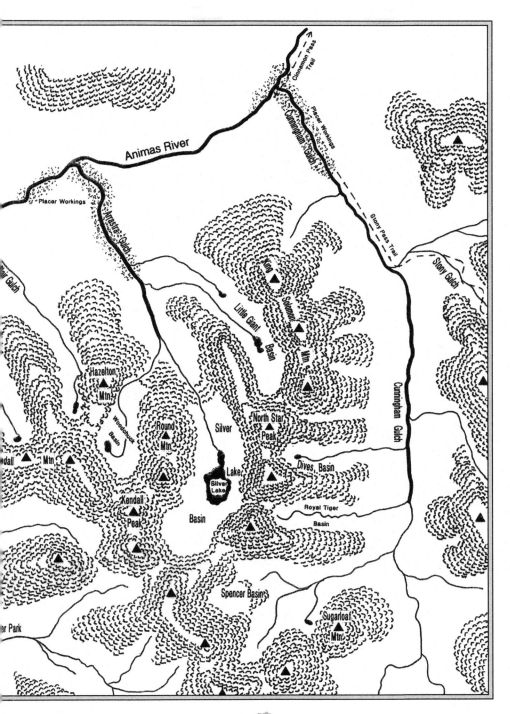

Awe inspiring, compelling, and yet intimidating, a panorama very similar to the one in the photograph greeted the Baker Party from the crest of Cinnamon Pass in 1860. Such a rugged wilderness was a reminder to prospectors that they were truly alone, isolated, and far from home. William Henry Jackson captured the northwestern view from the top of King Solomon Mountain in 1874. Source: U.S. Geological Survey, Jackson, W.H. 556.

These surrealistic rock formations were the eastern gateway into Baker's Park, which lay in the background. It was in this area that the Baker Party began its search for placer gold in 1860. When William Henry Jackson took the westerly view in 1874, the area had changed little. Source: U.S. Geological Survey, Jackson, W.H. 553.

Some of the 150 returned to familiar settlements in the San Luis Valley and at Abiquiu, while Baker's original party and others who had nowhere in particular to go stopped along the Animas River around thirty miles south of Baker's Park. There, they decided to erect a small settlement of crude cabins and wait out the winter. The large group named their settlement Animas City and felt some security in its strategic location (another town by the same name was founded during the mid-1870s down-river). The immediate area offered water, shelter, trees for cabins, and game. The settlement was as close to the gold discoveries as tolerable. If necessity required, healthy individuals could reach Abiquiu within a journey of several long days. However, reasons for insecurity certainly abounded. Animas City was by all accounts remote, the residents had only the most basic provisions, and of most concern, the settlement was within territory traditionally used by the Ute Indians, who were not altogether pleased with the prospectors' encroachment.[5]

Had the entire assemblage of 150 stayed together, the discoveries at Baker's Park and the location of Animas City may have remained only ambiguous rumors in the outside world. This would have countered Baker's interests in promoting the gold discoveries, which he did liberally during his descent in October. However, as various individuals and parties left the area in November and December, they conveyed information that contributed substance to the rumors. Some of the information was actually in contrast to Baker's intent. It seems that not all those who ascended into the Animas river drainage in October left impressed with the placer deposits. As they disbursed during winter, the prospectors, mostly credible individuals, spread many a discouraging word. J.C. Remington returned to Golden, on the Front Range, in December of 1860 and relayed his doubts to any who would listen. The highly seasoned Richard Sopris and partners left Animas City by December and returned to the Front Range to report that Baker's discoveries were a bust. Another prospector went so far as to write a series of letters to *The Rocky Mountain News* in January, 1861, arguing against Baker's finds.[6]

The resentful grumblings, however, fell on deaf ears. Toward the end of 1860, Colorado was ready for and in need of a new gold strike, especially in an uncharted and mysterious land such as the San Juans. The Pikes Peak Gold Rush was souring, the mountain discoveries made in 1860 were at their zenith, the older gold fields were completely claimed and showed signs of exhaustion, and optimistic wealth seekers continued to arrive in the territory. Those individuals who had little luck in Summit County, South Park, the upper Arkansas River Valley, and other areas immediately latched on to the reports of Baker's strike, which spread at an alarming pace following Baker's October contact with the outside world.

The extent and richness of Baker's strike grew each time the story was repeated until the tale was out of proportion with reality. While Baker did describe the strike with enthusiasm to anyone who would listen, his reports were apparently not exaggerations or fabrications. Further, in October, he sent dispatches to Kellogg & Company at California Gulch clearly noting that the discovery was limited, but that great potential existed because his party left much ground unexplored. Ready for new diggings, the unsuccessful, the optimistic, and the adventurous readied themselves for the protracted journey to the San Juans as early as October, 1860.[7]

George W. Howard was one of the first to respond to the stories that were floating around. Howard was born in Pittsburgh, Pennsylvania in 1840 and was seized with wanderlust at an early age. As a mature teenager, he worked as a trapper and hunted wolves on the plains during the 1850s, almost certainly developing relationships with Indian tribes there. Based on his intimacy with the vast grasslands, Howard became a valuable asset to travelers trekking west during the Pikes Peak Gold Rush in 1858 and 1859, and he made the dangerous journey at least twice.[8]

The year 1860 found Howard at Fort Garland in the San Luis Valley, where the post carpenter told him of a small placer gold deposit that he found in the Gunnison River Valley. The carpenter described the general location, the route there, and a broken wagon that approximated the deposit's place. Howard assembled a small party of adventurous characters and crossed over into the valley. They exhausted their supplies before finding the wagon and had to return. Back at Fort Garland, Howard's party heard of silver strikes in Santa Fe, lost interest in the broken wagon, and started south. At the town of San Luis, the group encountered several prospectors on the trail of Baker's entourage and took an interest in the reports of the confirmed placer gold. The prospectors suggested that they and Howard's partners join forces and organize a significant party of experienced individuals. Howard returned to Fort Garland one more time, possibly growing weary of the repeated trips, then went to the nearby Gray Back Diggings, which were just being prospected, and rallied sixty interested miners. By this time, the placer season was over and Baker and his entourage had settled at Animas City. The Howard party took a shortcut from the San Luis Valley, crossed the mountains above present Durango, and surprised Baker et al. at their settlement. With strength in numbers and the anticipation of mining, the inhabitants of Animas City, the first Euro-American settlers in the San Juans, bided their time and waited for winter to pass.[9]

Some popular publications claim that Howard met the Baker party in Baker's Park during the working season of 1860, and that Howard did not return to Fort Garland and instead continued down the Gunnison River to the Uncompahgre River. There, Howard supposedly turned south, ascended to the Uncompahgre's headwaters, and crossed over into Baker's Park via Red Mountain Pass.[10] Through extensive research, Allen Nossaman, undisputed Silverton historian, determined that this was not so and proposed the version of Howard's arrival as extracted above.

The makings of a rush to the San Juans gained momentum in California Gulch. Almost immediately after receiving Baker's dispatches in October, S.B. Kellogg felt confident that his grubstaked prospector's daring venture would become a real bonanza. He hastily returned East for his family, brought them to Colorado, and organized a party of 150 to 200 individuals eager for new diggings. Some of Colorado's most notable prospectors and placer miners were among the group, and their interest fostered a sense of confidence that Baker's Park would be the next bonanza. Abe Lee, the discoverer of California Gulch, Henry Allen, a founder of Auraria, and Thomas Pollock, one of Denver's first settlers and business operators, all thought enough of Baker's reports to join Kellogg. Hoping to arrive in advance of the rush that was sure to develop, Kellogg and party left for the San Juans in the cold of December with relatively few provisions. They went down to Pueblo, over La Veta Pass into the San Luis Valley, passed through Conejos, crossed over to Pagosa Springs, and struck west for the Animas River. Colorado's traditional January thaw granted the party a reprieve, but winter returned in February and March and stalled the travelers several times.[11]

Meanwhile, the residents at Animas City grew impatient and fidgety as they waited for winter to pass. Unfamiliar with the cycles of warmth and snow in the San Juans, many took a mild March as a sign of the coming spring and contemplated an early return to Baker's Park. Eager to be the first at the diggings, Baker and partners built sleds, hauled them the thirty miles up to the park, erected cabins, and made everything as ready as possible for the coming season. Much to everyone's surprise, Kellogg's massive party arrived at Animas City in early April with other bands of prospectors on their heels. After consulting with Baker, Kellogg joined Baker on what they thought would be the last trip up to the park, packing supplies and building cabins. Even though snow was on the ground, they tramped over to the scene of the discovery and actually began panning gravel in absolutely frigid water.[12]

After several days passed and Baker failed to return, many at Animas City grew agitated but felt paralyzed because snow coverage prevented prospecting and discouraged staking claims over unseen ground. Responding to the compulsion to do something, a few followed Baker's trail to the park, but most merely broke camp and moved their settlement up the Animas River during what they assumed to be the spring thaw. The idle prospectors erected another collection of crude cabins and named their new settlement Camp Pleasant.[13]

While many of the prospectors in both Camp Pleasant and Baker's Park were experienced outdoorsmen, they had not been in the Front Range, let alone the San Juans, long enough to understand the typical weather patterns. They mistook the unusual warm period for the spring thaw, and this fatal error almost became their undoing. Snowfall and cold resumed with full force in early April, taking all by surprise. Camp Pleasant became a scene of quite the opposite as provisions ran low, the hastily built cabins provided cramped and dark environments, and an air of discouragement and resignation pervaded the residents. Baker, Kellogg, and party were directly threatened as continued snow obscured their egress route despite efforts to keep the trail packed and visible. The fresh snow made prospecting and placering absolutely impossible, and so the prospectors in Baker's Park watched the weather and pondered their next move.

Those who followed Baker into the park ultimately decided what course the overall group took. Because the original Baker Party made the discoveries, common mining law granted the members the right to stake the first claims, which they had not yet done. Respecting this mining frontier institution, the other prospectors in Baker's Park waited for the party to stake its claims so they could then locate their own. However, as the snow began to accumulate, the prospectors grew panicky and implored Baker and his partners to take action. Aware of the potential uprising, Baker led his partners and members of Kellogg's party (since Kellogg provided the grubstake) to the site of the discoveries and reluctantly began erecting claim monuments in the snow. The group staked twenty claims ascending Cunningham Gulch from its confluence with the Animas River. A like set of claims were marked in Mason Gulch, and another twenty were staked on the Animas at a location the group named Eureka. Unceremonious as the event was, the Baker and Kellogg party staked the first claims in the San Juan Mountains. Although historian Allen Nossaman stated that the claims were 200 square feet, the properties were actually 200 by 200 feet in area, which was the common size for placer discovery claims recognized during the 1860s.[14]

The extraneous prospectors were free at last to stake their locations, which they quickly did adjoining the Baker and Kellogg assemblages. A few hardy individuals may have attempted to finish the winter in Baker's Park while the rest promptly descended to Camp Pleasant and joined their snowbound brethren. As winter began to abate in early May and granted travel at lower elevations, most of the Camp Pleasant residents returned to Animas City to wait for the thaw. There, they were confronted by bands of Utes who were unhappy to see the prospectors back on their land. Tensions and insecurity among the Animas City residents rose, as the Utes grew increasingly brave and began demanding goods that they then stole. On guard, the prospectors eagerly awaited their chance to return to the mountains as more individuals arrived from the Front Range.

Finally, the event that everyone impatiently awaited came late in May when scouts reported that the passes were negotiable. Within several days, Animas City emptied as its several hundred residents packed their goods and climbed deep into the San Juans. When they arrived in Baker's Park, some erected tents around Baker's supposed townsite while others continued on to the diggings. There, eager prospectors looked over the groups of claims staked in

April, added their own, and built crude shelters. Through May and into June, more prospectors continued to arrive from other parts of Colorado, in all constituting the first mineral rush to the San Juan Mountains. Allen Nossaman claims that more than 1,000 individuals were interested in Baker's Park in 1861, but not all came. In total, the rush probably drew between 500 and 700 prospectors who invested considerable emotion, capital, and time in the difficult journey.[15]

By the beginning of June, the creeks in Cunningham and Mason Gulches ran muddy, while those fortunate enough to possess claims began work in the icy water. As was the case with so many of Colorado's mineral rushes, the late comers found that the best ground had been staked and were forced to wander in search of additional placer deposits. It was probably common knowledge that the original Baker Party already examined the drainages descending into the Animas Valley, but the party was not thorough, which gave newly arriving prospectors some hope.

As a brilliant June progressed, clouds of doubt crept over Baker's Park. After backbreaking labor, many prospectors began to realize that the gravel deposits in the lower reaches of Cunningham and Mason gulches and at Eureka were the only ones that contained appreciable amounts of gold. All the rest offered nothing. Further, these deposits had been claimed by the Baker and Kellogg parties and the other prospectors who braved the April snows, leaving little for the hundreds of other individuals. Despair turned to anger, and the disenfranchised prospectors saw Baker as the cause of their overall failure. Baker defensively countered that he had been honest about the lack of indisputably rich placers since 1860, and that exaggerations of his factual reports stimulated the rush. Regardless, some prospectors attempted to foment rebellion and sought punishment of, and even threatened to hang, Baker. Most, however, conceded defeat and left the San Juans for the Front Range during June and early July, popularizing the event as the San Juan Humbug.[16]

As the last of the disenchanted prospectors left the San Juans, some Baker and Kellogg party members continued work but realized that they were not going to be wealthy. The party quickly exhausted its claims in Mason and Cunningham Gulches, then contracted around Eureka; but, after a number of weeks, the amount of labor finally outweighed the returns. With little to show for a year of hardship, Baker and partners left the San Juans, bringing to an end a gold rush in a land that would later yield millions of dollars in silver.

At Fort Garland, Baker learned of the outbreak of the Civil War, and feeling the call of duty, hastened to his native state of Virginia to enlist in the Confederacy. After the war's end, Baker returned to Colorado to resume prospecting and was drawn to the upper Arkansas River Valley in 1867 by gold discoveries at Granite. Probably still interested in his gold belt hypothesis, he and a small party began exploring the Western Slope and followed the Colorado River into Utah. There, Baker, who managed to survive the deadly Civil War, was killed by Indians.[17]

CHAPTER 3

Prospecting in a Howling Wilderness

THE FAILURE OF THE BAKER'S PARK RUSH indelibly blemished the San Juan Mountains in the minds of most Colorado prospectors, who continued to focus on the eastern mountain ranges. By the mid-1860s, miners had exhausted nearly all the placer fields there, causing the Pikes Peak Gold Rush to collapse. The region saw a mass migration of seasoned prospectors to new discoveries in Arizona, Montana, Idaho, and Oregon; the inexperienced and busted went back to settlements and farms in the East. Those individuals who stayed in Colorado became wage laborers in company placer operations and the few hardrock mines in operation, or they turned to other forms of business, such as ranching and farming. Few of the permanent miners and prospectors entertained the idea of further exploration of the San Juans, which was fine with the Utes who were happy to see the Whites go. The San Juans were to remain their mountains for at least another decade.

While most Coloradans ignored (and a few even disdained) the San Juans during the 1860s, the magic peaks still captured the imagination of a few prospectors in distant lands. In 1869, Adnah French,

John C. Dunn, Rodney McKinnon, and Solomon Shoup prospected together in west-central Arizona, hoping that a coordinated effort would find them a bonanza. French may have been the most experienced prospector among his compatriots. He was born in Brandon, Vermont, and in 1858 joined the famed Lawrence Party, one of the three original groups to find placer gold in Colorado and launch the Pikes Peak Gold Rush. As a member of the Lawrence Party, French was one of the founders of St. Charles City at the Cherry Creek diggings, and he went on to help found Denver. Two years later, French apparently hoped to repeat his good fortune and joined the Baker Party, where he became intimately familiar with Baker's Park. Dunn was born in New Brunswick in 1838, moved to Maine with his family five years later, then went to Lawrence, Kansas at the age of sixteen. Seeking adventure, he traveled over the Santa Fe Trail to wild New Mexico in 1862, and there he worked at the Apache-Navajo Indian Agency. Dunn served as an agent between 1864 and 1866, then went prospecting in Arizona. During his time in New Mexico, Dunn could not avoid hearing rumors of the San Juan Humbug, which raised a question about the potential for more minerals in Baker's Park.[18]

Corydon E. Cooley, Henry W. Dodd, and Dempsey Reese constituted another party in a similar state at Wickenburg, Arizona. Like French, Reese had direct experience as a prospector and was probably the patriarch of his respective party. He even participated in the Baker's Park excitement but never completed the journey to the San Juans. Reese was born in Henry County, Indiana, in 1835 and joined the Pikes Peak rush in 1860. Finding no gold, he worked for outfitters and helped Charles Baker begin his journey into failure. When the Pikes Peak rush went bust, Reese was among the migrants who left and joined a party to prospect Oregon. Still without luck, he returned to the East via Idaho, British Columbia, and Montana. Restless, Reese embarked on another whirlwind prospecting tour of Utah, California, Nevada, and Sonora, Mexico, and wound up in Arizona in 1868.[19]

After a wearisome and hot search around Wickenburg and Prescott, both groups were ready for better fields and became highly receptive to suggestions. Whether they held discussions together or came up with a common idea simultaneously is unknown, but the parties came to focus on the San Juans. French and Dunn probably infected their respective party with the legend of Baker's Park gold,

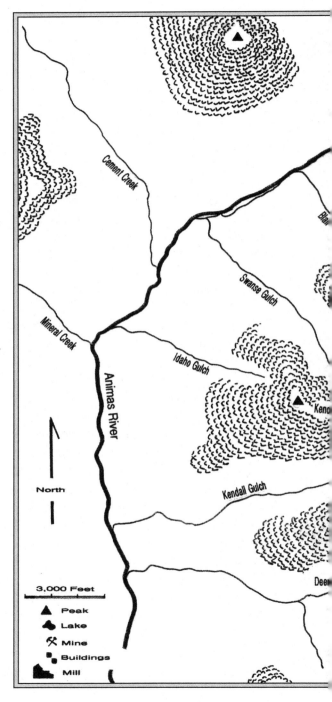

Principal mines and other places of activity, 1870 to 1874. Cunningham Gulch, the Animas River, and Deer Park and Spencer Basin formed the boundaries of the Las Animas Mining District. Source: Author.

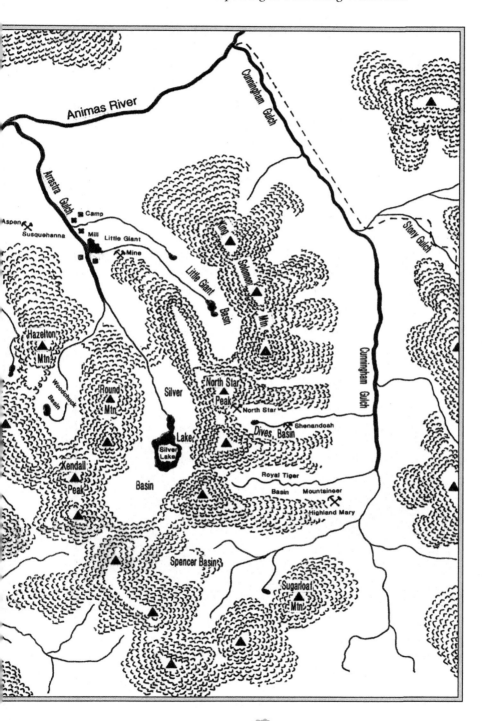

and Reese and Dodd, brother to a Baker's Park prospector, may have had a similar effect on their partners.

The reason why French, Dunn, and Reese enticed the parties, despite the legends of the San Juan Humbug, lay in a practical prospectors' education acquired during their eight subsequent years. Specifically, the men learned that placer gold consisted of particles loosened from a parent vein by physical weathering. Over eons, cycles of freezing and thawing, erosion from water, and natural disintegration fragmented all forms of rock, including gold veins, and mobilized the gold particles into waterways. Inert, the gold merely sifted down into stream gravel and awaited the prospector's shovel and pan. French, Dunn, and Reese surmised that the Baker's Park placers came from parent veins missed by the original miners, who focused only on the stream gravel. This basic geological knowledge gave the two groups of prospectors, now merged as one under Calvin Jackson, a reason to return to the San Juans.

Baker's Park was a prospectors' paradise, at least between May and October when the ground was thawed. The area offered enough drainages, rock outcrops, and peaks to keep prospectors busy for decades. William Henry Jackson took the southwesterly view in 1875, when Silverton was just beginning to grow. Source: U.S. Geological Survey, Jackson, W.H. 1689.

In 1869, the merged party began its long trek and quickly encountered problems. Their plan was to cross the desert into northern New Mexico, but this required traversing arid lands controlled by Apache tribes, who were among the most aggressive and hostile Indians in the Southwest. Water was difficult to find, and Apache raids and threats struck fear into the hearts of most of the party members, now numbering more than the original eight. Within a short time, all but eight turned back. While Jackson was the theoretical leader, Dunn rose to the fore and applied his experience as Indian agent to secure a treaty for safe passage through Apache territory. By October, the party finally reached the Animas River and ascended as far as Charles Baker's Animas City. They could not proceed further because of an early snow storm. Unwilling to stay the season in the crude camp, some of which had been destroyed by the Utes, the party continued to the safety of Fort Lowell in New Mexico.[20]

With no quarters, the prospectors were forced to camp. As winter gathered, they decided conditions were too cold and they traveled farther south. A few stayed at Santa Fe, several went on to Terra Amarilla, and Reese and others took up residence at San Juan Pueblo. There, Reese met Miles T. Johnson, an old Pikes Peak Gold Rush friend, and explained the party's plans. During the winter, Cooley arrived at San Juan Pueblo with several of the prospectors who had turned back, and all waited for the spring thaw.[21]

Finally, April arrived and warm weather swept the lower elevations, rousing the disseminated prospectors from their winter torpor. The party had grown and amassed supplies at Terra Amarilla, then left for the San Juans. They reoccupied the intact cabins at Animas City and waited for the snowpack on the passes to thaw. During their idle time, a schism developed, and while it was probably friendly, Dunn and most of the prospectors departed and traveled around the west base of the San Juans to the Dolores River drainage that was free of snow. This left French, Reese, Johnson, and a few others still fixated on Baker's Park.[22]

In April of 1870, Baker's Park saw the arrival of the first White prospectors since the rush nine years before. French and his partners at once returned to the scene of the original gold discoveries in Cunningham and Mason Gulches, and probably occupied one of the cabins built in 1861. Possibly working as a group, the prospectors tried panning the stream gravels again for gold but also eagerly began examining the sides of the gulches for mineral veins.

Below treeline, this proved difficult because the wet climate and dense, mature fir and spruce forest promoted the formation of thick soils that concealed bedrock. However, above treeline, at approximately 11,500 feet elevation, the region was a prospectors' paradise. Thin soils, expansive scree and talus slopes, and plenty of exposed bedrock provided the prospector with material for countless hours of examination. An increase in elevation brought more outcrops, and beginning at around 11,800 feet on some peaks, there were cliffs, spires, and buttresses of solid rock crisscrossed with bands, veins, and dykes. These formations soared to heights of more than 13,000 feet. The exposed rock seemed almost limitless and could consume a lifetime to peruse in detail, which some prospectors would ultimately do.

French, Reese, and Johnson chose to start their hardrock prospecting in Cunningham Gulch, and, probably in awe of their surroundings, ascended through the abandoned placer tailings to the gulch's head. They veered southwest up a tributary that they named Mountaineer Creek to an unusual geological formation on the north side and began close examination. Eureka! One of the party found a vein that carried metals, but they were different from free gold. Close examination suggested that the metal was silver, and the party claimed the formation as the Mountaineer. Probably aware of their place in history, French, Reese, and Johnson found the first hardrock lode and staked the first hardrock claim in the Animas drainage and probably the San Juan Mountains. On the way down and north out of the gulch, the party examined the steep walls and found another vein of similar character on the east side. It was staked as the Manderfield, which was the second lode and claim in the San Juans.[23]

That the prospectors did not heavily explore the area for more veins is curious. They were probably interested in gold and not silver, and resumed their search for the source of the placer deposits. In 1870, gold fetched an average of $20.70 per ounce and could be easily separated in the field with the crude methods of crushing and amalgamation with mercury. Silver, by contrast, was valued at $1.33 per ounce and usually required in-depth processing that involved roasting, leaching, and smelting. In addition, the exact process was dictated by the proportion of silver and other metals, which could

Arrastra Gulch, originally known as Mason Gulch, seemed like an unlikely place to find gold, but the Baker Party found economical placer deposits on the floor in 1860. The French party traced leftover gold flakes to the Little Giant lode in 1870, which became the first hardrock mine in the San Juans. The Little Giant was located on the left side of the gulch behind the forested slope. Silver Lake Basin lies behind the imposing headwall, and William Henry Jackson captured the view in September, when lower regions still enjoyed the warmth of summer. Source: U.S. Geological Survey, Jackson, W.H. 482.

only be determined through assay. Given this, the choice to pursue gold was understandable and the silver would have to wait; but the party claimed the vein anyway as a future investment.[24]

Within a short time, French, Reese, and Johnson focused on Mason Gulch, which offered the best placer gold in the past. At first, the prospectors clambered around the bedrock outcrops, cliffs, and scree slopes forming the imposing walls of the gulch. One of them climbed up onto a ridge on the gulch's west side and, amid bedrock outcrops at treeline, encountered a third silver vein. The group staked the region's third discovery as the Mammoth then resumed the search for gold.[25]

The party probably decided to employ a classic, planned strategy practiced by experienced hardrock prospectors. They sampled the gravel in the gulch for placer gold and slowly ascended upward and southeast until the gold disappeared. This marked the point where the gold was being introduced into the stream, and the prospectors responded by panning soil samples taken from the gulch sides. Gold flakes recovered well outside of the stream channel confirmed their suspicions, and they began closely examining the gulch sides for any sign of a mineral formation, vein, or fault. Possibly after additional sampling and identifying fragmented vein material, the party found that the gold came from a minor drainage on the gulch's east side, and after inspecting the bedrock outcrops, one of the prospectors finally found gold ore. Excited and optimistic, the party staked the find as the Little Giant, but was reluctant to declare absolute success until profitable ore had been proven. The claim was the fourth in the region and the only gold vein found up to that time.[26]

With hand-steels, hammers, and blasting powder, the prospectors drove a discovery cut into the vein and found, much to their delight, that the ore continued beyond sight. The length of the discovery workings that they blasted remains unknown, but it seems highly likely that the prospectors collected enough sacks of ore for assay and show. During the last month of summer, French, Reese, and Johnson must have been giddy and filled with tempered excitement. They were the first hardrock prospectors in Baker's Park with no pressure of competition, and they not only found the gold vein that they sought, but stumbled across three silver veins almost by accident! Experienced as they were, however, the three prospectors understood that hard work was ahead if they were to make the claims legal and profit from their finds. The turning aspen leaves told them that winter was on its way, and additional development would have to wait until 1871.

In September, French, Reese, and Johnson descended with light feet out of Baker's Park and met the Dunn party in Santa Fe. French imparted his group's success to Dunn, who reported optimistic news as well. Dunn's prospectors found some placer gold and at least one silver vein near what became Rico, but the find did not hold the potential offered by Baker's Park. Some of Dunn's prospectors made mental notes to ascend to Baker's Park the next season, others were discouraged by the hostility of Utes and Apaches, and all disbanded.

While wintering in Santa Fe, French was surprised to encounter William J. Mulholland, one of the prospectors who turned back to Wickenburg during the 1869 expedition. Mulholland was born in Ireland in 1837 and immigrated with his family to Canada in 1847 to seek a better life. As a young adult, Mulholland went to the southern United States in 1859, where he worked as a carpenter. He came to

Denver in 1865 and plied his trade at Buckskin Joe. When the boom there collapsed, he worked in Huerfano County then joined the rush to Elizabethtown, New Mexico. In 1869, Mulholland and partners went to Arizona to prospect, where they encountered French, Reese, and party. After abandoning French's expedition, Mulholland finally crossed the Southwest to Santa Fe, where he accepted a position as carpenter for the government and worked with the skilled Thomas Blair.[27]

An odd character, Blair embodied the western roustabout. He was born in Pond Mills, Ontario, probably during the 1830s, and may have served as a mercenary in the Civil War. Restless after the war ended, Blair sought adventure and excitement in the West, went to Wyoming, passed through Colorado, and ended up in New Mexico, working as a carpenter and prospecting along the way. In 1870, he found employment at Santa Fe as a government carpenter and worked with Mulholland.[28]

After meeting Mulholland and Blair, French realized that the two carpenters possessed construction skills, tools, and a little capital, which could be used to develop the Little Giant. The only item missing was enough capital for supplies, specific mining equipment, and materials. To interest the carpenters and additional capitalists, French, Reese, and Johnson divided the Little Giant into six shares and offered one each to Blair and Mulholland. They offered a third to merchant James H. Cook for $500 and a grubstake. French, Reese, and Johnson kept one share each for themselves, of course. The party realized, however, that yet more capital would be necessary, so French approached William A. Pile, New Mexico governor, and Joshua S. Fuller, Santa Fe merchant, and offered them a deed to half of the Little Giant.[29]

Early on an 1871 May morning, French, Reese, Johnson, Mulholland, Blair, and Cook quietly stole out of Santa Fe to bring the Little Giant into production. Their route was somewhat circuitous because the party made great effort to sneak around the scattered settlements to avoid tipping off prospectors and showing them the way to what was the party's personal treasure trove. After weaving through the juniper-pinion forest and expending energy climbing over hills, the party was far enough north to directly follow the Rio Grande River to its westerly headwaters. Physically fit like most prospectors, the party easily climbed out of the Rio Grande drainage, crossed over Stony Pass, and descended down into Cunningham Gulch. There, the six wealth-seekers pitched camp on the open, grassy floor, relocated the Mountaineer claim, conducted additional prospecting, and staked several more lodes. Afterward, the party returned to Mason Gulch and immediately set about planning the development of the Little Giant.[30]

The party members almost certainly built several cabins in the gulch, and French, Reese, and Cook probably began blasting ore from an open-cut on the vein. From the beginning, the party understood that the ore could not be economically packed to one of the handful of mills in New Mexico or Colorado's Front Range. Instead, the party came prepared to build their own facility, which was based on the ages-old Spanish arrastra. This simple apparatus consisted of a circular stone floor hemmed in by low sidewalls, a capstan at center, and a beam that rotated around the capstan. A draft animal walked a track around the arrastra and pulled the beam, which dragged stones around the floor. As the stones ground the ore, an attendant added water and mercury, which amalgamated with the gold as it became freed.

Under Johnson's direction, Mulholland and Blair began constructing the arrastra on the valley floor below the mine. Unlike the basic arrastra, theirs was fairly sophisticated and featured four drag beams powered by a side-shot waterwheel, more than likely linked with a leather belt. The arrastra floor was a relatively large fifteen feet in diameter, the sidewalls consisted of vertical planks, and the waterwheel was eighteen feet in diameter. A dam and flume provided the water, which flowed through a ditch. Before introducing the payrock into the arrastra, several of the party had to reduce it to gravel with hammers.[31]

While slow, cumbersome, and labor-intensive, the arrastra functioned from the start and promised gold in the form of silvery amalgam, which undoubtedly excited the party. When the first load of rock had been crushed, several of the members drained the excess water, shoveled off the depleted tailings, and marveled at the dark gray amalgam lining the stone floor. After scraping it into a leather bag, the liquid mercury was squeezed out and the pasty mass heated in a retort to drive off and condense additional mercury for reuse. With great anticipation, the retort's cover was cautiously removed to reveal the fruits of a protracted process – the first pure gold, or any metal for that matter, produced from ore in the San Juans. Of course, it almost needs no mention that the arrastra was also the first mill in the San Juans and Western Colorado.

The arrastra was an ancient milling apparatus for grinding gold and silver ore and extracting the metal content. The line drawing depicts the simplest version, which was powered by draft animals. Prospectors shoveled ore into the interior, and as the beams rotated, they dragged heavy stones around the floor, which ground the ore into sand. Periodically, the prospectors sprinkled mercury into the wet mix, which amalgamated with the gold and silver. While arrastras were slow and inefficient, they were ideal for remote locations such as the Las Animas Mining District. Source: Mining & Scientific Press 5/26/83.

During May and June, the inevitable finally occurred in the Animas River drainage. Another party of prospectors arrived in May, then a second in June, and a third shortly later in June. George Howard led the first party, and he, like members of the French party, had direct experience with the San Juan Humbug and probably hoped to return someday. Howard spent the winter of 1871 in Elizabethtown, New Mexico, when he learned of the gold discoveries at what became Summitville. He assembled a party at Loma, on the Rio Grande River, and traveled into the mountains where they were turned back by snow. When the party reappeared in Loma, Howard learned of the French party's quiet escape and set out after them only several days behind. Imitating French et al., the Howard party arrived in Cunningham Gulch, pitched camp, and prospected the area. Howard ascended the east flank of King Solomon Mountain, found a silver vein, and staked it as the Weminuche claim.[32]

The Howard party wasted little time searching for French et al. because they understood that, based on rumor, French and his partners had already found payrock. Given that prospectors think alike, the Howard party suspected that French and partners were most likely in Mason Gulch and in fact found them there hard at work. Within a short time, Howard and fellow prospectors had examined the area around the Little Giant, staked several adjoining claims, and examined the arrastra as a model for treating their own ore.[33]

Within several weeks of Howard's arrival, John Dunn brought the second party into Baker's Park. Disenchanted with the Dolores drainage and hearing of the prospectors bound for Baker's Park, Dunn formed a party and came to the Animas drainage based on descriptions imparted by Reese the previous year. The party consisted of George U. Ingersoll, David P. Quinn, Andrew Richardson, and Edwin Wilkinson. Ingersoll was born in Maine during 1847 and quickly assimilated into the frontier as a reporter in the wild railroad town of Cheyenne in 1867. The following year, Ingersoll went south through Colorado to New Mexico to prospect, and turned back north again to Gilpin County, where he worked as a miner until 1871. There, he honed his knowledge of prospecting for and mining gold. Rumors of strikes in and around the San Juans, particularly Summitville, drew him back south to Del Norte, where he apparently joined Dunn's party.[34]

Like the two parties already in Mason Gulch, Dunn and his compatriots examined Cunningham Gulch and perused the area around the Little Giant Mine. In Cunningham Gulch, they wandered up to the drainage head, may have encountered French's Mountaineer claim, and found a silver vein of their own in the same area staked as the Highland Mary. In Mason Gulch, the prospectors found another gold vein, claimed it as the Sampson (which should not be confused with the Sampson Mine on Cement Creek), and began development at once. After studying Miles Johnson's arrastra, Dunn and partners vainly erected a similar facility that probably relied on the traditional animal power. While Dunn's arrastra required the same hard work and provided the same anticipation as Johnson's during startup, it failed to recover a like proportion of gold.[35]

Ruben J. McNutt, Jim Pringle, George Rolbin, and Jack Munroe formed the core of the third prospecting party that arrived in the summer of 1871. McNutt had as much experience with the western frontier as anyone in Baker's Park. He was born on a farm in Albany, New York, in 1841, went west to California on the tail end of the Gold Rush in 1859, and found the placer fields mostly exhausted. To earn income, he worked as a miner at Placerville then joined the Fifth California Infantry in 1861 and participated in its Civil War march to New Mexico. After the war ended, McNutt remained on the plains as an Indian fighter, then returned to New York and tried integrating back into Eastern society. Unhappy with this, McNutt came to Colorado in 1870 and ended up at Loma, New Mexico, where he learned of the strikes in the San Juans.[36]

Pringle was another quintessential frontier prospector. He was born in Roxburghshire, Scotland, in 1838 and immigrated to the United States as a young man of seventeen years. Pringle spent a year in New York then went to western Canada in search of opportunity, adventure, and excitement. After only a brief time, he heard the siren call of riches, beckoning him south to the California gold fields. In 1857, Pringle sailed to San Francisco then up past Sacramento, where he mined placer gold on the American River. When he arrived, Pringle found that the era of the bearded miner with gold pan had passed and organized companies dominated the scene. He went to work for one of those companies until he saved enough money to move on. Hoping his luck would be better at distant, inland placer strikes, in 1865 he joined the rushes to Boise Basin and Montana. Still unsuccessful, he went to White Pine, Nevada, during its 1869 rush, and then prospected his way south through Utah and Arizona. When Pringle assessed his situation, he realized that Colorado was the only place of mineralogical significance he had yet to visit, so he traversed the dangerous southwest in 1871 and ascended through central New Mexico into the San Luis Valley. Impressed with the region's potential, he made a semi-permanent home in Canon City, worked during the cold months to replenish his coffers, and spent the warm months prospecting. On his way to Canon City, however, Pringle made the fateful diversion with McNutt and partners.[37]

During June, it became obvious that Baker's Park hosted enough prospectors, and would see more arrive, to justify the organization of a mining district. In general, this was a truly democratic system that prospectors throughout the West used to govern claim activity and keep records. The district boundaries and name, claim sizes and types, numbers of claims allotted to an individual, and requirements to hold a claim were defined by popular consensus. A recorder was appointed or elected to record the claim information and who the legal claimant was. In addition, mining district laws usually established a miner's court to hear, try, and punish offenses such as claim jumping and fraud. In the Animas River drainage, however, prospectors and miners were peaceable and tended to respect common law, so the court heard few cases.

During the early 1870s, prospectors, federal and territorial governments, and other individuals recognized five principal types of claims. The most elementary was the placer claim. It granted an individual a square tract 100 by 100 feet in area, and the discoverer was usually allowed an additional claim. The lode claim was slightly more complex and differed according to the mining district. However, most prospectors based their lode claim definitions on those developed on the Front Range during the early 1860s. In Boulder, Gilpin, and Summit Counties, most of the mining districts recognized the common lode claim as 50 feet on both sides of a vein and between 550 and 1,500 feet long. After passage of the 1872 mining law, the width expanded to 300 or 600 feet, depending on the generosity of a district's organizers. Prospectors who demonstrated the intent to mine were also allowed to stake a millsite claim on flat ground, usually on the floor of a drainage, for a mill and base camp. After proving the presence of ore, the claim owner could then pay a small fee to the General Land Office and complete the paperwork to patent the claim. This took the property out of the public domain and made it completely private above and below ground.

Because the French party consisted of seasoned members and was the first to find and develop ore in Baker's Park, the rest of the prospectors in the region looked to them as the governing body for the new mining district. Miles T. Johnson was appointed recorder and held a meeting in his tent on June 15 where the prospectors created the Las Animas Mining District around the main portion of the Animas River drainage. Initially, the district included the peaks and tributaries flanking the Animas River from the Continental Divide to the east, crossed by Cinnamon and Stony Passes, over to the west end of Baker's Park. To administer the intense activity of later years, this original geographic entity was carved into smaller mining districts and, over time, the Las Animas District contracted. The boundaries became somewhat nebulous and some historical references differed in terms of the district's exact extent. Ultimately, the cluster of peaks and basins bounded on the east by Cunningham Gulch, on the north by the Animas River, and on the south by Deer Park was the district's core.[38]

After the meeting, Johnson immediately began preparing documents that formally recognized the claims staked in the district up to that time. He alluded to some of the geographical place names that the overall body of prospectors used. Cunningham Gulch was named after Major Cunningham, who worked the drainage during the San Juan Humbug. King Solomon Mountain, also known as Solomon Mountain, rose along Cunningham Gulch's west side. Kendall Peak and Kendall Mountain were two peaks west of Solomon, and their names were derived from early arrival James W. Kendall. Mason Gulch, which separated the above mountains, became known as Arrastra Gulch after Johnson's arrastra.

By the height of summer, an estimated forty to fifty prospectors kept Johnson busy recording their claims when he was not at work on the Little Giant, which was the only truly profitable mine in the San Juans during 1871. Johnson also recorded several resources that only the French party and George Howard had the foresight to claim, which would figure prominently in later decades. Specifically, they claimed the water rights to Arrastra Creek. Thomas Blair was among the prospectors who submitted claim information to Johnson, and his was one of two Aspen locations staked during the summer. Blair was curious about the Mammoth Lode and ascended to Arrastra Gulch's west rim to examine the vein. He found that a second, more robust formation paralleled it to the west. Not only that, but this new vein cropped out on ground-surface. The fact that it had not yet been found indicated that Blair was one of the first prospectors to seriously examine the area.[39]

As the summer wore on, the nights cooled down, the aspens and arctic willows turned gold, and the days grew shorter. Nature signaled to the prospectors that their season was nearly over and most made preparations to leave before being stranded by winter snow.

The year 1871 was one of the most pivotal that the San Juans would see. Prospectors proved that there were more potential mineral veins than forty to fifty individuals could find, claim, and develop in a single season. The first mining district was created and many of its principal geographic features were named. A camp had been established in Arrastra Gulch, and it would serve as a base of operations for years to come. Most importantly, the first profitable mine and mill were brought into production, and by the end of the season yielded between $3,000 and $4,000, worth $45,000 and $60,000 today. These figures combined with the other factors mentioned drew attention to the San Juans but were not yet enough to stimulate a rush.[40]

Additional work and measurable volumes of ore were required for such an event, and nearly all the prospectors returned in the summer of 1872 to bring this to fruition.

Additional prospectors arrived during the summer, bringing the total to around 150, and arrangements were made for a long-term stay. Primitive log cabins went up in Arrastra Gulch, replacing the tents pitched the previous year, and prospectors working elsewhere erected similar structures. George Howard, unhappy with the increased population, removed himself to the mouth of Cunningham Gulch and built a small cabin where he could be alone. Someone else decided to join Howard, much to his dismay, and found no friend in Howard who took enough dislike to the neighbor to pressure him to move on.[41]

With 150 prospectors in the drainage, more mineral veins were claimed and developed so their content could be assessed at depth. In Cunningham Gulch, which was one of the centers of activity, prospectors began work on the Mountain Boy, Green Mountain, and others on the east side. In later years, these were developed into one of the most important mines in the Animas drainage, but they were absorbed into another mining district and are therefore part of a different story.

Possibly aware of Howard's discovery on Solomon Mountain, the original members of the Dunn party decided to see for themselves if more silver veins could be found in the area. They trekked up to Cunningham Gulch's head and ascended its precipitous west wall into a glaciated hanging valley. The floor of the valley started at around 12,000 feet in elevation and ascended west to a deep azure tarn, or glacial lake, surrounded by scree slopes. The valley was crowded on all sides with North Star Peak towering to 13,416 feet to the north, another peak rising to a similar height to the south, and a connecting arête, or knife-edged ridge, between.

Because the journey required hours and the total elevation gain was at least 2,000 feet from Cunningham Gulch, the party members almost certainly established a camp in the valley then went about the business of prospecting. Dunn, Ingersoll, Richardson, Quinn, James McKenzie, and several others fanned out and climbed across the valley's ragged bedrock walls. At times, these prospectors literally took their lives into their hands. Natural rock fall generated unpredictable projectiles that bounced down the steep slopes, loose rock provided poor footing, and a misstep could result in a lengthy tumble over cliffs. Thunderstorms materialized out of a crystal sky with little notice, and the lofty and exposed landscape offered absolutely no protection against the lightning. Further, hail and snow often fell during summer months, which complicated the already hazardous footing.

Despite the environmental barriers, one of the party found a rich silver vein within days, claimed it as the Shenandoah, and other members traced the vein northwest across the valley. They staked the extension with a series of claims that included the Dives and Shenandoah No.3, and then apparently returned to the main settlement in Arrastra Gulch where other prospectors learned of their success. Within a short time, a small rush converged on North Star Peak. Miles Johnson made the ascent early and staked the Miles Johnson claim on the peak, while Henry B. Adsit, John Goodwin, and the members of the Dunn party located additional properties.[42]

Two of the most interesting and important characters in what became known as Dives Basin were prospecting partners Theophile Benjovsky and Martin Van Buren Wason. Benjovski was born in Poland in 1854, immigrated to the United States when he was sixteen years old, and wasted little time in the East. He arrived in Colorado within a short time and journeyed to the Mosquito Mountains, possibly in response to the Moose silver discovery of 1871 and Fairplay's reputation for placer gold. The choice, however, was a poor one because little was actually happening in the area. A discouraged Benjovski thought his fortune would be better at Summitville. During 1871, Benjovsky staked and sold a few claims there and formed a partnership with Wason.[43]

The enigmatic Wason was one of the most widely traveled and cunning individuals in the San Juans during the 1870s, and could match almost anyone in terms of mining and prospecting experience. Wason was born in New Hampshire or Vermont in 1823, became a sailor at an early age, and saw Japan, China, and India. He weathered the dreaded Cape Horn numerous times and joined the California Gold Rush, during which he learned the basics of prospecting, placer mining, and the darker side of the mining frontier. Wason spent much time in Central and South America where he served as captain on a pearl boat, became a rancher in Argentina, and mined gold in Central and South America. Wason returned to the United States via California in 1870 and acquired a small herd of fine horses there because they could be readily converted into cash. In 1871, he drove his herd, accompanied by Vaqueros, through parts of the West until he arrived in the Rio Grande River Valley where he established a ranch. When gold was discovered at Summitville, Wason joined the small rush in 1871 in hopes that his experience would give him an advantage, and there he met Benjovsky. The partners staked several claims but were unsuccessful. The experience, however, whetted their appetites for prospecting, which they fulfilled the following year on North Star Peak.[44]

In Dives Basin, the partners enjoyed a streak of good fortune. They identified one of the best silver veins on the peak and claimed it as the North Star, then followed it northwest with the North Star Extension claim. Around the same time, they identified a spur off the Shenandoah vein and staked the Spotted Pup claim. In time, all these would yield handsomely, but not without a host of problems. In 1872, Wason and Benjovsky suspected that they possessed properties of substance because rich ore was revealed from the beginning of the shallow assessment work required to hold the claims.

Prospectors, and now miners, were as busy in Arrastra Basin as in Cunningham Gulch. Members of the Dunn party fed their inefficient arrastra with ore from the Sampson Lode, and another group worked the Little Giant Extension. The Little Giant Mine, however, continued to be the most profitable and served as a portal for the first serious investment in the region from the outside world.

As early as 1871, rumors of the strikes made in Summitville, Baker's Park, and the Dolores drainage drifted to the East and drew the attention of Emery Hamilton, who was a capitalist in New York City. Hamilton left the comfort of refined civilization for rough Loma, New Mexico, so he could be one of the first investors on the ground and acquire the most promising prospects. The Little Giant clearly offered the most potential, and he petitioned French et al. for an interest when they came to town. Hamilton offered a handsome deal that specified immediate payment of $1,000 to each party member (about $15,000 today) and another $4,500 to each by September 1, 1872.[45]

So certain was Hamilton of the Little Giant's potential, he ordered a stamp mill to replace the arrastra, and it was shipped in pieces over the Santa Fe Trail to Santa Fe during 1871 and 1872. Compared with hauling the heavy iron through the mountains into the Las Animas District, the months-long trip across the plains from the Midwest was relatively easy. However, a freighter willing to undertake the difficult task and deal with suspicious Ute Indians proved impossible to secure, and so the disassembled mill waited in Santa Fe through most of the 1872 working season. This frustrated Hamilton, who saw idle time as lost profits. Finally, Martin Van Buren Wason saved the day, but for a price. While in Santa Fe, Wason learned of the mill, and, since he was headed back to his ranch on the upper Rio Grande, made a costly proposition to Hamilton to haul the pieces onward. Hamilton agreed, Wason purchased ten heavy wagons and, with Hamilton, freighted the first substantial cargo into the Animas drainage. Unfortunately for Hamilton, the trip consumed two months and placed them in the mining district at the end of September, which was too late for construction.[46]

To complicate matters, when Hamilton arrived, he found that he had no mine for his mill! Probably because he was on the trail with Wason, Hamilton neglected to make the September 1st payment to French et al., and they assumed possession of the Little Giant. Horrified, Hamilton learned upon arrival that the owners sold their shares in his absence to Samuel S. Wallihan, Sterling P. Rounds, and George W. Bishop of Wisconsin, and Dan Castillo. To collect capital for operations, the four investors formed the Little Giant Gold & Silver Mining Company of Illinois, which was also known as the Chicago Company.[47]

After recovering from the shock, Hamilton engaged in quick footwork to force himself into the new organization. When representatives arrived in Loma with supplies and additional mill machinery, he made it known that the new owners would need his mill, which was still his property. Hamilton offered to trade the disassembled equipment for company stock and declared that he would, after all, pay for Cook's share of the mine, which had not been transferred. He even offered to throw the Mountaineer claim into the deal, although Hamilton neglected to disclose that the property was not his. After clashing with Wallihan, the rest of the owners consented and Hamilton was once again a driving force behind the Little Giant, or so he thought. Relieved of their burden, and with $5,500 in their purses from the sale alone, French et al. returned to their first love, which was prospecting in the Las Animas District.[48]

During 1872, the Las Animas prospectors faced a set of fundamental problems that they would have to overcome if they wished to see their efforts amount to anything substantial. Extreme isolation, vast distances to nodes of commerce and communication, and the lack of ore treatment facilities retarded development. In addition, Wason and Hamilton's two-month journey from Santa Fe made painfully clear the impossibility of efficient transportation. While these factors were not unique to new mining districts, the politics of prospecting in the San Juans exacerbated and even threatened the wealth-seekers' progress.

Simply put, the prospectors were squeezed between the Utes, who did not want them in the San Juans, and the United States government, which literally outlawed such activity there. During the 1860s, the Utes learned to mistrust Whites based on interactions of intolerance and violence, and on several treaties arranged to assume portions of their traditional territory. Aware that settlement and mining were inevitable in the southwestern and central portion of the Colorado Territory, the government and the Utes agreed to the Hunt Treaty in 1868. According to this act, the Utes would relinquish the central portion of the Colorado Territory and remove to the west. In exchange, the government outlawed permanent White settlement there. The government, however, made several fatal errors. First, officials perceived the Utes as a single entity when, in fact, they belonged to at least seven bands. Second, for the sake of political convenience, the government recognized Ouray as spokesman for all Utes, when he actually held limited power. Last, the government ignored the fact that the lust for gold and silver overpowered the Whites' respect for the law.[49]

The result in the San Juans was predictable. Prospectors came, the Utes became angry, individuals on both sides were suspicious, and tensions rose. In hopes of mollifying the Utes, the government passed an order during the Spring of 1873 to expel all prospectors and miners. Uncertainty pervaded those with interests in the Las Animas District, and their efforts were threatened for a short time. Understanding that expelling the prospectors from the San Juans would be unenforceable, the government saw bloodshed on the horizon and attempted to negotiate with the Utes once again. With Otto Mears as a mediator, the government met with Ouray and hammered out the Brunot Treaty in 1873. Mears and Ouray both understood that the Whites would inevitably come, and if the Utes could not reach an agreement, they stood to lose all. Instead of disaster, the Utes ceded the San Juans in exchange for annual interest on a $500,000 trust and a promise that the surrounding lands would remain theirs.[50]

The treaty had a major impact on prospecting and mining in the San Juans. With threat to life and limb eased, prospectors were free to wander the San Juans as best as the hostile environment permitted. The political stability instilled a sense of confidence among investors, and businessmen and merchants felt that their ventures could be permanent instead of tenuous. Under these conditions, the Las Animas District saw more prospecting and, finally, mining, in addition to that at the Little Giant, however primitive it was. The outside world began to take notice of the sacks of gold and silver ore packed out of the mountains, which began to cause a stir.

Arrastra Gulch was still the hub of activity, and rightly so. The new owners of the Little Giant invested a considerable amount of capital to make their operation as substantial and well-equipped as any other mine of similar size elsewhere in Colorado. Workers under Mulholland, who was appointed superintendent, finally erected the mill approximately 1,600 feet downslope from the mine in July, 1873. A Dodge crusher pulverized crude ore into small cobbles, a battery of stamps reduced the material to sand and gravel, and a ball mill pulverized the lot into slurry. With increased surface area, the particles flowed over amalgamating tables coated with mercury, which leached out the gold. A 115 horsepower steam engine powered the machinery, and the boiler was almost certainly a portable locomotive unit. As was the case with the earlier arrastra, workers recovered the amalgam and drove off the mercury in a retort.[51]

The mine and mill were separated by around 500 vertical feet, which presented a logistical problem that would plague most mines in the district. Instead of carrying the ore overland in canvas sacks by burro, which was slow and costly, the company sent the payrock down to a transfer station near the mill on a single-rope reversible tramway. A bucket on a pulley rode on a fixed track cable that spanned between the mine and station, and a worker winched the bucket up and lowered it down via a brake. To those in the Las Animas District, these improvements were nothing less than inspiring. The San Juans received their first steam-powered mill, and while the tramway was remarkably simple, it was the earliest in Western Colorado. Compared with what was to come, however, it would seem like a mere child's toy.[52]

What the Little Giant Mine featured in equipment and actual ore, adjacent properties had in promotion. One of the claims just in production, probably the Little Giant Extension, stimulated enough confidence to interest a group of capitalists to the sum of $450,000, or around $7 million today! Had the capitalists actually seen the property, which was no more than a short tunnel, they may not have been so eager. Thomas Blair's Aspen Lode, high up on the ridge west of Arrastra Gulch, attracted attention among prospectors again in 1873. Robert McGregor found yet another adjacent vein in what was becoming a complex series of narrow ore bodies, and named the claim after himself. He spent much of the summer mining ore from a shallow shaft equipped with a hand windlass. Several days later, Thomas P. Higgins and Z.H. Lawman, both of whom arrived in 1873, staked the nearby Susquehanna along the area's northwest-trending geology and began a tunnel downslope and east.[53]

At a time when prospectors searched for veins and miners focused on the handful of producing properties, several groups of individuals looked to the future and engaged in other activities. Envisioning the need for lumber for a boom which was sure to come, Henry F. Tower and Wesley A. Stevens brought the first sawmill into the Animas drainage and assembled the components on Mineral Creek, extending west from Baker's Park, where plenty of straight fir and spruce trees grew. The lumber was consumed almost as quickly as the partners could mill it.[54]

Probably tired of the hubbub of activity and the clatter of the stamp mill in Arrastra Gulch, Reese, Blair, and William Kearnes decided to move out to a quieter location. With the idea of claiming large tracts of land for ranching at the least and locating at townsite at the best, Reese filed an 80 acre homestead claim on the broad, open floor of Baker's Park, where a settlement was most likely to grow. Blair and Kearnes filed adjoining 160 acre homestead claims, and Reese was the first to actually build a cabin on the land. Sadly, Adnah French would not be joining them. Like a true prospector, French realized a dream with the discovery of the Little Giant and reveled in its sale. Flush, French spent his money on luxurious living and died of alcohol poisoning during the summer.[55]

By the end of the 1873 working season, Baker's Park was on the brink of a transition from prospecting to mining. A few investors expressed trepedatious interest and invested in minor claim development and the machinery at work on ore and lumber. Tower, Stevens, and Wason proved that heavy machinery could be hauled into the district, albeit slowly. Rumors of production were confirmed when silver ore and gold bullion emerged from the district for all to see. By the end of the year, the Little Giant yielded $12,000 in gold, or $183,387 today, with McGregor and others generating an additional $2,000 in silver. While the number of prospectors remained in the low hundreds, there was enough activity in the entire drainage to spur Andrew McNutt to carve the Eureka Mining District out of the Las Animas, which was then reduced to the peaks and gulches on the south side of the Animas River. The Las Animas District even saw the first permanent settlement when Superintendent George S. "Gassy" Thompson and his crew of five dared to weather the winter at the Little Giant—and a long one it would be.[56]

CHAPTER 4

A Mining Industry Takes Hold

AS 1873 PROGRESSED INTO 1874, Thompson and crew were not the only individuals who impatiently waited for old man winter to loosen his grip on the San Juans. Excited about the potential offered by a new and unexplored region, prospectors began massing in Del Norte and other settlements on the Rio Grande. Some paid for lodging, a few built cabins, others camped in tents, and all prepared their tools and equipment, planned their provisions, and contemplated what they would do once they made the big strike. While these prospectors idled away, some of the visionary entrepreneurs of the Las Animas District made preparations for the mining industry that would surely come of the prospectors' efforts.

Dempsey Reese may have been the busiest and was not even in Colorado. After discussing the idea of a townsite with Blair and Kearnes, Reese spent the winter in Chicago and Cedar Rapids, Iowa, promoting the mineral wealth of the Las Animas District and the profits that investment in the townsite would bring. Reese found a ready audience in George Greene, who was one of the founders of Cedar Rapids, a justice on the Iowa Supreme Court, and president of the Union Bank of Cedar Rapids. With only a handful of nascent mines and at least a dozen proven ore bodies under development, Reese must have painted a glowing picture of the Las Animas District's potential, and Greene, who had an interest in mining and previously published a mining periodical, listened intently. Reese undoubtedly went on to discuss the potential offered by the entire region, and how no ore treatment facilities existed. Which of the men first suggested a smelter is unknown, but Reese returned to Colorado victorious with not only the key element for the mining district's fruition, but also a major anchor business for his townsite.[57]

Reese and partners were not the only entrepreneurs planning a townsite for the coming boom. Unwilling to wait for the spring thaw, Donald Brown risked his life under threat of sudden winter storms to cross over the range from Del Norte into Cunningham Gulch. Most likely on snow shoes, which were actually crude skis, Brown descended to the gulch's mouth and located the townsite claim of Bullion City on the flat floor of the river valley. When Brown returned, he, Horton D. Chase, Theodore F. Braun, and others formed a townsite company and filed the location. Unlike Reese, Brown could not boast of a smelter even before a single building was erected, but Bullion City possessed a major competitive advantage. Specifically, it lay at one of the most important and busiest crossroads in the entire drainage. The trail over Stony Pass and down Cunningham Gulch was the principal artery into the drainage. At the gulch mouth, a trail ascended northeast along the Animas River to Cinnamon Pass, another important gateway, and to other areas under exploration. A third trail descended southwest into Baker's Park. Given its strategic location, Bullion City was poised to become the first stop in the deep San Juans.[58]

During the spring, the weather stabilized at last, and prospectors began trudging through the snow on Stony and Cinnamon Passes and dropping into the Animas River drainage. With the snow heavy above tree line (as most of the terrain was) the prospectors made camps, a few erected primitive log cabins, and all examined the snow-free areas. The prospectors advanced as the snow retreated, although blockades prevented access into the highest basins for months. Those individuals who were present the previous year returned to their claims and resumed drilling and blasting, and the fortunate few with proven ore bodies began production. Gassy Thompson and crew, of

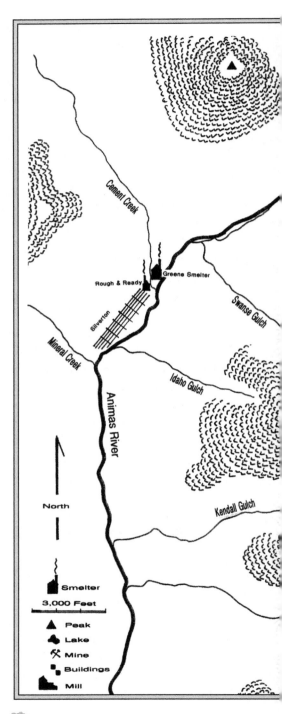

*Principal places of
activity, 1874 to 1880.
Source: Author.*

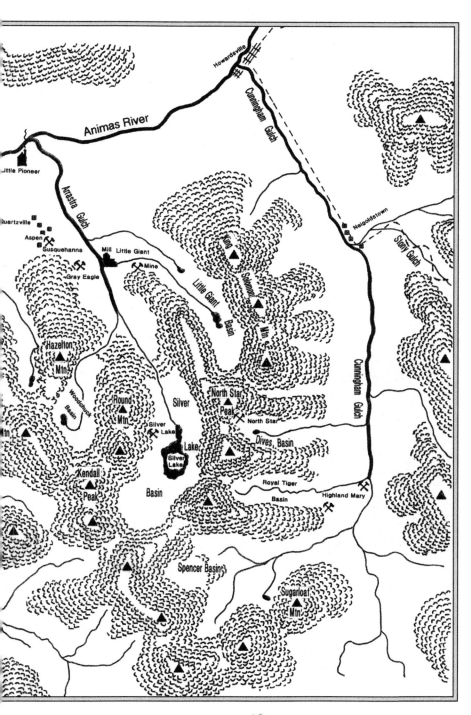

The plan view illustrates the Mammoth, Aspen, and Susquehanna claims, and the early mine workings associated with the Aspen ore system. Source: Adapted from Ransome, 1901:162.

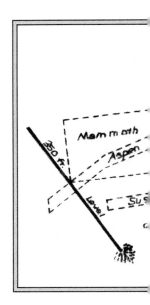

Colorado photographer William Henry Jackson captured these prospectors in their camp in 1874. The camp lies near treeline on the west side of Cunningham Gulch, in the vicinity of the Highland Mary and Mountaineer claims. The two prospectors could very well be members of John C. Dunn's party, who examined the area in 1874. In general, the prospectors' camp was a mining frontier institution, and the one in the photo was typical. Note the sacks of high-grade ore at the right. Source: Denver Public Library, Western History Collection, WHJ 10198.

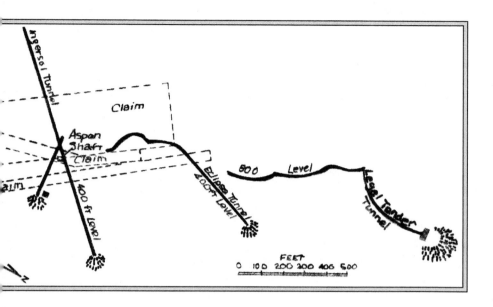

The Gray Eagle vein was directly exposed in the face of the cliff in the photograph, which made extracting the silver ore relatively easy since little development was required. As miners pursued the vein underground, they created the chasm-like open stope at center. Source: Author.

course, had been at work through the winter driving development workings and stockpiling ore. They welcomed the summer and the replenishment of the provisions it allowed.

Cunningham and Arrastra Gulches continued to be the centers of activity in the region, which was natural since they hosted the earliest discoveries. In Cunningham Gulch, Reese, Blair, and Mulholland prospected the high, barren, east side as the snow melted, and found a startlingly rich vein that they staked as the Green Mountain. Over the course of several months, they drove a tunnel and demonstrated that the vein held its value, then they began actual mining. With simple facilities, the partners realized enough ore to render the operation one of the region's most important for the time. Dunn, Quinn, and Richardson returned to their Highland Mary claim on the west side of the gulch's head, conducted development work, and relocated the property to ensure their title. Other matters, however, distracted them from drilling and blasting the vein's excellent ore. King Solomon Mountain, between Cunningham and Arrastra Gulches, drew interest and was a large enough mass that it was not overrun. W.S. Stratton was among the prospectors at work on the Cunningham side, and he staked and developed the Silver Cross and Black Crook claims. His visit to the Las Animas District was the beginning of a lifelong love of prospecting and mining that took him through most of Colorado's mountains. During the early 1890s, Stratton discovered the Independence Lode near Cripple Creek, raked in millions of dollars, and became known as the King of Cripple Creek. He never forgot his humble roots, however, of which his time in the Las Animas District was a formative part.[59]

On Hazelton Mountain, Blair, Mulholland, and Reese finally began sinking a shaft directly in ore on the Aspen Lode, and McGregor, Higgins, and Lawman went to work on their adjacent claims. This tight concentration of silver veins and the proof of rich ore stimulated a small rush to the mountain, and prospectors staked several additional claims. George Ingersoll, who was always on hand for the localized rushes, joined with Higgins to drive the Susquehanna Tunnel southwesterly to undercut the Susquehanna Lode. James L. Briggs, William E. Parsons, and Eugene Engley were among those who ascended Hazelton Mountain, and they found yet another vein extending southeast from the cluster. Instead of sinking a shaft like Blair et al., Briggs decided to drive a tunnel southwest like the Susquehanna.[60]

With the best ground on Hazelton Mountain claimed, other prospectors fanned out across the mountainside where they excavated exploratory workings in hopes of striking another cluster of veins. One partnership, Gregory and Brower, decided to pick their way along the cliffs that formed the shear west wall of Arrastra Gulch; and when nearly opposite the Little Giant Mine, they probably found float, or loose mineral samples, lying in the scree. By tracing the float up to the base of the cliff, the partners found a mineralized vein clearly exposed in the vertical wall, and one of them claimed it as the Gray Eagle. Staking the claim was almost as much work and more dangerous than mining the ore! Because the vein cropped out high on the cliff face, the prospectors had to scale the cliff to determine the vein's orientation, which would govern the direction of the claim. Once they accomplished this, the prospectors scrambled around to measure the claim boundaries and place corner monuments. This was all done with uncertain footing that threatened to plunge them several hundred feet down to certain death. Afterward, Gregory and Brower began production and shipped 1,200 pounds of high-grade ore to New York City for processing. This choice seems odd because the cost of sending the payrock across the country was exorbitant, and the Black Hawk Smelter in Clear Creek County could have treated the material.[61]

In contrast to the glamorized accounts of mining rushes, the prospectors and miners in the Las Animas District were peaceful, respectful of property and person, and adhered to the unspoken rules of frontier honesty. However, a combination of greed, confusion regarding claim ownership, poor records, and inadequate communication provided the conditions for several heated disputes that almost erupted in violence. The first occurred on Hazelton Mountain. When Thomas Higgins staked the Susquehanna Lode, he sank a shallow shaft on the vein as claim laws required; and, in 1874, he and Ingersoll began driving their Susquehanna Tunnel to intersect the vein. While they were away, partners of McGregor, whose claim was adjacent and slightly overlapping, assumed control of the Susquehanna shaft and were able to sack a little ore before discovery. Higgins and Ingersoll accused the sneaky miners of trespass, and the miners defended themselves by insisting that the shaft was on the McGregor claim. Instead of violence, both parties followed the mining frontier creed and took the matter before a miners' court. A panel was selected and the rough, grizzled, wool-clad men heard from McGregor and partners and Higgins and Ingersoll, and decided in favor of the latter.[62]

The second incident was not as easily solved as the first, nor were the parties involved as compliant as those on Hazelton Mountain. During the winter, Samuel Wallihan continued to question Emery Hamilton's involvement with the Little Giant and apparently managed to sway several of the other investors, including George Bishop, to his perspective. Wallihan, however, found it difficult to cleanly expel Hamilton from the company because Hamilton's mill was now an important part of the operation and had been used to turn out gold bullion. As a means of winning control over operations, Wallihan and Bishop hired Gassy Thompson and crew to work through the winter, hold the property, and turn it over when Wallihan and Bishop arrived in the spring.[63]

Sensing an erosion of his influence over the Little Giant and feeling that his source of profit was threatened, Hamilton panicked when he learned that Wallihan and Bishop were to take physical possession of the property. In Del Norte, Hamilton paid for an entourage of four gunmen, who were not difficult to find at that time, to accompany him to the mine in advance of Wallihan and Bishop. They crossed over into the Las Animas District, occupied the Little Giant under innocent pretenses, and smoothly assured Gassy Thompson that Hamilton was the proper owner. Thompson then turned the keys to the locks (which were only symbolic safety measures because the buildings were easily entered and the district was crime-free anyway) over to Hamilton. Leaving the gunmen in charge of the property, Hamilton accompanied Thompson to Del Norte, where he was supposed to meet Wallihan and Bishop. To better the case that the Little Giant was his, the wily Hamilton then filed claim amendments on the argument that the property had to be relocated when the Brunot Treaty conveyed Indian land to the Territorial Government in 1873. To those unaware of territorial land law, the fraud was excellent but, of course, it would never withstand legal scrutiny.[64]

Wallihan and Bishop arrived in Del Norte in June to meet Thompson, who was unaware of Hamilton's trickery. Thompson undoubtedly informed them of Hamilton's actions and the party hastened for the Las Animas District to reclaim their operation, leaving Hamilton behind in Del Norte. Once Hamilton learned of Wallihan and Bishop's departure, he hit the trail to overtake the party and beat them to the Little Giant. Hamilton was unable to sneak around the party and entered a direct race with Thompson, who was probably furious by now, on horses spurred to a full gallop.[65]

Hamilton beat Thompson and won the race but lost the mine. Hamilton was the first to arrive, and he barricaded himself in the tunnel then ordered his gunmen to form a shield. Thompson appealed to the miners' court, which met in special session, and relayed how Hamilton had jumped the Little Giant. This matter was of grave concern because claim jumping was a cardinal sin in any mining district, and William Kearnes and Alexander Wilson armed themselves for battle and crept up to the mine. They surprised the guard who was stationed at the tunnel portal, forced him to leave at gunpoint, and confronted Hamilton. More armed men arrived, the rest of the gunmen gave up, and the party threatened Hamilton with public hanging and banished him from the district without reimbursement for the property that he was forced to abandon. After several days, Wallihan and Bishop arrived to find the property in their possession, and they gladly paid their winter's debt to Thompson and crew. Hamilton, however, was not through with the Little Giant and seethed at the thought that his mill generated gold bullion for the treacherous company.[66]

During the summer of 1874, the Las Animas District boasted at least ten operations that generated ore. While the number was certainly greater than previous years, the mines were remarkably simple, shallow, and poorly developed. This included the Little Giant, excepting the steam-powered mill. The simplicity, lack of equipment, and minimal facilities limited the operators to the highest grades of ore because payrock of even medium-grade was uneconomical. This trend, however, was quite normal for remote and young mining districts of the era. Members of the original prospecting parties such as Reese et al. had enough experience to understand this, and Reese in particular put plan to action to further needed development in the region.

Two prominent mines, the Aspen and Gray Eagle, are excellent examples of the types of operations common to the Las Animas and other new districts during the mid-1870s. Archival information is not specific regarding the physical characteristics of either mine, but material evidence in the form of archaeological remnants clearly and accurately represents both operations today. The buildings, equipment, and items of value were removed from both mines long ago, leaving archaeological features and artifacts that, as is often the case with historic mines, compliment data gaps inherent in written records and allows us to interpret the facilities and reach conclusions regarding the workers.

As an archaeological site, the Aspen Mine features several parallel rows of prospect pits and several open-cuts, all aligned northwest-southwest. The rows are distinctly separated by around thirty-six feet, indicating that prospectors excavated them to track two separate veins, one of which was the Aspen. Blair and partners mined the Aspen from the top down, creating a series of open-cuts only as wide as the vein and around eighty feet long. As they progressed downward, Blair et al. drove drifts underground along the vein and had to install a hoist to raise an ore bucket out of the workings. As was common for simple operations, they installed a hand windlass that was no more than a spool with crank handles. To operate the windlass, one of the partners struggled with the crank and wound the spool until the ore bucket was at the open-cut's rim, then inserted a brace under the handle to arrest the movement. He grabbed the ore bucket's bail and hefted it onto the open-cut's edge, kicked out the brace, and dragged the bucket to flat ground where he emptied the vessel. The process was highly dangerous because if the windlass operator failed to catch the bucket or accidentally knocked out the brace, the full bucket could bounce down into the workings and crush anyone at the bottom.

To protect the windlass and the operator from the weather, Blair and partners erected a frame building over the main portion of the open-cut, undoubtedly with lumber from the new sawmill on Mineral Creek. Like all hardrock mines, the Aspen operation required a blacksmith shop to sharpen picks and drill-steels used to bore blast-holes. Currently, a platform for the shop lies on the open-cut's south rim, and its size and absence of structural materials indicate that the facility was a 9 by 9 foot wall tent equipped with a rock forge.[67]

Because the Aspen lay a considerable distance higher than and away from Blair's cabins in Arrastra Gulch, the partners constructed several impermanent residences near the workings. Building platforms and associated artifacts currently reflect three frame buildings that could have housed as many as nine workers. The Aspen site also features two earthen platforms for wall tents, which may have been the original residences occupied by Blair and partners when they initially developed the claim. A fireplace at one of the platforms indicates that the residents built large fires for outdoor cooking and to keep warm during cold nights, which were typical on Hazelton Mountain.[68]

The principal difference between the Aspen and Gray Eagle mines was that the workings were mostly horizontal on the Gray Eagle. Because the vein cropped out in a cliff face, miners at the Gray Eagle drilled and blasted the vein from several different levels at once and pursued the ore underground. As they went deeper, a tunnel undercutting the open stopes was most efficient, and miners hauled payrock out in wheelbarrows. As simplicity and austerity was the rule, the miners erected a single, 18 by 25 foot frame building against the cliff to house the necessary blacksmith shop and their residence, which occupied two small rooms. While coal smoke and grit pervaded the building's living quarters, which were extremely cramped, at least the forge helped to keep the interior warm.[69]

As can be surmised, the Aspen and Gray Eagle mines, like most of the operations in the Las Animas District, were primitive, small, and began with surface workings. After the surface ore had been extracted, miners pursued the payrock underground on a pay-as-you-go basis, and then only to shallow depths. The surface plants consisted of several structures at most that were crude, limited in size, and served multi-purposes. All work was carried out by hand and machinery was absent, and the surface facilities supported only the most elementary and basic needs of hardrock mining. The minimal development reflects the investment of little capital and the production of high-grade ore that miners sacked on-site for shipment over the range to Del Norte.

Despite the simplicity and primitive nature of the mines, they apparently generated enough ore to instill confidence among the Greenes and Reese in their smelter idea. Further, other properties elsewhere in the drainage showed all the signs of contributing payrock, which was a promise that many would fulfill. During the spring, Greene organized the firm of Greene & Company to build and operate the smelter, then hired John J. Epley and Thomas E. Bowman to accompany the disassembled smelter and a sawmill across the plains, through the San Luis Valley, and into Reese's new townsite. Epley was an expert with heavy machinery and understood how to assemble the basic components, and Bowman was a formally educated metallurgist and assayer.[70]

Unencumbered by the heavy steel and iron articles, Greene's son, Edward, arrived in advance of Epley and made preparations for groundbreaking on the north side of the Animas River. Part of the preparations involved establishing a supply business for the smelter and crew, which Edward did as Greene, Eberhart & Company. Seeing an opportunity to profit from sales as well as from smelting, the Greenes opened the supply business doors as a retail mercantile, which was gladly welcomed as the first in lower Baker's Park.[71]

Perhaps other milling entrepreneurs simultaneously saw the opportunity presented by the growing mining industry in the Animas River drainage, or the wintertime rumors of the coming Greene smelter spurred individuals into motion. In any case, two other parties constructed smelters during the summer of 1874 to compete with the Greenes. Christian Schoellkopf, Ashley Cooper, and Henry Remington constructed a facility, known both as the Little Pioneer Furnace and the Little Dutch Smelter, on flat ground immediately west of Arrastra Gulch's mouth. The facility was relatively primitive and relied on an arrastra made of brick to crush silver ore and a furnace to roast, then melt, the material. Schoellkopf, an ethnic German, probably based the furnace on designs he worked around in Swansea, Wales, which was the smelting capital of the world at the time. The choice of an arrastra for crushing was odd since machinery such as that used in the Little Giant Mill was superior in performance and required no manual labor such as shoveling. Given this, it seems likely that a lack of capital was the reason. Calder, Rouse & Company built the second facility, the Rough & Ready Smelter, on Cement Creek near the Greene operation. The Rough & Ready Smelter was small and as primitive as the Little Pioneer.[72]

When the three smelters of various sizes were finished, the Las Animas District, as well as the rest of the river drainage, finally saw the last crucial variable in the mining equation completed and ready to bring the nascent industry to fruition. The Greene Smelter was perceived as the best facility and used ore from the Gray Eagle Mine, stockpiled in eager anticipation, for its trial run. After the furnace had blown in, was heated for a time, and charged with ore, everyone was ready to see silver matte, an unrefined blend of silver and industrial metals, pour out of the ports. They were not disappointed, at first. After the matte had been run off into molds and the slag discharged, Brown, Epley, and Edward Greene were embarrassed to find that the smelter recovered only a fraction of the metals contained by some of the best ore mined in the Las Animas District. Word quickly circulated that the costly smelter, the hope of the river drainage, was a failure. Schoellkopf and partners had a similar experience, and the Rough & Ready Smelter produced a small amount of bullion then became tied up in litigation. Disappointment pervaded the region, the backers of the smelters lost precious capital, and confidence in the Las Animas District faltered. Greene & Company, however, refused to admit defeat and applied their capital and metallurgical expertise to identify a process that would work. One factor, discovered during this time, was that the ore in the Las Animas District was much more complex and resistant to treatment than anyone suspected.

To add to the disappointment, the Little Giant Mine failed by the end of 1874. During the summer, miners encountered an end to one portion of the gold-bearing vein after another in the workings. The company operated the mill fitfully and intermittently until the ore was simply gone. At the same time, Hamilton sued Wallihan over ownership and control, which was tantamount to fighting over a dead horse. Wallihan let a contract to have miners drive exploratory workings in search of more ore, but when the profits evaporated and legal fees mounted, Wallihan suspended operations. After miners extracted the last several hundred tons of ore, Wallihan closed the mill, sold some of the equipment to the Rough & Ready Smelter, and discharged the miners.[73]

While the Greene Smelter was on the trail into the river drainage, Reese continued to formalize and promote his townsite. Reese, Blair, and Kearnes interested William Mulholland, Francis M. Snowden, Nathaniel E. Slaymaker, and William Munroe in the venture, and they organized the Silverton Townsite Company as an umbrella for business affairs. Reese acted as townsite president and originally staked out the homestead claims, and Munroe, a surveyor, formally arranged the lots and streets on paper. Slaymaker, a lawyer who came to prospect, reverted to his former profession and administered the legal aspects.[74]

On slightly different dates, Blair, Snowden, and Slaymaker built the first three cabins in Silverton, in part to anchor additional construction. Greene & Company then erected its buildings in the area, followed by prospectors who constructed a few more cabins. By the height of summer, Silverton proper featured at least twelve residences and the Greene mercantile, while the smelter stood on the northern fringe.[75]

Just as 1874 was not a grand time for Silverton due in part to slow growth and the smelter failures, the year smiled on Bullion City, which saw nothing less than a boom. Donald Brown was correct in his assumption that the mouth of Cunningham Gulch was an excellent location, and because of this, Bullion City quickly became the region's principal hub. During the spring, a number of speculators and businessmen rushed to the townsite and claimed the best lots, while prospectors took up residence on the outskirts.

The heart of Bullion City, on the north side of Cunningham Creek, offered the best land, and a small business district materialized there. John C. Sullivan and James N. Galloway opened the first commercial blacksmith shop, Thomas Trippe established a surveying business, William Nichols brought an assaying business, and F.B. Hackett organized a law practice. All these men were experienced in their fields and they provided the services that were necessary for the successful evolution of a mining district. Trippe was born in Brooklyn in 1848, earned a degree in engineering and surveying, worked as a surveyor for a railroad, and came to Colorado in 1872. Nichols was an early arrival in Colorado, ran an assaying business in Clear Creek County, and closed shop to come to the Las Animas District. Due to his skill, he was later appointed Territorial Assayer for the San Juan region.[76]

Other businesses that catered to the needs of prospectors and miners quickly graced Bullion City. John and Amanda Cotton, the first permanent woman in the river drainage, opened a mercantile that evolved into a restaurant. Liquor, always in demand, was heavily represented. George Howard, who decided to make the best of his new neighbors, was the first to sell the precious liquid, followed by the formal saloons of George L. Wright and John Burrow. During the summer, additional businesses, including another mercantile, a boot maker, and a bakery, opened their doors. Located at the crossroads of important transportation arteries, Bullion City attracted a livery and the first cattle herd driven into the drainage as stock for a butchery.[77]

As the business district began to take form, the residents built cabins on surrounding lots and in a cluster near George Howard's establishment on the south side of Cunningham Creek. Based on this association, the southern residents named their suburb Howards, which was a name that grew in popularity until Bullion City was no longer recognized. During 1874, residents petitioned the Postal Service for a post office, which the administration granted under the name of Howardsville. The post office, the first in the river drainage, only furthered Howardsville's role as a center of commerce and communication.[78]

Images of Howardsville as a typical western mining town with a main street lined by false-fronted buildings and tidy houses could

William Henry Jackson took this impressive northeast view of Howardsville during his 1874 trip to the Las Animas Mining District. Howardsville, which was a commercial center, epitomized the types of towns on Colorado's mining frontier. The business district is at center, a few residences are scattered around, and Cunningham Creek flows through the foreground. The corral at the right may have been for one of Howardsville's packing services. Source: Denver Public Library, Western History Collection, WHJ 1582.

When Howardsville was designated the seat of new La Plata County in 1874, this primitive log cabin served as the first court house. The cabin illustrates just how informal frontier government administration could be. When Howardsville lost the seat to Silverton, the cabin saw other uses. The view is to the south, with the mouth of Cunningham Gulch in the background and Silverton Northern Railroad tracks at far left. The photograph was taken after 1906, when a branch of the railroad was graded up the gulch. Source: Denver Public Library, Western History Collection, X 9482.

not be less accurate. With lumber fetching high prices, residents and businessmen used locally harvested logs as much as possible for construction, and the businesses were only slightly larger than the tiny residential cabins. While a main street was taking shape, Howardsville actually consisted of several dozen crude buildings scattered almost haphazardly on both sides of Cunningham Gulch, with plenty of space between. Undoubtedly, Donald Brown hoped that these voids would soon be filled.

After the Brunot Treaty was signed, the Territorial Government realized that it possessed a considerable new tract of land that would be prospected and homesteaded in time. As had been demonstrated in the eastern half of Colorado during the previous fifteen years, the mining, settlement, increased population and commerce that followed prospecting and homesteading fostered a demand for government administration. Forecasting this for the southwest quarter of Colorado, the Territorial Legislature divided the region into La Plata, Rio Grande, and Hinsdale counties in 1874. La Plata County encompassed the Animas river drainage while Hinsdale County was its eastern neighbor.[79]

When the legislature surveyed La Plata County for the best county seat, they identified the largest, most promising town at the time, which was Howardsville. George Howard offered his small log cabin as the administrative building, and a second log cabin was rented for the court house. This must have perturbed Reese and partners, whose town of Silverton paled in comparison to Howardsville. The smelters were supposed to elevate Silverton to the level of "most important community," but instead their failure retarded Silverton's development. Probably through petitioning or lobbying the Territorial Legislature, Silverton organizers managed to have the county seat transferred to their young town.[80]

The smelter failures softened the outside world's confidence in the Animas River drainage, but the mystery of the San Juan Mountains and its untapped mineral potential still caused a stir. Prospectors made new strikes weekly, rich silver ore had been proven, the Animas River drainage possessed a local government and commerce, and residents now lived in the area year-round. The conditions finally came together for a rush, but developments elsewhere in Colorado siphoned off much of the outside world's interest as quickly as it developed. In 1873, Richard C. Irwin, William J. Robinson, and, ironically, the same James Pringle who was in Baker's Park two years earlier, proved rich silver in the Wet Mountain Valley, southwest of Canon City. Their discovery incited the Rosita rush of 1874, which was one of Colorado's most important silver excitements. At the same time, miners at Gold Hill in Boulder County realized that a dark material previously thrown out as waste rock was actually telluride gold. The county then saw its most intense period of prospecting since the initial gold rush of 1859. The development of the Moose, Dolly Varden, and other silver mines in the Mosquito Mountains stimulated a wave of prospecting west of Fairplay, and Montezuma in Summit County experienced a similar trend. As an added distraction for investors, mining in Nevada was doing extremely well and drew some of their attention and capital.

As had been proven elsewhere in Colorado, capital was absolutely necessary for mining, smelting, and transportation efficient enough to overcome isolation. Further, investment was the foundation for a positive feedback loop. Development and infrastructure on all levels, funded by capital, lowered the costs of mining, which allowed the production of higher volumes of lower grade ores. This fostered a reputation and confidence that drew additional investment, which in turn resulted in even greater production. Remote, new, and unproven, the Las Animas District could not compete with the rushes noted above, and the lack of capital from the outside world was dearly felt. As a result, the mining industry grew slowly during the mid-1870s and may have even become static were it not for several important developments.[81]

The Greenes were behind the first and most fundamental development, which began in 1875 when John A. Porter arrived at Silverton. Porter was born into privilege in Berlin, Connecticut, in 1850; and, as he grew to adulthood, he was captivated by the mining industry. Intent on entering the mining industry from the top, Porter attended the Columbia School of Mines for a time then moved on to study metallurgy at the Royal Academy of Mines in Germany, which offered one of the most prestigious mining education programs in the world. When finished with his studies, Porter returned to the United States in 1872 and went to wild and remote Eureka, Nevada, where he gained practical frontier experience as an assayer for the Richmond Consolidated Mining & Smelting Company. After working for Eureka's most profitable operation for several years, Porter moved on to Cherry Creek, Nevada, and served as assayer and assistant metallurgist. He then decided to expand his horizons and establish a consultancy. At the behest of investors, Porter traveled southeast through the barren Great Basin into the San Juans to report on the region's potential. Each day took him farther from his cultured roots and deeper into the lifestyle and acceptance of hardship required by the frontier. Porter approached the San Juans from the south and ascended along the Florida River, which took him through sedimentary geology rich with coal beds. As a mining expert and metallurgist, Porter took an interest in the coal, a resource always in demand, and noted the location for future reference. When Porter arrived in Silverton, he was probably given the red carpet treatment once it became known that he may be a source of capital.[82]

Edward Greene and John L. Pennington, manager of the business end of Greene & Company, treated Porter very well for other reasons. They saw in Porter, who had more practical metallurgical experience than anyone else in the region, the expert who could solve the smelter's problems. Within a short time, Greene & Company made Porter an offer that he could not refuse and secured him as chief metallurgist. Porter may have also sensed that sound employment in Silverton was the gateway to a very bright future in a treasure trove waiting to be opened by capitalists.[83]

During the summer, Porter refitted the smelter based on the designs that he worked around in Eureka. Repeating the sequence of events that preceded the 1874 failure, the furnace was blown in, charged with ore, and all gathered around to see what came out of the spouts. It was liquid metal, and in the proportions expected! The smelter was at last a success, Porter was a hero, and word spread through the Animas drainage like a shockwave. Even the Rough &

The Greene Smelter in Silverton was fundamental to the success of the Las Animas Mining District, and in this late 1870s view, the facility is in full blast. The square smokestacks for the smelter's two main furnaces belch fumes from the building at right. The warped rooflines on all the buildings illustrate that mining industry structures were far from perfect and often went out plumb within several years of completion. Source: Denver Public Library, Western History Collection, X 61438.

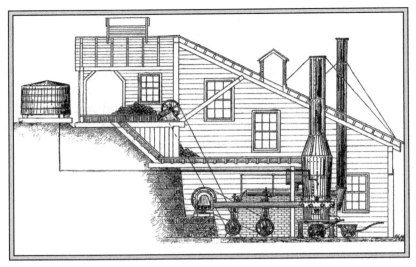

The profile illustrates the typical layout for a smelter, and we can assume that the Greene facility was similar. Workers received ore on the floor at the upper left and fed the material into a crusher. The pulverized material was stored on the floor at center, and workers periodically shoveled it into the tall smelting furnace on the floor at the lower right. The furnace was prefabricated and featured a powerful blower that fanned the fire within. Smelters such as the Greene facility usually had several furnaces. Source: Mining & Scientific Press *4/28/83, p281.*

Ready Smelter showed promise. The owners overcame their litigious behavior, rallied, and fired up the facility. The cooperation, however, was temporary, and after the furnace generated a ton of matte, they resumed fighting and suspended operations, leaving Greene & Company with a monopoly. Even though the Greene Smelter was the only regional ore treatment facility, the company wisely secured contracts with mines for ore and even went so far as to lease the Aspen from Blair and partners, who were glad for the effortless income from the royalty payments.[84]

The Greenes could not have expected their monopoly to last long. In 1875, when Porter worked on the Greene Smelter, the Crooke brothers engaged in similar activities in the Summitville Mining District, located over the range to the southeast. The Crookes were highly experienced, and Jonathan in particular was a New York City smelting and mining financier with a twenty-five year record. It seemed only logical for the brothers to make the short leap over to the San Juans as the mining industry showed promise. Instead of direct competition with the Greenes, the Crookes made haste to build a smelter in the Lake City area and capture the trade there before someone else did. The mines of the Lake Fork drainage, however, were part of what the Crookes hoped would be a larger empire that included the Animas River drainage.

Before the Crookes even started their smelter, they began their move toward an empire by aggressively soliciting contracts for ore in the Animas drainage, which initiated a war with the Greenes. The winner of the battle was, of course, the nascent mining industry as agents from both camps petitioned mine owners and even prospectors with claims known to feature ore. Further, the returns provided by the smelters to the mine owners were far greater than shipping the payrock to distant facilities, which rendered lower grades of material profitable. To ensure sources of ore, both organizations either leased or purchased mines outright during 1876. The Greenes invested $11,000 in mining properties in the Animas drainage, the Crookes purchased and consolidated the Ute and Ulay Mines in Hinsdale County, and both parties contracted for ore from areas high and low. They even went so far as to solicit contracts as far away as Imogene Basin and Howard's Fork.[86]

In the Las Animas District, the demand for ore and the superior financial returns finally fostered a long-awaited wave of mining, claim development, property transactions, and additional prospecting. The district even continued to be a place of contest between the two smelting organizations. Greene & Company was quick to claim Hazelton Mountain as its territory with the Aspen Mine as the centerpiece. The company continued to lease the Aspen and treated $40,000 worth of ore, or around $698,000 today, which was a figure limited only by the Aspen's primitive facilities. During the winter, prospectors driving a tunnel downslope from and north of the Aspen, on the same ore system, struck a vein then leased the property to Greene & Company. As a reflection of Greene & Company's presence in the area, the firm named the tunnel the J.L.P. after John L. Pennington. In 1877, Higgins and Ingersoll, aware that their Susquehanna Tunnel neared the anticipated vein, hired a small crew to expedite work. Finally, after penetrating 515 feet of rock, miners struck the ore formation, which featured a bonanza of silver, and they named the vein the Victor. Rewarded, Higgins and Ingersoll began enjoying significant profits and, around this time, renamed the operation the Ingersoll Tunnel. The ore, along with that from the Gray Eagle, went to Greene & Company.[87]

Just as Hazelton Mountain went to the Greenes, North Star Mountain, the other hot spot of activity in the Las Animas District, went to the Crookes. In 1876, James H. Winspear, a lawyer in Del Norte, purchased the North Star Mine originally as a source of ore for a smelter he proposed to build in Eureka on the upper reaches of the Animas River. Winspear's reputation as a debtor was poor, at best, and his law practice carried little respect. While the smelter was under construction, the Crookes contracted with Winspear for ore, then purchased a partial interest in the mine later in the year when he needed capital. In 1877, Winspear crossed over the range to Silverton to escape his debts but remained attached to the Crookes. The uneasy partnership developed the vein with a series of shallow tunnels, began production, and had workers divide the ore between Greene & Company and the Crooke Smelter according to the split ownership, which would change in favor of the Crookes within several years. Like most of the mines then open in the Las Animas District, the North Star was small, shallow, and labor-intensive.[88]

In addition to the North Star, the Crookes acquired several other claims around North Star Peak. The Royal Tiger and Royal Tiger No. 1 were among them, and they extended west from Royal Tiger Basin, which was a hanging valley adjacent to and south of Dives Basin. During 1877, the Crookes hired several miners who drove a tunnel into the Royal Tiger vein and shipped a batch of silver ore to the Crooke Smelter for testing.[89]

Prospectors throughout the region tried to profit from the smelting war by hitting the trail in search of new veins. By 1876, the Las Animas District still possessed plenty of potential because of the extreme terrain, short working seasons, and the limited acreage that the small population of existing residents was able to cover. Further, the ground that prospectors had already examined during previous years still possessed a likelihood of ore because initial efforts were cursory and incomplete. As an example, in 1875 assayer William Nichols prospected the north face of King Solomon Mountain a short distance above Howardsville, which had been examined once before. He found a small system of veins that offered silver and industrial metals, proved ore through a series of pits, and claimed the apex as the Little Nation.[90]

A few other prospectors made important discoveries, but in reality most of the wealth-seekers were unsuccessful like their brethren throughout Colorado. A few finds made by successful individuals drew attention to some of the deepest, most inaccessible portions of the mining district. Theophile Ressouches and Alfred Py were among the fortunate, and they were the first to spend an appreciable amount of time in Little Giant Basin. Ressouches and brother Louis were born in France to Laurent and Melanie, who came to Denver in 1866 in search of opportunity. Drawing on skills practiced in the Old World, Laurent found employment as a premier gardener, but Theophile and Louis, without skills, left for the San Juans when they were able and of age. The brothers arrived in the Las Animas District with little money, which forced them to work as miners until they had enough savings to prospect. Theophile met Py and, once they had sufficient funds, the partners ascended into Little Giant Basin and made camp on the valley floor.[91]

Little Giant Basin is actually a hanging valley where a glacier gouged out 1,000 vertical feet of solid rock and pushed the material northwest into Arrastra Gulch. King Solomon Mountain rises abruptly to the east and forms an imposing wall that features outcrops, scree slopes, and sheer cliffs. North Star Peak, with an equally harsh façade, forms the basin's south headwall, and an arête serves as the west side. When the glacier melted, it left several small lakes on natural terraces, which are separated by short and steep rises that feature waterfalls. At around 11,400 feet elevation, the lower lake was partially sheltered by a fir and spruce forest, but the upper lake, 12,100 feet high, was barren and perpetually windswept. Between the constant winds and the brief hours of sun, blocked by the high and steep walls, the valley's climate was neither the calmest nor the warmest.

Perhaps this is why Ressouches and Py were among the first to stay long enough to seriously examine Little Giant Basin. They wisely camped near the lower lake, embraced by the cliffs of King Solomon Mountain, and were rewarded for their efforts in 1875. They claimed a vein with a rich showing of silver as the Jura, but before the partners could explore the formation at depth, dwindling finances forced them back to work. The following year, they returned with Louis, continued to examine the same area, and staked the adjoining King Solomon. They repeated the pattern in 1877 with the Mountain Queen. Other prospectors joined the Ressouches brothers, picked over the opposite side of the valley, and found a vein so large they named it the Big Giant. While they were rich with claims and veins, the various parties lacked the capital or time for substantial development and waited instead to find investors.[92]

At the same time that Ressouches and Py examined King Solomon Mountain, several independent prospectors made the dangerous ascent into Arrastra Basin, a short distance south. As early as 1871, the prospectors working on the floor of Arrastra Gulch around the Little Giant Mine must have gazed up and south to the valley's imposing headwall cliff, locked in ice and snow for all but several months of the year, and wondered what lay beyond. In 1876, John Reed was the first prospector documented to put action behind curiosity.

What he found was another hanging valley carved by glaciers from between Kendall Peak and Round Mountain to the west and North Star and other peaks to the east. Their flanks, with 1,000 feet of relief, were even more sheer and rugged than in Little Giant Basin, and they presented a lacework of veins and dykes that must have excited Reed. At the valley's center lay a pristine glacial lake surrounded on most sides by exposed bedrock, and its outflow cascaded northward until it roared off the valley's precipitous north rim. With coarse scree slopes, jagged spires and outcrops, and little life, Arrastra Basin resembled a lunar landscape, especially during the nights, which were always cold and windy.

From the prospector's perspective, Arrastra Basin was ideal because the geology was plain for all to see. Examining the valley's west side on the flank of Round Mountain, Reed easily found more than one vein that carried silver and industrial metals. He claimed two on Round Mountain as the Whale, probably after its large size, and as the Round Mountain. He located the Silver Lake near the lake. Around the same time, another prospector working at the valley's head identified a huge fault and traced it southeast, where it featured a vein that he claimed as the Buckeye. During the summer, both men excavated shallow workings to prove ore and to retain title to the claims, then left for the season. When the prospectors returned the following year, Silver Lake Basin, as the valley came to be known, saw its first production, which was shipped by burro to the Greene Smelter. To the Greenes, the volume of ore was insignificant because the arduous and dangerous approach discouraged Reed and the other prospectors from packing much out and importing anything but the most essential materials. This limited production.[93]

CHAPTER 5

Silver, Gold and Psychics

IN 1875, EDWARD INNIS, an investor from New York City, developed the Highland Mary claim, at the head of Cunningham Gulch, into the most advanced operation yet in the Animas River drainage. Finally, the Las Animas District saw in Innis a serious capitalist from the outside world willing to pour money into claim development. Innis' motives, however, had nothing to do with the smelting war and its demand for ore, but instead began one of the strangest chapters in mining history.

Edward and brother, George, inherited a fortune and a set of profitable businesses in New York from their family. The businesses included a wood dye plant, investment banking, the Pennsylvania & Erie Railroad, and the Poughkeepsie Bridge over the Hudson River. Awash in money, luxury, and high society, the Innis brothers hungered for something more than money could buy, such as adventure. This they found in the Las Animas District, although not through normal means.[94]

During a portion of his business life, Edward kept an advisor on retainer who guided him in investments and important decisions. Interested in the potential offered by mining, Innis consulted his advisor, who suggested that he examine the Las Animas District because, there, he was sure to find a rich mine. What Innis kept to himself and a select few was that the advisor was actually a seeress, a psychic medium, whom he paid handsomely. She identified the Las Animas District not from a sound investment strategy, like most mining capitalists, but by placing her finger on a map and declaring that there lay a lake of gold awaiting discovery![95]

Probably slightly bewildered, Innis began his search for the Holy Grail by traveling to the Las Animas District and surveying the types of mines in production. It seemed to be a reasonable assumption that a lake of gold should offer some clue, which, in a mining district rife with silver veins, would logically be the only gold mine. When Innis consulted the psychic, she claimed that he was on the right track and that the lake of gold lay underneath a mountain in the area. However, she could not be specific about which one. Seeking further clarification, Innis examined several operations and consulted with Emery Hamilton, whom he may have known earlier, but did not divulge to Hamilton his secret. Hamilton informed Innis of extremely rich ore specimens collected from the Highland Mary claim, which Christian Schoellkopf had bonded for purchase. Possibly upon direction of the psychic, Innis moved quickly and purchased not only the Highland Mary, but also several adjoining claims to the west, which he felt lay over the lake of gold. Innis was happy to pay the $30,000 (around $500,000 today), and John C. Dunn, David Quinn, and Andrew Richardson, the original prospectors, were even more pleased to receive the funds.[96]

With little time to waste, Innis consulted with H.D. Whittemore to make preparations to drive a tunnel into the lake of gold. Whittemore was an agent of the Ingersoll Rock Drill Company in New York City. While he was conversant with compressed air technology and rockdrills, which had just been introduced, he was by no means an experienced mining engineer. Whittemore naturally made rockdrills a centerpiece of the operation and, while they were on order, he designed a surface plant to serve the Highland Mary Mine. Clearly larger and more advanced than anything the Animas River drainage had yet seen, the surface plant included an 18 by 25 foot compressor house constructed with logs and rock walls, a 26 by 34 foot stone boiler house, stables, an explosives magazine, and a store house. Whittemore planned a 22 by 30 foot mess hall and three 25 by 25 foot bunkhouses for a crew of thirty. For Innis an impressive log structure known as the Whitehouse was to be constructed. A two-story log building with a porch, the Whitehouse featured an office, superintendent's quarters, guest rooms, a kitchen, and many luxuries to make Innis feel at home.[97]

Today, archaeological aspects of the surface plant designed by Whittemore currently remain at the Highland Mary Mine site, and they reveal his limited competence in terms of mining engineering. In general, when planning a surface plant in anticipation of ore production, experienced mining engineers followed several rules for the organization of facilities. Usually, the tunnel was driven into a location that offered enough space for the storage of waste rock, the construction of critical support facilities, and a mill downslope. In so doing, ore could be moved from mine to mill by gravity, and critical facilities could be built adjacent to the opening. In addition, engineers usually arranged the surface plant components according to a master datum, or survey line, taken off the strike of the tunnel. Not so at the Highland Mary Mine. Whittemore sited the tunnel too low in elevation and too close to the floor of Cunningham Gulch to allow for a mill, the adjacent facilities, and waste rock storage. As a result, he built the facilities upslope in a haphazard arrangement, which engendered unnecessary and inefficient materials handling, servicing, and coordination. This was, however, an excellent representation of the state of Innis' mining operation.[98]

So sure was Innis that he would realize his Holy Grail within a short time, he financed the construction of a small smelter at Howardsville in 1875. With Hamilton on his side, Innis attempted to pillage the idle Little Giant Mill not to save capital, but because he did not want to wait for his machinery to make the long journey into the Las Animas District. Goaded by Hamilton, Innis sued Wallihan for possession and lost, forcing Innis to have mill machinery dispatched. Completion of the smelter undoubtedly excited Howardsville residents, who looked forward to challenging Silverton as an ore treatment center. Had they known Innis' pretenses, however, the residents would have been rightfully skeptical.[99]

In 1876, Whittemore arrived at the Highland Mary with the rockdrills and immediately put them to work driving the Innis Tunnel in a southwesterly direction. Satisfied with his handiwork, Whittemore returned to New York and appointed Thomas Mosely as the first superintendent in a series rife with rapid turnover. While Whittemore left much to be desired as a mining engineer, he made a significant and lasting impact on the western mining industry. Specifically, his introduction of rockdrills to the mine in 1876 was one of the earliest commercial applications of these apparatuses in Colorado and the Rocky Mountain West. For context, it was not until the 1890s that the mining industry truly embraced rockdrills, and ten more years passed before they were commonplace.[100]

A year after Innis began developing the Highland Mary, the lake of gold still eluded him, although the psychic kept him in a state of wonder and intrigue. Progress, however, was too slow, and Innis decided to approach the lake from two directions. He purchased the Little Giant Mine in hopes that it would lead to the gold. He even consulted the psychic regarding the direction that the Innis Tunnel should take, and because she was capricious, she often gave inconsistent directions. As a result, miners drove the tunnel this way, then that, until it was serpentine. When the miners penetrated perfectly fine, economical ore bodies, they were astounded when the superintendent, under Innis' orders, commanded them to leave the ore in place and drill and blast onward to some unknown destination.[101]

As mining and prospecting gathered steam during the smelting war, more people trickled into the Las Animas District. Most collected in Howardsville, Silverton, and the several other principal centers of activity. To house those with money, James Briggs took a break from his Briggs Tunnel on Hazelton Mountain and opened Silverton's first hotel in 1875. To quench their thirst, four saloons went into business. By 1876, Silverton mushroomed to 210 buildings and, as a reflection of community values of mining over God, a church was not among them, nor would one be for years. The town fathers did, however, erect a combination school, courtroom, and meeting hall. Howardsville also enjoyed growth and received a diverse array of businesses, however earthy they were. In 1876, Charles and John Pearson established the town's second slaughterhouse and a stockyard to supply regional butcher shops and mines with meat. John, James, and Joseph Gunsolus played to Howardsville's role as a transportation hub and ran packtrains into the Last Animas district. Charles Fischer and Henry P. Gill, acutely aware of the frontier penchant for drink, built Western Colorado's first brewery, known both as the Rocky

Thomas Blair developed the original Aspen Mine to the left of and above the large clearing near center. Prospectors drove a number of tunnels to the left, and established the camp of Quartzville around the disparate workings. The photo is a south view. Source: Author.

Mountain Brewery and Gill & Fischer. In 1877, Edward W. Johnstone and Andrew Bigger opened saloons and took different approaches toward the community. Johnstone was a family man and Bigger was a bully who shot a man in the back in Del Norte and came to Howardsville to hide. He went to prison for subsequent murders after he left Howardsville. To profit from the morally weak, a small troop of prostitutes even arrived and set up several tents on the edge of town. Because most individuals were too busy to bother, the ladies failed to return the following year.[102]

Some individuals who did not gravitate to Silverton or Howardsville in 1876 and 1877 found themselves in one of two new settlements that grew by default around the prospects and mines on Hazelton Mountain and in Cunningham Gulch. On Hazelton Mountain, local prospectors and miners began referring to their informal collection of cabins around the Aspen vein system as Quartzville, which the greater region then recognized.

Quartzville was, in many senses, a typical 1870s prospectors' camp, and today it manifests as a ghost town site represented by an excellent assemblage of archaeological features. Platforms and cabin remnants represent formal residences, fire hearths are left from open camps, and artifacts in the form of domestic refuse tell much regarding the inhabitants. Here, it is important to state that the settlement site has been thoroughly examined and the reader can rest assured that absolutely no buried treasure exists today. Anyone wishing to visit the site bears the moral responsibility of leaving everything exactly as they find it out of respect for history and future generations.

Quartzville never grew beyond being a handful of cabins, most located near the mines and prospects. The Aspen Mine, one of Quartzville's most important operations, featured three frame buildings and a wall tent that housed nine miners. William Kearnes, the principal operator, and his superintendent John McMahon were among the crew. The Ingersoll Tunnel, Quartzville's other important operation, featured a boardinghouse for George Ingersoll, Thomas Higgins, and around three or four other miners. James Briggs and Eugene Engley lived in a cabin at the Briggs Tunnel, and William E. Parsons had like accommodations at the adjacent IXL Tunnel. A few additional cabins or tents were built at three other tunnels with unknown names. The

While the photograph was intended to depict King Solomon Mountain, at center, it also shows a few buildings associated with Quartzville, at upper right. By around 1900, when the image was taken, Quartzville was largely abandoned but the cabins still remained. Edward and Lena Stoiber's mansion at Waldheim, built in 1895, stands at the lower right. Source: San Juan County, 1904; courtesy of Colorado School of Mines.

majority of Quartzville stood on a natural, flat area near the Legal Tender Tunnel, north of and downslope from the above mine workings. The flat area was less than 400 feet long and several hundred feet wide, and it featured an open camp, two frame buildings, and two log cabins. During the 1870s, unmarried workers in communal residences usually required around sixty square feet for bedding and personal possessions, which means that Quartzville housed about twenty miners and prospectors.[103]

Describing Quartzville as an informal mining camp almost seems to be an overstatement. Only a handful of its cabins were clustered together in the traditional sense of a settlement, and the rest were scattered among at least seven mines and prospects. Cumulatively, the disbursed residences housed a population of forty-five, which was much too small to support any businesses or a post office, which today's archaeological evidence confirms.

And what of Quartzville's residents? How did they live? Did the miners and prospectors there base their diets on canned beans and liquor as popular history portrays? Were the miners and prospectors the settlement's only residents? The answer lies with the artifacts, the domestic refuse, scattered around Quartzville's building features. In terms of diet and lifestyle, popular history is, in fact, partially correct,

Decades have passed since this tumble-down boardinghouse in Quartzville has seen residents other than squirrels and chipmunks. The log cabin typifies the types of buildings that constituted Quartzville. Source: Author.

Around 1906, this two-story boardinghouse was built at Quartzville for the Aspen Tunnel crew. Source: Author.

although grossly oversimplified. According to thousands of food cans on the site, Quartzville residents did rely to a great degree on pre-served food, which was necessary given the poor food-preservation environment and the lack of time between working shifts to prepare fresh meals. The cans, however, contained a variety of foods such as soups, stews, meat, vegetables, fruit, preserves, and milk. Interest-ingly, nearly all the residents did consume fresh foods when available, including pork, chicken, beef, and baked goods. If these repasts were served, then they were probably accompanied by vegetables and fruit, such as potatoes, corn, and apples, which stored well and could be cooked at altitude. In contrast to the myths regarding alcohol con-sumption, Quartzville residents were quite modest in their drinking, reflected by relatively few fragmented bottles and jugs amid the site today.[104] As can be expected at a camp such as Quartzville, most but not all of the residents were miners and prospectors of limited socio-economic status. Several individuals with disposable incomes lived at the Aspen Mine and the settlement core by the Legal Tender Tun-nel, and they were probably superintendents. Several women graced Quartzville as well, reflecting the ubiquitous presence of the fair gen-der on the mining frontier. According to archival sources, one was

Clara Parsons, the wife of William E. Parsons, who lived at the IXL Tunnel. Another was married to William Kearnes, who managed the Aspen Mine. Archaeological evidence confirms that Kearnes' wife or a third woman lived in the settlement core.[105]

A summary of a camp like Quartzville can become somewhat dry without the color of important events, such as life and death, that only archival sources can convey. For example, Kearnes' wife actually gave birth to a son in one of the primitive log cabins during 1878! Quartzville also saw death the previous year. The Parsons regularly invited Briggs to their cabin at the IXL for Sunday dinners. During the winter of 1877, Briggs started for the Parsons cabin through deep snow and realized that he could not make the trip on foot. He turned back for his snowshoes and, as he crossed a snowfield within twenty feet of his destination, Briggs triggered an avalanche that swept him down to the east base of the mountain and buried him head first. Despite the perceived dangers of mining, Briggs' grizzly demise was one of only several deaths in the Las Animas District during the mid-1870s.[106]

The other settlement that drew some of the region's prospectors and miners was Niegoldstown, located where Stony Gulch opened into Cunningham Gulch. Reinhard Niegold, the eldest of four ethnic German brothers, came to the Las Animas District in 1872 to prospect, and the second eldest brother, Gustave, joined him within a year or two. Despite the tardy arrival, Gustave found a vein rich with silver and industrial metals south of Stony Gulch in 1874, and the brothers claimed it as the Philadelphia and Little Fanny. Two other brothers joined the Niegolds in 1876, and they began production according to the simple, labor-intensive methods commonly employed in the mining district. The brothers had select ore samples assayed in Howardsville, probably by Nichols, and the reports indicated that the payrock featured as much as $1,100 in silver per ton. With visions of sugarplums dancing in their heads, the Niegolds hired a crew to increase output and hasten them on their way to fortune.[107]

In a move that was advanced for the Las Animas District's mining industry, the Niegolds decided to build a concentration mill at the mouth of Stony Gulch instead of sending the ore directly to a smelter. The concept behind a concentration mill was simple and economically prudent for mining companies with substantial ore reserves. Such a mill merely separated worthless waste, known as gangue, from the ore's metal content, and was not intended to generate matte or bullion. By shipping only the concentrates to a smelter for final treatment, the mining company saved the costs of freighting the waste, which consumed a significant share of the profits. The Niegolds' modest mill featured a Blake crusher that reduced crude ore to gravel, a battery of five stamps that pounded the material into sand and slurry, and a Frue vanner that carried out the concentration. In 1877 or early 1878, the brothers started the mill and it worked at first. But as the ore increased in complexity with depth, the mill lost too much of the metal content and forced the Niegolds to ship the payrock to a smelter anyway.[108]

The bunkhouses for the miners and mill workers became the seed for a small settlement that the brothers modestly named Niegoldstown. Taking advantage of opportunity, the brothers decided to formalize the settlement and requested a post office, which the Postal Service granted in 1878. They also built a sawmill for their operation and sold the surplus lumber, which was always in demand. The Niegolds' employees and a few prospectors and miners who moved into the settlement fostered enough demand to encourage a mercantile, saloon, and hotel, which may have been operated by the Niegolds. The town, however, remained small and primitive and never grew beyond a cluster of log buildings, even though it lay directly on the heavily traveled Stony Pass route.[109]

Following a pattern common to the mining frontier, influential individuals in the Las Animas District backed the development of a primitive infrastructure to assuage a sudden increase in the demand for goods and services. Because mining, milling, and settlement were functions of the movement of supplies, ore, and people, improvements to the transportation system were among the most important. Prior to the smelting war, the Animas River drainage lacked formal roads and, except for infrequent freight wagon expeditions, horses, mules, and burros were the principal movers of materials and people. Each animal had its advantages and limitations and was used to meet specific needs. Horses were the quickest and best trained, but carried limited weight, especially over the extreme terrain of the San Juans. As a result, they were used primarily as passenger vehicles by people traveling significant distances. Mules, by contrast, were slow but

Posed in downtown Silverton, this pack train illustrates the common methods used to carry, drag, and otherwise haul ungainly mining supplies into the Las Animas Mining District. Known as both mountain canaries and jacks, burros were the best-suited beasts of burden for the tortuous pack trails that led to the mines. The pack train, photographed during the 1880s, has a load of mine rails and an ore car. Source: Denver Public Library, Western History Collection, X 1771.

highly intelligent, powerful, and surefooted, and could heft as much as 400 pounds on gentle grades. Freight packers found them to be excellent for carrying heavy loads of equipment, building materials, supplies, and sacks of ore from shipping points to all parts of the San Juans. To make trips economical, freighting outfits usually assembled strings of mules led by a muleskinner who rode one of the lead animals or a horse. Prospectors and mining outfits, however, often preferred burros because these compact animals could scramble over the worst ground, were inexpensive, and could subsist on anything green. Because of their small sizes, burros were limited to loads of around 200 pounds but could easily navigate the narrowest of trails. On the few occasions where wagons penetrated the roadless San Juans, the ox was the preferred beast of burden because of its power, simple needs for fodder, and endurance. In addition, once an ox was no longer needed for hauling, it could always become dinner.

Given the reliance on draft animals to carry what people could not, it comes as no surprise that the original transportation system in the Animas River drainage consisted of a network of packtrails. As eluded to in the pages above, several well-beaten artery trails entered Baker's Park from the east over Stony, Cunningham, and Cinnamon Passes, and from the south over Molas Pass. The Stony Pass route crossed over from the head of the Rio Grande River, descended Stony Gulch, and entered the Animas River Valley via Cunningham Gulch. The Cinnamon Pass route crossed over from the Lake City area directly into the Animas River drainage; and the Molas Pass route roughly paralleled the descent of the Animas River south toward very old New Mexico settlements. By winter, each route became impassable to all but the most daring and resourceful on snowshoes who were able to pack mail and the odd specialty package at exorbitant prices. For a mining district with aspirations of notoriety and full-time ore production, this simply would not do.

Otto Mears, known as Pathfinder of the San Juans, understood this and saw great profit in toll roads. During the 1870s, he hired

Pack trains were as important for carrying ore down from the mines as they were for hauling supplies up. During the early 1890s, one pack train laden with sacks of ore passes down Greene Street in Silverton. To ship ore by pack train, miners had to sack the payrock in burlap bags, which were then lashed down to the burros. While transporting ore in this manner was costly and consumed much of a mining operation's profits, few economical alternatives existed. Source: Denver Public Library, Western History Collection, X 1769.

crews to grade a network of roads from the San Luis and Arkansas River valleys west toward the San Juans and the Gunnison area. The fathers of Lake City, including the Crookes, realized that roads were necessary for their wellbeing and graded several trunk lines in the eastern San Juans. The principal interests in the Animas River drainage, however, were slightly behind, even though their connections with the outside world were more tenuous.

Most of the goods consumed in the drainage came from shipping points in eastern Colorado, and so it would seem logical to improve the Stony and Cinnamon Pass trails first and establish links with the Lake City and Otto Mears road networks. Instead, Dempsey Reese and lumberman Henry F. Tower commissioned the first toll road, which took a route south and down the Animas River canyon to Hermosa and Animas City in 1876. Reese and Tower's direct experience with the region's weather superseded logic based on geographic distances. They understood that wagon roads over Stony and Cinnamon passes would become blocked by snow, while the Animas River Valley route, although much longer, was serviceable most of the year. Further, a road graded by the Park View & Fort Garland Freight Company already linked Conejos, in the San Luis Valley, with Animas City, and provided the essential connection with eastern Colorado. Reese and Tower saw their road carrying traffic by 1877, and began to recover construction costs by charging a lofty six dollars for teams and six dollars round trip for stages, which is around $100 today![110]

Almost as an embarrassment to the Animas River drainage interests, Lake City investors were the first to grade a road along the Cinnamon Pass Trail, but they stopped at Animas Forks, the river's headwaters. The motive was probably to capture some of the trade and make it easy to ship ore from the Animas River drainage to the Crooke Smelter. In 1877, San Juan County, created a year earlier, gathered its funds and finally completed a public road from Silverton up the river to Animas Forks, at last granting the desired shortcut over the range to Otto Mears' eastern network. The road, however, was poorly engineered and offered freighters plenty of opportunity to try the strength of team and harness in mud bogs.[111]

From the commercial and transportation hubs in the Animas River drainage, specifically Howardsville and Silverton, packtrails extended up all the major valleys and gulches to the mining centers.

The trails naturally followed the paths of least resistance and fewest obstacles and usually wound along the flattest ground. Feeder trails branched off the main avenues and zigzagged up to nearly every mine and prospect of note. Because these trails were the responsibility of the users, they tended to be well-constructed. Where the trails ascended across soil-laden slopes, prospectors and miners cut them with pick and shovel, and in areas of exposed rock and scree, the workers erected rock walls to maintain flat surfaces. Usually steep and exposed, these trails were the domain of mules, burros, and men on foot.

In the Las Animas District, several areas of mining were important enough to justify the construction of short spur roads. In 1876, the Innis brothers reasonably assumed that a toll road would be graded over Stony Pass and funded the first segment from Howardsville to Stony Gulch. Probably at the behest of the Greenes and Blair et al., the county graded a road up Hazelton Mountain to the Aspen vein system in 1877, which increased the volume of ore packed to the Greene Smelter.[112]

Communication with the outside world was a key institution of the mining frontier, and it saw great improvement in the Las Animas District during the mid-1870s. The system of packtrails and roads enhanced the spread of written notes, word-of-mouth, and even innuendo between the mines, Silverton, Howardsville, and communities elsewhere in the San Juans. The mail and newspapers, however, were the most important and reliable sources of information, and their arrival was more prompt and assured than in previous years. In the early 1870s, someone from the Animas River drainage had to fetch the mail from Del Norte, where the nearest post office lay. By 1875, two post offices at Howardsville and Silverton served the Las Animas District, and a carrier delivered the mail at regular intervals. When he arrived, he usually faced a crowd that anxiously milled around waiting for their names to be called. Many residents dropped what they were doing to receive precious news from loved ones, relatives, and business interests, and those unable to be present had to pick up their mail from the post master at a later time. Crews of miners working at locations too remote to gather on mail day had to rely on the benevolence of their employers to bring them the mail.

Newspapers generated almost as much excitement as the mail, and the pioneers of the Las Animas District enjoyed several, which they read, re-read, and passed on to others. The *Rocky Mountain News*, published in Denver, usually covered important national and territorial stories as well as cultural topics, but because it arrived with the mail, the news was less than fresh. In 1875, John R. Curry established the *La Plata Miner* in Silverton, which he changed to the *Silverton Miner* in 1879. Curry's paper, the first in the Animas River drainage, covered local news, extracted stories from Denver and Eastern publications, and served as an ebullient voice of the region.[113]

The assemblage of businesses in Howardsville and Silverton provided most of the immediate services that the pioneers needed when not at work on their claims. By the mid-1870s, district residents even had access to several doctors who had to practice frontier medicine given the lack of anything approaching a formal clinic. James Beaton, who arrived to prospect in 1872, was the first doctor in the region; and he was joined by others in subsequent years. Given the youth and health of the population, Beaton had plenty of time to attend to his mining interests.[114]

Many of those youthful and healthy individuals maintained their high fitness levels by working at a number of small mines scattered throughout the mountains. These operations shared a symbiotic relationship with the Greenes, who held their own as the smelting war continued through 1877 and into 1878. The Greenes had so many contracts and independent deliveries that metallurgist John Porter decided to add a second furnace. At the same time, W.G. Melville felt that the Animas drainage offered enough business to support a second ore treatment facility, which he began in 1876 as Melville & Summerfield. Melville's facility, however, relied on the lixiviation process, which used chemicals and water as a solvent to leach silver out of roasted payrock. While lixiviation had been proven to work with simple silver ores, it was no match for the complex material in the Animas drainage, and the mill's immediate failure in 1877 sent Melville back to the drawing board. He tried again in 1878 with the same result, then suspended operations. Interestingly, William H. Van Gieson followed a parallel path in Lake City.[115]

Edmund T. Sweet and Oliver Matthews also entered the Animas drainage's growing ore treatment industry, but they decided to open a facility that filled a specific niche. Specifically, Sweet and Matthews erected an ore sampler in 1878, which catered to small mines with sporadic production. A sampler was a combination assay house, smelter, and ore buyer, and it specialized in providing assays, testing batches of complex ore to identify the best treatment methods, and buying small lots of ore from outfits that needed immediate income. At the sampler, the purchased ore was segregated into piles by composition and, when enough of a single type had accumulated, the batch was smelted in a custom run. Samplers posed no immediate threat to smelters such as Greene & Company because the smelters, set up for large volumes of specific ore types, were unwilling to make process adjustments for small, specialty batches. Instead of building a facility anew, which would have been costly, Sweet and Matthews refitted the idle Rough & Ready Smelter. Because the Animas drainage possessed an array of small mines with complex ore, the Sweet Sampler enjoyed success from the start.[116]

To keep pace with new construction, several firms erected additional sawmills where the timber stood tall. In 1876, Greene & Company merged its logging operation with Tower & Stevens on Mineral Creek, and Melville & Summerfield set up another sawmill in the same area. After the company finished its lixiviation mill, it began selling the lumber in Silverton. H.F. Schenk brought a third sawmill into the Cement Creek drainage, whose trees had yet to fall to the axe. The San Juan Reduction Company erected a fourth sawmill at Gladstone in 1878, farther up Cement Creek from Schenk's facility.[117]

By 1877, both the promotion and proof of ore in the Animas River drainage finally created a sensation that spread through eastern Colorado and even the greater mining industry. The region possessed a small smelting industry, despite initial failures, as well as a primitive infrastructure, an increase in population, and formal settlements. Of this, one of the leading mining journals of the day noted:

> In the spring of 1872, when the San Juan excitement first began, few people regarded it in light of anything but a common mining stampede, which would shortly die out or prove to be only an ordinary furor over a fairly good mineral district. Instead of this, however, the five years that have passed since then have, in their results, not only upheld all but the most exaggerated of the assertions first made in regard to the wealth of the district, but have brought to light many

new resources which are at present being developed with an
energy equal to that found in any part of the West. In a word,
San Juan is an undoubted success. Its mines are not myths,
nor its rich ore products solely of the imagination.[118]

While the statement may have been slightly ahead of the actual situation in the San Juans, the Las Animas District seemed to be headed for greatness. The cornerstone, of course, was mining, which was why the inhabitants were in the district. By 1878, the district featured twelve principal operations and a handful of small producers worked by one or two individuals. Ore continued to trickle out of the Gray Eagle Mine and, during the height of summer, burros struggled down from Silver Lake Basin with sacks filled with rich payrock. Hazelton and North Star Mountains, however, remained the most productive centers of mining.

Quartzville held onto its status as one of the most consistent sources of ore for the Greenes, although this came into doubt for a brief time. As a general social rule, the original Las Animas pioneers tended to maintain close relationships based on their shared histories and hardships, business ventures, and the identity of being the founding spirits. Blair, Reese, and Mulholland may have been the most intimate, and they had an unspoken trust. When Reese organized the town of Silverton, he drew William Kearnes into the clique, and Kearnes then joined the partners in several mining interests. While they would not include Kearnes in ownership of the Aspen, they were willing to lease the mine to him, knowing full well that Kearnes would make handsome profits. Once Kearnes assumed operations, he made a deal with the Crookes where he would ship the ore to them in exchange for a loan of $4,000, to be repaid with a share of the profits. In debt, Kearnes was supposed to pay for supplies and miners' wages, but to everyone's astonishment, he quietly slipped out of the San Juans instead with full pockets. If this were not enough of a shock to a community that prized honesty, Kearnes' brother sold property that was not his to the Greenes and left as well. The damage was significant. The Kearnes brothers left a trail of debt to individuals with limited funds and angered the unpaid crew at the Aspen Mine. The miners threatened to strike and apply a miners' lien against the property, which would have required its sale for

Located at around 13,000 feet elevation, the North Star Mine was one of the most difficult properties to work in the San Juan Mountains. The climate, the topography, and the precipitous mountainside conspired against all efforts to profit from the rich silver vein. Regardless, miners developed the vein through several tunnels, which are denoted by the waste rock dumps and the shop buildings. Source: Denver Public Library, Western History Collection, X 62716.

restitution. Needless to say, Blair and partners promptly ascended to Quartzville, dug deep into their purses for back wages, and restored their good standing.[119]

North Star Mountain continued to be the domain of the Crookes, and they tightened their grasp on the productive operations there. In 1878, the Crookes sold a controlling interest in the Royal Tiger Mine to McPherson Lemoyne, who was a wealthy friend from Boston, assuming that he would cooperate with them. Loyal, Lemoyne brought the Royal Tiger into production, albeit on a limited scale, and had workers pack the payrock to Lake City for smelting.[120]

When James Winspear's Eureka Smelter failed due to misman-agement and ineffective processes in 1879, he decided to leave the region and sold his shares of the North Star Mine to the Crookes. To ensure possession over all the North Star vein and associated mineral formations, the Crookes, Lemoyne, and John N. Goodwin, one of the original prospectors on the mountain, joined forces, organized the North Star Mining & Smelting Company, and consolidated their various claims. Lewis Crooke was secretary and treasurer, John Crooke was the most influential board member, Lemoyne was president, and John Goodwin acted as vice-president. With power and money, the partners convinced Martin Van Buren Wason to part with his share of the North Star, which he probably did because he realized that the mine was simply too difficult to work himself.[121]

The mine was, in fact, difficult for anyone to work. As discussed in previous pages, the North Star vein trended northwest across North Star Peak, which rose to a lofty 13,416 feet in elevation. The southeast side of the peak, where Wason excavated his original workings, was steep, barren, and a mixture of cliffs, spires, and unstable scree slopes. Literally in the clouds during storms and subject to constant winds, which were hurricane force at times, the peak's environment of total exposure made surface work unpalatable and even life threatening during lightning storms. Further, because of the high elevation, snow was common in all months of the year and was guaranteed

In 1875, when Joseph Collier captured this northward view of the North Star Mine, the Crooke brothers owned the property and developed the vein through several tunnels. Miners in the lower tunnel, in the foreground, have been busy as evident by the stack of sacked ore around the portal. Pack trains of burros and mules were the only connection with the outside world, and they made regular ore shipments to the Crooke Smelter in Lake City. Source: Denver Public Library, Western History Collection, C 99.

William Henry Jackson was able to persuade this traveler and his horse to pause on one of the main packtrails to the North Star Mine in 1875. The trail began in upper Cunningham Gulch, wrapped north around the sheer cliff in the photo, then entered the safety of Dives Basin beyond. It seems unimaginable that trains of burros used this trail to carry down ore! The trail can still be walked today. Source: U.S. Geological Survey, Jackson, W.H. 1147.

This southeast view is of the remnants of the North Star ore bins at the mine's base camp on the floor of Dives Basin. Workers sorted the ore by grade and piled the material into one of several bins for crushing. Source: Author.

from October through May. As a result, work at the North Star was understandably seasonal, and even then the tolerable weather was a mere four months long.

Under Superintendent James Murdoch, workers erected a simple surface plant as early as 1877 on the north side of Dives Basin, a short distance southeast of the workings. The location offered enough flat space to allow muleskinners to assemble pack trains, which carried loads of ore down the basin and over the range to Lake City. Trails used by the miners ascended up to the North Star workings, and of course, the 13,000-foot elevation made even the shortest distances seem weary and long.

The surface plant consisted of four single-story buildings for the crew, pack animals, and ore storage. The main building, 15 by 42 feet in area, housed a small blacksmith shop, living quarters for six or seven workers, and a cooking and dining area. Another building downslope and south near the lake on the basin floor was a bunkhouse 9 by 25 feet in area that housed four workers. The ore storage structure was L-shaped and featured a row of eight flat-bottom ore bins totaling 12 by 42 feet in area. Workers stood by the bins and shoveled cobbles into a single stamp mill on a platform below that crushed the material into gravel. The advantage was that the gravel filled the canvas ore sacks to capacity and minimized the dead space that occurred between coarse cobbles. The stable, built away from the residences, was an 18 by 18 foot shed with an extension for several workers. It was surrounded by a corral. In general, the buildings

Workers fed crude ore from the North Star ore bins into a one-stamp mill for crushing because the resultant gravel was easier to sack for shipment. The photograph depicts the battery box for the single stamp as it exists today. Source: Author.

offered no amenities, had poor insulation, and were drafty given the area's fierce winds. The residential complex was, however, situated amid stunning beauty.[122]

During the working season of 1878, the Crookes increased development then pushed hard the following year. In 1879, they dispatched eighteen miners to the North Star, which was more than the flimsy residences could comfortably accommodate. They produced around three tons of excellent ore per day and drove development workings. Like the rest of the mines in the district, except for the Highland Mary, the workings were shallow and miners extracted ore directly from the vein with little extraneous effort.[123]

The North Star was not the only mine that yielded ore in Dives Basin in 1878 and 1879. After selling the North Star, Martin Van Buren Wason purchased an interest in Theophile Benjovsky's Shenandoah Mine, and they maintained a constant but limited production. At the same time, George Ingersoll took a break from his Quartzville operation and began developing the Dives claim, southeast of the North

Known as the Whitehouse, this two-story log building was Edward Innis' home away from home when he visited the Highland Mary Mine. The building served as a post office, polling place, mine office, and residence appointed with enough comforts to satisfy the wealthy Innis. The late 1870s view is to the north, the abyss of Cunningham Gulch extends into the background, and the mine is out of sight and behind the building. The pack train in the foreground was hauling lumber to one of the mine's upper tunnels. Source: Denver Public Library, Western History Collection, X 21782.

While Edward Innis enjoyed the Whitehouse, Highland Mary Mine workers settled for more modest accommodations, such as this log boardinghouse. For more than ten years, miners throughout the San Juans called these types of boardinghouses home. As a testament to the ubiquitous presence of women on the mining frontier, a member of the fair gender stands to the left of the doorway. She probably served as the hostler, which was a job almost as wearisome as mining. William Henry Jackson took this northwest view in 1875, and King Solomon Mountain rises in the background. Source: U.S. Geological Survey, Jackson, W.H. 1261.

Star group. He and several partners erected a tiny cabin, only 12 by 15 feet in area, as their residence, and completed a small tunnel house that enclosed a blacksmith shop. Because trees were nowhere to be seen around the basin, Ingersoll and partners had to haul lumber up to their claim for the buildings. By 1879, Ingersoll developed a vein and began minor production.[124]

Literally downslope and east of Dives Basin, a crew of as many as sixty workers was making a considerable din at the Highland Mary Mine in 1878. Still bent on finding the lake of gold, Innis had miners drive three additional tunnels higher in elevation than the

Innis Tunnel, which was termed Level No.1. The highest tunnel was Level No.4, and it was probably driven on the original Mountaineer claim far above the surface plant. Innis hoped that four tunnels would increase his likelihood of finding the lake of gold, but all that the miners encountered were fabulous silver veins, and then only by accident. Probably under the recommendations of superintendent Thomas Mosely, miners extracted a paltry twenty tons of silver ore and sent it to a smelter in St. Louis to be tested. The smelter reported excellent returns, but bent on finding the Holy Grail, Innis ordered that exploration continue and silver mining stop. Such behavior was simply unprecedented, and this, combined with constantly changing and poorly conceived mandates, completely undermined confidence in the operation. Superintendent Mosely left.[125]

The Highland Mary complex became a community hub by 1878, in part because Innis was generous with his Whitehouse, which cost around $10,000 to build and furnish, or $175,000 today. Innis took in an occasional guest, offered a few meals to prospectors and other mine owners, provided a polling place for elections, and obtained a post office under the name of Highland Mary. Probably on advice from the psychic, Innis ordered a stamp mill with a battery of twenty-five stamps and hired Lewis Schantl, expert metallurgist, to replace Mosely. Schantl was to oversee construction of the mill, but he quit within the year. The mill may have been built anyway under Schantl's replacement.[126]

Innis also used the Whitehouse as a hospital in the wake of a deadly disaster in 1879. During February, nine miners, including J.P. Anderson, Theophile Ressouches, Steven Toy, Ansalmo Giovanni, and Big Dave Olson, were eating lunch in the Level No.4 tunnel house when the frame building began to emit loud creaks and snaps. Olson, who understood winter in the mountains, instantly knew that the sounds harkened an avalanche and quickly kicked open the door and dashed into tunnel portal for safety. But since the building was cramped and the tunnel portal was limited in size, the other eight miners had difficulty crowding through. Before all were safely in the tunnel, the avalanche completely swept the building off its ledge, and, with it, Giovanni and Toy. Workers down at the Innis Tunnel saw the event and responded to Olson's stentorian voice beckoning for help. Superintendent Schantl organized a rescue party to find the miners entombed in the snow and debris and dispatched other workers up to Level No.4. Their route took them to a point above and to one side of the tunnel, and despite the danger of the remaining unreleased snowfield, Philip Uhl, John Klussman, G.T. Beall began traversing against their better judgment. Already weakened by the nearby avalanche, the snowfield released and created one of the most witnessed and deadly avalanches of the time. Uhl and Klussman plummeted 1,500 feet down into the gulch, but Beall was thrown to one side and saved himself by clinging to brush. Despite the cataclysmic event, after the avalanche finished, Beall resumed traversing the slope to rescue the workers. The injured were taken to the Whitehouse, and Toy's body was not found until an April thaw.[127]

In 1878 and 1879, the development of several trends set in motion events that permanently changed the social, industrial, and economic landscapes of the Animas River drainage and the Las Animas District. One of the trends had to do with the value of silver. In 1878, the Federal Government passed the Bland-Allison Act, which was, in essence, a massive subsidy for the silver mining industry. Initially, the government declared that the federal treasury would recognize a gold standard to the exclusion of silver. Concerned over the impact to silver mining, Western senators and representatives drafted the Bland-Allison Act, which reinstituted the partial monetization of silver, and required the government to buy the white metal at an average of $1.20 per ounce, or around $21 today. Previously, silver fetched $1.15 per ounce, and the increase in value coupled with the stability imparted by the Act instilled considerable confidence among investors, mine owners, ore buyers, and smelters. This should have generated considerable interest in the Animas River drainage, where rich silver ore proven at a number of mines was in want of serious development.[128]

A conspiracy of factors, however, prevented the interest from taking hold. First, Colorado hosted two of the most significant booms in the West in 1878 and 1879, which distracted silver-hungry investors. The first was Leadville and the second was Silver Cliff, ironically located only around eight miles from Rosita, whose boom caused a similar trend in 1874. Second, the wave of mill and smelter failures throughout the San Juans clouded the region's reputation among individuals knowledgeable about sound mining investment. The ore could be profitably treated, (as the Greenes, the Crookes, and Sweet's Sampler demonstrated), but investors instead saw the failures perpetrated by inexperienced and inept metallurgists. Third, the Meeker Massacre provided quite a fright for Coloradans, except among the seasoned pioneers of the San Juans. The Brunot Treaty granted the various bands of Ute Indians title to the lands surrounding the San Juans, but following a now tired pattern, White settlers encroached on the territory anyway, and the Utes were moved several times. The Southern Utes quietly settled on a reservation in southwestern Colorado. Nathaniel Meeker, in charge of the White River agency in northwestern Colorado, tried to force the Northern Utes into an agricultural lifestyle to which they were not accustomed. As tensions between the Northern Utes and Meeker escalated, Meeker sent a communication to the army, which headed for the White River area against warnings by the Utes. When the army arrived, the Utes attacked the agency,

An account of the Las Animas Mining District would be incomplete without at least one illustration of Silverton. The 1877 view is to the south, and the Greene Smelter stands at bottom, the Animas River courses beyond town, and Kendall Mountain towers on the left. Source: Denver Public Library, Western History Collection, X 11384.

killed Meeker, and took women as hostages. After a pitched battle, the Utes were subdued, but an anti-Indian hysteria developed and the outside world perceived the San Juans as wild, dangerous, and fraught with wild savages. In actuality, nothing could be farther from the truth, as the Utes were neither wild nor savage, and the Whites had been the perpetrators.

For the Animas River drainage, this conspiracy of factors proved to be very troublesome. Why, investors reasoned, should they risk capital on an under-developed and remote region where the climate was uncertain and problematic, when Leadville and Silver Cliff held great potential? As a result, the mining industry in the drainage remained static, and some of the small operations even ceased as their high-grade ore gave out. Competition between the smelters and mills, built on the expectation of an increase in ore production, intensified and casualties fell by the wayside. In a move that stunned the Animas River drainage, the Greenes decided to suspend their operations at Silverton in 1879. The smokestacks stopped belching their acrid fumes, the furnaces cooled, the machinery was stopped, and the valley became unsettlingly quiet. Financial troubles, emotional exhaustion, and the distance of the Greenes from Silverton were partially to blame, but competition and ore that grew increasingly complex and difficult to treat were the underlying reasons. The physical weakening and frailty of George Greene, the engine behind the business, certainly contributed as well.

Caught by complete surprise, the Las Animas District's miners tried to assess how the smelter's closure would impact them. The loss of their best and nearest treatment facility would be painful, and the district braced for a slowdown. Other mills and smelters existed at Lake City and Ouray, but the costs of shipping ore over the mountains consumed most of the profits. Sweet's Sampler and the San Juan Reducing Company lixiviation works at Gladstone, located on Cement Creek north of Silverton, were able to process some of the ore packed out of the Las Animas District, but the active mining companies relegated themselves to shipping only the highest grades of ore. As the district subsided into a depression, many wage laborers left. Visionary mine owners and business interests, however, held fast because an end to their problems was already in sight.

CHAPTER 6

Boom in the Basins

DURING THE MID-1870S, when the Animas River drainage entre-preneurs went begging for capital, few investors of significance seemed to listen. The success of the Greene Smelter and the proof of rich ore, however, did draw the attention of one of the most important orga-nizations for the development of any mining district. Specifically, the investors of the Denver & Rio Grande Railroad, with their hands on the pulse of the Rocky Mountains, clearly saw the inevitable growth of southwestern Colorado and the potential offered by mining in the mountains. William J. Palmer, William A. Bell, and others planned a line through the San Luis Valley and around the south side of the mountains to head off competing railroads such as the Atchison, Topeka & Santa Fe. With such a route, Palmer, Bell, and associates hoped to capture not only the business of the San Juan mines, but also the agrarian freight traffic, which was almost as important. The Denver & Rio Grande began grading its line in 1876, which increased the optimism of and confidence in the Animas River drainage.[129]

While the track gangs were at work, farmers and town builders were busy organizing a new Animas City on the broad, fertile, Animas River Valley at the south toe of the San Juans. The demand for goods, produce, and livestock in the San Juans was the foundation for the town's official establishment in 1876, and when the city fathers learned of the Denver & Rio Grande's plans, they naturally assumed that they would host the terminus. Unfortunately, the fathers knew not with whom they were dealing. Pursuing a highly aggressive policy for which the railroad would become known, Palmer and associates demanded concessions from Animas City such as free land, help with grading the track, a free right-of-way, and a mandate to buy company stock. Animas City fathers balked and the Denver & Rio Grande retaliated in 1879 by platting its own town, Durango, two miles to the south.[130]

Even though the Las Animas District was in depression during 1879, those individuals who remained understood that a revival, if not a total boom, was almost around the corner. The close proximity of the railroad would bring immeasurable benefit because trains could carry greater volumes of freight at much lower rates than wagons. Not only would this reduce the cost of living in the Las Animas District, but also ore could be shipped to the large smelters in Black Hawk, Golden, Denver, Pueblo, and Leadville. Further, these facilities were prepared to profitably treat the district's complex ore.

Interested in being more than just a glorified delivery service, Palmer, Bell, and other Denver & Rio Grande investors wanted nothing less than an empire, and quietly made plans to provide ore treatment in addition to rail service. In 1880, while track gangs pushed toward Durango, Palmer et al. contacted John Porter, who had returned to Eureka, Nevada, in 1877, and offered him the position as chief metallurgist and manager of their new smelting venture. Porter accepted, came to Durango during the year, and met with Denver & Rio Grande officials to flesh out their scheme. The plan, of course, was to build a massive smelter in Durango capable of treating the most resilient ores that the San Juans had to offer, and do so at rates that would undercut the local facilities scattered throughout the mountains. A railroad would carry ore out of the mountains and send supplies and coal up, with the Denver & Rio Grande, its investors, and select associates such as Porter being the beneficiaries. The idea was grand and may have even originally been Porter's, because years prior he saw the logic of building a smelter on the lower Animas River where flat land, water, and coal were available.

As a first step, Palmer, Bell, and associates organized the New York & San Juan Mining & Smelting Company in 1880 and, under Porter,

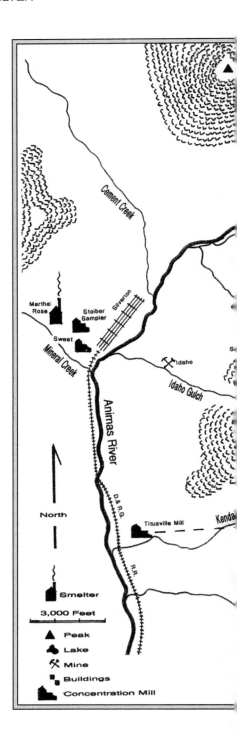

Principal places of activity in the Las Animas Mining District, 1880 to 1893. Source: Author.

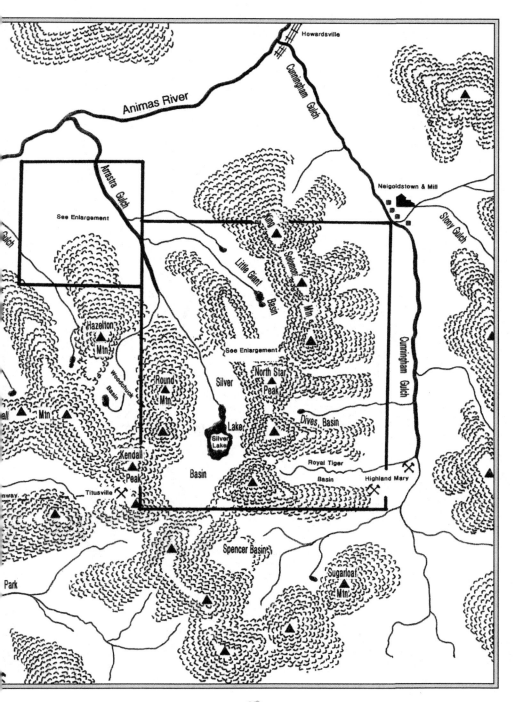

secured the Greene Smelter. Porter then hired Thomas Bowen and John Pennington as metallurgists, probably under a secret agreement, and began securing contracts for ore at highly competitive rates. Porter fired up the Greene Smelter merely to test processes proposed for the new smelter. That action, the organization of New York & San Juan, and the drive for contracts, all imparted the impression that the smelter was back in business. The region celebrated and excitement swept the Las Animas District; but this proved premature because, just as quickly as

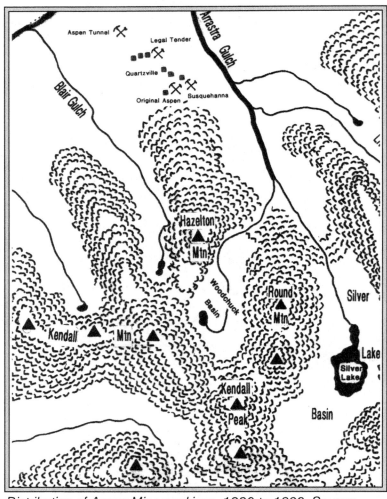

Distribution of Aspen Mine workings, 1880 to 1893. Source: Author.

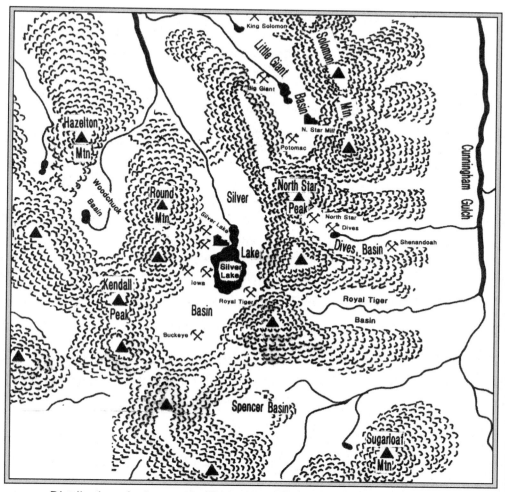

Distribution of mines and mills in the central portion of the Las Animas Mining District, 1880 to 1893. Source: Author.

Porter started the smelter, he shut it down. Then, completely dashing local hopes, the Animas River drainage saw a crew of workers arrive in Silverton, and actually dismantle the smelter and haul it away. A dark cloud of uncertainty crept over the region.[131]

   News traveled fast in the San Juans, and the inhabitants of the Las Animas District quickly learned of events that would change the region forever. Porter saw the Greene equipment freighted down to a large site on the lower Animas at Durango, then unloaded. At the same time, the company came to an agreement with Edmund Sweet where Sweet would serve as ore buyer if he forwent any plans to expand his sampler into a smelter. To ensure a constant supply of ore, the company surveyed the best mines in the Animas River drainage and came to the conclusion that the Aspen, Ingersoll, Legal Tender, and the other mines on Hazelton Mountain offered the greatest potential. In 1880, the company approached Blair, Ingersoll, Higgins, and the other claim owners with an offer of $60,000, or $1,073,483 today, for their interests.[132]

The furor of construction activity regarding the smelting and railroad empire around Durango reached a crescendo in 1881. The track gang building the railroad set up a camp on the townsite as a pioneer village of sorts and received the first train to arrive in the valley. At the same time, John Porter secured the services of renowned mining engineer J.H. Earnest Waters to help him design and build

The New York & San Juan Smelter, also known as the Durango Smelter, radically changed mining in the Animas River drainage. The smelter treated ore at competitive prices and provided high returns, which rendered marginal grades of ore economical to produce. The New York & San Juan facility also undercut Silverton's local smelting industry. Source: Denver Public Library, Western History Collection, Z 4858.

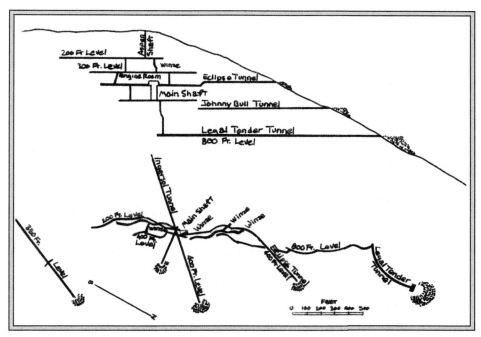

The plan view and elevation illustrates the principal Aspen Mine workings developed by the New York & San Juan company during the early 1880s. Source: Adapted from Ransome, 1901:162.

the new smelter with much of the old Greene equipment. Waters' reputation preceded him, and in many ways, he was a pioneer mining engineer in the San Juans.[133]

Waters was born in Parsonstown, Ireland, in 1851, son of prominent physician John Waters. Interested in mining and not medicine, he received a formal education at the Royal School of Mines in London and the School of Mines at Freiberg, Germany. In 1872, Waters became an apprentice in the machine shops of John & Henry Gwynne in London for practical experience with machinery. Ready for the field, Waters traveled far and wide. Under the employment of a London investment syndicate, he traveled to Gilpin County in 1873 and examined mines there, then went to Japan where the imperial government hired him to serve as State Mining Engineer and build the Japanese Imperial Mint. In 1875, Waters resumed his practice as a consulting engineer and examined mines in the Lake Superior area and Mexico. He then came to Colorado and joined the Leadville rush in 1877 when the district was still wild. He spent the next four years primarily in Leadville and the San Juans, where he made his mark. Waters first engineered the San Juan Reduction Company's lixiviation mill at Gladstone, which became a blemish on his record when the facility failed. Regardless, Waters was of great assistance to Porter, and when finished with the New York & San Juan Smelter, he went on to other projects of note, all the while increasing his affair with the bottle. This became Waters' undoing and, in a deep depression, he poisoned himself in Denver in 1893.[134]

As if the physical presence of the railroad in Durango was not enough good news for the Animas River drainage, the region learned it was to have direct service! In 1881, the Denver & Rio Grande Railroad organized the subsidiary Denver & Rio Grande Extension for the explicit purpose of grading a narrow gauge line up the Animas River canyon from Durango to Silverton, located on the north edge of the Las Animas District. Track gangs began work during the year, and what had seemed an engineering impossibility and distant dream was on the way to becoming a reality.

During 1880 and 1881, outside capital in the form of a railroad and smelter finally arrived and, while both were located in Durango for the time being, they directly impacted the Animas River drainage. The greater mining industry finally accepted the region as legitimate, which drew long-awaited attention. Prospectors returned, investors examined proven properties, optimistic individuals cautiously invested in new properties and existing companies, and the successful mines saw greater development. The Las Animas District, in particular, felt the wave of confidence as prospectors made several new strikes and the number of profitable operations increased.

In keeping with the expectations of the New York & San Juan Company, the Aspen complex remained one of the district's most important mines. In 1880, the company consolidated the 4,000 feet of disparate workings into a single operation, and the Ingersoll Tunnel became the principal entry into the upper workings. The Legal Tender Tunnel accessed a lower portion of the Aspen vein. Under John Porter, foreman C.M. Osman kept a crew of thirty-five miners busy driving development workings and stockpiling ore in anticipation of the railroad's arrival. They lived in buildings left over from Quartzville. By 1881, the Ingersoll (Susquehanna) Tunnel served as the main working level, and 600 feet in, where the tunnel intersected the Victor vein, miners blasted out a hoisting chamber and sank a winze 140 feet down on the ore body. At the 100-foot level, they drove around 400 feet of drifts along the vein, which the company termed Level No.1. They also drove a raise upward into old stopes mined in past years and blasted another series of drifts termed Level A. To raise an ore bucket in the winze, miners installed a small steam hoist and upright boiler in the hoist chamber. Smoke was routed up the raise where it left the mine altogether through the original Blair workings. At the tunnel portal, miners erected a simple surface plant that consisted of a 16 by 40 foot tunnel house and a 20 by 50 foot boardinghouse. The Legal Tender Tunnel was under development and struck the Aspen vein 500 feet in. A 16 by 40 foot frame tunnel house sheltered the tunnel portal, a timber dressing area, and a blacksmith shop, and the miners lived in several buildings in Quartzville's central portion.[135]

North Star Peak and Dives Basin remained the Las Animas District's other key centers of ore production. During the summer, Martin Van Buren Wason, Theophile Benjovsky, George Ingersoll, and others maintained production from the Shenandoah and Dives mines, as well as several surface operations. In complete control of the North Star, the Crooke brothers became unsatisfied with the seasonality of operations and, in 1880, decided to consult with a professional mining engineer. At this time, Ebenezer Olcott, equal in every way to J.H. Earnest Waters, serendipitously arrived in Lake City at the Crookes' doorstep.

Like Waters, Olcott came from an upper socioeconomic status, although he was born in New York. From an early age, Olcott was interested in mining and had the opportunity to enter the industry from the top. He studied engineering and metallurgy at Columbia School of Mines in New York, graduated in 1874, and took a job as a chemist for the Ore Knob Copper Company in North Carolina. In 1875, Olcott accepted a position as superintendent of the Pennsylvania Lead Company, in Mansfield, Pennsylvania, then jumped at an offer after a year to work as an engineer. He sailed for Venezuela and filled a position of responsibility in the Orinoco Exploring & Mining Company, which held his interest for several more years. In 1879, Olcott returned to the United States, decided to establish a consulting practice, and had no trouble securing several important clients due to his practical experience. D. Willis James of Phelps, Dodge &

Company was one of Olcott's best clients, and Olcott quickly packed his bags when Willis requested a survey of a number of significant mining districts in the West. Olcott started in Colorado and perused Leadville, Silver Cliff, and Caribou, then came to Lake City in 1880 specifically to examine the Crooke Mining & Smelting Company.[136]

The Crookes were not particularly interested in cooperating with Phelps, Dodge & Company, but they were more than open to showing Olcott the North Star Mine in hopes of securing additional investment from the firm. The North Star was probably unlike anything that Olcott had yet seen, and during his visit, he was immediately possessed by the extremely harsh environment. Seemingly as an act of God telling him that the North Star was to play a role in his future, Olcott was literally struck by a small lightning charge, which electrified him all the more. When Olcott returned to Lake City, he and the Crookes came to a mutual understanding. They realized that Olcott had what it took to embrace the mine and bring it into substantial production, and Olcott saw the Crookes and the mine as a gateway into an exciting physical and management challenge in a magical land.[137]

Olcott negotiated a sound deal with the Crookes that included a $25,000 investment in the North Star from Willis and associates in exchange for a monthly salary of $500, or $8,946 today, plus expenses. Olcott immediately set about correcting what he observed as poor development at the North Star in terms of both the surface plant and the workings. To improve efficiency, he oversaw the construction of a small surface plant at the main tunnel high on the southeast side of North Star Peak. Within the financial constraints imposed by the Crookes, Olcott had workers erect a combination tunnel house, boardinghouse, ore-sorting house, stable, supply shed, and shop. The workers had to blast a terrace 30 by 94 feet out of the cliff for the building, which was a two-story, informal affair tailored to fit against the cliff. Aware of the hurricane-force winds that were to come later in the year, Olcott literally bolted the building down to the cliff with iron rods. He also strung a double-rope reversible tramway from the building down to the original cluster of buildings on the valley floor to replace the packtrains.[138]

With a crew of eight miners, Olcott formally developed the North Star vein from three principal levels with the main tunnel serving as Level No.1. During the summer, an increased crew of twenty miners sent more ore than ever via the tramway down to the small one-stamp mill for crushing. Even though the operation was seasonal in theory, winter came early at 13,000 feet and presented the crew with considerable challenges. To maintain production, Olcott instituted the use of a sled to lower ore to the stamp mill, where workers had to stockpile the processed material because snow blocked the trails down to Cunningham Gulch.[139]

As the temperatures plummeted and the winds picked up, the large crew quickly came to realize that the tunnel house was perhaps more than a little cramped. The interior was more like a ship than a boardinghouse. One large room served as the living quarters where miners spent nearly all their time when not at work because the outside was intolerable. They slept in a set of five bunks three tiers high, warmed themselves around a single stove, ate meals together, and competed for the few pieces of furniture during leisure time. Sacks of provisions were suspended from the ceiling, boxes were stacked along the walls, and tools leaned against the corners. On windy nights, warm air promptly left the drafty building, the stove was insufficient for heat, damp rags froze, and the workers could see their breath. The crew simply had no escape from each other, the ambiance of mining, and the cold. Yet they labored on until Olcott called an end to the working season.[140]

When Olcott returned in the spring of 1881, many of the miners followed him and resumed their arduous lifestyle. Their solace, in addition to excellent pay, was three large meals per day, which consisted of a fare similar to that consumed by the miners at the Aspen, discussed previously. In August, Olcott abruptly quit for the warmth of a mine in Mexico. He was satisfied with his adventure and found great frustration with the Crookes, North Star Peak, and the seasonality of the work. While the Crookes were sorry to see Olcott go, they were certainly pleased with the state in which he left the mine, which was now ready for regular production. L.P. Burrows inherited Olcott's improvements, hired a crew of forty to continue development and production, and built a second boardinghouse for the newcomers.[141]

On the opposite side of North Star Peak in Little Giant Basin, the positive climate of 1880 and 1881 fostered not only prospecting, but also the development of several of the ore veins discovered earlier. Prospectors searching the rock formations at the gulch's head found a rich vein that carried silver and industrial metals exposed at the surface. They claimed it as the Potomac. They had no trouble finding buyers, who organized the Potomac Silver Mining Company and immediately began production. With the vein literally traversing bedrock, miners went right to work extracting the ore from an open-cut and a shallow tunnel, which must have pleased the company since almost no infrastructure and, hence, capital were required. According to archaeological features remaining today, miners erected a remarkably simple surface plant at the mouth of the open-cut, and it consisted of a tiny blacksmith shop and an open-air plank floor where they sorted and sacked ore for shipment by pack train. The residential accommodations were equally primitive and impermanent. A crew of six to seven miners lived in two wall tents and a 15 by 20 foot frame cabin, and even though the work was seasonal, they were exposed and cold.[142]

As early as 1879, prospectors were driving a tunnel south into a cliff on the floor of Little Giant Basin to undercut the Big Giant vein at depth. They erected several buildings including a tunnel house to support activity underground, and in 1880 found investors who furnished capital for major development. A small crew of miners drove the tunnel to the impressive length of 400 feet where they struck a vein laced with gray copper and silver ore. Excited, the investors increased the crew to seven miners who began extracting and stockpiling the ore in anticipation of the railroad and smelter at Durango. Down the gulch to the north, a party of prospectors hoping for the same result was at work driving an exploratory tunnel toward the Black Prince vein.[143]

The King Solomon Mine was Little Giant Basin's most impressive operation, although it, like most of the producers in the Las Animas District, remained small, shallow, and labor-intensive. In 1879, the Ressouches brothers realized that their King Solomon would never pay in desirable quantities without capital for development. Despite the regional economic slump at the time, they interested Robert Hook, a lawyer who practiced in Silverton during the warm months and in Chicago during the winter. Through connections in the Windy City, Hook convinced William Kneip and Eugene J. Fellows of the King Solomon's potential, and together they organized the Solomon Silver Mining Company to work the property. The

Ressouches brothers retained a significant share of the company and probably personally oversaw development in 1880 by a small crew, while Hook acted as superintendent. Because the vein was close to the surface, miners had to drive only several short tunnels in preparation to extract the rich copper and silver payrock.[144]

Once the King Solomon began proving its potential in 1881, the Ressouches and Hook had little difficulty convincing the Chicago investors to pay for an expert engineer capable of increasing production. The nationalistic Ressouches brothers had just such an individual in mind, Victor Vincent, a fellow Frenchman. While Vincent actually had little direct experience with mining, he was an accomplished structural engineer in France, as well as a talented artist. Vincent had aspirations of becoming a well-practiced American mining engineer and came to the Animas River drainage during the growing mining curiosity of the late 1870s, where he met the Ressouches. Hoping that the King Solomon would be his first stepping stone in mining, Vincent convinced the Ressouches to hire him. During the year, Vincent was given charge of a crew of sixteen miners, who increased development of the vein while bringing ore to daylight.[145]

In addition to Little Giant Basin, the movement of prospecting and claim development crept over to the northwest face of Kendall Mountain, which loomed over Silverton. After the sale of the Ingersoll Tunnel, Thomas Higgins was free to pursue other interests and had the capital to see them become reality. One of his projects was backing his wife Mary Anne in a lease on the Grand Central Hotel in Silverton in 1881. The other was investing in the development of two highly promising claims staked in Swansea Gulch during the late 1870s. One, the Lackawanna, was within a short walk from Silverton and consisted of a group of claims that covered several veins on the gulch's east side. The other, the Scranton City, lay at treeline at the base of a cliff on the gulch's west side. In light of the coming railroad and the smelter in Durango, Higgins sensed that the time was right to bring the claims into production and hired several miners to work with him in initial development. At the same time, prospectors were at work driving tunnels and sinking shafts into one-half dozen other claims on Kendall Mountain.[146]

In the summer of 1882, high times finally "chuffed" into Silverton in the form of the eagerly awaited train with its heavy load of powerful capitalists and dignitaries. As the narrow-gauge engine rolled down the final length of track, it was greeted by a throng of jubilant spectators, as well as 1,200 tons of precious ore that had been stockpiled in anticipation of the railroad's completion. Finally, the Animas River drainage had an all-season link with the outside world and with the New York & San Juan Smelter, the largest ore treatment facility in southwestern Colorado. The railroad's impact was northing less than revolutionary for day-to-day life, business, and of course, mining.

The residents of the Animas River drainage also realized that a wider array of goods were available than ever, and for only a fraction of the price. During the mid-1870s, residents had to pay as much as $400 per ton for freight imported from Denver. This fell to as low as $100 when the Denver & Rio Grande established its railhead at Durango. The Denver & Rio Grande Extension, also known as the Silverton Railroad, reduced the total cost to as low as $16 per ton, which tumbled farther to $12 when regional business interests vehemently protested the rates! The railroad also opened the Animas drainage to capitalists acclimatized to comfort, as most were, because they rarely had to leave their Pullman palaces. In short, the drainage, and especially Silverton, moved several steps farther away from being a wild frontier.[147]

At the same time, John Porter and Thomas Bowman brought the New York & San Juan Smelter, also known as the Durango Smelter, into action. The smelter was large enough to process ore in economies of scale, which allowed the New York & San Juan company to undercut the smaller facilities in the mountains. The combination of rail service and the discounts offered by the Durango Smelter dramatically reduced the costs of mining. Whereas freighting outfits charged $35 to $40 to haul a ton of crude ore to the Front Range for treatment, a mere $12 would send the same material to Durango. Delighted, mining companies throughout the Animas River drainage had to reassess the worth of their properties because medium-grade ores were now economical and the stuff that barely paid the bills in the past was now considered to be bonanza quality.[148]

While popular history claims that the discount service offered by New York & San Juan crushed smelters local to the mining centers, this was not completely true. Smelters continued to operate in Lake City, Ouray, and Telluride because the cost of freighting the ore over to Silverton for shipment remained high. In Silverton the industry did not collapse, it merely adjusted. The complex ore and numerous small mines in the Animas River drainage guaranteed a market for a few custom independent smelters and samplers.

As early as 1881, Seth R. Beckwith forecasted the need for a local smelter in the vacuum left by the removal of the Greene facility. He, Edward C. Dean, Lemon G. Hine, and Almon M. and Henry H. Clapp organized the Martha Rose Smelting & Mining Company in hopes of filling the void, despite the coming Durango Smelter. Beckwith was an experienced metallurgist who surveyed mining districts in Arizona, Nevada, and Colorado for an up and coming market and settled on the Animas River drainage. With British capital, Beckwith and Arthur Macy, another metallurgist, began construction on the northwest edge of Silverton in 1882, and competed aggressively with New York & San Juan for ore contracts. They locked in several new mines including the Potomac, the Silver Lake, the Gray Eagle, and a few nascent operations in the Ophir area, which cumulatively generated enough ore to keep the Martha Rose busy. At the high cost of $150,000, or close to $3 million today, they equipped the facility with a crusher and Cornish rolls to pulverize the ore, two roasters to oxidize the material, a blast furnace to complete the smelting, and a steam engine to power the machinery.[149]

With great fanfare, Beckwith started the Martha Rose in September, confirming pronouncements that the Animas River drainage's mining industry was at last prolific enough to support both a local facility and the Durango Smelter. Impressed with the Martha Rose, a *Rocky Mountain News* reporter described the event:

> *The machinery of the Martha Rose smelting works was started up Thursday afternoon, and the mammoth crusher and Cornish rolls put in operation. The machinery worked to a charm, running as smoothly as though it had been in operation for months, and reflects credit upon the mechanical skill of Mr. Macy, under whose careful and pains-taking supervision it has been put in place.*[150]

During the trial run, a crowd of dignitaries watched as the first silver bar was poured into a mold cast with M.R.S. & M. Co.

Afterward, Beckwith and Macy ordered their workers to dig into the 1,000 tons of stockpiled ore and feed the clanking machinery. After each run, the smelter had to be stopped to remove slag and charge the furnace, but on the third or fourth day, no new charges were added. Instead of stoking the furnace and roasters for another run, Beckwith and Macy let them cool. Sadly, even though the Martha Rose was effective from the beginning, unlike many of the region's other smelters, the business collapsed under the weight of financial, legal, and management issues. The Animas River drainage was not to have two smelters after all.[151]

Ore samplers, however, continued to serve the needs of the small mines with limited production of complex ore. While the

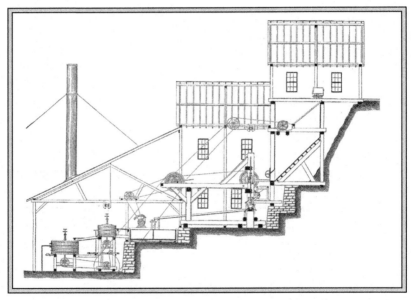

The profile illustrates a silver ore concentration mill. Workers input crude ore on the top right floor, and it passed through a jaw crusher then descended to a battery of stamps for additional pulverization. The sand and slurry continued down to concentration machinery on the lower floors, which separated out waste. In the illustrated mill, grinding pans achieved the separation, and they were one of several machines typically employed. Note the mill's stairstep profile, which utilized gravity to draw the ore through the various treatment stages. Source: Mining & Scientific Press 5/17/90.

New York & San Juan certainly wanted the business of these small operations, their limited and funky batches of ore were not worth the trouble of the adjustments and interruptions required for custom treatment. Because of this, Sweet's Sampler thrived. Sweet also wisely adapted to the combination of the Durango Smelter and the railroad by expanding the sampler's role, but staying within the deal he had with the New York & San Juan company. In addition to providing custom treatment, Sweet bought ore, tested it to identify the best smelting methods, segregated the payrock, and then sent large shipments down to the Durango Smelter with his treatment advice. This business strategy was so effective that, in 1883, Edward G. and Gustavus H. Stoiber came west from Leadville to open their own sampler near the Martha Rose. The Stoiber Brothers Sampling Works became a stepping stone on the way to greatness for these Germans.[152]

The rise of concentration mills in the Animas River drainage was another form of adjustment in response to the competition imposed by New York & San Juan. As noted previously, concentration mills were never intended to produce matte or refined metals, and instead merely carried out the step of separating the metalliferous content of ore from waste. By concentrating their ore, mining companies could avoid the costs of shipping waste-laden payrock to the Durango Smelter and the fees levied for full treatment. The concentrating process began when crushers pulverized crude ore into gravel, and a variety of apparatuses such as Cornish rolls, pan grinders, stamp mills, and ball mills gradually reduced the gravel into particles ranging from sand to slurry. Screens segregated the particles by size, and the particles went on for concentration in jigs, vanners, and other appliances that used combinations of gravity and water currents. While the process seems simple, it was nothing of the sort. The character of the ore's host rock, the chemical compounds of the metals, and the different types of metals conspired to render concentration in the Animas River drainage a science fraught with difficulty and failure. Particle size, the behavior of crushed material and metals, and the specific gravity of the rock types and metals complicated the process and required calculation, experience with machinery and metallurgy, experimentation, and outright cunning to win them from the host rock.

Few metallurgists and engineers in the Animas River drainage possessed all these abilities, but several persevered during 1882 and 1883 and made concentration a viable adaptation to the changed ore treatment industry. While the Niegolds pioneered ore concentration at Niegoldstown, the credit for truly effective methods in the region goes to Theodore B. Comstock, who was a renaissance man of his time. Described as energetic and even hyperactive, Comstock was born into an upper class family at Cutahago Falls, Ohio, in 1849 and immediately embraced the sciences. He gravitated toward geology, studied at Cornell University, and proved so advanced in his thinking that he established the school's renowned geological department. In 1873, Comstock combined a lust for adventure with his penchant for science and joined Captain W.A. Jones' exploration party to Yellowstone in 1873 and produced the first geological report of the area. He even led his own expedition into Canada's Northwest Territory and made some of the first scientific observations of the far north. Afterward, Comstock decided to use his geological knowledge for profit, and came to the Animas River drainage to examine the possibilities of establishing an ore treatment facility knowing that this would be difficult due to the troublesome ore. In 1879, he established an office at Eureka, collected data, and, once the railroad arrived in 1882, prepared to build a sampler in Silverton.[153]

As a direct competitor to Sweet, Comstock applied his vast knowledge and understanding of the scientific process to complete an excellent facility. Through the sampler, Comstock experimented and determined a concentration process that seemed effective, and then built a full scale mill for the North Star Mine on Sultan Mountain, west of Silverton. Unwilling to involve himself in the New York & San Juan monopoly, Comstock contracted with the North Star and other mines for ore and shipped the concentrates to smelters in Denver, Omaha, and St. Louis for final refining.[154]

Comstock's precedent began to take hold in the region, and the Las Animas District hosted three additional concentration mills. Late in 1882, George Ingersoll erected a small facility at the Green Mountain Mine in Cunningham Gulch, and the Solomon Silver Mining Company built a second in the western portion of Howardsville. Patrick O'Brien apparently erected the facility, which relied on a jaw crusher for coarse reduction, a set of Cornish rolls for pulverization, and several jigs and vanners to carry out the concentration. Ingersoll's mill proved a success probably because the Green Mountain ore was fairly straightforward while the Solomon Mill was a total failure even though it featured the correct equipment. The mill's simplicity, the complexity of the ore, and improper adjustments were probably to blame. A third mill was built at the mouth of Maggie Gulch, a short distance east of the Las Animas District.[155]

By 1882, the Las Animas District possessed all the elements necessary for its mining industry to blossom. Within the span of around ten years, it witnessed the development of the key elements necessary to bring mining in the basins to a boom. The district had two major towns, two minor settlements, a network of roads, and direct rail access literally at its doorstep. A local ore treatment industry, the railroad, and the Durango Smelter provided a market for many ores that were previously uneconomical due to grade and complexity. The railroad not only lowered the costs of living and ore production, but also made the mining district accessible to investors who were unwilling to brave frontier conditions while, ironically, gladly accepting the profits of its industries.

In the Las Animas District, the roster of active mines increased only slightly during 1882, although the many prospectors at work were hoping to add their contributions. The main difference in the district from previous years was the intensity of activity as almost every significant operation began sending ore down to Silverton. At the Aspen, the New York & San Juan company appointed Thomas Hackett as foreman because he had experience with the property as one of the original miners who helped drive the Ingersoll Tunnel. Under Hackett, a large crew of miners drilled and blasted six to seven tons of ore per day, which Sweet's Sampling Works prepared for shipment to the Durango Smelter. By 1883, the Aspen featured at least 7,000 feet of underground workings.[156]

To the southwest, the new properties high on the flank of Kendall Mountain began to make good on their promise of ore. In 1882, the Lackawanna Tunnel & Mining Company drove two tunnels to undercut the J.B. Smith and A.J. Craine veins. After driving one of the tunnels 350 feet, miners struck ore rich enough to justify development, and they sent samples to Silverton for testing. A short distance up Swansea Gulch, several miners were at work driving Higgins'

Scranton City Tunnel toward another vein. Almost one mile to the west, prospectors examining bedrock exposed in Idaho Gulch discovered a vein with potential and staked the Idaho and Idaho No.1 to No.4 claims. During 1882, they drove two tunnels 100 feet long each into the extremely steep mountainside and found that the vein offered excellent ore at depth. A small party of miners leased the Idaho the following year and began production. However, when they shipped the ore to a Denver smelter for testing and treatment, the reports were disappointing. While visually impressive, the ore was difficult to treat and less profitable than the lessees hoped for.[157]

The operators of the Big Giant Mine in Little Giant Basin experienced similar problems. It must have been very frustrating to own a mine with ore that assayed well but was too complex to treat at a profit. As the Big Giant operation withered, the Solomon and Potomac Mines more than made up for its lack of production. At the Potomac, miners enjoyed the relatively easy work of drilling and blasting ore from the vein's surface outcrop then pursued the vein underground. After the failure of the Martha Rose Smelter in 1882, the Potomac Company shipped its notably rich payrock to Durango.[158]

Still aspiring to become a mining engineer and operator, Victor Vincent deepened his involvement with the Solomon Mine, which proved his undoing. In 1882, Vincent interested fellow Frenchmen Jules Rifflard and Richard Salembier in the Solomon and discussed the idea of leasing the property from the Solomon Silver Mining Company. The trio agreed, Vincent appealed to the wealthy Arthur C. King in New York City for capital, and they organized the French Boys Silver Mining Company. The outfit retained the Solomon Company's crew of twenty miners and kept them busy all winter producing ore and developing a handsome vein. After encountering a ten inch wide vein of solid copper and galena ore, the French Boys were so excited that they petitioned the Ressouches brothers and the Solomon Silver Mining Company to sell the claims. The owners agreed, but only on the condition of regular payments and specified underground development should the French Boys default and abandon operations.[159]

After signing the sale contract, Vincent was suddenly caught in a difficult position. In an unrealistically short time, King started making noise about returns on his investment while the Ressouches reminded Vincent about their payment schedule. To meet the

Little remains today of the boardinghouses built in 1882 for the Iowa Mine's first crew except for structural debris. The southeast view depicts the platform, hewed out of bedrock, on which the buildings stood. The location was on the brink of a cliff at an altitude greater than 12,000 feet. Source: Author.

financial obligations, Vincent abandoned the required development and directed all twenty of the miners to extract ore as fast as they could. After several months, Vincent fell behind and the Ressouches found out about the neglected development. They immediately ordered a stop to ore production, which left Vincent in a Catch 22 situation. He was not allowed to produce ore until he paid the Ressouches, and he could not pay the Ressouches without mining ore. According to the Ressouches, the French Boys defaulted on the contract and the Ressouches attempted to reclaim the Solomon Mine, but the French Boys would not let the property and their hard work go. At a deadlock, both parties filed suit at the end of 1883 and shut the operation down, with the laid off miners as the principal casualties. Deflated, Vincent quit the French Boys and returned to France where he enjoyed success as a mechanical and architectural engineer.[160]

To the southwest, Silver Lake Basin began to resound with the hammers and drill-steels of several parties in addition to John Reed. In 1881, several prospectors imitated Reed and made the dangerous ascent into the basin, where they were no doubt awed by the sheer walls laced with mineral formations. The prospectors examined the flank of Kendall Peak a short distance south of Reed's Silver Lake claim and, after climbing among and between rock cornices, found a rich vein at around 12,800 feet. They staked the find as the Iowa and Stag claims and blasted a tunnel and a shaft to explore the vein at depth.[161]

At the end of the season, the party had ore samples assayed in Silverton, and to everyone's surprise, the report found that the ore was not only rich with silver and industrial metals, but also gold, which was unusual. In 1882, the party returned as soon as the spring thaw rendered the snowbound headwall negotiable and began production. Somehow, the members enticed a crew of around ten miners to make the Iowa their home for the working season, and they brought up all the supplies and lumber necessary to build a basic surface plant. The location and environment were equally repelling in every way to the North Star Mine, except that the approach from the bottom of Silver Lake Basin was longer and more arduous. A narrow bench gouged flat by glaciers lay near the Iowa workings and was an acceptable site for the mine's modest blacksmith shop. It, however, caused too much insecurity among the workers for permanent residences. While the bench offered plenty of ground for outdoor activities, it was abysmally windswept and exposed to avalanches. The miners, therefore, blasted a protected terrace out of bedrock a short distance north, and erected three frame boardinghouses for their living quarters. The buildings were so close to the edge of a cliff that the miners certainly risked life and limb walking around at night or on extremely windy days, which were common.[162]

While the Iowa miners acclimated to the breathtaking heights, John Reed labored away a short distance to the north. During 1880 and 1881, he traced the Silver Lake vein for a considerable distance with shallow excavations hewed into solid bedrock. In 1882, Reed produced several tons of ore from a tunnel that he drove for a distance of around fifty feet directly on the vein, and lamented the slothful progress due to the short working seasons. To be caught by a heavy snow in the basin was a life-threatening event, which forced him down relatively early each year.

During a stay in Silverton in 1883, Reed convinced John W. Collins that the Silver Lake and Round Mountain claims would pay well if worked by a small crew of miners, which required an initial investment. For a share of the Silver Lake, Collins and Reed formed a partnership, ascended into the basin, and began production together. Around this time, Reed and Collins packed in enough lumber and equipment to build a small blacksmith shop and a cabin. He then hired a crew of three or four miners who began a second tunnel. Once the miners reached the vein, the party produced around five tons of ore per day, which one of the workers packed down to Sweet's Sampler. Somehow, Reed and Collins convinced a reporter compiling data for the director of the United States Mint to examine the property, probably for promotional purposes. Impressed, the reporter noted that "One of the biggest veins and best showings of mineral in San Juan is to be found in the Silver Lake, on Round Mountain."[164]

On the other side of the basin, Julius Johnson was at work driving a tunnel east underneath the Royal Tiger claim. Johnson, an old-time prospector, leased the property from owner McPherson Lemoyne, who grew tired of dealing with the difficult-to-work property. Johnson's lease ended around 1883 when Lemoyne sold the Royal Tiger to Innis, who hoped to approach his fabled lake of gold from the opposite side of the mountain should the Highland Mary fail to make the discovery, which it was doing.[165]

At the Highland Mary, Superintendent Henry Guillette finished building a mill in 1882, although the miners had not yet reached the lake of gold. By August of 1883, they drove the tunnel for a total length of 2,680 feet along a meandering course dictated to Innis by his psychic, and Innis kept the miners going. Mining journals assumed that Innis targeted the Bald Eagle Lode, which was another 2,200 feet away, but Innis kept his secret. During their work deep underground miners pierced several more rich silver veins in November and shook their heads over Innis' instructions to ignore that which usually elated normal mine owners.[166]

The gathering boom in the Las Animas and other mining districts, the presence of the railroad, and the arrival of opportunists had a dramatic impact on the Animas River drainage. As the regional railhead, Silverton took the brunt of the change, and Thomas Blair and Dempsey Reese saw their quiet, crime-free hamlet evolve into a noisy hub of industry, freight, commerce, finance, and communication. In 1881, at the same time that Denver, metropolis of Colorado, received its first telephone system, the Colorado Telephone Company strung a line between Silverton and Lake City, then expanded the service during the next several years. By the end of 1882, Silverton had eleven telephone subscribers including a hotel, the Western Union office, the San Juan County Bank, and Theodore Comstock's sampler and residence. In 1883, the San Juan County Bank was formally chartered as the First National Bank of Silverton, which handled all manner of financial transactions. Green Street became the commercial district, and its side streets offered all the basic forms of businesses and services needed by a diverse population. Silverton even hosted the first mining business exchange in the San Juans. Cushing M. Bryant, a successful metallurgist from Boston, opened Bryant's Mining Exchange in 1882, an information clearinghouse stocked with reference books and periodicals with access to investment opportunities. There was even talk of providing gas and electric lighting. In 1883, Henry Adsit, Edmund Sweet, W.G. Melville, and other investors organized the Silverton Electric & Gas Light Company, but they did little more when the reality of building a power plant set in.[167]

Of course, as the crown jewel of the San Juans, Silverton was the Animas River drainage's cultural center. John and Amanda Cotton ran the Cotton House, which was a community performance and celebration hall of sorts. The saloon was one of the most important social institutions in any mining camp, and Silverton featured around thirty of them, as well as two dance halls, mostly on Blair Street. The saloons catered to specific segments of the population, and like most mining towns, the establishments in Silverton served as communication centers, public meeting halls, and entertainment centers. Silverton's residents finally found time for God during the early 1880s. The Congregational Church Society built the first church in 1881, and the Catholics built their church in 1883. Many of Silverton's residents brought the tradition of fraternal orders with them, which was another important institution on the mining frontier. Fraternal orders provided social contact, assistance, guidance, death benefits, and even a primitive form of unemployment support. Men joined the Masons, the Odd Fellows, the Order of Eastern Star, and the Woodmen of World, while some women belonged to the Women of Woodcraft and the Rathbone Sisters.[168]

These organizations and others served as surrogate families for the few residents bold enough to stay the winter, and the organizations hosted holiday celebrations. Silvertonians and regional residents made sure that they enjoyed every holiday to the fullest, and orchestrated social events on the slightest pretense. In 1876, young men established a baseball league, and the older residents organized dances that drew men from miles away. Often, the Moyle brothers, Cornish immigrants, played at the dances. Summer was a time for the Animas River drainage residents to celebrate their mining culture and, starting in 1882, miners' contests became a part of every July Fourth celebration. During the region's first drilling event, Jake C. Brewer, foreman of the Gray Eagle Mine, was captain of the winning team. Even prospectors had an opportunity to showcase their skills by enlisting their burros in races.[169]

A few visionary residents, mostly from Silverton, continued Dempsey Reese's low-level promotional campaign during the early 1880s, although by now, Silverton had earned a name in the greater mining industry. As a showing of local pride, some of the mine owners in the Las Animas District contributed show-quality ore specimens for presentation and a contest at the National Exhibition in Denver in 1882. Reporters from the *Rocky Mountain News* admired the samples contributed by the Aspen, Idaho, Iowa, and Silver Lake Mines. Several local voices and experts maintained contact with reporters for the *Rocky Mountain News*, various mining industry journals, and the United States Mint. The most reputable individuals such as Theodore Comstock even produced their own articles on the region for publication.[170]

Paralleling the rise of positive attributes, crime and vice increased in the Animas River drainage, although it never approached the levels misrepresented by popular history. Through 1878, Howardsville, Silverton, and greater San Juan County were able to claim only one shooting each. By 1881, there were certainly more violent crimes such as shootings, but it was proportional to the overall increase in population and occurred mostly among the rough element in Silverton. Robbery and theft, reliant on the anonymity of a large population, also increased. To prevent crime from reaching the epidemic proportions experienced in other boom towns, Silverton fathers hired legendary Bat Masterson to keep order, while other concerned citizens formed midnight vigilance committees, which made use of the noose on more than one occasion. In contrast to another myth of the mining frontier, the Animas River drainage was nearly bereft of prostitutes. "Aunt Jane" Bowen brought the first of these service workers to Silverton around 1878 as the town grew. She found the market quite limited. The entire Animas River drainage was unable to support more than twelve prostitutes into the early 1880s, when their numbers probably increased slightly. To be near the potential customers, the prostitutes set up shop on Blair Street, which was the region's only red light district. Amusingly, to distinguish themselves apart from the strip of sin, those respectable citizens who already lived on Blair Street renamed both ends of the avenue Empire Street.[171]

The Las Animas District proper saw relatively few of Silverton's social problems because of the demography of its prospectors and miners, who were too busy, honest, and reliant on each other for survival. Scattered on the mountains, in the basins, and at Howardsville and Quartzville, they constituted a significant share of San Juan County's population, which almost doubled from around 1,100 people in 1880 to 2,000 in five years. While we can imagine what the residents of the town of Silverton were like, popular history seems to have glossed over the types of people who were willing to live and work deep in the Las Animas District, and exactly what their lifestyle consisted of. Modern society knows few characters like them.[172]

Nearly all the residents in the Las Animas District were men ranging in age from their 20s to their 40s, and it comes as no surprise that most worked in the mining industry. In contrast to popular misconceptions, the miners and prospectors tended to be educated and could read, write, and do basic mathematics. Most were single, and an average of only twenty percent were or had been married. The individuals in positions of management, such as foremen, superintendents, managers, and engineers, tended to be slightly older and married.[173]

Around sixty-five percent of the miners and prospectors were Americans who came primarily from the East and Midwest, with a small contingent from Colorado and the Southeastern states. The remainder was foreign and immigrated from England, Ireland, Scotland, Germany, and other northern European countries; and a few were Italian and French such as the Ressouches brothers. Racism toward different skin shades was common in the Las Animas District as it was elsewhere in the hardrock mining industry. The region's only four Chinese were grudgingly permitted to run a laundry in Silverton, while several Blacks were allowed to operate businesses that were higher in profile. Thomas Smith, one of the first Blacks in the region, worked as a barber in 1880; and Albert Tennyson, the first Black business owner, established a bath house in 1882. Hispanics may have been the most accepted, primarily because the remote mines and prospectors may not have functioned without them. Specifically, many of the best packers and mule skinners were Hispanic, exemplified by the misspelled Gonsolus brothers of Howardsville. All experienced racism to some degree or another, although this was mostly a function of Silvertonians.[174]

Divisions by ethnicity were only slightly more subtle at the mines. Americans, Germans, and some English held the highest labor positions due in large part to education and familiarity with the sciences, engineering, and workplace culture. Miners and prospectors came from a variety of ethnic backgrounds, although Chinese and Blacks were not tolerated. While hardrock mines of the 1880s were more egalitarian than in later decades, the crews were also divided according to socioeconomic status, which was in part a function of position. Managers and engineers were accorded the greatest luxury while superintendents and foremen were slightly behind. In the Las Animas District, private sleeping quarters, special meals, delicacies, and freedom to move about the mine at will were tantamount to luxury.

Interestingly, in the Las Animas District, immigrants from some of the countries noted above left identifiable material evidence at several of today's historic mine sites, which confirms their presence. In general, immigrants on the mining frontier often consumed products and foods from their homeland, when available, out of familiarity, preference, and comfort. In so doing, the immigrants generated specific types of refuse in the form of fragmented bottles, cans, clothing parts, and butchered bones that can provide clues regarding their origin. According to this material evidence, during the early 1880s, a significant proportion of the crew at the Iowa Mine were British, while some of the prospectors at work on the northwest slope of Kendall Mountain were Italian.[175]

We know that women were certainly present in the Animas River drainage during the early 1880s, and almost twenty percent of the 1,100 people in San Juan County counted in 1880 belonged to the fair gender. But how many of them actually lived among the miners and prospectors deep in the Las Animas District? The question can be a difficult one to answer because women received little documentation by the records-keepers of the past. Here, archaeological information is key because women tended to leave specific types of artifacts such as clothing parts, and decorative tableware and household items. In prior pages, we found out that several women in fact lived in Quartzville during the late 1870s and early 1880s as the wives of miners and the superintendent; and we know that married couples ran businesses in Howardsville. According to the material evidence, few if any women lived at the mines, leaving the rest of the Las Animas as a man's world.[176]

And exactly where did these men live? Popular history often mistakenly describes towns like Silverton and Howardsville as being full of miners; and while miners were certainly present in these settlements, they constituted a small portion of the population. The adverse environment of the San Juans required miners to live at or near their points of work, and only a handful of mines were within an easy walk of these two towns. Silverton and Howardsville certainly accommodated workers employed in the mining industry, but they also held jobs at the samplers, mills, and related businesses.

The men of the Las Animas District lived in cabins and boardinghouses at or near the mines, wherever and in whatever environment they lay. At the small mines and prospects, the cabins tended to be low, cramped, and featured at most several rooms. At the substantial operations, such as the Aspen and North Star mines, companies provided boardinghouses divided into multiple rooms and lofts for sleeping, domestic activities, dining, and leisure. Below treeline, workers usually used logs for construction because they were free and made for a tight, warm structure. Above treeline, mining companies hauled in lumber for frame buildings, which were often drafty and vibrated in the wind. These structures were so cold in the winter that residents often saw their breath and standing water froze, even when the wood stove, the only source of heat, was at full-blast.

Because of the frigid temperatures from November through April, miners and prospectors wore entire wardrobes of woolen and cotton clothing, as well as heavy boots and slouch hats. While today's society considers temperatures in the '40s and '30s as cold, the human body has an amazing capacity to acclimatize, and the men of the Las Animas District adapted somewhat to the low temperatures. The cardiovascular nature of mining, travel by foot, and life at altitude helped many to maintain high metabolic rates, which made the cold less acute.

Because space in the cabins and boardinghouses was limited, the prospectors and miners kept relatively few personal possessions. They maintained only several changes of clothing with the oldest and dirtiest dedicated for work. When the crew came off shift at the end of the day, they usually changed into their cleanest clothes and washed their hands and faces but bathed fully only once per week, temperatures permitting. Imagine the smell that pervaded the small rooms and cabins during the winter when damp work clothes hung out to dry, unwashed bodies warmed around a stove that leaked stringers of smoke, kerosene lamps emitted fumes, and odors from dinner still hung in the air. In such an atmosphere, miners spent their few hours before bed reading, playing card games, spinning yarns, and mending clothing.

The interiors of the cabins and boardinghouses were brisk when the miners awoke early in the morning. After they were stirred by the sounds of cooking, the first individuals to rise, or by a human alarm system, the men dressed in their baggy wool trousers and undershirts. Those working underground wore pull-on boots, some with hobnail soles, as well as rain slickers for wet conditions. The 1880s were decades in advance of hardhats, and instead, nearly all miners used shapeless felt hats that offered no protection from falling rocks. Candles held by forged steel candlesticks were the only sources of light, and they featured a hook that the miner punched into his hat to free his hands.

At work, miners engaged in a limited variety of tasks that revolved around bringing ore to daylight. They spent most of their time using hammers and drill-steels to bore blast-holes, which they loaded with dynamite or blasting powder. Here, experience and skill were prized. Competent and efficient miners drilled only enough holes and used just the right amount of explosive to blast the desired block of ground into a heap of rock for removal with a shovel. In shallow workings, miners may have used wheelbarrows to cart off the waste rock while they did so with ore cars in the deeper operations. With this process, miners were able to advance their workings a painfully slow average of one to three feet per shift, depending on the density of the rock.

Because of the extreme terrain of the Las Animas District, prospectors and mining companies alike preferred to drive tunnels to intersect veins instead of sinking shafts, which were more expensive and prone to flooding. The veins, however, were vertical, which usually required raises driven upward from the tunnel and winzes sunk from the floor level. Through the raises and winzes, miners blocked out sections of the vein for extraction and usually worked the ore body from the bottom upward at properly engineered operations. In so doing, gravity drew the blasted payrock down into bins or bulkheads built over the tunnel for easy loading into ore cars. A trammer filled the cars, pushed them out of the tunnel, and discharged the contents into outside bins or floors, where another worker sorted through the material and cast off the waste. Of note, miners drilled and blasted hundreds of tons of waste rock for every ton of ore and ejected the unwanted material at the mine entrance, forming large dumps. The greater the dump, the more extensive were the underground workings.

As we can infer, mining was one of the most physically demanding jobs available, and when this is combined with the altitude and climate of the San Juans, miners and prospectors consumed a tremendous amount of calories. Rare was the overweight miner. Meals were a centerpiece of existence in the Las Animas District in part to satisfy the craving for calories, and in part for the camaraderie, rest, and pleasure that they provided. Popular history and stereotypes have grossly oversimplified exactly what miners ate, and here a combination of archival and archaeological information allows us to interpret their common diet.

During the latter portion of the nineteenth century, the dominant American work culture favored certain types of foods that can be termed the *Victorian diet,* which evolved from traditional Northern European cuisine. Meals emphasized fat, protein, carbohydrates, and starches usually in the form of meat, egg dishes, baked goods, grains, vegetables, and fruit. Beef was favored over other meats, pork was least desirable, and fresh meats and vegetables were preferred over preserved foods. Meat dishes often took form as roasts, stews, and fried cuts, while vegetables tended to be boiled and potatoes fried or roasted.

The prospectors and miners in the Las Animas District were no different from other workers in their preference for the Victorian diet, and many were probably raised on such fare, but a number of factors confounded its duplication. First, many of the ingredients were unavailable, especially during the winter, although the railroad and the slaughter business in Howardsville offered a partial solution. Second, hauling fresh food from Silverton and Howardsville into the backcountry was fraught with trouble. Vegetables, fruit, and eggs were either smashed or frozen, depending on the season, and meat had a short life in summer. Third, fresh produce came at a price too dear for small outfits. Fourth, many independent miners and prospectors were too busy to take the time necessary to prepare fresh foods.

In addition, many prized dishes simply could not be cooked due to the climate, altitude, and temperamental woodstoves. Because water boiled at only 194 degrees, Fahrenheit, at 10,000 feet, beans, rice, and potatoes usually did not soften and hardboiled eggs were nothing of the sort. Baking was tantamount to an adventure. At altitude, yeast rose abruptly, sourdough tended to crystallize, other types of dough dried too quickly, and muffins and cakes collapsed. Cooks tried compensating with excess salt and eggs, but many resigned themselves to scrap leavened items in favor of biscuits and flapjacks. Preparing meat dishes was equally difficult because cooking depended on the evolution of the water content under pressure. Roasts and fried foods required more time than usual and tended to dry on the outside while being underdone on the inside. Given this, tender meats and large fried items remained the domain of lower altitudes.[178]

Within the above limitations, what did the miners and prospectors eat? Did they subsist on canned beans, flapjacks, and sourdough as popular stereotypes portray? Once again, the answer lies in an examination of archaeological and archival evidence. According to material evidence, prospectors and miners employed by small outfits relied on preserved food and baked goods because they lacked the time and resources to prepare fresh ingredients. For breakfast, they probably consumed coffee, canned milk, flapjacks, biscuits, preserves, syrup, preserved meat such as bacon or ham, and canned fruit. Lunches may have featured sandwiches, salami, a baked good, or canned food. Dinners were similar and included canned soups, stews, beans, meats, vegetables, and fruits. Organized mining companies, by contrast, were able to provide superior meals because the companies possessed the financing to purchase fresh ingredients and the labor to haul in and prepare the meals while the miners were at work. The organized companies served meals with a much higher proportion of stews, roasts, fried meat and eggs, and vegetables that were easily shipped and stored such as potatoes and corn. They also provided soft grains such as oats.[179]

The miner's penchant for liquor and tobacco is another subject currently surrounded by myth. In contrast to today's misconceptions, the miners and prospectors in the Las Animas District, as elsewhere in Colorado, were actually quite modest in their consumption of alcohol, although they almost certainly overindulged when they came down to town during days off. How did we come to this conclusion? The amount of fragmented liquor bottles and jugs at the mine sites today is relatively light, especially compared with the sizes of the crews—even when we consider that many bottles and jugs were reused and refilled. The reasons may lie with Victorian values of moderation, the difficulty of packing fragile bottles into the backcountry, and company policies intended to minimize the ingredients for social problems. The crew at the North Star Mine was an exception and openly enjoyed plenty of liquor and beer.[180]

In the Las Animas District, most miners worked shifts that were ten hours long for six days a week, and for this they were paid between $3.50 and $4.00 per shift. Unlike coal miners whose living expenses matched or slightly exceeded their dismal pay, the Las Animas miners were able to save money when frugal. Room and board cost them between $1.00 and $3.00 per day, which was the average on the mining frontier; while the replacement of clothing, boots, and other items consumed some of the leftover money. For example, a flannel shirt fetched around $2.00; leather boots were $5.00; and blankets cost $3.00. Of course, many miners purchased at least some substances of pleasure and delicacies to help them cope with their austere living environments, and these took an additional bite out of their savings. Depending on the brand and quality, miners paid between $3.50 and $10 for a bottle of liquor and $.50 for a gallon of beer, not including the container. When in town, the miner who visited the saloons could expect to pay between $.12 and $.25 per drink, depending on the establishment, and just one was usually insufficient. Total expenses considered, at the end of a month, a miner's pay went far enough to attract prospectors and other individuals hoping to accumulate savings for future adventures.[181]

CHAPTER 7

The Boom Continues

DURING THE MID-1880S, a change began to creep through the
Las Animas District, and it was so subtle that no one took immediate
alarm. At the principal operations, miners sent a continuous flow of
ore down out of the basins to the samplers and the railroad at Silverton. The North Star Mine was the exception. After developing the vein
above and below the main tunnel level during 1883, the miners there
split the ore shipments between the Crooke Smelter and the Durango
Smelter during the next several years. The northwest flank of Kendall
Mountain continued to show promise. At the Lackawanna Mine, the
Lackawanna Tunnel & Mining Company drove development workings on one of the many veins and shipped some ore during 1884 and
1885. At the same time, a group of lessees engaged in similar activities
at the Idaho Mine. Lessees in the Gray Eagle Mine maintained a limited but steady production. In November, at the eleventh hour of the
1885 working season, they made an excellent strike in new workings.
Sure that the property owner would not renew their lease, the miners
decided to work the ore through the winter.[182]

The subtle change in the district was that many of the small
pocket mines and shallow operations either curtailed production or
suspended work altogether. Despite a fine start and some fanfare,

Silver Lake Basin quieted during the mid-1880s. The Iowa Mine was idle, and George Reed and John Collins stopped production at the Silver Lake Mine in 1885. By this time, the Royal Tiger Mine was the only active operation, which a small party leased from Edward Innis. Little Giant Basin was mostly vacant. The Big Giant failed to pan out; the King Solomon property was locked up in litigation; and the owners of the Potomac Mine suspended operations in hopes that the price of silver would increase. In Dives Basin, only the North Star showed signs of life.[183]

From outward appearances, the Las Animas District showed signs of contraction, but several events probably distracted people from noticing the gradual change. One of these was another period of unrest at the Aspen Mine. The crew there was content with their lifestyle and financial situation. The company paid them the going rate of $3.50 per shift, provided a few dining luxuries such as canned fruit, and charged the miners the common $1.00 per day for room-and-board. In an attempt to cut back on operating costs, manager John Porter tried reducing the wages to $3.25, revoking the special comestibles, and also reducing the room-and-board. Pay and food being sacred to miners, they naturally threatened to strike; and Porter, unwilling to negotiate, tested the miners' will.[184]

Unfortunately for Porter, he underestimated the power of the miners and set in motion a juggernaut that impacted most of the mine owners throughout the Animas River drainage. Specifically, the Aspen crew appealed en masse to the Silverton chapter of the Knights of Labor, which was the most powerful miners' union in Colorado during the 1880s. The union met with Porter and, when he continued to balk, word spread to other miners throughout the drainage, who threatened to strike in sympathy. Their reason was simple. If Porter could reduce wages at the Aspen, why would the other mine owners not follow suit? Then, Silverton witnessed a mass gathering of miners who showed support to their Aspen brethren and pressured Porter to accede. Tensions ran high and the fate of the region's entire mining industry teetered on one man's decision.[185] Backing up their threat in writing, a reporter for the *Engineering & Mining Journal* noted: "At a meeting of miners held at Silverton, a resolution was passed and signed by all who were present, pledging themselves not to work for less than $3.50 a day."[186] Unwilling to precipitate a catastrophe over a few dollars, Porter finally caved in and all went back to work.

Another event that distracted the Las Animas District was the inevitable collapse of the Highland Mary operation. After ten years of confusing instructions, conflicting orders, and decisions that railed against common sense, Edward Innis finally ran out of money and hope in 1885 and closed the mine. Somehow, Innis let slip his reliance on a psychic, which confirmed the suspicions of the workers and caused a minor sensation in the Colorado press. Repeating a story reported in Silverton, the *Rocky Mountain News* announced for all to read: "The Silverton *Miner* pronounces the Highland Mary Mine a howling failure. This mine has been worked, says the *Miner*, under the direction of spirits." In their amusement, everyone forgot that, despite the complete lack of ore production, Innis made the Highland Mary one of the most advanced and deepest operations in the San Juans at the time. This came at a price so dear that it ruined Innis. He squandered around one million dollars, or $18,971,034 today, and paid his trusted seeress $50,000 for his troubles![188]

The last event of note in the Las Animas District was the discovery of yet another promising vein in 1884. During this time, prospectors penetrated deep into the mining district and examined the south side of Kendall Peak, west of Silver Lake Basin. They clambered around the mountain's southern spine and found a large mineralized vein that they claimed as the Titusville. While only the portion of the vein within the claim featured ore, the prospectors were able to trace the associated fault northwest to Idaho Gulch, where the Idaho Mine lay. This caused a minor excitement because, as other prospectors reasoned, the fault probably offered additional ore formations. Dodging lightning, parties of prospectors scrambled up Kendall Mountain and Kendall Peak and staked claims the length of the fault. The discoverers of the Titusville had no problem selling the claim, but the owners did little with the property and waited for the value of silver to increase.[189]

In 1886, the Las Animas District had to confront a combination of internal and external problems that abruptly cooled the boom in the basins. Inside the district, inhabitants finally noticed that many of the small operations had either suspended work or scaled back operations, and the significant producers appeared to be in trouble as well. The exhaustion of payrock was to blame in some cases, such as the Gray Eagle; and the overestimation of ore reserves at other mines, such as the Big Giant, was another reason. A few properties still had ore, but it decreased in value and increased in complexity with depth, and was uneconomical to treat. It appears that the Silver Lake, Idaho, Royal Tiger, Dives, and Shenandoah Mines befell this fate. From a broad perspective, the overall change in the district was that miners had finally finished off the easily treated, shallow ore and found the deeper material unprofitable. The richest and most promising mines, however, were able to maintain some level of production.

Outside the district, a synergy of forces at first exacerbated the gathering condition, then brought the region close to collapse. As early as 1884, anti-silver sentiments in the Federal Government shifted treasury policy in favor of paper currency; and, the following year, fiscal administrators loudly opposed the free coinage of silver. Together, these events eroded confidence in the silver market and not only caused the value of the white metal to slip, but also made investors wary of silver mining. In 1885, the value of silver decreased from $1.12 per ounce to $1.06 and continued a downward trend until it bottomed out at $.94 by 1888. The watershed year, however, was 1886, when Cleveland's stance became well known and silver reached $1.00 per ounce, which seemed to be the threshold for mining investors. At the same time, the prices for industrial metals fell, and they constituted a significant portion of Las Animas ore. Copper dropped from $.21 to $.16 per pound, and lead decreased by a penny from $.05 per pound.[190]

The net result of the internal and external troubles was that the mine owners and operators of the Las Animas District saw their profits evaporate. The impact was direct, noticeable, and frightening. Of the eight substantial mines active during 1885, only the North Star, the Lackawanna, and several small operations carried on through 1886. The Aspen Mine, a bellwether of the Las Animas District, was apparently silent for the first time in over ten years, indicating that the ore sampling and smelting industry was in trouble as well.

Perhaps out of confidence or maybe ignorance, regional investors organized two substantial ventures during 1886, despite the poor economic climate. Development of the Titusville vein was one of the ventures. Thomas Trippe, the Howardsville assayer, led a group of

distant investors in the operation. Trippe probably personally examined the property, hired a group of miners, and put them to work
building a small surface plant, developing the vein, and extracting
ore.[191]

The Buckeye Mine, silent since around 1879, was the scene of the
second venture. Otto Mears, Pathfinder of the San Juans and toll road
king, felt confident enough in the Buckeye to lease the property, probably because the owners suspended operations around 1879 before
they exhausted the vein. The mine had a history of troublesome ore,
so the owners were more than happy to accommodate Mears because
they were in debt. Interestingly, the mining industry in the San Juans
was as dependent on Mears as he was on it. His transportation empire
handled all manner of mining traffic and goods, but Mears had kept
a distance from the actual mines themselves. In 1886, Mears relented
and took on the Buckeye as his first direct experience.[192]

He could not have selected a more difficult property. The mine
lay at the head of Silver Lake Basin in an environment only slightly
better than the Iowa and North Star mines, and equal in terms of
inaccessibility. Regardless, through the Buckeye Mining Company,
Mears invested in what was the best surface plant in the basin to sustain a crew of ten and ore production all year long. Because the two
existing tunnels were exposed to rockslides and avalanches, Mears
had his miners drive a third tunnel, protected by a cliff, to undercut
the vein at depth. A split-level tunnel house, approximately 42 by
50 feet in area, covered the tunnel portal, a blacksmith shop, an
ore sorting area, and living quarters that neatly divided the building into separate sections. The engineer who designed the structure
was wise in the ways of San Juan winters and arranged the living
quarters (15 by 50 feet in area) directly against the cliff where the
crew had the greatest protection against avalanches. He also imitated Olcott's North Star buildings and tied the tunnel house to the
cliff with iron braces. Relative to the era, the Buckeye company was
progressive and featured a ventilation blower that forced fresh air
underground and provided warming boxes so miners could thaw
frozen dynamite prior to use. In general, frozen dynamite was one
of the greatest hazards underground, because it often failed to completely detonate in the drill-hole, providing the miner with the life-
taking opportunity of picking it out bit by bit. Frozen dynamite also

was unequaled in its ability to foul mine atmospheres with toxic gas when it exploded.[193]

By 1887, Mears had the Buckeye Mine in full production, and Trippe petitioned his investors to fund a concentration mill at the Titusville. Meanwhile, prospectors made an amazing discovery in the deep reaches of the Las Animas District. During early spring, they examined rock outcrops at treeline on the south edge of Deer Park, in the district's southwest corner, and found something immune to the issues with silver. Specifically, the prospectors encountered one of the richest gold veins identified in the region and claimed it as the Mabel, also spelled Maybelle. Within a short time, they leased and bonded the property to a group of New York City capitalists for a handsome $35,000, or $675,635 today. The property was an investor's dream because the vein cropped out on the ground-surface and required minimal work (or so the capitalists thought). They quickly hired several miners who found the vein to be a treasure trove of free gold laced with glittering specimens of leaf- and wire-gold, which had been seen in only a few other regions of Colorado up to that time. Within a short vertical distance, however, the miners encountered a watertable that flowed so freely that their hand pumps were unable to keep pace, and operations were suspended. A small steam pump may have been installed with equally ineffective results, leaving the capitalists with the decision of investing further or abandoning operations. Because the ore seemed to lose value at the watertable and the pockets were small, they waited.[194]

Other prospectors, however, were keenly interested in the unexpected find and came to see the area for themselves. With silver mining declining, the discovery of gold was a welcome breath of fresh air, and they hoped to find veins in addition to the Mabel. During the small excitement, a party encountered a second vein in similar conditions to the northeast and claimed it as the Montana, although it was not nearly as rich. Unfortunately, groundwater quickly fouled prospecting.

In 1888, the economic outlook for silver mining was no better, and in fact had grown worse. The principal mining interests of the Animas River drainage had every reason to believe that silver's value would continue sliding, yet they instituted a handful of projects using mostly their own capital. The projects did not involve fabulous discoveries, new veins, or rich ore, but were instead an attempt to improve the efficiency of existing operations in hopes of squeezing out profits. Thomas Trippe spearheaded one of the most important when he finally convinced his Titusville investors to provide $50,000 for a concentration mill. Because the environment at the mine was extreme, the wintertime accessibility limited to men on snowshoes, and the water supply unreliable, Trippe sited the mill on Deer Creek near the Animas River. Moving the ore to the mill, however, remained a problem; and in response, Trippe contracted for a Huson aerial tramway to carry the ore over the ground in all weather for a distance of around 8,000 feet. The firm of Smith McKay, which built the Mickey Breen Mill in Ouray, planned and built the mill. When finished, the facility was relatively small at 45 by 90 feet in area, and stood over a series of terraces so that gravity could draw the ore through the various stages of treatment. A Blake crusher reduced the ore to gravel and cobbles, and two sets of Cornish rolls and a battery of stamps pulverized the material to sand and slurry. Seven Hartz jigs and additional bumping tables carried out the concentration, and a steam heater dried the concentrates for shipment. A Pelton waterwheel ran the machinery and a steam engine was kept on standby.[195]

Because the construction season was short, the mill was not ready when winter set in. Regardless, a group of lessees maintained production at the mine and probably stockpiled the ore for 1889 when the mill would be ready. Trippe, however, had been courting St. Louis investors who accepted his word as an experienced mining expert that the operation was one of the best in the region. There was certainly some truth in this sentiment because the tramway was the second ever built in the district and the mill was one of a few constructed within the last five years. Trippe must have been a smooth salesman, because he negotiated a deal for an astounding $250,000, or $4,956,396 today.[196]

At the time that Trippe was working on his mill, the New York & San Juan Mining & Smelting Company was reorganized as the San Juan Smelting & Mining Company and consolidated its assets to achieve the business practice known as vertical integration. The massive company controlled coal mines, coke ovens, the Durango Smelter, transportation, and several silver mines including the Aspen complex. Given the low price of silver, San Juan Smelting & Mining decided to remedy the awkwardness of managing the Aspen's five separate tunnels and improve efficiency by driving a central haul-ageway to undercut the workings at great depth. In 1888, the company commissioned the Amy Tunnel, named for Henry Amy, manager of the Durango Smelter under John Porter, on the north base of Hazel-ton Mountain, 1,000 feet lower than the mine's early workings. In so doing, miners could work the ore veins from the bottom up and haul the ore through the tunnel to a proposed concentration mill. By 1889, miners drove the tunnel more than 1,000 feet where they struck the Aspen ore system, which brought the property back into profitability. In later years, the tunnel was renamed the Aspen to reflect its associa-tion with the Aspen ore system.[197]

The North Star Mine was one of the few operations in the Las Animas District that weathered the 1886 recession, but not without problems. The Crookes scaled back activity in 1887, but apparently continued to develop several veins. By this time, miners drove the main tunnel to the impressive length of 800 feet, sank an internal shaft almost as long, and blasted five levels off the shaft. The levels were intended to develop different sections of several veins, but at this depth, the veins manifested as irregular stringers that were dif-ficult to follow. Further, the ore changed in character from a lead sulfate to a galena that was difficult to treat. In March, 1888, min-ers working on the main level encountered amazingly rich ore that featured masses of brilliant wire- and brittle silver, which excited the entire crew because it demonstrated that excellent material could still be found at any time deep underground. The stringer, however, was easily lost and the miners invested at least a month of drilling and blasting before they found the vein again.[198]

As had been the case for years, the early winter at 13,000 feet prevented muleskinners from packing ore down after November, which required the crew to stockpile the full sacks until the spring. The Crookes accepted the reality that sending the ore down to the Durango Smelter was more economical than Lake City, and the team-sters took the shortest route to Silverton. Specifically, they led their mule trains on a well-built trail that wound around the exposed east summit of North Star Peak, descended through Little Giant Basin to Arrastra Creek, and continued to Silverton.

After paying the heavy cost of packing crude ore to Silverton and Lake City for fifteen years, the Crookes finally decided to invest in a concentration mill to separate out some of the waste prior to shipment. Why they waited until 1889 is a mystery since the benefits of concentrating ore for a mine such as the North Star were well known by then. Regardless, the Crookes invested $40,000 to $50,000 in a facility that was similar in scale to Thomas Trippe's Titusville Mill. The North Star facility, however, was not nearly as well planned. Oddly, the Crookes could have followed Trippe's example and sited the facility on the floor of Cunningham Gulch, which was accessible by packtrail and had the ideal fall-line for an aerial tramway. Instead, the Crookes chose a location at the head of Little Giant Basin along the Silverton route, which required that the crude ore be packed over North Star Peak first. In addition, the physical environment presented the same impediments that convinced Trippe to build his mill lower down on the Animas River. When finished during 1889, the *Engineering & Mining Journal* praised the mill as the highest in the nation at 12,700 feet. This, however, was an exaggeration because the mill actually lay at around 12,160 feet.[199]

Curiously, the North Star Mill received little more documentation than the notations above, despite its importance. For further information, we must turn to the archaeological features and artifacts that currently represent the facility. According to a set of terraces and foundations, the mill was L-shaped, around 40 by 60 feet in area, and stood over three platforms incised into the base of a low cliff, which offered protection against avalanches. As was common for concentration facilities, a jaw crusher reduced crude ore into cobbles and two sets of Cornish rolls pulverized the material into sand and slurry, which passed through trommel screens for sizing. The concentration machinery and drying facility were located on the lowest terrace, and a steam engine powered by a portable boiler drove the machinery. Workers lived in a frame building adjacent to and south of the mill, and a blacksmith shop stood adjacent and north.[200]

It remains uncertain how long the mill operated before the Crookes realized that it was not recovering enough of the ore's metal content. They operated the facility during 1889 and through the winter of 1890, when the *Engineering & Mining Journal* noted the unusual practice of lowering ore down from the North Star Mine on a giant toboggan. While the destination was never mentioned, it seems likely that it was the mill. By 1894, the Crookes apparently shut the mill down. Fine gray tailings ejected from the mill currently lie on the floor of Little Giant Basin near the site.[201]

Otto Mears was behind the last significant project that impressed the Animas River drainage in 1888 and 1889. In a game of one-upmanship with himself, the heady Mears proposed grading a railroad from Silverton northwest up Mineral Creek, over Red Mountain Pass, and down into the famed Red Mountain Mining District. No one but Mears, John Porter, and several of the most powerful mine owners in the district thought that it could be done; but they brought their capital to bear and completed the Silverton Railroad in 1888. The organizers were quite proud of themselves because the railroad astonished the mining industry and the Denver & Rio Grande, which claimed that such a venture was simply impossible. The mine owners had a direct interest in the new line because the railroad reduced their high operating costs and restored profitability even given the low value of silver at the time. Porter in particular wanted the railroad because he needed the ore for the Durango Smelter, which had trouble securing enough payrock; and he could send more coal up to the San Juans from his mines near Durango. While Mears was not dependent on the railroad, he saw the project as the next logical step in his San Juan transportation empire.[202]

Even though the Silverton Railroad had no direct impact on the Las Animas District, it set Mears in motion for a second line on the floor of the Animas River, which would bring great benefit to the district. In 1889, the district was abuzz with the news that Charles W. Gibbs was surveying a route from Silverton through Howardsville and up to Eureka. After Gibbs, who had experience engineering railroads on the Front Range, charted a feasible route along the river, Mears came to the realization that he was already beyond his financial comfort zone with the Silverton Railroad and decided to wait.[203]

While the Las Animas District would not see a new railroad after all during the late 1880s, the other projects completed at this time in fact stabilized the impending decline to a degree. The Las Animas District, however, still suffered as the mining industry continued to contract around the principal companies, who maintained production primarily by improving efficiency and saving costs. The smaller operations were less fortunate. In 1889, the Lackawanna Mine and Mears' Buckeye Mine closed, but the resumption of mining at the

Iowa partially offset the loss. The rest of the Animas River drainage experienced the same overall contraction, which changes in the population confirmed. In 1885, San Juan County was home to around 2,000 people, and around 400 (or 20 percent) left after the value of silver fell. Of these optimistic individuals, approximately 1,210 lived in Silverton and 61 resided at Howardsville, which was one of the most stabile settlements in the Las Animas District. Quartzville was largely abandoned after 1886, although a few miners employed at the Aspen Tunnel occupied several of the cabins at the nearby Legal Tender Tunnel. Niegoldstown was relatively unaffected by the silver problem because the town was virtually nonexistent by 1886. The Niegolds' empire collapsed in 1881, and an avalanche wrecked the town's commercial buildings in 1884.[204]

Finally, the Las Animas District's residents were rewarded for their perseverance through hard times when the political instability of silver's value turned in their favor. During the late 1880s, Western legislators clamored for a return to a pro-silver policy to bolster sagging mining industries in their states, as well as their own personal silver stock portfolios. Well organized, they succeeded in 1890 and passed the Sherman Silver Purchase Act, which required the Federal Government to buy 54 million ounces of silver per year at $1.05 per ounce. The figures fostered a demand and price capable of resuscitating the West's silver mining industry, which created jobs, revitalized regional economies, and, of course, improved the popularity of the legislators among their constituents.[205]

Busy times returned to the Las Animas District, and its basins literally boomed again with the sounds of mining, milling, and construction. Almost overnight, the number of significant operations, increased to four and at least as many small mines. The Titusville and North Star were among the significant operations and they became highly profitable given the increased value of silver. At the North Star, the Crookes found that the ore, which was ordinary shipping grade payrock, provided excellent returns; and in 1891, miners blundered into a vein rich with high-grade material, further boosting profits. To make up for lost time, the Crookes increased the workforce to thirty, who continued mining, followed the veins downward, and sent some of the ore to Lake City.[206]

The Titusville Mine experienced a similar trend. The new director Thomas Kane started up the mill and tramway in 1890 on stockpiled ore; and when production presented the pleasing problem of exceeding the mill's capacity, Kane ordered the mill to operate around the clock. Of note, the *Silverton Standard* mentioned Kane as the mine's owner, but it seems likely that he was merely a director appointed by the St. Louis investors who bought the operation from Thomas Trippe in 1889. Kane, who had operated several mines at Mineral Point since the late 1870s, was probably unable to come up with the $250,000 paid to Trippe. During his watch, however, miners blasted into a stringer of gold, which excited the owners.[207]

Several of the small operations that had been priced out of activity during the late 1880s saw renewed activity. Pleased with themselves for not selling the Dives Mine to the Crookes, Martin Van Buren Wason and Theophile Benjovsky finally reopened the property in 1890 after patiently waiting for the value of silver to increase enough. They may have worked the property themselves, and if so, they had the help of several hired miners. At the same time, the King Soloman Tunnel & Mining Company acquired and began developing the Little Nation Mine, on the northeast flank of King Solomon Mountain over Howardsville. The company began work probably where Winfield Scott Stratton left off, and felt confident enough to continue during 1891 when the directors patented the Mother of Solomon and Hancock claims. In the depths of the Las Animas District, B.O. Driscoll reopened the Mabel Mine and had an easy time gathering 200 tons of gold ore and packing it to the Titusville Mill for treatment.[208]

In 1891, the French Boys Silver Mining Company, apparently out of litigation and without the King Solomon Mine, turned its attention to a handful of claims that it possessed in Little Giant Basin, including the Big Giant, Mountain Quail, and Republic, and prepared for minor development. William B. Steven and Thomas Merrill did likewise with their Black Prince claim, located on the basin floor below the idle King Solomon. At the same time, W.C. Watson leased the Lackawanna Mine and invested mostly labor in an attempt to find a continuation of a vein mined several years earlier. Watson was wise to avoid sinking much money into the property because he enjoyed only meager production for around one year. The Highland

Mary Mine lost its stigma by 1892, and several parties of lessees wisely remembered that miners encountered several silver veins that Innis left in place in the upper workings. They had an easy time bringing the workings into minor production, since Innis had already completed the initial development work years ago.[209]

More than any other area in the Las Animas District, Silver Lake Basin and the surrounding peaks again resounded with drill-steels, dynamite, carpenters' hammers, and saws. Benjamin W. Thayer and James H. Robin thought that they had outsmarted the silver recession when they found that a vein in the Iowa Mine offered enough gold to offset silver's declining value. Why previous parties missed the vein is a mystery, but they leased the property in 1889 and prepared to develop the richest part of the vein when silver's value was more than restored. Elated, Thayer and Robin hired several miners to expedite development, and they not only confirmed sufficient gold ore in 1890, but also discovered a vein of galena that ensured greater profits than expected.[210]

Thayer and Robin were well on their way to realizing a dream shared by other local businessmen who dabbled in mining, as many Silvertonians did. Thayer arrived in Silverton in 1881, literally with the railroad, and found a job in a mercantile. Dissatisfied, he migrated down to Durango in search of opportunity in the boom town and married Nellie Pennington, daughter of John L. Pennington. Probably with Pennington's capital, Thayer returned to Silverton in 1883, opened his own mercantile, and invested in real estate. As a solid businessman, Thayer ascended into Silverton society, where he met Robin.[211]

Born on the Isle of Jersey in New York, Robin was one of the first entrepreneurs to establish a business other than a mine in the Animas River drainage. In 1875, Robin and brothers George and Charles E. leased a brickyard being assembled near Silverton, which was a wise business move. By leasing the yard, they realized immediate income with a minimal outlay of capital, which they reinvested in real estate. The brickyard also demonstrated that construction materials, always in demand, provided a surer income than uncertain mining ventures. With this in mind, Robin and John Pennington pooled their resources, established a sawmill on Cement Creek in 1880, and sold the lumber in their yard in Silverton. At the same time,

Robin maintained a real estate office and continued to speculate with his own money. He cemented his role in Silverton society by entering local politics and working as a community activist along with his wife Amelia. Once Robin had enough capital, he felt free to venture into the uncertain mining projects from which he mostly refrained, including the Iowa.[212]

During the summer of 1891, the Iowa consumed more and more of Robin and Thayer's attention. They hastily repaired the buildings up on Kendall Peak's cliff, brought in additional supplies, and made arrangements for a small crew of miners to stay the long and lonely winter. At the same time, the crew on-site maintained a steady but small production. As winter set in and the mine became snowbound, all the crew could do was develop the several veins and stockpile sacks of ore for the coming thaw. And when it arrived in June, Robin and Thayer eagerly received the precious payrock and also reports that the veins looked better than ever. During the short summer, the miners sent down another 250 tons.[213]

Thayer and Robin realized that their meager investments would always constrain production and that more money was necessary for the mine to blossom. Further, the veins gave every appearance of running deep underground, and their exploration and development would be a function of further capital. With this understanding, Robin approached Gustavus Stoiber because he was a trained mining expert with funds, and Robin found him to be a ready audience. Together, the men organized the Iowa Gold Mining & Milling Company in 1893 and drew in H.W. King and R.W. Watson. Stoiber served as president, King was vice-president, and Robin acted as secretary.[214]

While the Iowa was proving to be a confirmed bonanza, developments on the Silver Lake group of claims (a short distance north) simply dwarfed Robin and Thayer's relatively simple operation. After running the Stoiber Brothers Sampling Works for four years, the brothers Edward and Gustavus Stoiber had a falling out in 1887 that cleaved what had been a harmonious relationship. Lore suggests that the brothers' wives fueled a disagreement that exploded into a conflagration, and Edward and Gustavus decided to take a vacation from their relationship and divide their assets. Gustavus assumed the sampling works and Edward took the Silver Lake group of claims, which they had acquired a short time earlier. Gustavus' choice was the safer of the two since the sampling works would provide a reliable source of income, and Edward based his decision on the educated guess that the Silver Lake would provide great rewards for such a high-risk venture. Edward lived his life on calculation and educated decisions, and, at least in mining matters, he was rarely wrong.[215]

The Stoibers were proper, stiff, conservative Germans reared in an upper socioeconomic climate. Edward was born in 1854, began studies in engineering at a young age, and attended the famed School of Mines at Freiberg. In 1879, he and Gustavus sought their fortune in Leadville where Edward experienced immediate success as a mining engineer and metallurgist. When competition among professionals increased in Leadville, while the Animas River drainage begged for metallurgists, the Stoibers responded in 1883 by building their sampling works.[216]

While on business in Denver, Edward met Lena Allen Webster, who has been described as a "very liberated divorcee." Lena came from humble beginnings, a Kansas farm according to some and a whore house according to others, and embodied the image of the frontier woman. Lena was completely out of her element in Denver and felt more comfortable driving a team of horses and carousing with mountain characters.[217]

What she and Edward saw in each other is a mystery, since they were polar opposites—fire and ice. Edward was quiet, reclusive, very handsome, and the quintessential German engineer. He was meticulous and exacting, and left little room for spontaneity and surprise. In fact, Edward was so formal, dry, and grouchy that the extremely conservative *Mining & Scientific Press* politely described him as "not at all gregarious." Perhaps the juxtaposition of Lena and Edward was their mutual attraction, which led to marriage in 1884 followed by a very rocky relationship. Lena felt more at home in Silverton than Denver, although she certainly had clashes with the neighbors on Reese Street and probably with Gustavus' wife. Lena soured the neighbors so much that she erected a twelve-foot high "spite" fence to block them out of her life. Silvertonians had trouble making sense of this odd woman who swore, was tough, freely expressed both good and unflattering opinions, and acted as Santa Claus for local children. They tacitly summed up their sentiments by giving Lena the nickname of Captain Jack, which she probably relished.[218]

After the 1887 split, Edward had to move quickly on the Silver Lake since his resources were limited and needed to be maximized. Edward's interpretation of quick, however, meant two years of sampling, examining the property's geological features, conducting assays, staking claims with Lena, and calculating the most cost efficient manner of development. Unlike most mine owners, Edward took a primary interest in the low-grade ore and considered the high-grade material to be merely a bonus, since plenty of low-grade ore existed. The main problem, however, was that the costs of shipping the low-grade payrock and processing it exceeded the returns. In response, Stoiber thought big. If he could mine and concentrate the ore in large volumes with a highly efficient system, the economies of scale would render the low-grade material profitable through a nominal cost per ton. Devising an efficient system and working out the economic calculations was easy for the stuffy German engineer, and by 1890 he had a plan that fit within his personal finances.

During the late spring when Silver Lake Basin's snow blockade consolidated, a small army of workers ascended with mule trains that carried equipment and supplies up to the Silver Lake Mine. They brought thousands of board-feet of lumber, tons of construction hardware and bricks, and the basic necessities of life, which they assembled into a properly engineered surface plant larger than anything yet seen in the Las Animas District. The living quarters consisted of a handsome story-and-a-half boardinghouse 30 by 80 feet in area, which accommodated a crew of forty. Some of the workers ascended up to the original shaft, enclosed it in a shaft house, and began developing the vein. Other parties did likewise in a tunnel located between the shaft and the basin floor. The largest party of workers, however, blasted a broad terrace at the base of a cliff above the boardinghouse, began a main haulageway tunnel, and erected a basic blacksmith shop 20 by 20 feet in area near the opening. At the same time, additional workers manipulated heavy timbers for a stout tunnel house that would enclose blacksmith, carpentry, and machine shops.[219]

After workers finished the basic infrastructure, they hauled up all the equipment necessary for the largest mill yet to be built in the Las Animas District. Why Stoiber chose to bring the mill up to the mine instead of using a tramway to carry ore down to a better site in

Arrastra Gulch is a mystery. Regardless, considering the weight and bulk of some of the equipment, such as stamp rods and boilers, the only way workers could have defied gravity was winching them up on sleds over snowfields during the spring. They blasted a platform 150 feet wide out of bedrock immediately below the haulageway and pushed the waste rock to the east for the mill building's platform. When finished, the mill was an impressive edifice, especially in the perspective of its lunar landscape setting.

According to archaeological features remaining today, the structure was T-shaped and featured at least three stairstep terraces that allowed gravity to draw ore through the carefully designed treatment steps. The main portion of the mill building was 90 by 150 feet in area, and the top floor featured a row of sorting stations where

This northwest view clearly depicts the lunar landscape in which Edward Stoiber developed his beloved Silver Lake Mine. In 1890 or 1891, when the photograph was taken, workers recently finished both the mill and a boardinghouse adjacent and right. Miners also formally developed several veins on the cliffs at the upper left, which are denoted by the two shaft houses. The long chute at left delivered ore from a mid-level tunnel, and the Stoiber Tunnel, which would become the mine's principal entry, penetrated the mountain immediately above the mill. The man on the boat's bow appears to be Edward Stoiber, and he is accompanied by engineers. Source: Colorado Historical Society, CHS X 7880.

workers manually separated fresh crude ore by purity and threw out the waste. They dropped recovered payrock into bins that fed the material into two Blake crushers, which pulverized it into gravel and sand. Adhering to his high-volume strategy, Stoiber installed five batteries of ten stamps each for an impressive total of fifty, and they further reduced the crushed payrock. Rotating trommel screens classified the fines by size; and here is where Stoiber's mineralogical acumen set him apart from the less experienced metallurgists prone to failure. The segregated particles entered specific treatment paths depending on their sizes. Large clasts proceeded through four sets of Cornish rolls that reduced them to a desired consistency, and the rest went directly for concentration. The stem of the T-shaped mill building housed the concentration machinery, and Stoiber carefully selected specific apparatuses that he knew would achieve the desired results. A row of eight Hartz jigs separated the fines by specific gravity, and eight Woodbury tables and eighteen end-shake slimes tables finished the concentration. Troughs carried the heavy black material away in the form of slurry, which was dried and sacked for shipment.[220]

In addition to the crushing equipment, the main portion of the mill also enclosed the power plant, which Stoiber engineered to perfection. A bank of three 100 horsepower return-tube boilers generated enough steam for an unstoppable 150 horsepower main engine, pumps, several donkey engines, and heat for the mill and boardinghouse. A heater also warmed fresh water for the boilers to minimize shock and temperature fluctuations, prolonging their lives. A room 60 by 60 feet in area enclosed the complex power system, and workers fed the perpetually hungry boilers from a bank of coal bins on the terrace above. Currently, archaeological features represent all aspects of this steam system except for the main engine, which rested on a timber foundation, now gone.[221]

When finished, the mill was able to generate fifty tons of concentrates per day, which provided Stoiber his economies of scale. This translated to five railroad cars of freight, assuming that one car could carry ten to twelve tons.[222] Because Silverton lacked a facility or storage area capable of accommodating the hundreds of tons that Stoiber expected to store at a time, he built his own. Stoiber chose the abandoned Little Dutch Smelter site located on a flat terrace west of

Arrastra Gulch's mouth. While the exact facilities and structures remain unknown, they certainly included large bins, freight platforms, and a corral and stable for the constant procession of draft animals.

The crown jewel to Stoiber's instant empire was an electric power plant that he commissioned on the Animas River. In 1890, electricity was a revolutionary technology under experimentation, and the San Juans served as the cradle for its application to mining. In 1888, the Sunnyside Extension Mining Company installed the first electric plant in the San Juans for its mill near Eureka, followed within months by the Virginius and Tomboy mines above Telluride. These early power plants were small and generated Direct Current (DC), which was able to run variable speed motors but only could be transmitted short distances before suffering a debilitating power loss. As a result, DC current had to be consumed near the point of generation, giving mining engineers pause for thought. What, they reasoned, was the advantage of electricity if it had to be generated on-site? Provided that a DC power plant could be run by hydropower, a costly steam engine and boiler usually had to be kept on standby in case the water system failed. Why not do away with the electrical equipment and merely use the steam engine alone to operate mine machinery for a fraction of the cost? Alternating Current (AC) provided a partial answer to this problem. AC current could be transmitted for miles without a power loss, but as of 1890, AC motors were unable to run variable speed equipment. AC current could, however, energize lighting and run constant speed motors that operated with little drag, such as those used in machine shops and some mill applications. With this in mind, progressive electrical engineers near Telluride finished the first AC power plant in the San Juans and Colorado at Ames in 1891, which set a precedent for others to follow.[223]

Stoiber was not far behind. Around the same time, he completed what appears to have been the second AC power plant in the San Juans and Colorado, which is of great historical significance. According to archival references, a power plant was built on the Animas River, most likely at the concentrates storage terminal, and power lines carried the electricity at least two miles up to Silver Lake Basin, which was too far for DC current. Given this, Stoiber's power plant had to generate AC current, which lit the interiors of the buildings and ran several small motors in the mill.[224]

At the beginning of November 1890, Stoiber started the mill, and it ran to perfection, although the electrical equipment may not have been working yet. The quiet of Silver Lake Basin was permanently broken, and the din of the machinery filled the air with a rumble that could be heard for miles around. While workers put the finishing touches on the facility, muleskinners hauled up hundreds of tons of supplies and coal so Stoiber's empire could weather the gathering winter. After around a year, Stoiber and Lena pored over the balance sheets of the Silver Lake Mines Company to assess how well the empire functioned. They came to the conclusion that it functioned quite well and netted $255,000, or around $5,148,286 today, which constituted around 25 percent of San Juan County's total production! This was far from pure profit, however, because an operation as large as the Silver Lake Mines Company in the environment of 12,000 feet was very costly.[225]

After two years of clockwork production and milling, Stoiber declared the Silver Lake a success. Stoiber's Germanic work ethic and penchant for constant improvements got the better of him and he declined the path of retirement sought by other successful mine owners. Instead, Stoiber took his empire along the next logical step and expanded operations in 1893. Lena, who was the human resources manager for the company, increased the workforce to 130 and had Stoiber build a second boardinghouse. Stoiber sited the structure adjacent to and east of the first boardinghouse and provided amenities unseen in the Las Animas District. The building was an imposing two-story structure 40 by 60 feet in area finished on the interior with ribbed paneling. The bottom floor featured a dining hall, a kitchen equipped with a brick oven, and bunkrooms, while the top floor consisted of more bunkrooms. A water tank suspended in the rafters provided running water for sinks and probably flush toilets, and steam radiators provided heat.[226]

Not all the 130 workers lived in Silver Lake Basin, nor were all the workers in the basin miners. Many worked in the mill and around the surface plant, and a handful staffed the concentrates storage facility and the power plant. As a unit, however, they met Stoiber's expectations and generated at least one railroad car of concentrates per day. The production was so constant, and the mine's future was so sure that, at Stoiber's behest, Mears extended the Silverton Railroad up the Animas River and over to the concentrates terminal. While Stoiber paid little attention to accolades, his Silver Lake empire was the first mining operation in the Las Animas District to receive direct rail service.[227]

The boom in the basins fostered a sense of optimism and prosperity that pervaded the entire Animas River drainage during the early 1890s. In 1891, San Juan County miners generated $761,850 in silver and $192,109 in gold, which was more than any previous year. While the figure fell the following year, the average ore production showed every sign of remaining high. Proud of the increasing sophistication of Silverton, a handful of prominent businessmen decided that the conditions were right to plan a few modern services. Not to be outdone by his brother, Gustavus Stoiber joined James H. Robin and others in organizing the Silverton Electric Light & Power Company in 1890. During the year, the Edison General Electric Company built a power plant equipped with two dynamos powered by a forty horsepower steam engine and a boiler. While Stoiber and Robin

In 1892, Otto Mears and Red Mountain Mining District investors completed the Standard Smelter at Durango to compete with the San Juan Smelting & Refining Company facility, also known as the Durango Smelter. While the Standard Smelter mostly treated Red Mountain ores, it also accepted payrock from the Animas River drainage and drove smelting fees down. Source: Denver Public Library, Western History Collection, X 61433.

In response to Otto Mears' new Standard Smelter, the San Juan Smelting & Refining Company expanded and improved the efficiency of its Durango Smelter during the early 1890s. By comparing this photograph with the one on the pages above, it becomes apparent that a new furnace and buildings have been added. Source: Colorado Historical Society, CHS B 369.

initially planned to energize 450 lights, they chose AC current for its long distance transmission potential in hopes of securing mining companies as customers.[228]

During the boom, mining companies in the Animas River drainage and the Red Mountain District sent more ore through Silverton than the Durango Smelter could handle. Otto Mears quickly seized the opportunity in 1892 and organized the Standard Smelting & Refining Company, which built a second smelter in Durango. While the facility was equipped to treat the copper-rich ores of the Red Mountain District, it also accepted custom orders. Mears' strategy was threefold. First, he attempted to compete directly with the Durango Smelter and subsume a share of the smelting business, and second, Mears operated the smelter in coordination with his Silverton Railroad, which strengthened both companies. Last, Mears wanted to provide a low-cost treatment facility for the mines that he and friends operated, while pocketing the savings. The San Juan Smelting & Mining Company responded in short order by adding several furnaces to its Durango Smelter, lowering its fees, and improving the returns.

At the same time, the Crookes made a reappearance in the Animas River drainage and, after twelve years of dawdling, finally built a silver leaching mill at the mouth of Boulder Gulch, near Howardsville. Even though the Crooke mill was on the north side of the Animas River, the mining companies in the Las Animas District, including the Crookes' North Star, had yet another outlet for their ore.[229]

CHAPTER 8

The Great Silver Crash of 1893

THE RESIDENTS OF THE ANIMAS RIVER DRAINAGE easily settled into the prosperity that they seemed entitled to after investing years of hard labor in the San Juan wilderness. Perhaps the prosperity distracted them a little too much, because few individuals noticed that dark forces were at work to bring prosperity to an end. Almost immediately after the Sherman Silver Purchase Act was signed into law in 1890, reformers grew angry with what amounted to a massive government subsidy for mining and profiteering among powerful capitalists, and they clamored for the repeal of the Act. At the same time, a general economic crisis loomed, which created political instability and factions in both the Federal Government and Great Britain, which was one of the main consumers of American silver. Repeating the cycle of the mid-1880s, the increasingly dour climate contaminated investment in silver and the industries that depended on it, causing the metal's value to slip. In 1891, the price of silver eroded from a high of $1.09 to $.99 and kept going down to $.78 by mid-1893, an all time low that gave the Las Animas District a moment for pause. As with the 1886 cycle, some of the small operations closed, but many companies were able to get by because they were more

Principal places of activity, 1893 to 1898. Source: Author.

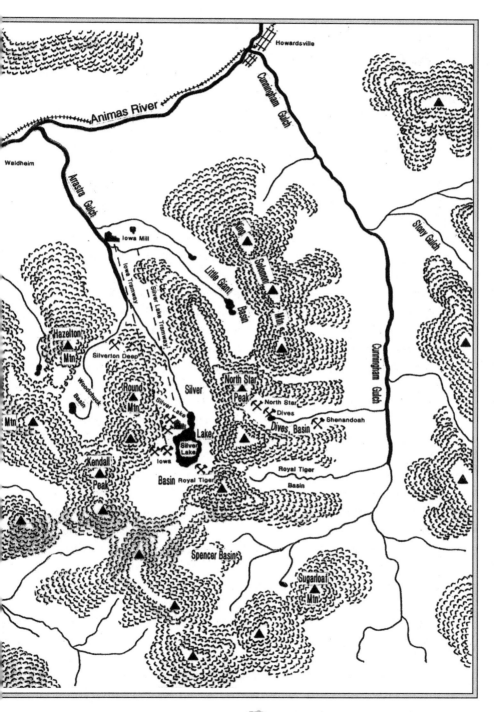

efficient than before and the two smelters in Durango improved their recovery of copper and lead. To make matters worse, however, the value of these metals fell in parallel with silver.[230]

Then, in 1893, the political factors noted above came together to bring at first the ruination of the western mining industry, followed by a nationwide depression. President Grover Cleveland called a special session of Congress to repeal the Sherman Silver Purchase Act, which became a reality in November of 1893, hoping that it would stop an impending economic crash. At the same time, Britain decided to adopt a gold standard and abolish its silver standard, as well as minting no more Indian rupees for its empire in the Far East. The market for silver promptly evaporated and the metal's value plummeted to an abysmal $.64 by March, 1894. The result was cataclysmic. Mines across the West suspended operations and thousands of workers suddenly found themselves jobless. A financial panic then swept the West and rippled out to the rest of the nation, ushering in a depression that lasted through much of the 1890s. [232]

Like the rest of Colorado, the entire San Juan region, which relied to a great degree on silver, was devastated. Almost every mining company in the Las Animas District closed, and the rest of the region faired little better. Some estimates suggest that around 1,000 workers lost their jobs, which seems slightly high given that the population of San Juan County was around 1,600 in 1890. Regardless, those residents able to hang on witnessed nothing less than an exodus of the best, brightest, and healthiest who were forced to find work elsewhere. With little ore coming down from the mountains and few supplies going up, the San Juan Smelting & Mining Company and Otto Mears shuttered their smelters in Durango, and Mears and the Denver & Rio Grande reduced service on their railroads. This sealed the fate of the Animas River drainage. The few mining companies willing to try maintaining some semblance of production no longer had low-cost treatment available, and at $.64 per ounce, the silver ore would barely even pay the cost of bringing it out of the ground. The Stoiber and Sweet sampling works, fortunately, received just enough business to prevent them from closing.[233]

Curiously, while an unsettling quiet hung in the air, the residents who remained looked up to Silver Lake Basin in awe, because it still resounded with the dull roar of Edward Stoiber's mill. Upon

Some of the most important dignitaries at the Silver Lake Mine - the cook and his staff - pose in front of mine workers in this mid-1890s photograph. Many of these rugged individuals were Italian immigrants. The mine's two boardinghouses stand at right and at center, and a portion of the mill is visible at left. The numerous electrical lines traversing the scene reflect Edward Stoiber's prized power system, and the avalanche fences on the mountainside in the background offered some protection from heavy snows. Source: Denver Public Library, Western History Collection, X 60864.

investigation, it became apparent that a small crew of miners continued to labor underground at the Iowa as well. How were the Stoibers able to keep their operations alive and well? The answer lay in the ore that miners found in the system of parallel veins. The payrock contained a higher proportion of gold than most of the other ore bodies in the region, and the value of this precious metal retained a constant value of around $20.70 per ounce despite the collapse of silver. Theophile Benjovsky came to this realization and, with the region in a depression, returned to his Dives Mine for needed income from its gold-bearing ore.[234]

If the smelters in Durango were idle, where could the Stoibers, Benjovsky, and the region's few other gold producers send their ore for treatment? In most cases, the ore was not rich enough to pay the costs of shipping it to the Front Range smelters. The two samplers in Silverton may have taken custom orders, but the region suffered a deep void in terms of ore treatment. Thomas F. Walsh saw this as an opportunity, albeit risky given the poor economic climate, and assembled the resources in 1894 to open a new smelter at Silverton. He felt that if he provided relatively low cost ore treatment, companies in the Animas River drainage and the Red Mountain district would generate enough payrock to keep the facility afloat until

Waldheim, built in 1895, was the crown jewel of Edward Stoiber's Silver Lake Mines Company. Stoiber's mansion at left was reportedly the largest brick residence in the San Juans, and it featured hot and cold running water and steam heat. The building on the right was a powerhouse, which was one of the most advanced Alternating Current generators of its time. The large structure was a boiler house, and the low, adjacent building featured dynamos, Pelton waterwheels, and a massive steam engine. The Aspen Tunnel is visible on the mountainside above and behind. Source: Denver Public Library, Western History Collection, X 62272.

The photograph, taken from the same vantage point as the historic image, depicts Waldheim as it exists today. Source: Author.

A complex set of machine foundations currently represents the Waldheim powerplant. Dynamos were anchored to the four large pads extending across photo-center, and a steam engine rested on the pad at the upper left. Source: Author.

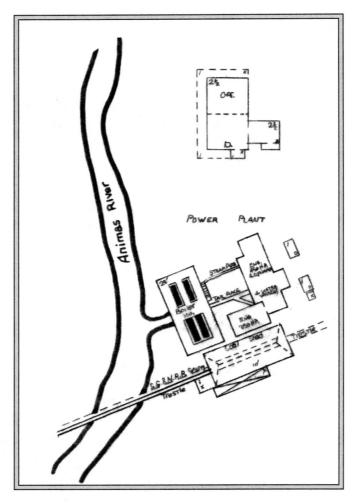

*The plan view depicts the facilities that made up
Waldheim. The lower complex is the powerplant, and
from left to right are the boiler house, channels for spent
water, the dynamo house, and two offices. The dynamo
house featured four dynamos driven by an equal
number of Pelton waterwheels, and a steam engine kept
on standby. The Silverton Railroad delivered fuel coal
to the shed at bottom. Source: Sanborn Fire Insurance
Map, 1902.*

A Pelton waterwheel spun in the channel at center, and the pipe behind provided a high-pressure jet to turn the apparatus. A total of four Pelton wheels drove the powerhouse's dynamos. Source: Author.

The lithograph illustrates a Pelton wheel and belt pulley. Source: Mining & Scientific Press *5/26/88, p325.*

better times returned. In addition, Walsh had a personal stake, since the mines he invested in were not doing very well and needed a smelter.

In 1894, Walsh, Charles J. Hughes, and Albert Smith incorporated the Silverton Smelting & Mining Company to formalize the project, which gave the residents in the Animas River drainage a ray of optimism. Walsh obtained the rights to the abandoned Martha Rose Smelter on the northwest edge of Silverton, because it featured a well-built structure and some of the original infrastructure, which saved him badly needed capital. During the first half of the year, workers repaired the facility and installed new equipment, and by the spring, Walsh was ready to treat the first load of ore. With little more to do than busy work, many Silvertonians found the time to examine Walsh's efforts and were on hand for the final pour of silver. Walsh had an easy time convincing independent miners such as Benjovsky, as well as companies, to send their ore; and after several weeks of successful operation, Silvertonians felt reassured by the return of smog, the acrid smell of sulfur, and the clatter of the mill. Walsh was nothing less than a hero for delivering a functional smelter to the Animas River drainage in its darkest hour of need, and his reward came several years later with the development of the famed Camp Bird Mine near Ouray.[235]

The Stoiber brothers were also celebrities, although Edward renounced any fanfare and remained fixated on his Silver Lake Mine. The Stoibers gained notoriety not only on a local level, but also in the greater mining industry for their skills in running their respective mines in the dismal economic climate of the Silver Crash. Given that brothers often think alike, both Edward and Gustavus responded to the Silver Crash not by curtailing operations but by taking the opposite approach and expanding operations beyond all proportions of the time. The philosophy was an extension of Edward's original idea where mechanization on a massive scale, and the production and concentration of high volumes of ore would reduce the cost per ton and render low-grade ore profitable. And with the value of silver at an all time low, the time for such practices was never better.

Fascinated with the potential offered by electricity, Edward planned a second powerplant for his Silver Lake Mine, so he could install more motors, as well as providing some current to his brother's Iowa Mine. In 1894, he chose a site on the south side of the Animas

River between Arrastra Gulch and Silverton and probably contracted with an electrical firm for the design. Workers built a dam on the Animas River near Howardsville, and it directed water into a large flume that crossed the mouth of Arrastra Gulch on a high trestle. The flume continued to a point over the powerhouse site and fed the water into pipes that descended into the powerhouse building.[236]

Archival sources document some aspects of the powerplant, and when combined with today's archaeological evidence (mostly in the form of foundations), we can clearly interpret what the facility consisted of. The powerplant featured three separate, neatly arranged buildings dedicated for specific functions. The actual powerhouse was 42 by 100 feet in area and featured four dynamos powered by four Pelton waterwheels that spun in channels in the building's southwest corner. High pressure water jets turned the Pelton wheels, which were geared to a central driveshaft extending along the length of the powerhouse's west side. Belts transferred motion from the driveshaft to the dynamos and, in case the water system failed or froze, a titanic 450 horsepower steam engine was kept on standby in the building's northeast quarter. As the demand for electricity increased, and the water system in fact failed, a second engine and several more dynamos were added. A boiler house stood 45 feet to the west and was a stately brick building 45 by 90 feet in area. Originally, a pair of return-tube boilers for the first steam engine was in the building's north portion, and workers added an efficient water-tube boiler in the south portion to power the supplemental steam engine. The powerplant also featured a set of coal bins south of the other two buildings to store the mountain of fossil fuel necessary for the boilers. Otto Mears' workers built a trestle over the Animas River for a spur track that ended in the large coal shed for the efficient transfer of freight. Several years after construction, newspapers claimed that the powerplant was the most complete of the privately owned AC facilities in the nation and saved Edward $15,000 in coal per year, or $330,096 today, which was more than just pocket change.[237]

Completely absorbed by his Silver Lake empire, Edward needed to meld as one with the operation and found that living by the powerplant was the closest he could get. Along with the powerplant buildings, in 1895 masons also erected what was the largest and best appointed private mansion in the San Juans. The brick

building was L-shaped and two stories high, not including a full basement and loft, and the main portion was around 50 by 90 feet in
area. Edward spared no expense and installed a complex plumbing
system complete with hot and cold water, sinks, bathtubs, toilets, and
steam heat. Lena demanded an upstairs ballroom, and she accented
most of the mansion's twenty-nine other rooms with different woods
such as maple and oak. Edward designed his own play room upstairs
complete with a billiards room, a large office, and a vault downstairs.
Edward and Lena named the heart of their Silver Lake empire Waldheim, which was German for forest home. The mansion's location

*Tram terminals were dark, drafty, cold, and loud. Such an environment
combined with the labor of pushing full buckets around the interior
was exhausting and dangerous. Source: Colorado Historical Society,
CHS 84-192.583.*

was a tacit statement of their attitude toward the community. Specifically, Waldheim lay more than one mile east of Silverton and across the Animas River, which resembled a moat, and there Lena was free to be as profane as she wanted with no repercussions, while the pulse of the power plant's titanic steam engines soothed Edward.[238]

Improving the efficiency of the Silver Lake operation also meant defying the impossible winters by sending concentrates down from the mill regardless of conditions. To do so, the material had to be treated as if it was liquid to achieve a continuous flow from the mill to the terminal and into Mears' railroad cars. The best way, Edward surmised, was to imitate Thomas Trippe's Titusville operation, which was now idle, and install an aerial tramway to levitate the concentrates above the nearly impassable valley floor as if by magic. A tramway was no easy or inexpensive undertaking, especially in Arrastra Gulch, and Round Mountain complicated matters by presenting an obstruction between Silver Lake Basin and the mouth of the gulch where Edward's terminal lay. After surveying a route around Round Mountain, Edward came to the conclusion that the most effective tramway would have to consist of two segments linked by a turning station in the gulch.

Based on the enormous distances and the necessary carrying capacity, Edward chose the Bleichert Double Rope tramway, which was designed by two equally imaginative and meticulous German engineers. The ingenuity of the Bleichert system was that it featured a constant procession of ore buckets tugged around a circuit by an endless loop traction rope. The buckets coasted over a separate track rope on special carriages featuring guide wheels, and a series of regular tram towers supported both cables. If the system had an adequate fall-line, the weight of the full buckets theoretically pulled the light, empty ones up. In some cases, clever engineers harnessed the gravity-drawn system to generate electricity. In the system's top terminal, mine workers uncoupled incoming buckets, pushed them across a hanging rail, and stopped them underneath chutes to fill them with ore. Once full, the workers recoupled the buckets onto the traction cable, and they left the upper terminal. Workers in the bottom terminal uncoupled the incoming buckets and emptied them. Both terminals also featured massive cast iron sheave wheels for the traction cable, brakes to stop the system, anchors for the fixed track cables, telephones, and stoves to ward off the cold. However, the exposure of most terminals to wind, their draftiness, and the air drawn in by the buckets guaranteed a chilly interior, which was deafeningly noisy as well.

When Edward made the arrangements to build the Las Animas District's fourth major tramway, he listened to his inner voice of Germanic frugality and found that his readily available funds would only pay for the first segment. So it had to be, and in 1895, Edward contracted with William M. Frey, tramway expert from Leadville, to begin construction. Probably at Edward's insistence, Frey engineered the system components for long-term durability and high capacity, and wisely took into account the physical environment. According to structural debris and a few surviving engineering features currently remaining from the tramway, Frey built four-legged pyramid towers for the cables and erected them on formal masonry foundations instead of the less expensive, common timber footers. At approximately 8,700 feet in length, the tramway could not help but to cross one avalanche chute after another, any of which had the potential to completely wreck the system. Understanding this, Frey protected each vulnerable tower with a triangular-shaped avalanche deflector constructed of cribbing filled with cobble ballast. In theory, the tram tower stood in the shadow of the deflector, which forced the avalanche around both sides and away. By November, Frey was done with construction and watched with newspaper and journal reporters as the system started with perfection. Edward would tolerate nothing less.[239]

Meanwhile, Gustavus Stoiber and James Robin were as busy pouring money into their Iowa Mine as Edward was with the Silver Lake. Following Edward's example, they hatched a grand plan for long-term production, which included improvements at the mine, the widespread adoption of mechanization, a mill, and a tramway. And, like Edward, Gustavus was also frugal and insisted on enacting the plan in manageable steps. The first was the construction of a concentration mill to immediately reduce transportation costs and retain a portion of the treatment fees that they paid to smelters.

Unlike Edward, Gustavus and Robin sited their mill on the floor of Arrastra Gulch almost directly over the obsolete Little Giant arrastra. This location was inefficient in the beginning because it required mule trains to deliver ore, but the planned tramway would remedy this, and the location made shipping out concentrates easier. Workers broke ground for the mill early in 1895 and pushed hard on finishing the facility by the end of the year. At a reasonable cost of $25,000, or only $544,713 today, Gustavus and Robin built a highly functional mill capable of concentrating 150 tons of ore per day. Rising on the northeast side of the gulch floor, the mill building was 32 feet wide and 127 feet long with a 30 by 26 foot wing that enclosed the steam engine and boiler. The flow path for the ore was slightly different from the region's other mills because the Iowa facility was geared toward recovering gold as a metal while producing silver and industrial metals concentrates. Workers dumped crude ore into a receiving bin that fed the material into a jaw crusher, and the resultant gravel passed through several sets of Cornish rolls. Trommel screens classified the sand by size and a row of seven jigs sorted it by specific gravity. Gold-bearing particles were diverted into a Huntington mill, which was an excellent gold recovery apparatus with rollers that rotated around the interior of a large cast iron pan. As the rollers revolved around the floor, they crushed the ore particles into a slurry and the heavy gold amalgamated with mercury while the light gangue passed through several screens. In the Iowa Mill, two vibrating Woodbury tables concentrated the silver-bearing sand and slurry, and a drying table prepared the concentrates for sacking.[240]

By early 1896, workers finished the mill, and it recovered a high percentage of the ore's metal content, which reflected the mineralogical prowess of the metallurgist who most likely was Gustavus. This, evidence that the veins appeared to hold their value at depth, and the fact that the Iowa produced an impressive $300,000 by 1896, or around $6,601,920 today, baited Gustavus and Robin to take the next step in their master plan. They wanted to replace the mule trains that carried ore down to the mill because the cost was $4 per ton, which consumed nearly half the value of the ore. A tramway was the logical choice, and they contracted with the Trenton Iron Works of New Jersey for a Bleichert system in the spring.[241]

With the tramway under construction, Gustavus and partners directed their attention to mining operations and claim development. They hired on more miners who drove two tunnels to penetrate the vein and work it simultaneously at different elevations. In keeping with proper mining engineering, Gustavus planned to drive a deep haulage tunnel from the lowest elevation possible, develop the vein system from several levels linked by raises, and allow the payrock to roll down the raises to bins over the haulageway. From there, miners could send it in ore cars out of the tunnel directly to the tramway. While this was expensive and ambitious, it would ultimately lower production costs and create a lasting underground infrastructure. At the same time, an external infrastructure in the form of surface plants was also necessary at the tunnels. Driving the two new tunnels and the surface work constituted quite an expense that taxed the company's coffers.

The original workings high on the side of Kendall Peak became known as Level No.1, and while miners continued to access the old stopes through the level, they relied primarily on the two new tunnels. During 1896, miners drove the new Level No.2 Tunnel on the precipitous mountainside around 120 feet below Level No.1, and Level No.3 Tunnel, also known as the Selzner Tunnel, around 100 feet farther down. The Iowa Tunnel, which was to serve as the haulageway, was also known as Level No.4. Miners drove it into the base of a natural bedrock terrace near the basin floor.[242]

While workers assembled the permanent surface plant for the tunnels, they quickly completed temporary facilities to support actual mining. One of the most important facilities was a simple compressed air system that allowed miners to expedite driving the Level No.3 and Level No.4 tunnels with piston rockdrills. While archival sources merely noted the use of drills, archaeological and engineering features clearly reflect the original compressed air system. Workers excavated a platform southeast of and below the Iowa Tunnel and installed a 2 by 10 foot straight-line steam compressor capable of powering four drills. A small return-tube boiler farther downslope and to the southeast powered the compressor, and because it was an excellent source of heat, workers abutted several residences against the boiler's brick setting.[243]

In the chill of December, workers put the finishing touches on the tramway, although several miscalculations slowed work. Poor footing in the snow and the laws of physics contributed to the worst blunder, which was almost catastrophic. In preparation for lowering the track cables down onto the towers, a capstan holding one of the cables stretched taught was chocked to lock it in place. The foreman ordered workers to man the sweeps on the capstan and gently lower the cable down, then the chock was gingerly removed. The workers were insufficient to resist the immense tug of the cable, and the capstan spun wildly with the sweeps suddenly acting as clubs and catapults. Workers were thrown from the device, some were beaten, and Joe Dresback was struck on the head. Most of the injured had to walk down from the mine for medical assistance, while the severely injured were carried out on stretchers.[244]

Once a second team of workers successfully fastened the track cables, the system was tested and worked as expected. By this time, Gustavus and partners increased the workforce to 125, and while not all worked underground, the expert crew produced around 125 tons of ore per day, which exceeded the normal average per miner. The tramway carried the material down to the mill, where the workers treated eighty tons and stored the remainder for periods of bad weather when the tramway could not run. By reinvesting profits and spending capital wisely, Gustavus and partners made the Iowa Mine into one of the best in the Las Animas District, second only to Edward's Silver Lake operation.[245]

Just as Edward assembled a mining empire, so too did Gustavus. In 1896, he, Robin, and the other Iowa investors purchased the Tiger Mining & Milling Company, which began work on the Royal Tiger Mine, directly across Silver Lake. The previous outfit had done little with the property and was eager to sell because it found that operating in the basin was more complicated than supposed. Gustavus and Robin immediately put a crew to work erecting a surface plant capable of withstanding the environmental rigors of the basin. Miners blasted a bench at the base of a large cliff and erected a single, large building on the flat area. The building, 18 by 95 feet in area, was stout and featured a heavy post-and-girt timber frame bolted together and buttressed by diagonal braces. The northern portion served as living quarters, the center portion housed a stable, and the southern section enclosed a tunnel and a shop. To the knowledgeable miner, everything about the building spoke of the expectation that it would be struck by avalanches at some time. By nestling the building against the cliff, it was hoped that avalanches would skim over its top, and the heavy frame and diagonal buttresses were intended to withstand impact from above. Like Edward's boardinghouses, Gustavus equipped the quarters with a kitchen and dining hall appointed with a brick oven and a water heater. After abandonment, an avalanche in fact smashed the structure into splinters.[246]

In the climate of the mid-1890s depression, the success of the Stoiber brothers was nothing less than astounding and railed against the trend followed by the rest of Colorado. If asked how, both of the brothers probably would have cited their Germanic work ethic and frugality, as well as careful attention to investment strategy, expenses, management, and operations. Their high level of success also depended on a coordinated effort, which brought the brothers back into each other's good graces. When Gustavus talked of making the Iowa great during 1894, Edward took a keen interest and extended his hand, and Gustavus responded in kind. Edward and Lena were several of the largest stockholders in Gustavus' Iowa company, and when Edward built the Waldheim powerplant, he intended to provide electricity to the Iowa Mine. Edward also offered no objection when Gustavus convinced the Postal Service to locate the misspelled post office of Arastra at the Iowa in 1895, even though Edward had a larger workforce at the Silver Lake. At the same time, Gustavus, Robin, Joseph Bordeleau, Frank B. Brown, and R.S. Courtney organized the Silverton Deep Mining & Tunnel Company to drive an ambitious haulage tunnel from Arrastra Gulch underneath Round Mountain and Kendall Peak. They intended to undercut the Silver Lake, Iowa, and Titusville ore systems and fully expected to encounter Edward's Silver Lake first. In the spring, miners began the tunnel high up on the gulch's west side and worked into the fall, when other matters distracted Gustavus and Robin.[247]

In 1897, the brothers' cooperation reached a crescendo as each installed massive and complimentary facilities intended to serve both mines. At the Iowa, workers finished a giant surface plant that resembled a factory, and which featured three enormous frame buildings as well as ancillary structures. A two-story compressor house built on the shore of Silver Lake was among these, and its main floor featured the largest, most expensive, and most advanced compressed air system in the Las Animas District, if not the greater area. A titanic multi-stage Norwalk compressor and a smaller Rand Imperial Type 10 compressor were at the heart of the system, and they pressurized a maze of pipes extending into the Iowa, Silver Lake, and Royal Tiger mines. The system allowed miners in distant areas of work to use rockdrills and other compressed air machines. A steam engine drove the compressors and other machinery via a system of driveshafts and belts, and two highly efficient and costly water-tube boilers provided steam for motive power and heat in other buildings.[248]

A single-story tunnel house at the Iowa Tunnel was another of the surface plant's principal structures. The building, 58 by 95 feet in area, consisted of a heavy timber frame intended to withstand any snowslides that a special cable avalanche fence erected upslope could not catch. According to archaeological evidence, the tunnel house was divided into shops capable of meeting the advanced needs of a mine as large as the Iowa. The southwest quarter housed a machine shop, the northern portion enclosed blacksmith and carpentry shops and a transformer station, and the northwest corner featured the heavily timbered portal of the Iowa Tunnel. The demand for shop work grew so intense that workers erected a second shop 12 by 20 feet in area to the north for blacksmithing and general carpentry.[249]

Rail lines extended throughout the surface plant so miners could shuttle ore to the tram terminal, which was the most imposing building, and send heavy items underground. Nearly as much ore came out of the Level No.3 Tunnel as the Iowa Tunnel, and special structures were built to accommodate its transfer down to the main surface plant. Specifically, an inclined tramway on an elaborate trestle carried pay-rock down to ore bins, which miners tapped into ore cars.

With the advanced facilities, miners developed no fewer than three principal ore formations that included the Iowa, West Iowa, and Collins veins with a maze of workings. Through hard labor, they kept the tramway operating at its 175 ton per day capacity and provided the company with a total of $225,000 in gold, $80,000 in lead, and $60,000 in silver for 1897 alone. Gustavus' strategy was paying off handsomely, to say the least.

Whereas Gustavus provided his brother with compressed air, Edward provided housing for their combined army of miners. During 1897, Edward employed between 220 and 275 workers, Gustavus retained around 120, and of the total, more than 300 lived in Silver Lake Basin. The mere workforce for Silver Lake Basin's three mines was larger than the population of many towns on the mining frontier![250]

Despite his grouchy façade, Edward deeply understood the value of his miners and, perceiving himself as a benevolent mine owner on par with Thomas Walsh, he extended himself to treat the workers well. Edward clearly demonstrated these sentiments by providing comforts, unheard of in most mining districts, in the two existing boardinghouses at the Silver Lake; and herein forced his growing reputation when he built the third boardinghouse in 1897. Miners accustomed to flimsy frame structures and cramped cabins were amazed at what Edward provided, and reporting journalists used words like "hotel" and "A Model Miners' Home" to describe Edward's contribution.[251] A reporter gathering data for the United States Mint examined the new boardinghouse and summed up the accommodations best:

> The comfort of the miners has been most carefully studied. The boarding house at the Silver Lake properties, largest in the district, is a five-storied structure, with ground floor space of 80 by 90 feet, and the four upper stories, 40 by 90 feet, lighted throughout by electricity, heated by steam, provided with hot and cold water, bath, laundry, and other modern conveniences. Fire hose lines run through the house, and two tanks, of 5,000 gallons capacity each, are located on the roof. The dining room is 40 by 90 feet and seats 250 persons. In the large and well-equipped kitchen all cooking, save meat, is done by steam. Dishwashing machines and drying tables prevail. The garbage is burned daily. Just off from the model merchandise store is Arastra post-office, a money-order office accommodating over 500 men employed in Silver Lake Basin.[252]

Structural remains from the collapsed building and other forms of archaeological evidence provide additional details that make the boardinghouse all the more impressive. To prepare meals for the throng waiting twice daily in the dining hall, the kitchen, on the bottom floor, featured running water and two brick ovens vented by chimneys. A primitive sewer system, virtually unknown on the mining frontier, except in the most metropolitan cities, served the hotel-like boardinghouse and its western neighbor. According to material evidence, sewer pipes fed offal into plank culverts that emptied into septic tanks buried by mill tailings to the north. The sewer is particularly noteworthy because it reflects Edward's aware-ness of water pollution and the potential for a population of 300 to create unhealthy conditions at the mine as well as downstream. Instead of relying on small basement boilers to provide the board-inghouses with hot water and steam heat, Edward perhaps went overboard and installed a water-tube boiler in a freestanding boiler house. This type of steam generator was not only the most efficient type, but also the most expensive and above and beyond what was necessary.[253]

Despite the amenities of the Silver Lake boardinghouses, they seem somewhat less than idyllic when the reality of the physical set-ting is considered. Originally, the "hotel" stood on the edge of Silver Lake, but with one of the largest mines in the San Juans crowding the building, the setting was nothing less than a gritty, noisy, industrial atmosphere. Over time, waste began to engulf the boardinghouses. Mill tailings blanketed the surrounding ground, a gigantic dump of ashy boiler clinker extended east into Silver Lake, and the residents were not the tidiest with their household garbage. Smoke from the adjacent boiler wafted across the hotel at times and dust certainly blew through the complex daily. Beauty is in the eye of the beholder, however, and most of the miners almost certainly considered the boardinghouses and greater Silver Lake Basin a far cry from what they were used to.

Viewed from the summit of one of the overlooking peaks, activ-ity at the Silver Lake Mine must have appeared similar to a giant ant colony. A constant stream of miners poured into and out of the Sil-ver Lake Tunnel and another entry on the mountainside above, and they found their way through the mine's ten miles of underground passages to their points of work. The Silver Lake Tunnel, 6 by 7 feet in-the-clear, was the main entry underground, and it extended more than 1,250 feet northwest along the Silver Lake Vein and, near the end, a 900 foot crosscut tunnel penetrated one vein after another including the L.A.S., E.G.S., Royal, Selzner, and New York City. Miners drove another drift northwest until they punched a hole completely through Round Mountain and into Woodchuck Basin. Edward's miners were every bit as skilled as Gustavus', and they gen-erated more than the average of one ton per man per shift, for a total of 300 tons per day! The volume was the benchmark of economies of scale and exceeded the mill's 250 ton-per-day treatment capacity, which Edward increased during 1897. To provide power for the additional machinery in the mill and at the mine, Edward installed two 120 horsepower water-tube boilers, which saved fuel in the long run but cost a small fortune.[254]

As operations grew almost out of control, Edward hired the expert metallurgist Robert J. McCartney from Leadville, who was never satisfied with a mill until it recovered an unrealistic 100 percent of an ore's metal content. To this end, McCartney looked at problems from the scale of an entire mill down to the performance of an individual machine. He was Edward's man, and together they spent hours and days romancing the Silver Lake Mine and tinkering with improvements to the concentration process. As part of this, they literally invented one of the best vibrating tables for concentrating San Juan ores, which the mining industry recognized as the Stoiber-McCartney table.[255]

As we can infer by now, the Silver Lake surface plant was every bit as complex and well-equipped as the Iowa Mine. A heavily framed tunnel house, protected at the base of a cliff, featured advanced and motorized shop equipment for all types of work, as well as a blacksmith station for sharpening drill-steels. To handle overflow work, McCartney maintained the mine's original blacksmith shop, as well as a machinery repair facility and stable combined into a single, handsome gabled building. Because the Silver Lake Mine was the first stop on Edward's crown jewel electrical grid, the surface plant included at least three humming transformer stations. The mine's other entries upslope also had dedicated buildings, as well.[256]

By the end of 1897, the Stoibers transformed Silver Lake Basin into an industrial landscape of epic proportion. The original bedrock texture of the west side became lost amid a veneer of waste rock created by the coalescence of one dump after another. The three mines took on the odd appearance of massive factories completely out of place in the barren landscape of the basin. An octopus of roads and packtrails radiated outward from the mines, wrapped around the basin, and went over nearly every low point on the surrounding walls. A small forest of smokestacks belched out acrid smoke, which swirled through the basin before being sucked away by the high-altitude winds. The noise could be heard from all the surrounding basins as screeches, clangs, and rhythmic thumps from the Silver Lake Mill, and a general background roar.

Several other mines made small noises of their own during the depths of the depression, despite the abysmal value of silver. Italian miner Louis Sartore faced a future of no income and, since mining was the profession he knew best and he wanted to remain in the area, Sartore decided that producing silver for pennies was better than nothing. In 1894, he leased the idle Lackawanna and managed to eke out an existence on small batches of ore that he packed to the Walsh Smelter. Thus Sartore survived through 1896.[257]

In Little Giant Basin, construction crews, probably employed by William Keith, were busy building a new surface plant at the Big Giant Mine. Where the capital came from is a mystery, but Keith was able to fund a tunnel house, a boardinghouse, and a new concentration mill. According to archaeological evidence, he saved a considerable amount of money by using a high volume of salvaged lumber for the structures, probably taken from the abandoned King Solomon Mine and North Star Mill at the head of the basin. The Big Giant Mill

While this north view of the North Star Mine's tunnel house was reportedly taken around 1900, the building changed little from when Eben Olcott erected it in 1881. The structure housed the mine's tunnel portal, blacksmith shop, ore sorting station, and living quarters under one cramped, sooty, and drafty roof. The building is actually larger than it appears and was as deep as it was long. Source: Denver Public Library, Western History Collection, X 62714.

The transportation system for shipping ore from the North Star Mine to the railroad at Silverton was slow and cumbersome. Pack trains carried the payrock in sacks over and around North Star Peak, through Little Giant Basin, and down to a transfer station in Arrastra Basin, where it was loaded into wagons for the final descent to Silverton. This 1890 view captures the transfer station. Arrastra Basin forms the impressive backdrop, and Round Mountain looms at center. Source: Colorado Historical Society, CHS X 9254.

featured a jaw crusher, Cornish rolls, and a grinding pan to pulverize the ore, and other pieces of machinery to concentrate the fines. A steam engine powered by a portable boiler ran the equipment. The boardinghouse was 18 by 80 feet, included a stable, lacked amenities, and was able to accommodate sixteen miners.[258]

After finishing the surface facilities and developing the Big Giant vein through 1896, Keith persuaded the French Boys Silver Mining Company to sell the property the next year. By 1897, he was ready to produce ore, and when his miners began work in the old stope, they found something that the last crew missed. Specifically, Keith's miners encountered a vein of high-grade ore that promised to pay the costs of the property improvements. Unfortunately for Keith, the mill proved to be a dismal failure from the beginning, and he found himself paying for something that was unable to treat the rebellious ore. Regardless, Keith maintained production through the rest of the 1890s.[259]

During 1896, measurable life returned to Dives Basin, and with it came a face that the original generation of miners in the Las Animas District were not fond of. The Crookes hired William A. Kearnes to lead a crew of twenty miners thankful for jobs up to the North Star Mine and resume production. Kearnes must have atoned for the $4,000 he took from the Crookes in 1878, although he had yet to return to the good graces of Thomas Blair, who may not have been aware of Kearnes' return. The remote and isolated North Star was a great place to hide out while employed, and Kearnes apparently satisfied the Crookes with the amount and quality of ore that he sent them. This was due in part to a rich strike that Kearnes took credit for. He directed several miners to drive a crosscut tunnel into the wall along a meager vein, and after a short distance, they found a parallel ore formation that glittered with a complex blend of silver, lead, and copper. Kearnes hired another fifteen miners, who drilled and blasted thirty tons of both the fresh ore and the regular material per day through 1897.[260]

Immediately below the North Star, Theophile Benjovsky was at work in the Dives Mine, which was controlled by the Dives Mining Company. Probably in 1895, he and friend Martin Van Buren Wason consolidated their claims, including the Shenandoah and Dives, and organized a company to manage the assets and provide capital for formal development. Benjovsky did so well with the Dives in 1895 that he hired a small crew to extract ore from the primitive workings. At the same time, Henry M. Bennett paid a visit to the Shenandoah to assess its potential and see if Wason's descriptions of the ore body were accurate.[261]

Bennett exemplified how some rough prospectors matured from frontiersmen to settled and established mine operators, and adapted to regional changes as they grew older. Bennett was among the early prospectors who were intrigued with the San Juans and formed a partnership with the legendary John C. McKenzie. They spent much time on the eastern side of the mountains; and, in 1876, when they were passing through the Rio Grande River Valley, the partners took a few days to examine the Willow Creek area. There, they discovered the first silver formations at what became Creede and staked them as the Alpha and Corsair. Bennett and McKenzie tried working the ore in an arrastra with little success, but returned for additional forays during the next several years. In 1885, Bennett, McKenzie, and James A. Wilson found a second silver vein on West Willow Creek that they named the Bachelor. When the rush to Creede let loose in 1891, Bennett saw the Bachelor become one of the richest mines in the area, and he may have profited from its sale. He continued to live in Creede and, as a pioneer, came to know Martin Van Buren Wason, whose ranch lay at Creede's gateway. Wason probably described the Shenandoah to Bennett, who took an interest in the property.[262]

As Wason may have promised, the Shenandoah was barely developed and saw its last significant activity during the 1880s, which left Bennett with the impression that the vein was as yet untapped and held great potential. Bennett and Wason struck a mutually beneficial deal in 1896 where Bennett leased the property. Wason has finally found someone who would face the climate of Dives Basin and develop this fallow fortune, and Bennett had the rare opportunity of being the first to seriously open up a vein proven to possess excellent ore.

In general, Colorado miners and mine owners came to prefer the leasing system during the 1890s for different reasons. A lease was an arrangement where an individual such as Bennett paid the mine owner a fee for the right, by legal contract, to work the property. The fee varied and ranged from a percentage of the gross income, to a flat rate, to a combination of the two. A fee of twenty percent was common, although it varied from as low as ten percent to as high as sixty percent, based on the quantity and quality of ore. By leasing out a mine, the owner realized income while investing little effort and shifted the operating costs over to the lessee. The owners of idle properties, such as Wason, were often more than willing to have someone else do the work, especially when they lacked capital. Lessees stood to benefit because they had the potential to make more money than company wages, at the least, and strike bonanza ore, at the best. Leasing, however, had its pitfalls. The potential for dishonesty among all parties fostered a sense of insecurity. Some lessees tried to hide their production levels, and on more than one occasion, the owner attempted to cancel a lease after the lessees made a rich strike. Because the lessees had to pay their own operating costs, they had a tendency to ignore the infrastructure necessary for a mine's long-term wellbeing, as well as the safety of the workers. In their haste, some lessees even damaged the underground workings through poor practices and left them in a state that required costly improvements. In some cases, the mine owner or company maintained the mine and operated the surface plant, while leasing blocks of ground or sections of the workings to individual miners, who tried to extract ore as fast as they could.[263]

Because Bennett and Wason were acquaintances and probably friends, the Shenandoah lease held little potential for problems. During the summer of 1896, Bennett sent a crew up to the Shenandoah to build a basic surface plant and begin development. As they pursued the vein underground, the miners proved Bennett's hunch correct — they made a strike so rich that it was reported in mining journals. Eager for more finds, Bennett increased the workforce to eight miners the following year, and they produced around five tons of ore per day, drove development workings, and constructed a boardinghouse for an even larger crew. By mid-summer, ten miners sent ore down to be milled and found another excellent vein. With silver fetching a mere $.61 per ounce, the ore in the Shenandoah must have been extremely rich to provide Bennett and Wason with enough profits to keep the arrangement going.[264]

One of the fundamental reasons why mining companies were able to produce ore during the mid-1890s depression was that the Durango Smelter was back in business, and it provided relatively low-cost treatment. The Omaha & Grant Smelting & Refining Company, one of the most powerful smelting firms in the Rocky Mountain West, saw the void left by the closure of the Durango Smelter in 1894. The success of the Walsh Smelter probably convinced the directors that a sound market existed in the San Juans, and with aspirations of an empire, Omaha & Grant leased the Durango Smelter from the San Juan Smelting & Mining Company the following year. Walsh cringed at the competition, but the mine owners and operators in the Animas River drainage were elated that low-cost treatment finally returned. The residents of Durango, also known as the Smelter City, gleefully inhaled the noxious fumes that once again filled their confined valley when the smelter fired up its furnaces. Forecasting a revival of mining in the San Juans, Omaha & Grant made San Juan Smelting &

Mining an offer it could not refuse in 1896 and purchased the Durango Smelter.[265]

Out of a conflicted sense of both selflessness and deep self interest, Otto Mears made major contributions that helped the central San Juans weather the depression. He understood that his transportation empire and financial interests could make or break the mining industry, which depended on his roads, railroads, ore production, and financing. To prevent a complete shut down of the Red Mountain district, he maintained railroad service even though it was unprofitable. On his roads, Mears softened his tolls and even suspended them at times, and he continued production at his mines to keep ore going through Silverton.

Mears' greatest contribution at this time, however, was the construction of another railroad, even though the project extended his finances beyond comfort. In 1895, Mears, Fred Walsen, Alexander Anderson, Jerome B. Frank, Thomas L. Wiswall, and Moses Liverman, most of whom were established Colorado capitalists, incorporated the Silverton Northern Railroad. Mears planned the line to ascend the north side of the Animas River up to Animas Forks, and to include a spur to Howardsville and the existing tracks to Waldheim and the Silver Lake ore terminal. Because Edward Stoiber would see direct service to his terminal and the railroad would carry John Porter's coal, both men were heavy investors. Further, Stoiber promised Mears all the ore traffic that he could generate, and in return, Mears provided him with a fifty percent discount.[266]

The railroad company then purchased Mears' Animas Forks Toll Road as the bed and began construction in the fall of 1895. With the region in depression, the project created quite a stir, and the Las Animas District was excited at the prospect of direct rail access all along its northern boundary. Dignitaries and the general public turned out at the mouth of Arrastra Gulch for the commencement ceremonies, and railroad officials requested a lovely lady to drive the first spike. Up stepped Lena Stoiber, who was more than qualified to hammer the spike all the way down. Track gangs labored between snowstorms throughout the winter until they finished the line to Howardsville by May. The following month saw the crew move camp to Eureka, where Mears stopped work due to the financial burden. Ironically, the Silverton Northern would prove to be Mears' most profitable railroad despite its short length, because it served one of the richest portions of the San Juans.[267]

CHAPTER 9

Heavy Industry in the Wilderness

AS THE DECADE OF THE 1890S WANED, the economic out-
look for silver mining in general grew worse, if such things could be
imagined. Even though the foreign demand for silver returned as
India and China sought the metal for their treasuries, silver's value
hovered at around $.60 per ounce. From outward appearances, the
situation seemed hopeless, but a variety of factors came together to
spell a revival of silver mining across the West and especially in Colorado. Almost as if by magic and defying logic, the residents of the
Animas River drainage had seen their mining industry ascend to epic
proportions, and with the exception of several isolated years earlier
in the decade, the miners of San Juan County produced more gold,
silver, and lead than any time in the past. Averages of $1 million in
gold, $400,000 to $500,000 in silver, $300,000 to $400,000 in copper,
and as much in lead per year became the norm.[268] Given the poor
economic climate, how could this be? The reasons are complex, but
we will make an attempt to simplify them.

First, the nation's economy recovered from the depression; and,
while the rebound started in the East, it rippled westward by the late

1890s. As the economic climate stabilized, investors felt secure again and were willing to risk capital. Mining companies were able to find other forms of financing, such as loans and credit, for their projects. In addition, transportation improved, railroad traffic increased, and goods and services were readily available again. Second, mine and mill owners, tired of bearing the costs of idle, profitless properties, were more than willing to extend themselves to bring their operations back into production or sell or lease them to investors who would. Third, the demand for industrial metals such as copper, lead, and zinc greatly increased due to the revival of industry and consumerism. Fourth, advances in mining technology and engineering decreased the costs of mineral production; and improved milling methods permitted ores greater in complexity and lower in grade than ever to be profitably concentrated.

The last and fifth factor instrumental to the West's great mining revival of the late 1890s started at home in the Animas River drainage. Specifically, mining experts credit Edward Stoiber and John H. Terry, owner of the fabulous Sunnyside Mine near Eureka, with pioneering the production and concentration of low-grade ores in economies of scale through massive investment and mechanization. The Silver Lake and Sunnyside Mines in essence became models that mining companies across the West imitated by the late 1890s, and by employing like strategies, the companies were able to offset the low values of silver and industrial metals. Stoiber, Terry, and almost certainly a few other progressive and visionary mine operators started a movement that propelled mining forward, at least in Colorado, if not in other states. While the movement gave rise to gigantic operations, even smaller outfits were able to profit when they supplanted labor with machinery and ensured the production of high volumes of ore per shift. The main lesson that many companies missed, however, was that the Silver Lake Mine was a function of frugality on a grand scale.[269]

The staff of the *Silverton Standard* was acutely aware of Stoiber's role in the late 1890s boom in the San Juans and summed up his contribution well.

In 1893, when the price of silver was cut in two, or reduced nearly one-half, many of the low-grade products

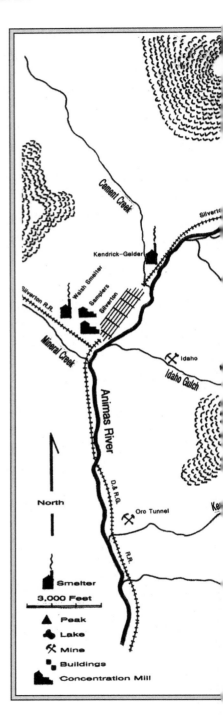

Principal places of activity,
1898 to 1914. Source: Author.

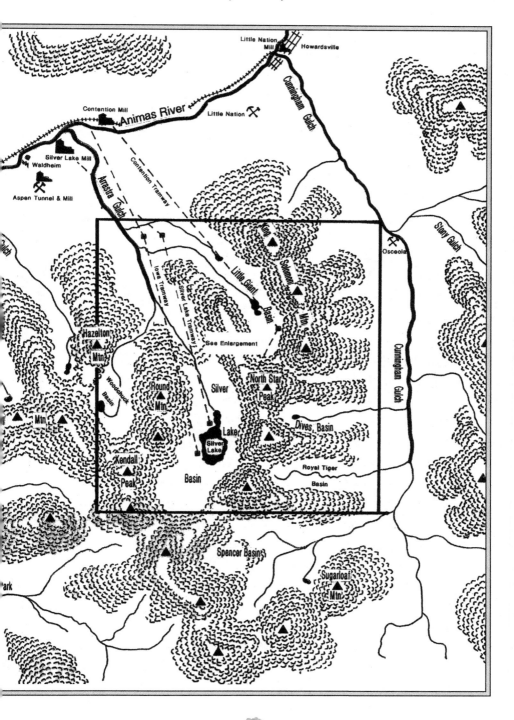

were closed, but about all of these have resumed operation, and many more new producers of like character have been added to the list. At the time the operators of the silver mines were confronted with a situation which seemed to preclude further effort. Edward G. Stoiber, then proprietor of the Silver Lake plunged into the problem with more than a million to lose if he failed, but emerged successfully, after employing every close value-saving appliance which the character of his

Principal mines and mills in the central portion of the Last Animas Mining District. Source: Author.

low-grade lead-silver ores suggested. He saved the values so well that his concentrates of $7 ores enabled him to continue mining profitably. When this had been done the other owners of low-grade mines proceeded to the building or alteration of mills which enable them to operate, and all along the line, throughout the entire San Juan region, there has been a marked advancement in the economy and better value saving of mill enterprises.[270]

When the conditions conducive to mining finally returned to the Las Animas District, the mining outfits there generally responded to the low metals values in several ways. Some decreased

By around 1900, the brothers Edward and Gustavus Stoiber had transformed Silver Lake Basin into an industrial landscape. The edifice near center was a five-story boardinghouse for both Silver Lake and Iowa mine workers. Two additional boardinghouses, built during the early 1890s, stand to the right amid mine buildings, all of which were steam-heated. The rocky slope at far right was one of the Stoiber Tunnel's massive waste rock dumps, and the Iowa Mine is visible in the background. Source: Denver Public Library, Western History Collection, X 62273.

622. MIDWAY. SILVER LAKE TRAM © Colorado Historical Society

Known as a turning station, this building linked the two segments of the Silver Lake Mine's tramway, which was one of the longest in the San Juan Mountains. The entrance behind and left of the tower received a second tramway from the Unity Tunnel. The view is to the north and the timeframe around 1900. Source: Colorado Historical Society, CHS 84-192.657.

their operating costs through simplicity, which also meant very limited production. Others attempted to employ efficient technology only where necessary while maintaining simplicity under the understanding that production would not be grand. A substantial number of companies, however, created costly and substantial surface plants and mills designed to produce and concentrate ores in economies of scale. Such operations tended to be the domain of powerful capitalists and trained engineers. In contrast to the handful of mines active during the depression, the Las Animas District boasted at least six major and six minor operations, and the number kept climbing past the turn-of-the-century.

Despite his success, Edward Stoiber by no means relaxed his pace, in part because his Germanic work ethic and his obsession with the Silver Lake Mine would not let him rest. In 1898, he reinvested even more capital to improve operations and bring his master plan closer to completion. As noted previously, almost from the beginning, Edward planned a tramway from the mine down to an ore storage terminal at the mouth of Arrastra Gulch. The first segment, 8,700 feet long, was built to a temporary station a short distance above the Iowa Mill. The time was finally at hand to finish the system.

Edward contracted again with William Frey who began construction not only on the tramway's second segment, but also on a massive terminal that replaced the original one. When finished in August, the terminal bore the mark of ingenuity and the clear understanding of efficiency. The facility featured an imposing structure similar to a grain elevator, and it was 50 by 100 feet in area, four stories high, and divided into eight bins. The tramway entered the top, workers discharged the tram buckets into a set of receiving bins, and bucket-lines directed the material into one of the eight bins, depending on the type and grade of the ore. In total, the bins had the capacity for 16,000 tons of material, which could have kept Otto Mears' railroad busy all year.[271]

In addition to receiving ore, the terminal served as a base station of sorts for the Silver Lake Mine. An assayer tested samples in a shop on the main building's ground floor, workers conducted some machining and blacksmithing in a separate facility, and freight outfits dropped off lumber, coal, and other supplies for the mine in a storage yard. All was sent up via the tramway. Workers had to use a special crane to lift heavy items up to the terminal. Of course, when the new tramway segment was started, it ran perfectly, and the station above the Iowa Mill became the link between the two segments. Inside, workers transferred tramcars from one line to the next in a constant, tiresome procession. Together, the two segments totaled almost 15,000 feet, making it one of the longest in the state.[272]

In preparation for the terminal, Edward turned his attention to fine-tuning exactly what was done with the ore, since the eight ore bins allowed better segregation of the mine's products. During the winter, McCartney stopped the mill, expanded its capacity, and installed new machinery. Huntington mills augmented the batteries of stamps and twenty Stoiber-McCartney vibrating tables enhanced concentration. In the sorting house at the head of the mill, McCartney directed the workers to separate the ore by richness. Low-grade material continued to pass into the mill, but rich ore ended up in a bin at the upper tram terminal for shipment down to a smelter. By segregating the ore, Edward's army of miners, 275 strong, were now free to out-produce the mill's 250 ton per day treatment capacity.[2733]

Curiously, an aspect of ore production that Edward paid little attention to was one of the most fundamental activities at any mine: the cycle of drilling and blasting. Ever since Edward developed the Silver Lake, his miners drilled blast-holes by hand, which was slow but the norm in most mines. Rockdrills were available by the 1890s, and while they proved themselves much faster than hammer and steel, Edward made little effort to introduce them into the Silver Lake workings. The exact reasons are unknown, although Edward may have been wary of the high cost of the necessary compressed air systems. The chattering machines required an air compressor, a power source, and plumbing installed right up to the miners' points of work, which would have been costly in the Silver Lake's ten miles

The Silver Lake Mine was one of the most complex and advanced operations in the San Juans, as this circa 1900 westward view reflects. Miners literally turned Round Mountain inside out, evident by the sprawling waste rock dumps, and workers treated enough ore in the mill to create an artificial beach with the resultant tailings. The mill stands at center, and the low building immediately above and left was the tunnel house for the Stoiber Tunnel, which was the mine's principal entry. The tunnel house enclosed full machine, carpentry, and blacksmith shops. The buildings on the waste rock dump at center-right included a stable, a repair shop, a storehouse, and a transformer station. Two shaft houses and the mid-level tunnel are at the upper left, and the three boardinghouses stand at the lower right. In total, the mine employed around 300 workers. Source: Denver Public Library, Western History Collection, X 62189.

The northeast view depicts the Silver Lake Mine complex as it exists today. The large mounds left of center are waste rock dumps associated with the Stoiber Tunnel. The Silver Lake Mill stood between the dumps, and the boardinghouses were located at center. Technically, the mine can be described as an archaeological site. Source: Author.

The Silver Lake Mine is now a ghostly assemblage of buildings and wreckage. Source: Author.

of passages. Edward's brother Gustavus, by contrast, immediately embraced rockdrills and installed the most advanced compressed air system in the Las Animas District, as noted above. Once the system was in place, Edward then introduced some drills into his mine, primarily to expedite the driving of horizontal passages.

The drills must have made an impression on Edward, because at the end of 1898 he decided to purchase more. However, in keeping with his progressive attitude, Edward decided to experiment with revolutionary electric models, which were perfect for the Silver Lake because the mine already had an electrical infrastructure and Edward would not have to install a compressor. The technology was unproven and only several years old, leaving Edward with few manufacturers to choose from. He imported Siemens and Weissner drills from Germany and purchased several Halske units from a domestic firm. By January, 1899, miners were using the drills with qualified success. In many cases, they were not as durable or as fast as conventional American compressed air types, but they proved their worth in the stopes.[274] By using a significant number of electric drills, Edward was

Structural debris and the battery boxes for 50 stamps mark the site of the Silver Lake Mill in Silver Lake Basin. Each battery box accommodated 10 stamps. The Stoiber Tunnel is located above and right out of view. Source: Author.

View down and east of the Silver Lake Mill site. A complex array of concentration machinery occupied photo-center. Source: Author.

The southeast view illustrates what currently remains of the Silver Lake Mine's three massive boardinghouses, which manifest as the rectangular debris piles at center. A heating boiler stands at left and a transformer station is at right. Source: Author.

This boiler provided steam heat for the Silver Lake Mine's boardinghouses and other buildings. Source: Author.

Edward Stoiber created one of the most advanced Alternating Current electrical systems of its time in the San Juans. These two buildings were transformer stations at the Silver Lake Mine. Source: Author.

once again on the forefront of the mining industry. In regards to this, the *Engineering & Mining Journal* stated: "The eight Weissner electric drills recently imported from Germany are working satisfactorily and their operation will be carefully monitored by mining men."[275]

Edward could not supply all his miners with mechanical drills, and those who continued to bore blast-holes by hand should be credited with the state that the Silver Lake workings were in by the late 1890s. The workings took the form of an underground ore factory with more than a dozen miles of passages and levels linked by a central internal shaft. An electric hoist raised a cage in the shaft, and miners pushed loaded cars off the cage and across a long set of ore bins directly over the Stoiber Tunnel. Mules pulled trains of cars under the bins, where workers filled them, and continued on to the mill. Edward's concern for efficiency and lost ore extended beyond the mill into the underground workings, where miners laid canvas tarps on the ground prior to blasting to prevent the metal-rich fine material from sifting down into unwanted waste rock.[276]

In 1900, ten years after Edward began his involvement with the Silver Lake, he finally finished his master plan. When the *Silverton Standard* received the news of the tram terminal under construction on the Animas River at the beginning of 1898, the paper postulated

The tidy 1903 line drawing illustrates the relationship between the Silver Lake Mine, at upper left, with the new Silver Lake Mill, at right. The artist accurately depicted the mill but compressed the rugged landscape. The tall structure at the lower right was the original ore storage bin and tram terminal built in advance of the mill in 1898. Source: Mines and Minerals *April, 1903:390.*

Edward Stoiber personally designed and supervised construction of the sprawling Silver Lake Mill on the Animas River in 1900. Because Stoiber was one of Otto Mears' best customers and invested in Mears' Silverton Northern Railroad, Mears provided the mill with direct rail service. At far left stands the ore receiving bins and tram terminal built prior to the mill, and to the structure's right are two shop buildings. The small building with tall smokestack at photo-center was an electrical powerhouse, and the large building at lower right was the crew's boardinghouse. The tall and complex building to the left of the mill's head was a new tram terminal that received and crushed ore from the Silver Lake Mine, and a conveyor carried the crushed material into the mill. Note how the mill building proper fans out to accommodate the increased number of concentration machines for each processing stage. Source: Denver Public Library, Western History Collection, X 62275.

Today, the Silver Lake Mill has been reduced to archaeological features. The photo was taken from the same vantage point as the previous photograph. Source: Author.

A series of masonry terraces currently represents the Silver Lake Mill. Source: Author.

that he would eventually build a mill on the site. The newspaper knew Edward too well, because he did just that in 1900. With McCartney's assistance, Edward personally designed the new mill and selected the equipment, then pushed its construction around the clock through the year, in all weather.[277]

The mill and associated facilities were one of the largest and possibly the most advanced ore treatment complex in the San Juans and Colorado. The mill building alone covered two acres and descended from several large holding bins on flat ground down over a series of ten stair-step terraces to the valley floor. According to the plans, the tramway passed along the mill's east side and delivered crude ore to receiving bins that fed the material into two jaw crushers. A conveyor sent the pulverized rock into the mill's holding bins, and the material proceeded through eight sets of Cornish rolls and three Chilean mills, which featured large wheels that chased each other around the base of a cast iron pan. Rotating trommel screens sorted the ore between each crushing stage and bucket-line elevators sent the oversized particles back for crushing. A bank of twelve Hartz jigs separated the metalliferous material according to specific gravity, which in essence segregated the particles by metal type. Depending on the type, the particles proceeded in the form of slurry to thirty-four vibrating tables, six Frue vanners, and forty-two canvas tables for concentration. After the concentrates were dried, a worker trammed them over to the storage bins. With the array of equipment, the mill was able to treat an astounding 1,000 tons of ore every twenty-four hours, which was more ore than many mines generated in a month![278]

The infrastructure that Edward designed for the mill was enough to support a small town. A 4-foot wide flume delivered water from the dam on the Animas River at Howardsville and another pipeline carried water over from the Aspen Tunnel. They emptied into a reservoir on a natural terrace above the mill. Three motors totaling 200 horsepower drove the machinery, other motors powered small apparatuses such as pumps, and electric lights illuminated the entire complex. To provide the electricity, Edward erected a smaller version of the Waldheim Powerplant, which was tied into the mine's grid, and individual shops provided blacksmithing, machine, and carpentry services. Until the complex was finished, which Edward forecasted for the spring of 1901, the mill in Silver Lake Basin continued to operate.[279]

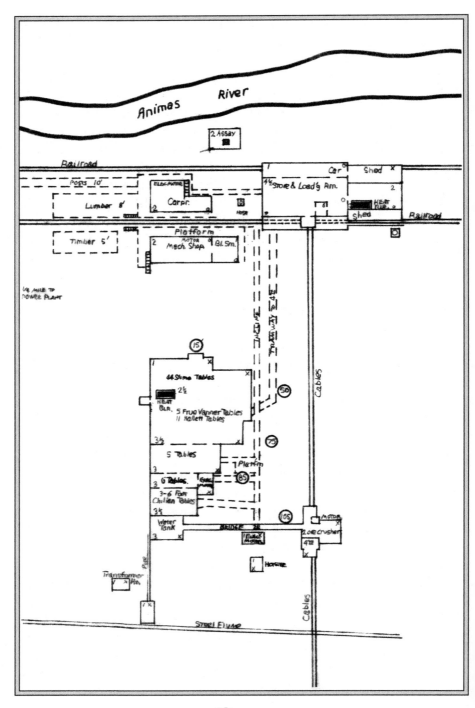

While the Iowa Mine was not quite as extravagant as the Silver Lake, Gustavus was almost matching Edward's improvements one-for-one. By 1898, miners had driven around 8,000 feet of underground workings in the Iowa on the four different levels, and during the year, a crew of 110 generated 30,000 tons of ore worth $300,000, or around $6,601,920 today. With an eye to the future, Gustavus and James Robin understood that such a rate of production would exhaust the veins of the Iowa company's claims, so they aggressively pursued adjoining properties owned by individuals at one time associated with the Iowa, such as Benjamin Thayer. During the year, they were successful, but at a high cost. They acquired the Black Diamond and other claims for $60,000, which gave the company new ground and more ore.[280]

Left: The plan view documents in detail the content of the Silver Lake Mill complex as built by Edward Stoiber. The structure at the upper right was the original ore and concentrates storage bin and tram terminal constructed in 1898, and the accompanying assay shop is adjacent and left. The parallel lines that extend left are Silverton Northern Railroad tracks, and the lines extending down are tram cables. It is interesting to note that the mill building's footprint fanned out in concert with each stage of concentration. Source: Sanborn Fire Insurance Map, 1902.

The foundations for the 1898 ore bins at the Silver Lake Mill are currently outlined by structural debris. Source: Author.

With the Iowa in better condition than ever, Gustavus and Robin turned their attention to the Royal Tiger Mine across Silver Lake. The fine surface plant was finished, but the lack of mechanization and the use of mule trains to haul ore around the lake to the Iowa tram restricted production. To remedy the problem, Gustavus, Robin, and the other Iowa directors reorganized the Tiger Mining & Milling Company to raise more capital. R.W. Watson served as president and manager, Robin was vice-president, and Stoiber acted as secretary and treasurer of the new company.[281]

The directors spent the capital wisely, and some of the money went to formal underground development similar to that at the Iowa. The haulageway at the main surface plant was known as A Level, early tunnels above were B through D Levels, and the highest workings,

This north view captures Silver Lake Basin with the Iowa Mine at left and the Silver Lake Mine in the right background. The photograph was taken in 1898 immediately after Edward Stoiber built his modern five-story boardinghouse, visible at far right, but before the Iowa company erected its important compressor house (see following photo). The building at left was the terminal for the Iowa Mine's tramway, which carried crude ore to the right and past the Silver Lake Mine. The cupola on top was for a second tramway that extended right and over Silver Lake to the Royal Tiger Mine, which is out of view. Source: San Juan County, 1899; courtesy of Colorado School of Mines.

On a remarkably calm day in June or July of 1898, a photographer captured this south view of Silver Lake Basin and the Iowa Mine. At this time, the Iowa was near its peak and featured a highly advanced and costly surface plant. The large building at left was a compressor house and electrical generator, and the long structure at the upper right enclosed shops, an ore transfer system, and the portal of the Iowa Tunnel. The mine's aerial tram terminal is the complex assemblage between. Source: Denver Public Library, Western History Collection, X 62274.

which cropped out on the surface were E Level. Miners linked the levels with raises and chutes, built bins over A Level, and followed the vein southeast into the mountain. From these workings, the crew brought $50,000 worth of ore to the surface.[282]

A substantial portion of the new capital went to additional surface improvements. A small boiler provided steam for a blower and heat in the avalanche-proof boardinghouse, while electricity wired from Waldheim powered shop equipment and electric lighting. Workers also constructed an interesting boardinghouse for newly hired miners. Workers cut three tiers out of the waste rock dump and the mountainside below and built a stairstep building 36 by 70 feet in area similar in appearance to a small mill. The top story stood

*This westward view neatly depicts the Iowa Mine's principal workings
and surface facilities around 1900. The Selzner Tunnel is at the upper
right, and its shop and ore transfer station are visible on the waste rock
dump. An inclined railway lowered payrock down to the Iowa's aerial
tramway terminal behind the tall smokestacks. The large building at
center was a compressor house, and it served both the Iowa and Silver
Lake mines. The open cupola on top was the tram terminal for the
Iowa-Royal tiger system, which crossed over Silver Lake. The cluster
of buildings at right-center were shop facilities built around the Iowa
Tunnel, which was the mine's principal haulageway. Source: San Juan
County, 1904; courtesy of Colorado School of Mines.*

*The southeast view depicts the Iowa Mine, center, as it exists today.
The large waste rock dump marks the Iowa Tunnel, and the debris at
left was the compressor house. Source: Author.*

View down and east of the Iowa Mine as it exists today. The Iowa Tunnel and the remnants of its tunnel house are left of center, and the wreckage of the compressor house is at center. Source: Author.

The Iowa Mine's compressor house enclosed a complex assemblage of boilers, air compressors, and other machinery. The building is in ruins, but the machinery remains in place. Source: Author.

The Iowa Mine featured two highly efficient but costly water-tube boilers, which provided steam both for heat and to run machinery. Source: Author.

The miners who worked the Iowa's upper levels lived in this boardinghouse high above the mine surface plant. The building, located near the original 1882 camp at Level No.1, was bolted down to bedrock. Source: Author.

exposed on the waste rock dump's surface and enclosed a storage area and an office, while the lower tiers served as bunkrooms. The idea of the stairstep arrangement was to hide the building below the dump and keep the structure low to the ground in hopes that avalanches would strike the dump first and skim over the roof.[283]

One of the most important improvements was a tramway to replace the cumbersome and seasonal mule trains. During the spring, workers built a terminal below the new boardinghouse, installed new hardware and bins for the double-rope system in the Iowa terminal, and floated cables across Silver Lake in a skiff. In the Iowa terminal, workers dumped the buckets from the Tiger system into the new bins, and transferred the ore to the Iowa system for the trip down to the mill in Arrastra Gulch. By August, workers finished the double-rope tramway, bringing the Royal Tiger into full production.[284]

Interestingly, Edward and Gustavus had similar master plans for concentration mills and tramway service down to the Animas River. While each brother sited their mills in different locations, both stopped their tramways at almost the same point during the mid-1890s. Slightly behind Edward, Gustavus decided to finish the Iowa's tramway system in 1899, although he had no intention of building another mill on the river. Gustavus chose a site for the bottom

Another view of the boardinghouse for the upper level miners. The building was dark and perpetually drafty. Source: Author.

terminal on a natural terrace on the north side of the river slightly east of Arrastra Gulch. Crews worked furiously during the year to finish the facility, which featured a number of bins for concentrates and crude ore to be sent to a smelter. When the terminal was finished, Otto Mears extended a spur off the Silverton Northern to provide direct service.[285]

The Royal Tiger Mine was a significant component of Silver Lake Basin's industrial landscape, and it lay directly across the lake from and east of the Iowa complex. The buildings clustered around the main tunnel include, left to right, a boardinghouse and dining hall, mule stables, a shop, and at bottom, an aerial tram terminal. The tramway replaced the mules used to carry sacked ore around the lake to the Iowa. The view is southeast and the year around 1898. Source: Colorado Historical Society, CHS 84-192.642.

The Royal Tiger Mine as it exists today is an archaeological site. Miners developed the vein through a series of tunnels ascending through the cleft at center. The debris at bottom marks the main tunnel. The photograph was taken from the same vantage point as the previous illustration. Source: Author.

Feeling rather impoverished after two years of costly improvements, the Iowa directors decided to reorganize the company for more capital and to absorb the Tiger Mining & Milling Company. In 1900, they formed the grandly named Iowa-Tiger Consolidated Mining & Milling Company, but the principal officers remained the same. The company continued to enjoy heavy production, as the miners in the Iowa generated around 120 tons of ore per day while those in the Tiger offered an additional 75 tons. Around this time, Gustavus made one last improvement to the Iowa when he increased the capacity of the compressed air system to accommodate more rockdrills. The Iowa complex was at its zenith in terms of facilities and production.[286]

In addition to aggressively pursuing their master plans, Edward and Gustavus continued to fiddle around with their joint tunnel project originally known as the Silverton Deep. The idea behind the tunnel was to undercut the ore systems of both mines at great depth, provide a platform for miners to stope the veins 700 feet upward to the existing workings, and serve as a central artery through which the deep ore

91375 IOWA MILL - SILVERTON, COLO.

The Iowa Mill was not as large or complex as the Silver
Lake facility, but was vital to the mines in Silver Lake Basin.
The south view depicts the Iowa Mill, Arrastra Gulch's
imposing headwall, and the confusion of tram towers in
the gulch around 1900. The towers in the left background
descended from the Iowa and Silver Lake mines, located
above and beyond the headwall, and the tower at right
carried the Unity Tunnel tramway. The cupola on top of the
mill was a terminal for yet another tramway that carried
finished concentrates down to a station on the Animas
River. Source: Denver Public Library, Western History
Collection, Z 2560.

could be hauled out. Such a project would be an engineering feat on par with similar tunnels in Creede, Idaho Springs, and other important mining districts. After they started the tunnel in 1895, the Stoibers were reluctant to pour their resources into the project when there was so much yet to accomplish at the Silver Lake and Iowa. But once the brothers approached the ends of their master plans, they renewed their interest in the tunnel and, in 1897, renamed it the Unity, probably to reflect and even celebrate their intimate cooperation.

For the first several years, the operation was relatively simple and consisted of several teams of miners drilling and blasting around 100 feet per month, which was a significant rate given that the tunnel was 5 by 6 1/2 feet in-the-clear. By the end of 1898, the tunnel was 1,500 feet in with an equal distance required to reach the Silver Lake workings. After several years, the time was at hand to build a surface plant to accommodate the anticipated production, and the Stoibers spared no expense and included many of the same components as at the Iowa and Silver Lake. One building 100 by 300 feet in area enclosed a number of facilities. It was nestled against a cliff and featured a sloped roof for protection against avalanches. The upper level housed a drainage

While Arrastra Gulch is too large lend itself to panoramas, this 1898 photograph portrays the relationship between the Iowa Mill, lower right, and the turning station for the Silver Lake Tramway, center-left. Source: San Juan County, 1904; courtesy of Colorado School of Mines.

system, a duplex air compressor, and an advanced shop with a drill-steel sharpener, which had just been introduced. The middle and lower levels were dedicated to ore treatment and handling, and the system bore the Stoibers' attention to efficiency. Miners input ore into a sorting station on the middle level where grizzlies, which were course screens, and workers separated obvious waste. The recovered ore passed through a jaw crusher that pulverized the pay rock so tram buckets could be filled to maximum capacity. The bottom level featured the terminal for a tramway that extended over to the station on the Silver Lake system, and it also housed a water-tube boiler that provided steam for heat, the compressor, and a ventilation blower.[287]

The miners and surface workers lived in a two-story boarding-house 18 by 55 feet in area that was bolted to the cliff above the main

Almost from its first day of operations, the Iowa Mill was a success, unlike many other concentration facilities in the area. This easterly view depicts the mill around 1900. An aerial tramway on the right delivered crude ore from the Iowa Mine, and the material descended through multiple stages of crushing and concentration in the multi-terraced mill. A steam engine and boiler, marked by the smokestacks at center, powered the machinery via canvas belts and driveshafts. The long building at left recovered metals from tailings. The high tower was the top terminal for an aerial tramway built in 1899 to carry finished concentrates down to a station on the Animas River. Source: San Juan County, 1904; courtesy of Colorado School of Mines.

In 1899, Gustavus Stoiber and fellow investors financed a tramway to carry finished concentrates from the Iowa Mill down to a terminal on the Animas River. Otto Mears graded a railroad spur to the terminal, and box cars are parked at the building's foot. Note the cable spools, for the tramway, and the stacked lumber above the building. Source: San Juan County, 1904; courtesy of Colorado School of Mines.

building. Edward extended his benevolent mine ownership to the Unity crew and provided plumbing, steam heat, and electric lighting. The floorspace of the platform existing today suggests that the crew consisted of twelve miners.[288]

Linking the Unity Tunnel with the Silver Lake workings, after boring through 3,000 feet of solid rock, was like finding a needle in a haystack. Yet, through expert surveying and tunnel driving, miners made the connection in 1901. With the tramway operational, the surface plant complete, and the connections made, the Unity was ready to fulfill its role.

While the Iowa and Silver Lake were clearly the largest mines in the Las Animas District during the late 1890s revival, they were by no means the only operations. The unbridled success of the Silver Lake and Iowa Mines demonstrated that the vein systems in

Silver Lake Basin held great potential, but the Stoibers had most of the land locked up. They did not, however, possess the old Buckeye Mine, which was idle since Mears quit his lease in 1889. A partnership realized this, found the mine's owners, and managed to secure a lease in 1899. The partners rehabilitated the critical workings and began production, which lasted for several years.[289]

The central portions of Arrastra and Little Giant Gulches saw activity that seemed promising, although most of it turned out to be nothing more than speculation. W.H. James and James Perchard organized the Bill Jim Mining Company in 1898 and employed a crew of seven miners to drive exploratory workings in search of missed gold veins in the Little Giant Mine. Amid the cliffs on the east side of Arrastra Gulch, opposite the Unity Tunnel, James W. Kendall was busy with a short tunnel on the Mayflower claim. It seems that Kendall, who was one of the first prospectors in Arrastra Gulch thirty years earlier, never gave up the search for the mother lode. In Little Giant Gulch, Theodore Grabowski, an early prospector, sold the Black Prince to Louis Pelow during 1900; and William Keith sold the Big Giant Mine back to the French Boys Silver Mining Company because he was fed up with the complex ore, the difficult to follow vein, and his failed mill.[290]

Outside Silver Lake Basin, the northwest flank of Kendall Mountain saw the most activity and the mines and prospects there serenaded Silverton with the sounds of prosperity. In 1898, sheriff and community activist John Rogers invested his own money developing the Mighty Monarch literally on the south edge of Silverton, only to be confounded by ore too rich with zinc to be easily treated. Rogers quickly understood that the claim required more capital than he possessed. He sold it to the Gold King Consolidated Mining Company, which operated one of the richest mines in the Animas River drainage. At the same time, prospectors were at work in at least six other tunnels and shafts, hoping that their mineral veins would become another Silver Lake or Iowa. The old Aspen workings were among these, and partnerships leased blocks of ground in nearly every principal tunnel and sent around forty tons of ore to the smelter per day.[291]

The Lackawanna and Idaho Mines, with their proven but inconsistent veins, were promising enough to draw significant investments from the outside world. In 1898, George Whitelaw and John Norton, principals with the Four Metals Mining Company based in Pueblo, acquired the two properties and hired a crew of four miners to rehabilitate the decayed portions of the Lackawanna. The company found that plenty of ore still existed and increased the workforce to eight miners, who drove exploratory workings and generated at least several tons of ore per day. To permit the mine to operate all year, despite heavy snows, the company erected a double-rope reversible tramway to a set of ore bins on the Animas River. Meanwhile, O.C. Hanson kept a small crew busy at the Idaho on similar work, sans tramway.[292]

Not all of the companies spawned during the late 1890s boom were there to mine the mountains; and while the Las Animas District saw little obvious fraud, the district, because of its overall richness, provided a sound setting for some highly dubious shenanigans. In 1897, B.F. Kelly and W.H. Bush organized a project so preposterous that only investors as out of touch with reality as Edward Innis could possibly see its merit. With other people's money, naturally, Kelly and Bush established the Gold Tunnel & Railway Company to drive a tunnel no less than 20,000 feet long under Deer Park, Silver Lake Basin, and the Highland Mary Mine! From the mouth of Deer Creek, the tunnel would extend east and pierce vein after vein, repaying the investors many times over. In 1898, Kelly and Bush collected enough money to secure a site for the surface plant, and then hired miners who began driving the Oro Tunnel.[293] Silvertonians, who were intimate with real mining, shook their heads at the fraud, and of the project, the *Silverton Standard* stated: "B.F. Kelly, better known as 'Tunnel Kelly,' if he never was thought of before as being a rustler and 'smart' man, will be now since he and W.H. Bush, the promulgators of the famous Oro Tunnel scheme, have realized out of their enterprise $400,000."[294] The project was a clear sign to the Las Animas District that investors, in fact, had plenty of capital and were eager to spend it during the late 1890s.

While the strategy of mining and milling in economies of scale saved the Animas River drainage and the rest of the San Juans, it brought with it unforeseen consequences. The massive amounts of capital that were required to implement the strategy, and the proportional profits to be made, became a breeding ground for large companies and powerful capitalists. Some of them were satisfied with the growth of their businesses and an edge on their competition, while others sought domination on local, regional, and even statewide levels. The American Smelting & Refining Company (ASARCo) fell into the last category. It was organized in 1899 by some of Colorado's and the nation's most powerful smelter men. They were bent on nothing less than the domination of the smelting industry across the country, which they hoped to achieve through the business trust of ASARCo. James B. Grant of the Omaha & Grant Smelting & Refining Company was among the organizers, and he included the Durango Smelter in the new trust. In the same year, ASARCo acquired Otto Mears' Standard Smelter, and in so doing, controlled a significant share of the smelting capacity that served the San Juans.[295]

The company was adamantly anti-labor and had a friend in the form of Frank Guiterman at the Durango Smelter. Guiterman detested organized labor, had personal experience quashing strikes at Telluride, and carried his policies over to the Durango Smelter as manager. In 1899, the State of Colorado mandated the eight-hour law for mill workers, and clever Guiterman told his workers that he would uphold the law but pay them for only eight hours instead of the usual ten hour shift, in essence reducing their wages. Guiterman underestimated the power and unity of the workers, who belonged to the Mill and Smelterworkers' Union, and they struck and literally shut down both plants. Chapters in Pueblo, Denver, and other smelting centers in Colorado followed in sympathy, and the Western Federation of Miners threatened similar action at many mines in Colorado.[296]

The result of the massive strike was awesome. At first it paralyzed Colorado's mining industry, and as mines began to close, the demand for coal slackened and railroads curtailed traffic. Some of the mining districts in the San Juans were definitely in trouble, although Silverton offered enough ore treatment to soften the blow in the Animas River drainage. The mining industry became polarized as pro-labor individuals sided with the strikers and anti-labor forces (mostly mine owners) argued that the action was to everyone's ruin. In the Las Animas District, where union membership was a requisite for work, mine owners felt threatened by the potential for sympathy strikes. Newspapers fed the fires of tension and harped on the fact that if the strike in Durango forced the closure of mines, 500 workers alone in Silver Lake Basin and Arrastra Gulch would be jobless. After several weeks, the Colorado Supreme Court declared the eight-hour day unconstitutional, and the wages and shift issue was back to where it started. The strike collapsed. Everyone breathed a sigh of relief as mining returned to normal in the Las Animas District.[297]

Despite the near monopoly that ASARCo held over the smelting industry, mining companies in the Animas River drainage continued to generate enough ore to support at least one niche smelter. Unable to compete, Thomas Walsh closed his Silverton Smelter in 1898 or 1899, but the San Juan Smelting & Refining Company built the Kendrick-Gelder Smelter at the mouth of Cement Creek in 1900. Like Walsh's facility, the Kendrick-Gelder Smelter specialized in treating ores rich in pyrite and copper, which attracted mining companies in the Red Mountain District. Because some of the operations in the Las Animas District had similar payrock, they also found the smelter to be of benefit. Unfortunately nature was against the Kendrick-Gelder facility and blocked the feed water ditch with an avalanche at the beginning of 1901. Without water, the smelter suspended operations and the mining companies that provided it with ore turned to ASARCo.[298]

The rise of large companies in the Animas River drainage was not necessarily a bad trend since the boom was a function of their practices, but it irrevocably changed the fabric of the region on a fundamental level. Among other things, the companies employed a larger workforce than in years past, which translated into a higher population. In 1900, 2,300 souls called San Juan County home, which should be compared with the 1,600 residents of 1890. Silverton claimed the greatest share at 1,400, with most of the rest living in the Las Animas District. The Stoibers employed about 370 workers, Howardsville accommodated ninety residents, and almost as many miners were scattered throughout the rest of the district.[299]

Of the communities in the Las Animas District, Silverton experienced the most change due to both the larger population and the evolving demography. Newspapers noted that Silverton was busier than ever, which brought congestion, noise, pollution, and an increase in petty crime. Longtime residents lamented that Silverton's personal and quiet frontier culture, ambiance, and roots were slipping away; and that the prosperity was changing the social climate to that of the East. If Lena Stoiber had trouble with Silverton society during the 1880s, she would not have fit in at all by around 1900. The crush of new arrivals became so intense that Silverton experienced a housing shortage, which stimulated a new construction. The drive to become metropolitan in addition to the increased population fostered a demand for modern services. In response, the town improved its water system during the late 1890s and organized a water company by 1902. The number and sophistication of social institutions also increased, such as the construction of a union hall for the 1,300 members of the Silverton chapter of the Western Federation of Miners. A well-appointed library followed the next year.[300]

The demography of the region changed with the boom, and nowhere was this more obvious than in the Las Animas District. In 1890, women constituted almost twenty-five percent of San Juan County's population, and most lived in Silverton and the other county settlements. By 1900, the proportion of women was higher, and they now could be found among the large mines deep in the district, where both single and married women worked for wages or helped their husbands. Because mining was a man's world and Victorian society frowned on women who dirtied their hands, most of the working women held jobs that were deemed acceptable. It was not uncommon to find women cooks, hostlers, maids, and even boardinghouse managers. Lena Stoiber was the queen of female labor at

Miners are at work drilling blast-holes in a stope deep in the Royal Tiger Mine around 1898. Source: San Juan County, 1899; courtesy of Colorado School of Mines.

the mines, and attended to the human resources for nearly all of Silver Lake Basin. In Silverton and Howardsville, women had greater latitude for employment and ran or worked in restaurants, bakeries, hotels, boardinghouses, mercantiles, tailor shops, and schools.[301]

Even though women were able to hold fewer positions than men, their work was every bit as hard. For those running boardinghouses at mines or hotels in town, their working day started earlier than their patrons. The women prepared, then served breakfast, washed the dishes, made the beds, cleaned the establishment, baked foods, did the wash, mended sheets and other items, then cooked and served dinner. Married women who lived in town also served meals to workers, sold them baked goods and other food for midday meals, and accepted some wash and clothes for mending.[302]

The proportion of foreign workers also increased in San Juan County. In 1890, around twenty-eight percent of the population came from the British Isles and northern Europe, and by 1900, the total skyrocketed to around thirty-five percent. By this time, Italian miners made up a large percentage, and the Stoibers played a significant role in this. According to archaeological evidence in the form of artifacts of Italian origin, the Stoibers employed more Italian miners than all the other companies in the Las Animas District combined, probably because the Stoibers were aware of the Italian work ethic and tolerance for dangerous and difficult conditions both above and below ground. The Italian miners were also highly pro-union, which did not concern the Stoibers too much because they readily acceded to reasonable requests such as an eight-hour workday. And, although mining experts credited Edward Stoiber with initiating ore production in economies of scale, he may have devised the strategy, but his Italian miners did the physical work.[303]

The specific tasks that miners did and the nature of the workplace at the medium- and small-sized mines changed little from earlier years. Technology and the lower cost of equipment brought the miners some benefits, such as improved ventilation and proper thawing of frozen dynamite, but the main purpose was to increase the tonnage of rock brought to daylight. Any one miner filled a variety of capacities during a given week, such as driller, trammer, timber man, and blacksmith. The large companies, however, found that producing ore in economies of scale required managing their workforces as if they were machines with individual miners being no more than components. As a result, the social structure and corporate culture of most of the large mines evolved into stratification and hierarchy. Specialization of labor positions became part of this, and miners found themselves doing a limited variety of tasks and repeating the same thing more often, just like the parts comprising a machine. For example, large companies hired workers to fill the positions of driller, trammer, mucker, machinist, electrician, and so forth, with few miners attending to all these duties over the course of a single shift. Some companies with absentee management took the perspective that the workers were easily replaced and interchangeable despite their position, but the hands-on officials such as the Stoibers knew otherwise. They understood that miners were happier and better at some tasks than others, and were more productive when working at their best. The large mines became, in essence, underground ore factories, and the variety of tasks that the average worker carried out was inversely proportional to the size of the operation.

All things being relative, many of the immigrant workers were perfectly content with this arrangement. The residential accommodations at most of the mines were adequate, the food was often great, the work was invigorating, and the pay was better than other forms of employment. According to an agreement between the Western Federation of Miners and a regional mine owners' association, common miners and unskilled workers were paid $3.00 per day while skilled workers such as drill operators, timber men, hoistmen, and machinists were given $3.50 to $4.00. By contrast, factory workers and unskilled labor in the East received at best $1.50 to $2.00 per day, which, even though the cost of living in the East was less, made mining in the West an attractive proposition.[304]

It almost goes without saying that the miners forfeited a certain level of safety and comfort for the money. It was well known that danger lurked around nearly every corner and in every crevice of a mine, but hazard was a function of management's concern and progressiveness. According to common perceptions of the time, miners were blamed for most accidents, and if the workplace was inherently hazardous, they were free to find other jobs. As a result, mining companies were rarely held liable even in the most egregious cases of negligence. Progressive management, however, understood that accidents and deaths not only impeded production in the short term, but also created long-term inefficiency through fear, wariness, and general malaise among the surviving miners.

Accidents in the Las Animas District were inevitable, though, and several miners died and dozens were injured every year during the late 1890s and early 1900s boom. Cave-ins and falling objects were a common problem; and, in some cases, miners numb to danger were as much to blame as any other reasons. In 1898, Gus Morrison was killed in a stope in the Silver Lake Mine when a boulder dropped onto him. According to the *Silverton Standard*: "The skull was literally smashed and the poor fellow evidently never knew what hurt him."[305] In 1901, Thomas Hodge, Edward Tressider, and August C. Johnson were timber men replacing rotten stulls in an old stope deep in the North Star Mine. The men cut several of the new timbers too long, and Hodge had to knock the existing stulls completely out to fit in the new beams. Without the support, the walls collapsed and crushed all three. With only dim and flickering candles for light, miners often failed to see or misjudged yawning pits, stopes, and winzes, and fell into them with alarming frequency. So it was for Joseph Steffani, one of Edward Stoiber's Italian miners, when he fell into a raise and tumbled 160 feet to his death in the Unity Tunnel.[306]

Tampering with unexploded dynamite charges was one of the most common sources of misery in the Las Animas District and across the West. Too often, dynamite packed tightly in drill-holes failed to detonate when frozen, when a damaged fuse failed to burn, or when inexperienced miners did not ignite the fuse at all. In blasts that involved numerous charges, the misfire of one often went unnoticed until an unsuspecting miner bored into it. In the Unity Tunnel stopes, Charles Morse drilled into such a missed charge that hurled him several feet and rendered him unconscious when it detonated. Morse lost an eye, broke his cheek, and his chest was peppered with quartz.[307] In 1897, the *Silverton Standard* reported the fate of miners who were aware of missed shots and tried to remediate the problem in an article aptly titled "Another Accident in the Basin."

> *It would appear that there is to be no end to the frightful accidents in the great mines of Silver Lake Basin. This time the scene to casualty is the Silver Lake Mine. Walter*

Eales and John Olson were working together there as part-
ners. Tuesday noon the usual rounds of blasts were fired. An
hour elapsed, during which time the smoke cleared away and
the men returned to duty. Eales and Olson commenced pick-
ing away at a missed hole, which we learn remained intact
by reason of a short fuse that had not ignited. The explosion
that followed sent both men spinning across the drift and
prostrating them to the ground. Judging from the injuries
sustained, Eales must have taken the blast squarely in the
face as the sight of one eye has gone forever; the other eye
also being badly injured, although he can see a little out of
it. Olson's legs were terribly mutilated and upon the arrival
of the men at the hospital the surgeons in charge were of the
opinion that amputation of the right leg would be necessary.
At this writing, however, Dr. Prewitt informs us that the
leg can be saved and that Olson is out of danger. Mr. Eales
departed, accompanied by Wm. Stanger, on Wednesday's
train for Denver where his parents reside.[308]

The underground workings were not the only source of danger, as workers also fell prey to hazards associated with surface facilities, mostly mechanical. In the Iowa Mill, Peter Libon was riding an elevator with a load when the car fell eighty feet. The sudden deceleration crushed Libon from the inside, and he suffered four hours in agony before dying. Victor Sapp was oiling the pulleys on one of the Iowa tram system towers when he fell and died. Ben Johnson, Ed Tandstad, and Ralph Kaffka were riding the tram between the Iowa and Royal Tiger Mines when the bolts clamping the counterweight to the track cable gave way, plunging the bucket occupants eighty-five feet down into icy Silver Lake. Johnson suffered two broken ribs and a leg, and Kaffka sprained his ankle. A dog and workers rushed to the rescue, and the dog jumped in to save the immersed. After the three were retrieved, the dog ran down the road into Arrastra Gulch and encountered the two doctors summoned by phone, and led them to the building where the three were recovering.[309]

The physical environment of the San Juans featured its own hazards, especially during the winters, and with most mountain-sides treeless and at the ideal pitch, avalanches were very common.

Identifying avalanche chutes and staying clear was the only response possible, but some companies had little choice in where they could locate their surface facilities. As a result, disasters, mostly financial, were guaranteed. In 1891, for example, Dave Purdy and another worker were in the Titusville Mill's boardinghouse when an avalanche roared down, smashed the building, and tore off the kitchen. The remainder of the building was filled with snow, and the men had to walk to Silverton for shelter. In 1918, an avalanche swept over the Trilby Mine and took all its buildings except for an ore bin. A bunkhouse and compressor house were carried off but, fortunately, no one was at the mine at the time. Because of dozens of such incidents, in 1906 the *Silverton Standard* went so far as to propose an avalanche inspector who would consider the potential risk to life posed by the locations of some mine facilities.[310]

Even on the move during the winter, Las Animas District prospectors and miners had no choice but to put themselves at risk. In 1900, six workers were transporting Clarence Coburn in a toboggan from the Tiger Mine, due to an illness, when a slide broke loose above them. Rightly fearing for their lives, the six promptly abandoned poor and helpless Coburn right in the middle of the slide's path, but because the toboggan provided Coburn with flotation, he was carried down around 100 feet and lived. In December of 1904, Ludwig Vota started down the trail from a lease he had on Solomon Mountain near the North Star Mine when an avalanche swept him off his feet. The snow carried him several hundred feet down to the edge of a cliff. Vota frantically grabbed at anything he could to save himself. On the very edge of the precipice, he managed to snag several rocks to prevent cascading down with the snow slide to certain death. After the avalanche passed, Vota amazingly hung by his hands in freezing weather for an hour as he tried to regain his footing. Vota eventually succeeded and returned to Silverton to tell the tale.[311]

Temperature was another problem. Between snowstorms, the thermometer would plummet below zero for days, which when combined with wind, made life miserable. During 1897 and 1898, the Las Animas District saw temperatures as low as minus forty-six degrees, Fahrenheit! This threatened life and limb with hypothermia and frostbite, and rendered many frame buildings uninhabitable. In such temperatures, one coal stove per building was inadequate unless the structure was buried by snow, which trapped warm air. How tolerable the cabins and boardinghouses remained during such temperatures became a measure that miners used to identify the desirable employers from those who cared little for their workers. When a miner looked forward to his damp, clammy, and dangerous shift underground as an escape from a freezing boardinghouse, he knew that he worked for an uncaring company.[312]

One of the benefits that miners insisted on in exchange for the difficult work, reflected by the 1885 strike at the Aspen Mine, was hearty food, and lots of it. While the diet of miners and prospectors at the small operations changed little from two decades prior, miners employed by the organized companies could look forward to a greater proportion of fresh food and a wider variety of dishes prepared within the parameters of high-altitude cooking. Most of the miners in the Las Animas District continued to practice moderation in terms of alcohol consumption, except for the miners in Silver Lake Basin. According to archaeological evidence, they consumed not only more liquor than most other crews, but the Italian miners drank highly alcoholic bitters imported from their homeland.[313]

To the average wage-earning miner, housing was second in importance only to meals, and those in the Las Animas District during the late 1890s boom enjoyed better conditions than in the past. While residential accommodations at the small mines and prospects continued to be austere and primitive, the large companies invested capital in well-built boardinghouses. Many companies provided electric lighting, cold running water, abundant natural light, multiple stoves, and spacious kitchens. Overall, the boardinghouses offered more personal space per worker as well as common areas and dining halls. Stoiber, however, was the only mine owner who offered hot running water, showers, and flush toilets.[314]

CHAPTER 10

Progress Continues

AS THE LATE 1890S BOOM carried on into the early 1900s, the Las Animas District saw a wave of large companies assume not only the well-developed properties, but also many nascent mines with little record of production. Like excitements of the past, the recent boom fostered a buoyant atmosphere rife with speculation, exemplified by B.F. Kelly and his crazy Oro Tunnel project. In most cases, however, a majority of the large companies applied their capital wisely and realized some level of success, industrializing the wilderness of the Las Animas District in the process.

The North Star Mine was one of the first major properties caught up in the wave of large companies. After operating the property for more than twenty-five years, the Crookes decided to sell after realizing around $2.5 million in ore. While the high operating costs consumed much of this, the Crookes certainly enjoyed substantial profits. They searched for a buyer through 1900 and were finally approached by experienced mining investors who were impressed with the North Star's record of production. Some of the investors were from Boston, others were associated with the powerful Calumet & Hecla Mining Company in Michigan, and the rest were local to the San Juans. Together they constituted the Smuggler-Union Mining Company. This outfit was one of the largest in Telluride and held the Contention Mining Company as a subsidiary, which operated the Contention Group there and the

229

Sunnyside Extension Mine near Eureka. Depending on the information source, the Contention directors, many of whom were also with the Smuggler-Union, offered the Crookes $75,000 or $95,000, which is $1.6 or $2 million today. The Crookes, ready for retirement, accepted, and the North Star passed into the hands of a company that had grand plans for the property.[315]

Like Edward Stoiber, the Contention Mining Company intended to build a mill on the Animas River, secure a siding from the Silverton Northern Railroad, and send the ore down via a tramway. The company also assembled a quiltwork of claims around the North Star to maximize its amount of ore-bearing ground. Core claims in the North Star group were nearing exhaustion. To this end, Louis Pelow, who was with the Contention Company, purchased the Black Prince Mine in Little Giant Basin and participated in buying the Big Giant Mine from the French Boys Silver Mining Company in 1901. The Contention directors approached Martin Van Buren Wason with a fine deal for the Shenandoah group; but instead of consummating a deal right away, Wason leased his claims with an option to sell.[316]

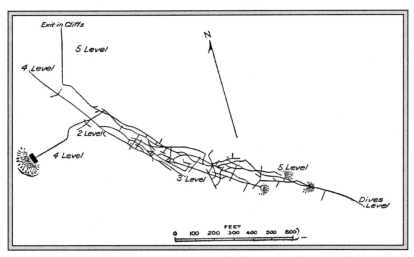

The plan view depicts the maze-like North Star workings as of around 1901. The Dives Tunnel is at the lower right, and 4 Level and 5 Level were the North Star's main entries. The tunnel noted as "Exit in Cliffs" housed the upper terminal for the Contention Tramway, built in 1901. Source: Ransome, 1901:164.

The Contention Company wasted no time in pursuing its grand production scheme. During the fall, workers labored furiously to build the tramway and the mill, a short distance east of Arrastra Gulch. The tramway was one of the strangest contraptions in the Las Animas District. The main problem that the Contention engineer faced was that the very summit of North Star Peak lay between the mine's surface plant and the route to the mill. The route, therefore, was not straight and featured a crook like Stoiber's Silver Lake system. After considering these factors, the engineer bored a tunnel from the North Star workings through the peak and blasted a room out of the peak's north cliff. Workers erected two ore bins and the mechanism for a double-rope reversible tramway in the room and covered the opening with a plank façade. This served as the system's top terminal. The double-rope tramway descended to the abandoned North Star Mill in Little Giant Basin, which workers apparently refitted with tram hardware. A Bleichert system then continued down to what was known as the Contention Mill on the Animas River. The North Star Mill, which treated no ore by this time, was merely a union between the two systems. [317]

The Contention company blasted a room out of the north face of North Star Mountain to house the upper terminal for a tramway. The room is left of center and a boardinghouse is bolted to the cliff right of center. Source: Author.

Once the mill and tramway were finished, William Kearnes, who came with the North Star purchase, increased the workforce to 100. Miners engaged in development and ore production, and other workers braved the bitter weather of late fall to collect waste rock from the North Star's dump, which offered a lot of low-grade material that the Crookes cast off as waste. Some of the workforce also manned the funky union station in the North Star Mill, while the rest started up the Contention Mill on the river. From outward appearances, the Contention Mill featured a flow path that was similar to other concentration facilities in the region. Jaw crushers reduced crude ore, Chilean wheels pulverized it, screens and jigs separated the particles by size and specific gravity, and vibrating tables concentrated the fines.[318]

Only a year after the Contention Company invested a considerable sum of money in the North Star, the entire operation collapsed. Bulkley Wells, the dashing and spoiled manager of Smuggler-Union, was mostly to blame because he neglected important details. First, he failed to adequately develop the ore veins in the North Star workings for production, and second, he did not ensure that the concentration

The Contention company installed a steam hoist and upright boiler to power a short tramway at the North Star Mine in Dives Basin. Source: Author.

A party of lessees placed this cable spool between two rock pylons at the North Star Mine's base camp. They intended to pay the cable out for a tramway but abandoned the project. Source: Author.

process was truly effective, which it was not. During the winter of 1902, Wells closed the mine and mill as a monumental failure and let go the workforce of 100.[319]

The miners who were laid off had no trouble finding work in one of the other ventures active in 1902. William Kearnes & Company leased the North Star from the Contention Company through 1903, and William Barkow leased the mine when Kearnes left for Telluride the following year. The North Star, however, was past its prime and the Black Prince in Little Giant Basin and the Shenandoah in Dives Basin quickly took its place.[320]

When the Contention Company took an option on the Shenandoah, it fully expected to purchase the property and use the Spotted Pup Tunnel as a haulageway for North Star ore. To this end, the company invested in a mechanized surface plant complete with blacksmith and machine shops, an air compressor, and a battery of stamps to crush ore in a large tunnel house. Like the Stoibers' Unity Tunnel, the crushing station at the Shenandoah was intended to reduce the bulk of crude ore for efficient shipment to the Contention Mill. After building the surface plant, Contention then subleased the

Shenandoah to A.S. Sturgeon and James Gordon, who made a rich strike in the Spotted Pup Tunnel. When the Contention Company failed in 1902, the property reverted to Wason, and Sturgeon and Gordon's lease expired. They kept working the mine anyway, hoping to keep all the proceeds. As a mine operator of some experience, Sturgeon knew better, but he weakened under the weight of the rich ore. Wason learned of Sturgeon's deceit and hurried over the range from his ranch on the Rio Grande River straight to the Contention Mill, where he intercepted Sturgeon's payment.[321]

Somehow, Sturgeon persuaded Wason that the payment confusion was only a mistake and renewed his lease for 1903. In November alone, Sturgeon's miners drilled and blasted a handsome $1,400 in ore with additional low-grade material being treated in the revised Contention Mill, operated by the Black Prince Gold Mining Company. When Sturgeon's lease ended in 1904, Wason failed to renew in favor of his old friend Henry Bennett, who was glad to be back at the Shenandoah. Bennett enjoyed great success and found that the mine possessed more workings than before. With new machinery, he produced a substantial twenty tons of ore per week through 1905. At the same time, Daniel McLean, of whom we will learn more later, started his involvement with mining by leasing the Shenandoah No.3 and the Dives.[322]

As was usual, Bennett and McLean kept crews at the mine through the winter of 1906, which had all the appearance of being an unusually severe one. One storm after another roared through, blowing the heat out of the living quarters, making work at the surface plant miserable, and leaving thick layers of snow on the ground. As a harbinger of events to come, more mining companies than ever reported damage to their facilities due to avalanches, and the Shenandoah would join the roster. In March, a heavy storm dumped at least several feet of snow and wind-loaded the slopes above the mine. While the miners were trying to stay warm in the boardinghouse at night, a snow slide quietly let loose above them and began to rumble as it approached and gathered speed. The miners were caught by surprise when the avalanche mowed the boardinghouse down like a house of cards and carried the men, contents, and splintered wreckage downhill. When the snow slide stopped, it solidified and entombed twelve of the miners. The survivors frantically searched the debris for their workmates, but with no luck. Help was then summoned from the Highland Mary. Braving additional avalanches, the fresh hands arrived. Ora Kirk was among them, whose brother was among the missing. The twelve lost souls were too scattered and deeply buried for recovery, and it was decided that nature would have to exhume them during the spring thaw. Mournful, Kirk labored for a week until he finally found his frozen brother along with most of the other bodies. This was the single deadliest tragedy in the Las Animas District, although avalanches would continue to cause terror and destruction in subsequent years.[323]

If some of the 100 miners that the Contention Company discharged in 1902 were unable to find work at the Shenandoah, they could have continued down Dives Basin to the Highland Mary Mine, which was hiring. When Innis went bankrupt in 1885, he left the property as a "ready-made" mine, because workers had pierced several silver veins on the way to the fabled lake of gold. Curiously, although residents in the Las Animas District knew this, the stigma of the Highland Mary's past overrode anyone's desire to develop the veins on a significant basis.

In 1901, the property resumed its association with unusual characters and drew not psychics or unhinged millionaires, but instead Mary B. Murrell of Denver. During the previous year, B.F. Kelly and W.H. Bush apparently abandoned the Gold Tunnel & Railway Company, leaving the outfit to Murrell, Toledo investor C.W. Everett, and New York City capitalist John R. Wyatt. Murrell was probably the first of the partners to realize that Innis left more than one silver vein undeveloped and convinced Everett and Wyatt to redirect their resources to explore the idea further. Wyatt began purchasing the necessary claims, and Murrell did likewise through the Highland Mary Gold Mining & Railway Company, until they held the most important properties.[324]

Because she was in Denver and knew something about mining, Murrell assumed the position of manager during initial operations. A woman managing a mine? To many in the industry, this was preposterous. Regardless, she hired George Leiner and fifteen miners who repaired the surface buildings, installed a new steam compressor, and began rehabilitating all 6,500 tortuous feet of the Innis Tunnel. Exactly as Murrell expected, the miners found several ore veins, which they developed with new Durkee rockdrills and traditional hand drilling. One was the Lookout vein in one of the upper tunnels, the other lay deep in the Innis Tunnel, and both began to yield high-grade ore.[325]

The investors must have had bottomless pockets, because at the same time, they amazingly funded the Oro Tunnel on the opposite side of the mining district. By 1902, miners drove the passage to a length of 3,000 feet and prepared the ground for a mill at the portal, even though they had yet to penetrate a single vein of economic worth. Instead, reason prevailed, and they secured J.A. Snedaker to build the mill adjacent to the Innis Tunnel where it was actually needed. Snedaker must have been experienced because he designed an excellent facility that not only effectively concentrated ore, but also included a small hydropower generator for electricity. By the end of 1902, the

Primarily through the initiation of Denver mining investor Mary B. Murrell, the Gold Tunnel & Railway Company brought the Highland Mary Mine into its first meaningful production and built this mill in 1902. The large waste rock dump came out of the Innis Tunnel, located at right, and the building with twin smokestacks adjacent to and right of the mill was the original compressor house built in 1875. The head of Cunningham Gulch rises in the background, and the roof of Edward Innis old Whitehouse can be seen at the end of the water pipe. Source: Denver Public Library, Western History Collection, X 62209.

The Highland Mary Mill site as it exists today. The photograph was taken from the same vantage point as the previous illustration. Source: Author.

modern mill began treating ore from the Lookout level. With veins ready for mining and a mill capable of winning metals from the ore, the company increased the workforce to thirty. Their stay was short, however, because an avalanche roared down onto the surface plant, wrecked several buildings, and scared most of the miners away.[326]

A crew was back at work by spring and began production. However, because the workings were disorganized, the mine was a long way from being truly profitable. Under Superintendent W.E. Wilson, miners split their duties between production and trying to link the disparate levels together through vertical workings. By 1904, the miners made enough headway to produce a significant sixty tons of ore during a shift, which was an impressive fifty percent higher than the average per person. Once Wilson felt that the amount of development was sufficient, he reduced the crew and saw a steady stream of ore flow into the mill through 1906. The operation enjoyed reduced transportation costs when the Silverton Northern graded a line up Cunningham Gulch to the nearby Green Mountain Mill.[327]

On the other side of North Star Mountain, the Black Prince had all the signs of becoming a major operation. In 1902, W.B. Severn,

L.H. Chadwick, and other investors from Chicago and Michigan organized the Black Prince Gold Mining Company with the intent of developing the forgotten Black Prince vein. Severn and partners found that, with Contention's mill and the tramway, the Black Prince was almost a ready-made mine. Eager to be done with the North Star debacle and minimize its losses, the Contention Company was more than willing to sell the Black Prince claims, the tramway, and the mill to Severn and partners.[328] With a little promotion on the part of the Black Prince Company, the press gave glowing reports of the coming operation. The conservative *Engineering & Mining Journal* noted: "Black Prince. This company has purchased the possessions of the Contention Mining Company on King Solomon Mountain, near Silverton, and is making many improvements. The old Contention tram is also being extended to the Black Prince lode."[329]

In actuality, the tramway was not exactly "extended." It was, in fact, shortened. When the snow cleared in lower Little Giant Basin, workers erected a new terminal directly under the original Contention system and adapted the existing components. According to archaeological evidence and engineering features existing today, the new terminal was well designed, nestled into a niche blasted out of bedrock for protection against snow slides, and appeared similar to a

The Black Prince Mine, center, was nestled in the lowest basin of Little Giant Gulch near the abandoned King Solomon Mine. Source: Author.

mill. Miners input ore into bins at the top and fed pay rock down to sorting stations where workers dropped the recovered ore into holding bins below. On the bottom level, more workers loaded tram buckets from the holding bins.[330]

During autumn, a large crew began driving the main tunnel toward the vein and erected a well-appointed surface plant. Workers blasted a bench at the base of a cliff for a stout tunnel house, 25 by 60 feet in area, erected a frame snow shed for a rail line east to the tram terminal, and constructed a two-story boardinghouse for twenty residents. When finished, the Black Prince Company operated the mine and mill, at first, with success. However, the investors were probably too distant and inexperienced to have learned just how complicated mining was in the San Juans. The ore increased in complexity with depth, the mill recovered only a fraction of the metals content, and the mine proved very expensive to operate. Had they looked into the histories of the operations that surrounded the Black Prince, they may have been more thorough in their planning. By 1904, the mine closed, but the mill continued to treat custom orders.[331]

In 1901, the entire Animas River drainage was stunned by the news in March that Edward Stoiber was selling his Silver Lake empire. The mine was producing ore in unprecedented volumes, the operation ran as smooth as clockwork, and it was the marvel of the greater mining industry. Why, everyone wondered, would Edward sell so quickly after completing the last stage of his master plan? The reason was simple. After amassing a fortune, Edward needed no more money. He had remained fixated on building the greatest one-man mining system in the nation, and, once he accomplished this, Edward was ready to move on. Selling the mine and moving to Denver left Edward, and probably Lena, with an emptiness in their souls.

Their bank accounts, however, were overflowing. The Guggenheims, empire builders on a national scale, offered Edward a stunning $2.5 million for the Silver Lake collection, which is $54 million today. Some sources claim that Edward accepted around $1.3 million in cash and the rest in stock. Regardless of form, he would have to work hard to spend it all in the years he had left. The only stipulation that Edward had was that he be retained as a consultant until the mill was finished and treating ore successfully. This happened in May.[332]

The Black Prince Gold Mining Company erected a spacious two-story boardinghouse for its crew in 1902. The building is currently in ruins. Source: Author.

An explosives magazine such as this one at the Black Prince Mine provided a safe alternative to the usual practice of storing dynamite in boardinghouses and blacksmith shops. Source: Author.

The Guggenheims, who epitomized the large organizations moving into the district, took Edward's empire-building several steps farther. They purchased the Titusville for $500,000 and the Scranton City because these mines lay along the same geological features

The Black Prince Gold Mining Company purchased the Contention Tramway to carry ore from the Black Prince Mine down to the Contention Mill on the Animas River. The company adapted the tramway by shortening it, and continued to use the original towers below the mine. Source: Author.

that passed through the Silver Lake workings. Immediately after the transactions, Samuel I. Hallett, a talented mining engineer and metallurgist, arrived from Aspen to replace Robert McCartney as manager over the empire. Hallett maintained the Silver Lake Mines Company structure, kept the various employees, and found a position in the mill for McCartney. Amusingly, one of the first changes that Hallett instituted was the replacement of some of the concentration machinery in the mill with Hallett tables, which were apparatuses of his own design.[333]

The Guggenheims did not have the personal interest or purity of motive that possessed Stoiber, which created an atmosphere for one problem after another. The first drew Stoiber's honesty into question. Within three months of the sale, the principal ore vein pinched out and the miners lost it, leaving the costly operation with much less payrock than had been supposed. Whether Stoiber forecasted this and sold the mine anyway remains uncertain. Possibly at Stoiber's recommendation, Hallett did not reduce the workforce and instead directed nearly all the miners to extract the existing ore and drive exploratory workings in search of the lost vein and others. The miners triumphed, Hallett was relieved, and Stoiber was off the hook.[334]

Because Hallett was not as intimate with the mine as Stoiber, he was not nearly as adept at forecasting where miners should explore for ore or how best to coordinate production from the existing veins. As a result, the workforce produced 260 tons of ore per day through 1902, which was only one-quarter of the new mill's capacity. Around thirty percent flowed out of the Unity Tunnel, which was now a haulageway for the Silver Lake's lower workings; and the remainder came from Silver Lake Basin. While Hallett wanted more, the figure was not shabby, especially given that the mill reduced the ore to sixty tons of concentrates. This required daily removal by rail. With all the ore descending to the Silver Lake Mill, Hallett decided to mothball the old facility in Silver Lake Basin.[335]

While Hallett may not have been the best at finding ore within the mine, he certainly spent time and money exploring the ore systems extending outside of Silver Lake Basin. Shortly after the Guggenheims bought the Titusville Mine, Hallett put a crew to work rehabilitating the workings and making ready for an underground exploration campaign. Thomas Higgins' old Scranton City

Mine drew Hallett's attention next. During the summer of 1902, he dispatched a crew of around twenty workers, who erected a surface plant that forecasted an expectation of ore. The workers constructed a tunnel house 24 by 75 feet in area with a timber frame heavy enough to withstand avalanches. The structure enclosed the tunnel portal, a machine shop, a compressor, and a timber dressing area. The compressor was a powerful duplex model that could power up to eleven drills, while the rail line could accommodate small locomotives. This could only mean that Hallett had big plans for the Scranton City. In keeping with the rest of the Silver Lake empire, electricity provided lighting and power for the machinery.[336]

After workers finished the surface plant, superintendent Robert Hines kept three shifts of miners driving the tunnel through 1902

Thomas P. Higgins began the Scranton City Tunnel during the 1880s and abandoned work after investing more than he took out. By 1903, when this northwest view was taken, the Silver Lake Mines Company owned the property and planned to drive the tunnel almost two miles to undercut Silver Lake Basin. The company invested in a powerful air compressor and shop buildings, at lower left, and amassed supplies for the effort. With several years, the project was cancelled. The mine's boardinghouse stands out of view to the right. Source: Denver Public Library, Western History Collection, X 62200.

and into 1903. Using rockdrills, they drilled and blasted around eight feet per day until the tunnel was 800 feet long. Hallett was secretive about the operation, but word circulated that he intended to connect the Scranton City with the Unity, drive it father underneath the Silver Lake workings, and use the Scranton City as a deep drain and haulageway. Of course, because the tunnel followed one of the vein systems, it would naturally encounter ore. The project was definitely doable as the Roosevelt Tunnel in Cripple Creek, the Nelson Tunnel at Creede, and the Argo Tunnel at Idaho Springs demonstrated.[337]

Hallett did not last to see the outcome of his projects. In the middle of 1903, the Guggenheims dispatched him to Mexico to examine several promising mines there, and Rowland Cox of Ouray took his place. Cox dropped the fantastic Scranton City project and focused his energy on the Silver Lake and the Titusville workings. By this time, ASARCo controlled the Silver Lake empire because the Guggenheims had merged with the smelting giant. ASARCo dispatched the famed engineer John Hays Hammond to personally examine the Titusville and render an opinion. Hammond reviewed the mine, compared it with what was known about the Silver Lake, and declared that the Titusville had great potential. Responsive, Cox put a crew to work driving exploratory workings.[338]

The Scranton City Tunnel's boardinghouse saw little use after the tunnel was abandoned, and it then fell into ruin. Source: Author.

Then, Cox found himself mitigating one problem after another, with each being more catastrophic than the last. Robert McCartney and a Mr. Pickel, the two managers of the Silver Lake Mill, did not get along and were constantly at odds. Repeated arguments between the two turned into such a heated debate that, by the fall of 1903, they had poisoned the work environment. The workers finally had enough and walked out en masse, which naturally shut down the mill and infuriated Cox. After enough profits were lost to downtime, Pickel resigned and left McCartney in charge, which was for the better because McCartney had the most experience with the mill. Only four months later, the workers suffered a terrible tragedy that shut down the mill again. One of the workers found McCartney dead of natural causes in his office, which sent the workers into mourning since he was well liked. McCartney, who helped Stoiber design the mill for Silver Lake ore, proved difficult to replace.[339]

On a cold and windy October day in 1904, the workers who manned the tramway's turning station above the Iowa Mill were cooking on their woodstove and stoked the fire a little too high. The wind blew sparks out of the stovepipe onto the turning station, which caught fire and burned to the ground. The anchors for the track cables released. When the cables became suddenly free, they responded like taut rubber bands and pulled over several tram towers on the Silver Lake and Unity segments. In addition, the traction cables that held the buckets collapsed, dropping the buckets all along both tramlines. The system was a total wreck, and the conflagration suspended the entire mining operation. The Silver Lake Mill, of course, was shut down until the tram system could be repaired; and instead of bringing the old mill in Silver Lake Basin back into operation to treat the ore, Cox laid off around 150 miners, half the workforce, curtailing activity at the mine. The Las Animas District panged at the loss of production and the sudden surge of miners in need of work.[340]

Possibly because of his inefficient response to the catastrophe, Cox resigned early in 1905 and H.A. Guess, assayer at the mill, took his place. From a comfortable office in the Waldheim mansion, Guess oversaw reconstruction of the tram system and brought the mine back into full production. Miners sent 300 tons of ore down to the mill per day, which approached Stoiber's maximum. Under his management, around 350 souls worked amid the Silver Lake empire, making Guess the largest employer in the Animas River drainage. The Gold King Mine was second with a mere 175 workers. Perhaps Guess loosely followed the mold of Stoiber, because he adopted an eight-hour day for the mill workers instead of the usual ten-hour shift.[341]

Despite his generosity to the mill workers, Guess was not immune to the series of cataclysms that plagued the Silver Lake empire under ASARCo. At 4:00 in the morning on April 20, 1906, workers noticed that a fire had been deliberately started in the mill office and sounded the alarm. They frantically rushed to the hydrants only to find that someone had purposefully cut the hoses! With no way to control the fire, the blaze quickly spread to other parts of the mill until the entire building and some of the ancillary structures were enveloped. The flames and smoke could be seen from miles around, and those up at that hour of the morning knew what had happened. When the ashes cooled, Guess took stock of the wreckage and tallied the loss at $100,000 to $250,000. The mill was gone, the tramway was wrecked again, the loading sheds no longer existed, and tons of ore and concentrates littered the ground. The devastation was not total, however, because the ore elevators, the powerhouse, the shops, and the boardinghouse remained intact but charred. Operations at the Silver Lake were suspended yet again while Guess figured out the best way to continue production.[342]

Occasionally, important events can be so inextricably parallel that they defy coincidence. On April 21, the day after the mill burned, Edward Stoiber died in Paris of typhoid fever while on vacation. It seems highly unlikely that Stoiber could have learned of the disaster so quickly since he was no longer involved with the Silver Lake and was probably too delirious to make much sense of the news anyway. The timing was, however, nothing less than eerie.[343]

Although the Silver Lake operation faced one difficulty after another during the early 1900s, the Iowa Gold Mining & Milling Company faired even worse. If asked about the continuing boom and excitement in the mining district, Gustavus Stoiber, James Robin, and fellow directors would have probably complained that it passed them by. The main problem with producing ore in economies of scale, they realized, was that if the ore reserves were limited, the mine's life was relatively short. By 1901, the Iowa showed signs of exhaustion after only six years of intensive mining, in contrast to more than fourteen at the Silver

Lake. To the amazement of nearly everyone in the Las Animas District, Gustavus and Robin curtailed operations and let go more than half of the workforce almost overnight during the beginning of 1902. For a brief time, Gustavus and Robin thought they could save the operation through an exploration and development campaign on some of the geological features, but this failed. Even the Guggenheims, who bought the Silver Lake on one side of the Iowa and the Titusville on the other, were only tepidly interested in the Iowa.[344]

While the complex ore system was not yet completely exhausted, Gustavus and Robin took the option that companies reserved for times of trouble and leased both the Iowa and Royal Tiger properties. They even suspended the mill and tramway because the meager volume of ore that the lessees generated was not enough to pay for daily operations. During the depths of winter, around forty workers sought ore in both mines, where each had over twice that several years prior. Al Kunkle presided over the Royal Tiger lease, and in 1902 his miners struck a fabulous vein over five feet wide that was rich with gold and silver. However, it lasted only around a year, then gave out, and with it Kunkle's interest in the mine. He moved on to another operation in San Juan County, followed by the lessees at the Iowa. The surface plant was not completely vacant because ASARCo workers had to keep the compressors running to supply the Silver Lake Mine.[345]

Interestingly, Gustavus and Robin shared relationships with the Iowa that were almost as intimate as Edward Stoiber's, and as the operation crumbled and failed, so did they. Robin was the first to succumb, and he grew increasingly depressed and despondent over the impending failure of the Iowa; and, in a state of mental instability in 1903, he shot himself. Gustavus was next. He could not cope with the beginning of a series of catastrophes on par with those at the Silver Lake. In 1905, a spring storm dumped several feet of snow on Hazelton Mountain, resulting in an avalanche coming down directly on the Iowa Mill. The avalanche wrecked the tailings plant, engine room, and shop, and buried much of the mill. And, even though the facility was idle, the event added insult to injury. The stress proved to be too much, and Gustavus died of a massive stroke on the train from the Red Mountain District down to Silverton.[346]

During the early 1900s, the boom in the Las Animas District was by no means limited to the melodrama of the large companies.

The investors with moderate resources, who greatly outnumbered the Stoibers, Robins, and Guggenheims of the industry, financed and even personally worked a number of small to medium-sized operations. Some of these were continuations from the late 1890s, while a substantial proportion were new, reflecting how hope sprang eternal. While significant fortunes were not won or lost on these mines, the financial stakes were important to the owners and investors, who were greatly pained when some of the operations failed.

The Four Metals Mining Company was having such a grand time with the Lackawanna Mine that one of the directors proposed a concentration mill at the base of the mountain. After several years of regular production convinced the other directors that the mine's future seemed sure, they agreed in 1902 to build the mill. In frigid winter weather, a construction gang cleared snow off a parcel at the mouth of Swansea Gulch and prepared the ground. Director George Whitelaw took the plan a step farther and suggested a haulage tunnel be driven from the mill site. He was satisfied when workers finished the small mill at the end of the year. The construction and then operation of the mill, on the east outskirts of Silverton, may have annoyed some residents, but that was the price of living in a prosperous mining town. Unfortunately for Whitelaw and partners, the mill saw little use because miners were unable to find ore in the anticipated volumes. They spent most of 1903 driving exploratory workings and bringing payrock to daylight; but like Gustavus Stoiber and the Iowa Mine, Four Metals found that operating costs eclipsed production. By 1904, Whitelaw and partners had to stop work and let their miners go.[347]

After sinking a considerable sum of money into the Idaho, Four Metals realized that the property was a failure and decided to sell while the vein still showed ore. In 1901, Abe and Isaac Shiffer of Alamosa, who had very little experience with mining, relieved the company of the property. After investing their own money and coming to the same conclusion as Four Metals, the brothers began releasing statements to the press in 1902 to gradually create a sense of excitement regarding the Idaho. First, they claimed that they had "big plans" for the property, then the brothers "discovered" enough ore to justify a mill, and finally in 1903, they were discussing a smelter. It remains unknown how long it took the brothers to finally sell, but the Idaho saw no further activity of note and certainly consumed more money than it ever returned.[348]

During 1901, optimistic wealth-seekers were at work prospecting the Osceola and Montana Mines. The Osceola was a vein bearing primarily industrial metals that no one had seriously explored, and A.M. Munder finally unwatered a shaft on the Montana in Deer Park and found enticing gold samples. In 1899 or 1900, the brothers G.H. and Augustus Malchus of Silverton acquired the Mayflower claim from James Kendall and began what they appropriately referred to as the Cliff Dweller Tunnel, which literally penetrated a sheer cliff. Accessing the tunnel was infinitely more dangerous than the work underground, but they toiled away until the season closed them out. While the Mayflower vein awaited the miner who was fortunate enough to reach it, the Malchuses did little with the property for several years. In 1905, John C. O'Neill, a Chicago capitalist who successfully leased the North Star Mine on Sultan Mountain, recognized the Mayflower as a rare opportunity because it was still undeveloped. He leased the property, organized the Mayflower Mining Company for capital, and began driving a tunnel the mere 300 feet required to pierce the vein. By summer, miners not only struck the ore body but also drove 600 feet of drifts along it. O'Neill was obviously disappointed, because he did little more with the Mayflower. The Malchus brothers, however, gladly accepted the development workings. Around this time, according to archaeological evidence, someone reopened the long-idle Potomac Mine at the head of Little Giant Basin. A small party of miners accompanied by a woman (probably the wife of the superintendent) repaired the residential buildings and moved in, refitted the simple surface plant, and began mining. The partnership managed to eke out a living for a few years at most, then quit because the ore was truly exhausted.[349]

The Trilby Mine was one of the new, small operations that investors of limited means funded during the early 1900s. Yet, from these humble beginnings, the Trilby became one of the most important mines in the Dives Basin area. As was the case with the Mayflower, the Trilby drew keen interest because its miners pushed a tunnel toward a poorly explored area literally surrounded by proven mines. Imagining the riches that were surely locked in the Trilby Vein that traversed the mystery ground, Martin Houk organized the Trilby Mining &

Milling Company in 1901 or 1902 to buy the necessary claims and stake more south of the Shenandoah Mine. He hired six workers who drove shallow workings on the claims, then began a deep tunnel almost directly above the Highland Mary Mine before being frozen off the mountain. Houk and another crew were back by the summer of 1903, and they erected several buildings on a narrow terrace literally blasted out of the precipitous mountainside. For the time being, Houk's only goal was to undercut the vein, which lay around 2,000 feet to the east, so he paid several teams of miners to work through 1904 and 1905. They averaged around two feet per day in the hard rock and kept drilling and blasting until the fateful year of 1907 gave them moment for pause.

During the 1890s, two power plants served Silverton. One was the Silverton Electric Light Company and the other was the Silver Lake Mines Company, which diverted some of the electricity generated at Waldheim. In Silverton, businesses and individuals with disposable income were the principal consumers, while several mines in the immediate area received power as well. Given the extreme demand by the Silver Lake properties and the Iowa and Royal Tiger Mines, however, there was not enough power to go around. As the region's boom continued into the early 1900s, the demand only increased, spurring the Silverton Electric Light Company to add another dynamo to its Silverton power plant in 1903. Mining companies outside of town began to demand even more power for lighting and industrial uses such as milling equipment, tramways, and air compressors. In 1903, P.J. Brown and P.H. Scott of Denver, and other capitalists from Indiana and Tennessee hatched one of the most ambitious electrification projects yet proposed in Colorado to tap this growing market. While the project may not have been Scott's idea, he was the mastermind behind its actual implementation.[350]

Scott started in mining as a lowly placer prospector during the California Gold Rush, and during this time he struck an association with John W. Mackey and John O'Brien, who went on to reap a fortune from Nevada's Comstock boom. Mackey hired Scott as a master mechanic at the Comstock Mine, where he served for fifteen years and learned the skills of an engineer. Scott gravitated to Colorado during the 1880s and served as both a consulting and employed mining engineer. Over the course of the next fifteen years, he designed and built a number of concentration mills, all the while learning the rich potential that electricity offered. From this perspective, Scott easily forecasted the growing need for electricity in the San Juans and helped to seize the opportunity.[351]

Scott, Brown, and fellow investors organized the Baker Bridge Electric Company with the intent of damming the Animas River for a massive hydropower plant that would distribute electricity to mines throughout the southern mountains. When the company was well on its way to building the plant, Scott died in 1904, which may have stalled the project. No matter, because Henry T. Henderson was several steps ahead. A few years earlier, Henderson, J.W. Adams, and A.H. Mundee organized the Animas Canal, Reservoir, Water, Power & Investment Company and had made significant headway with the arrangements for an even larger project than the one envisioned by Scott and partners. Henderson's firm planned to divert Cascade Creek to run one hydro-plant at Tacoma, and to use several other creeks, and even the Animas River, for two more generation facilities both upstream and downstream.[352]

In 1905, the company completed the most important components of what was one of the most advanced hydro power plants in the San Juan Mountains. A complex system of flumes and reservoirs collected and distributed water to a large generation building at Tacoma, and workers strung powerlines up the Animas River to a stately brick substation in Silverton. However, unexpectedly high costs forced Henderson and partners to both limit the project to the Tacoma plant and reorganize the company in 1905 as the Animas Power & Water Company. Some archival sources mistakenly mention the firm as the Animas Electric Light & Power Company. The *Silverton Standard* correctly claimed that the company would revolutionize the mining industry because mines, large and small, would be able to electrify at a reasonable cost.[353]

Because hydropower required no fuel and Animas Power & Water only had to pay for its infrastructure, the company was able to undercut the other electrical suppliers in the Animas River drainage. During 1905, the company already signed contracts with the Silver Lake, Gold King, and Gold Prince Mines as customers. These mines generated their own electricity and had, in essence, been competitors. In so doing, Animas Power & Water already signed away half of its capacity, which required an expansion before a single switch was ever thrown. By 1906, the Tacoma plant was finished, and the powerlines were energized. Ironically, the company had to temporarily contract with one of its best customers, the Silver Lake Mines Company, as a supplier because the power plant's penstock failed in September. Finally, the Tacoma plant was permanently on line and consumers saw their electricity bills fall by as much as fifty percent, which brought the cost-saving technology within reach of many mining operations that relied on kerosene lights, steam, and muscle.[354]

In 1907, the vagaries of economic cycles impacted the Las Animas District once again. This time, a national recession struck; and while it had little to with mining, it directed the district toward the

In 1905, the Animas Power & Water Company built this brick substation, center, and shop, right, to receive high voltage power from its Tacoma hydro powerplant. From the substation, transmission lines carried electricity to most of the principal mines throughout the Animas River drainage. Rates were so affordable that the Silver Lake Mines Company subscribed and placed its three powerplants on standby. Source: Denver Public Library, Western History Collection, X 1779.

slippery slope of decline. In terms of production, the year was one of the best for all of San Juan County since the late 1890s. Mining companies generated almost $1 million in gold and $105,000 in zinc, which was now being recovered as an important industrial metal. Miners also produced $776,000 in silver, $490,000 in copper, and $662,000 in lead, significantly more than during the previous several years. Further, the companies were so productive that the county was second only to Leadville in terms of lead and copper. As the recession set in, metals prices ebbed until silver averaged a lowly $.56 per ounce and copper dropped from $.17 to $.13 per pound. At the same time, many mining companies saw their days of high- and even medium-grade ore come to an end, leaving only the unromantic low-grade deposits. The large companies with concentration mills were able to subsist on ore valued at six to twelve dollars per ton; but for those companies without mills, which were usually the small outfits, the value of the ore had to be double. Many of the small outfits simply lacked such payrock, and in such cases they were forced to close. As the first decade of the twentieth century progressed, mining in the Las Animas District centered around those large companies wise and wealthy enough to profit from their low-grade ore reserves.[355]

One of the approaches that some companies took in the face of low metals prices and poor economic conditions was a close examination of all operating costs, including labor. In keeping with what was becoming a wearisome business pattern, the mining companies tried to get more out of their workers for less money by either increasing their hours or reducing their pay. Both sides of the labor issue were well organized for disputes. Willis Z. Kinney and Franklin L. Ross represented the San Juan Mine Owners' Association, and the Silverton Chapter of the Western Federation of Miners was a shield for the miners. Kinney was an interesting study in how some anti-labor mine owners rose from the bottom to prominence in the mining industry. He was born in New York in 1860, the son of a leather merchant who worked the family farm. In search of opportunity he journeyed to Pueblo in 1880, and worked in one of the smelters there. After traveling the short distance west to Silver Cliff and prospecting during the rush, Kinney moved to the San Juans in 1883. Ten years later, wealthy investors Henry Soule and Cyrus Davis gave Kinney a fortunate opportunity to manage their Harrison Mine; and, as Kinney proved himself, they accepted his opinion that they should buy the Gold King Mine near Gladstone. During the 1890s, Kinney developed that property into one of the richest operations in the Animas River drainage with more than a little help from his hardworking miners.[356]

In response to the mining companies' desire to either extend the miner's workday or reduce pay, the miners' union demanded a wage of three dollars per eight-hour shift. The owners' association vehemently protested. As tensions rose and a strike seemed imminent in 1907, the Deputy State Labor Commissioner made a trip to Silverton to mediate between the powerful forces. The miners' union and its body of more than 1,000 members proved to be a juggernaut of an opponent, and had demonstrated its might in the past. To avoid a shutdown of the mining industry, which may have been fatal in the poor climate of the recession, Kinney and Ross acceded to the miners' demands. With labor tensions defused, the region was ready to get on with the business of mining again.[357]

When the Silver Lake Mill burned in 1906, ASARCo had every intention of rebuilding the facility because the ore from the company's Las Animas District mines required concentration for profitability. Instead of replicating Stoiber's design, ASARCo probably consulted with manager H.A. Guess to revise the original operating strategy and design a new mill accordingly. Guess knew that he would continue production at the Silver Lake, and ASARCo floated the idea of reopening the long-quiet Amy Tunnel, which still offered low-grade ore with high zinc content. A single mill, however, would not be very efficient for both types of ore since they differed greatly. This sparked Guess' mineralogical creativity. Why not build a mill with two separate flow-paths? One path would be tailored to ore from the Silver Lake, and the other could treat not only high zinc payrock from the Aspen, but also custom orders. Most likely, Guess helped to design the mill because he had the most experience with Silver Lake payrock and was familiar with the workings of the original facility.

Once the matter was settled, he put a crew together to do the horribly dirty and sooty job of sifting through the charred debris in search of equipment that had survived the fire. What a miserable job it must have been, soot turning to black sludge as the snow melted, and being whipped up by breezes when freed from the debris. The workers found that most of the important machinery was sound enough for salvage, which saved ASARCo a considerable expense. During 1906, workers began building the new mill, but before they finished, ASARCo transferred Guess to Mexico to manage the Cananea Consolidated Copper Company, and C.T. Van Winkle took the helm at Waldheim. By April of 1907, the reincarnated Silver Lake Mill was finished and featured split flow paths as planned. The one for Silver Lake ore could treat 200 tons per day and the other half that. This was a large step backward from Stoiber's original design of 1,000 tons per day.[358]

In 1906, the mighty Silver Lake Mill burned to the ground, and the American Smelting & Refining Company, which bought the property, built a new facility on the old foundations. According to this circa 1910 photograph, the fire spared the 1898 ore storage structure at lower right. The cupola on top of the storage structure was the bottom terminal for the original aerial tramway. Note that the new mill is smaller than Stoiber's 1899 version illustrated near the beginning of the chapter. Because the Silver Lake Mine was no longer a reliable producer by this time, the mill took custom ores from local companies. The Aspen Tunnel and mill are visible in the trees at far right. Source: Denver Public Library, Western History Collection, X 62198.

At the same time, miners employed by the Garfield Smelting Company, which was a subsidiary of ASARCo, reopened the Amy Tunnel and rehabilitated the critical areas underground. After an engineer examined the low-grade ore left by the previous groups of lessees, the miners began production and shipped the ore over to the Silver Lake Mill via a new tramway. The arrangement, however, was short-lived to the detriment of the entire Silver Lake empire. Apparently, both sides of the new mill did not recover all the metals content of the ore; and, as the 1907 recession deepened in 1908, ASARCo found that the facility was simply not profitable enough and suspended operations. Without a treatment facility, ASARCo leased out blocks of ground in the Silver Lake Mine instead of working the mine itself, and Garfield decided to continue with its Aspen project and erected a mill at the Amy Tunnel. Garfield's metallurgist had no better luck with the zinc-rich ore; and, after spending a small fortune on a brand new mill, Garfield stopped work at the Aspen altogether.[359]

ASARCo was by no means ready to concede defeat, and the local managers agreed that the split treatment concept in the Silver Lake Mill held great potential. They went back to the drawing board to

In 1907, workers are clearing debris off and modifying the original foundation for the new Silver Lake Mill. Source: Colorado Historical Society, CHS 92.24.192.

The new Silver Lake Mill was equipped with rows of efficient concentration appliances, such as these special tables designed to recover metalliferous material from otherwise spent tailings. This was one of the last stages of a lengthy and complex series of concentration steps. The view is across a row of tables. Source: Colorado Historical Society, CHS 92.24.190.

refit the facility. It seems likely that the task fell to Louis O. Bastian, a milling expert who served as one of the superintendents for much of the decade and had experience with the facility. Garfield was one step behind and attempted to improve its new mill at the Aspen rather than scrap the facility. By late winter of 1909, ASARCo was ready to try again and brought ore down from the Silver Lake and over from the Aspen. Probably in fear for their jobs, Van Winkle, Bastian, and the other metallurgists nervously watched the first run of ore. They must have been highly relieved when the metals recovery met expectations. Finally, normal operations could resume at the Silver Lake Mine, but they did not. The tramway's turning station burned again and wrecked the system, shutting down regular mining operations and frustrating ASARCo to no end.[360]

ASARCo continued to lease out the Silver Lake Mine and may have become bitter over several rich strikes that it could have claimed had the turning station remained intact. In October, a party of lessees mined ore from one of the veins and broke into a pocket worth $2,100, or $42,398 today, which was a fine bonus. The various lessees sent this and their usual low-grade material down to the mill, which survived in large part on the ore from the Aspen. Because Garfield still had trouble with its new mill at the Amy Tunnel, the company decided to send the complex ore to the Silver Lake facility and treat the rest at the Amy Tunnel until 1911 when Garfield decided that the Aspen was no longer profitable. [361]

Almost as if the Silver Lake operation was cursed, disaster struck yet again when a series of avalanches let go in Arrastra Basin following a powerful spring storm in 1911. One slide took out towers for both the Silver Lake and Iowa tramways and laid one of the powerlines on the ground, which shorted out and started a fire at a transformer station. By now, ASARCo learned to keep plenty of repair workers on hand, and they fixed the tramway relatively quickly. Lessees continued to work the mine; but during the summer, ASARCo

A charred tram tower still standing today serves as a witness of the fire that consumed the Silver Lake Mill in 1906. Source: Author.

realized it needed ore rich with lead as a flux for the Durango Smelter, which was attempting to treat complex low-grade silver and copper payrock from elsewhere in the San Juans. In general, when metallurgists tried smelting resilient ores in blast furnaces, they mixed in soft ores with a low melting temperature such as lead. When the soft ore melted first, it ran over and coated the resistant material and helped it soften and then liquefy. ASARCo knew that the Silver Lake Mine offered such ore and decided to work the property on a large scale again for the necessary tonnage.[362]

In June, ASARCo sent a crew of eighteen miners to join the lessees at the Silver Lake, and they assessed which mine workings would yield the needed ore. The miners naturally took up residence in one of the boardinghouses; and, while the residential complex was not filled to capacity, they were certainly not alone. Silver Lake lessees and a considerable crew of miners employed at the Iowa made for a population of several hundred, which maintained a sense of life and purpose in the basin. The population, however, was too transitory and insufficient for the Postal Service to justify maintaining the *Arrastra* office, which was closed in 1910. By July, the ASARCo miners began production. As the demand at the Durango Smelter increased, ASARCo sent up additional teams until the workforce was around 100 by the fall. The atmosphere of Silver Lake Basin approached its heyday years, and the tramway carried as much as 100 tons of ore per day down to the mill.[363]

The last and final disaster for ASARCo struck in the summer of 1912, and it was an event to behold. Leaving out the intense drama and excitement, the *Mining & Scientific Press* dryly reported that: "A fire occurred on June 30 at the Silver Lake Mine, near Silverton, owned by the American S.&R. Co. Practically all the mine buildings were destroyed, except the boardinghouse, which was saved by dynamiting smaller buildings between it and the blacksmith shop, where the fire started. The upper terminal of the tramway was destroyed, necessitating the closing of the mill."[364] According to archaeological evidence in the form of charred wreckage and foundations, the fire actually consumed the tunnel house, the tram terminal, and the mill that Stoiber built in 1890 in one giant conflagration that rivaled the 1906 disaster at the main mill. The scene must have been impressive as the surface workers scurried about trying to extinguish

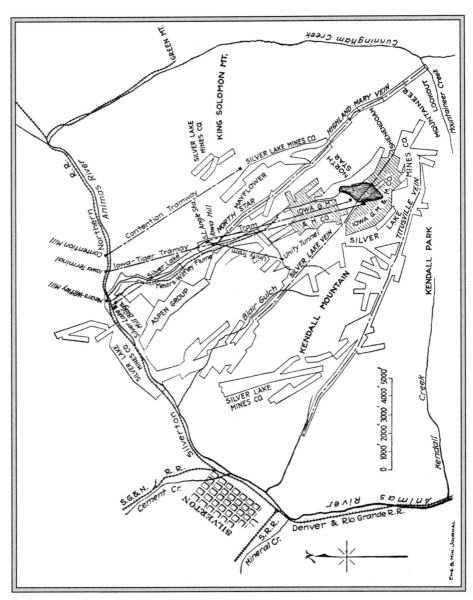

Even after the American Smelting & Refining Company acquired Edward Stoiber's Silver Lake Mines Company by 1902, ASARCo continued to acquire claims along the area's principal veins and faults. The map neatly illustrates the tramways, railroads, and Silver Lake facilities. Source: Prosser, 1914.

the blaze, blowing up the buildings in an attempt to save their temporary home. It remains a mystery how the residential complex was spared, even though some buildings were dynamited, because it was so close to the roaring flames.[365]

This was the last straw for ASARCo. The company gave up on the mine, continued to lease out blocks of ground to small parties, and wondered what it would do with the Silver Lake Mill. In hopes of keeping the costly facility in operation, ASARCo turned to the Unity Tunnel as a means of mining the Silver Lake ore system. The tunnel had been idle for several years, so a party of workers assessed what would be needed to use the tunnel as the haulageway that Stoiber had in mind. Workers relocated several towers from the Silver Lake system over to the Unity, rehabilitated key facilities, and finally tried producing ore. Within a year, the attempt proved to be a failure.[366]

Ironically, the Silver Lake and Iowa Mines literally traded roles in the Las Animas District after the 1907 recession. The poor economic conditions created an environment for the juxtaposed relationship; but the greatest factor was the difference of management strategy between the conservative ASARCo at the Silver Lake and a new organization that operated the Iowa. Of course, ASARCo's horrible run of luck with the Silver Lake played heavily into the reversed roles, as well.

After Gustavus Stoiber died, his heirs, James Robin's heirs, and the surviving Iowa Tiger Consolidated Mining & Milling Company directors declared both the Royal Tiger and Iowa properties bereft of profitable payrock. Otto Mears suspected otherwise and reasoned that if the Iowa and Silver Lake Mines were neighbors on the same general ore system, there was no logical reason why the Iowa should not match the Silver Lake's eighteen solid years of production. The ore, however, was not going to readily jump into waiting ore cars, and, instead, would require expertise and an attentive management to find and produce. With this in mind, in 1908, Mears and Jack Slattery approached the Iowa owners with a proposal to lease the entire idle operation. The owners accepted, and Mears and Slattery organized both the Iowa-Tiger Leasing Company and the Mellville Leasing Company, the beginning of a long-lasting and highly lucrative leasing syndicate.[367]

Formally known as John H. Slattery, Jack was a dyed-in-the-wool Silvertonian with experience in business and mining. Slattery worked as a civil and mining engineer in the Red Mountain District during the early 1890s, and decided to leave when the Silver Crash of 1893 struck. The collapse of mining made engineering jobs difficult to find, so Slattery chose an industry that would always be in demand. Specifically, he moved down to Silverton and operated the Bucket of Blood Saloon, then the Hub Saloon, followed by the Grand Hotel. In charge of several of Silverton's key public institutions, Slattery became a community figure, started a baseball club, and even served in the state legislature as a proponent of the San Juans. Slattery's capital, popularity, business experience, and knowledge of mining made him an excellent leasing partner.[368]

Instead of viewing labor as a resource to be tolerated only by necessity like most conventional mine owners, Mears and Slattery understood that their success hinged on their miners. Given this, the partners hired the best workforce that could be assembled, and gave the miners incentive to find ore and produce it efficiently through a profit-sharing program. During the summer, Mears and Slattery applied capital and their crack miners to rehabilitate the necessary surface plant components and areas underground at both the Royal Tiger and Iowa. They then pursued an organized exploration program for ore. Contrary to the property owners' misconception, the miners found plenty of low-grade material available in the old stopes and began production.

The workforce divided itself into six groups. The first two brought the existing ore out of the Iowa and Royal Tiger Mines for shipment down to the Iowa Mill, which the third group repaired then operated. The fourth group outfitted the surface plants at both mines, and the last two groups carried out a planned and educated exploration campaign in the mines. One of these last groups made a major contribution that ensured the future of the Iowa-Tiger Leasing Company. Specifically, several knowledgeable individuals realized that the original Iowa company paid little attention to the geology below the Iowa Tunnel level and assumed that ore surely lay deep in the ground. In 1909, miners sank a shaft on the top of a natural bedrock bench immediately west of the tram terminal to a depth of 350 feet, where they discovered an extension of the Melville Vein, which had been identified and mined in the upper levels in years past. The discovery was exactly what Mears and Slattery hoped for, and additional development demonstrated at least six months' worth of ore and a fat stock dividend. The Melville, however, yielded for years.[369]

While sinking the shaft may seem like a straightforward affair, the natural environment at the Iowa complicated the project. The bedrock shelf was one of the most exposed locations in the area in terms of avalanches; and, for this reason, the original Iowa company erected a stout cable net on its crest to arrest the cascading snow slides. Given this, the Iowa-Tiger Leasing Company worked feverishly during the summer to complete the shaft before the snow accumulated, because the hoist house stood on the worst spot. Once miners finished the shaft, they built an avalanche deflector on the upslope side and bored a tunnel below to make an underground connection. In so doing, miners could push ore cars from the shaft through the tunnel and directly out to the tram terminal with little risk. Workers installed the shaft's headframe underground and the permanent hoist, a powerful electric unit, in the massive tunnel house by the tram terminal. Such an arrangement required an expert and attentive hoist operator, because he could not actually see the shaft and had to rely on an exact level gauge and signal bells.[370]

Whereas 1909 met Mears and Slattery's expectations, 1910 surpassed them and vindicated the progressive approach of paying expert miners well for their acumen. The educated exploration campaign in the Iowa provided grand returns with a crew discovering not a pocket, but an entire vein of ore valued at $1,200 per ton, about $40,000 today! During the early summer, Louis Quanstrom, the metallurgist in the Iowa Mill, noticed that the proportion of gold recovered from Royal Tiger ore constantly increased and suspected that the miners must have been encountering stringers too fine to be obvious. Quanstrom relayed this to the Royal Tiger foreman, who decided to test the idea by blasting a chamber out of the vein's hanging wall on Level D. To everyone's surprise, ore rich with free gold came down with the first shot.[371]

With all the new ore that the Iowa owners had originally asserted did not exist, Mears and Slattery kept over 100 employees busy through 1911 and 1912. The mill workers tried to keep up with the 100 tons of ore sent down to them every day, and the miners made several additional discoveries. The same avalanche that damaged the Silver Lake system in

1911 also stopped the Iowa tramway for about one month. This, however, was merely a hiccup given the operation's overall success. One of the beneficiaries of the leasing arrangement was Mears' old friend Lena Stoiber. Even though Edward had died, she remained interested in the Las Animas District and held onto her Iowa stock. When E.P. Watson resigned as treasurer of the Iowa Tiger Consolidated Mining & Milling Company in 1912, Lena quickly took his place and helped administer to Mears' lease. While she did not need the money, she accepted a share of the $50,000 royalty paid to the company by Mears, who netted an astounding $400,000 from the mine.[372]

After five years of continuous production, Mears and Slattery saw operations at the Iowa finally slow down. Further, the winter of 1913 provided an omen of what was to become of the Royal Tiger. In keeping with the predictions of the engineer who built the original surface plant, an avalanche crashed down directly onto the boardinghouse, and its stout timber frame was no match for the impact. The structure was smashed. Everything inside was either ruined or buried by snow and debris, except for the occupants who were fortunately at work. The problem, however, was that all the Royal Tiger miners lived in the building and were now homeless. Salvaging what they could, the crew moved over to the Silver Lake complex and commuted across the valley on the tramway, which carried them slowly through blowing snow and driving rain. The miners had to endure this inconvenience only a short while, however, because Mears and Slattery finally exhausted most of the profitable payrock in the Royal Tiger, leaving further operations as an enervating drag.[373]

The 1907 recession did little to stop the momentum of the Shenandoah and Trilby Mines in Dives Basin. During the spring of 1908, Martin Houk's Trilby Tunnel was an impressive 2,000 feet long; and, as anticipated, miners finally struck the sought-after vein. The findings were troubling, however, as Houk realized that the vein was not quite as rich as he expected. Hoping to find a better section of the Trilby vein and other ore formations after investing a considerable sum, Houk decided to take a two-pronged approach. One was to drive development workings along the vein from the Trilby Tunnel, and the other was to mine known ore and find new veins in the Shenandoah through the Spotted Pup Tunnel. For the Shenandoah end of his plan, Houk organized the Danville Leasing Company with investors from Danville, Illinois, and began production to turn an immediate profit. The miners brought ore out of both tunnels for a while; and, when winter closed the packtrails to ore shipments, Houk ordered his miners into an exploration and development phase.[374]

Houk's gamble with the investors' money paid off in April 1909, when miners finally struck a rich copper vein in the Shenandoah ground. However, the crew exhausted the payrock within several months, forcing Houk to ask the investors for more money, which was always an unpleasant task. They provided, and Houk applied the funds to more exploration in both the Shenandoah and the Trilby, with qualified success again. By October of 1910, ore started emerging from the tunnels; and, while the material in the Trilby proved uneconomical, Houk kept the Shenandoah in constant but limited production. Wondering why the Trilby came up short, Houk convinced his backers to lease the Highland Mary Mine, whose deep workings should have penetrated or neared one of the veins. By 1910, the Highland Mary was largely idle, having been closed by a disagreement among its stockholders. During the year, Houk's miners completed a connection between the Trilby Tunnel and the highest level in the Highland Mary workings, while a crew gathered and shipped up to fifty tons of ore to please the Danville investors. The geology exposed by the Highland Mary workings brought no answers, and Houk focused on the Shenandoah through 1912 when he called it quits and moved on.[375]

When the Shenandoah became available, Daniel McLean (often misspelled as MacLean) jumped at the chance to lease the historic producer, especially because past lessees had already developed the property. McLean, who lived in Durango, leased the Dives several years earlier and felt that the basin still had much to offer if mining operations were managed correctly. In 1913, McLean organized the Dives Leasing Company, sent a crew of miners up to the Shenandoah, and continued where Houk left off. McLean's miners had no trouble finding enough ore to assemble a shipment, and sent 132 tons down on mules when the trails were free of snow. McLean would be in Dives Basin long enough to test his opinion of its resources.[376]

While some of the large operations were able to weather the 1907 recession, several of the small mines that held great promise became the scenes of busted dreams. Such was the case with the Lackawanna

Mine. A group of miners optimistically took a lease on the property early in 1907 and shipped at least fifty tons of ore. However, they lacked an effective mill, which limited the party to medium-grade ore. As the economic climate disintegrated and metal prices slipped, they were probably unable to find the capital necessary for exploration and suspended operations. At the same time, Henry Frecker, who purchased the Little Nation Mine above Howardsville in 1900, was finally ready for production. During the past seven years, he had pushed the Tom Trippe Tunnel, the lowest of three entries, in fits and starts as capital became available, toward the Royal Charter Vein. In 1907, he finally reached his destination, drove drifts along the vein, and declared eureka. With proof of rich ore, Frecker rounded up the capital for formal development and even a mill, which he planned at Howardsville.[377]

Howardsville was alive and well during 1907; and, while it was not forgotten, the town remained fairly static as Silverton usurped the attention, business, and infrastructure. Howardsville continued its role as a hub for the Cunningham Gulch area and supported a number of service businesses, a railroad station on the Silverton

During the late 1890s, Howardsville was a small, quiet commercial and service center for Cunningham Gulch and surrounding area. The town may have actually contracted from its late 1870s heyday. The business district is at center, one of several slaughter yards lies in the right background, and Cunningham Gulch is left and out of view. Source: San Juan County, 1899; courtesy of Colorado School of Mines.

Time has been unkind to Howardsville. The Pride of the West Mill was built near the center of town in recent decades and the rest of Howardsville was buried underneath a large tailings pond. Source: Author.

Northern, freight outfits, and slaughterhouses. The late 1890s boom had a limited impact and brought more people and Rickett's Mill, which was a concentration facility that failed within a few years. By 1907, the population was quiet, mostly working-class, and numbered around 150 to 170 men and women. When Frecker made his discovery in the Little Nation and proposed building a mill on the edge of town, the residents were certainly excited.[378]

As soon as the snow of 1908 melted, Frecker hired a construction gang to build the mill. By July, the facility was complete and featured an old-fashioned battery of ten stamps to crush ore and concentration machinery to separate out the metals. Frecker proudly led pack trains of ore down from the mine, dumped the payrock at the mill, and started the facility when he had enough on hand. After a week of testing, the mill seemed to fulfill its promise, and the *Mining & Scientific Press* hesitantly declared it a success. In actuality, the ore was too complex for the limited facility. The lack of further coverage suggests that Fecker had to close it sometime during the year; and the poor economic climate and low metals values ensured that he would not find the capital to try again. Unfortunately for Frecker, he sold the Little Nation before seeing it become one of the most important operations during the region's greatest hour of need.[379]

The economic climate created by the 1907 recession was very unkind to the Animas River drainage's milling industry. Most of the large and profitable mining companies remained such only because they concentrated their own ores in-house, while the small mining companies struggled to find enough ore above the twelve to twenty-four dollar per ton threshold. In addition, the treatment fees went up for the small companies, because the increasingly complex ores were costly to process. As a result, the demand for custom treatment slumped, which caused the independent milling business to collapse. Only a few samplers operated in Silverton. The Silver Lake Mill accepted custom orders, and the Kendrick-Gelder Smelter hung on. Overall, the available payrock was so low in grade that the *Engineering & Mining Journal* noted how crude ore was no longer economical to send to the Durango Smelter and everything had to be concentrated prior to shipment. This did not bode well for the future.[380]

The reason why the Kendrick-Gelder Smelter survived was because it was a niche facility and accepted only ores rich in copper and pyrite. In 1906, J.B. Ross purchased the smelter from the San Juan Smelting & Refining Company, which was in trouble, to treat ore from his mines in the Red Mountain District. Ross was apparently unsuccessful and sold the facility to wealthy investor W.B. Lowe of New York City in 1909, who attempted to modify the furnaces to treat lead-rich ore. Among the sources of payrock was the North Star Mine, which Lowe purchased from the Arpad Mining & Milling Company.[381]

Theodore Grabowski was behind the Arpad company, and he purchased the Contention Mining Company property, including the North Star Mine, the Contention Mill, the confusing tramway, and the Black Prince assets when they came up for sale in 1906. Where Grabowski found the capital is a mystery, because he spent most of his time, dating back to the late 1870s, as a prospector and contract miner. Regardless, Grabowski revived the Contention Company strategy of sending ore from the North Star down to the mill on the river with the same poor result. After several years, Grabowski suspended operations and sold the Contention properties to Lowe in 1908.[382]

Lowe tried operating the Contention Mill with mediocre results and bought the Kendrick-Gelder Smelter as an alternative. He tried adding new furnaces, but the facility proved unable to treat his ore or that from other mines within the stringent efficiency requirements dictated by the economic conditions. In 1910, Lowe closed Silverton's last independent smelter.[383]

CHAPTER 11

Over Here: The World War I Boom

THOSE WHO REMAINED IN THE ANIMAS RIVER drainage after the dark times that followed 1907 ultimately persevered when political unrest in Europe set the stage for a revival reminiscent of years past. When World War I began in 1914, manufacturing industries at first in Europe and then in the United States mobilized to meet a heavy wartime demand. As the war progressed and devastated Europe's economy, governments there sought stability in silver. To the delight of the greater mining industry, the value of industrial metals and silver slowly rose during the first years of the war then shot upward as the war dragged on. Silver ascended from an abysmal $.54 per ounce to $.73 by 1916. It then rose to $.84, a price not seen since the Silver Crash of 1893. Lead and zinc, which never fetched high values, almost doubled. Around 1910, zinc was valued at $.05 per pound and leaped to $.08 by 1917, while lead doubled from $.04 to $.08 per pound.[384]

Silver and industrial metal mining districts across Colorado experienced a sudden surge of activity. Ores that were merely eco-nomical by 1910 standards became almost the stuff of bonanza, while previously uneconomical ores, by far the highest in volume, were profitable. In the context of these high values, a sense of optimism, purpose, and prosperity returned to the Las Animas district.

By World War I, Colorado's mining industry had evolved away from the pattern of intense booms around new discoveries, overnight millionaires, and investment schemes, to one where new generations of speculators, investors, and laborers mixed with the old, and together picked through areas already subject to decades of mining. The Las Animas district was no different, and several distinct groups of new and old brought the region's mining industry back from decline. One group consisted of experienced miners and claim owners who were intimate with the histories of many mines, in some cases as far back as the original 1880s boom. Based on their accumulated knowledge, the older individuals innately understood which mines still possessed low-grade ore and how much effort would be required to bring a given property back into production.

Another group was a new generation of speculators, many of whom resided outside the district. The speculator of past decades usually sought out promising prospects, acquired the associated claims, and found investors to provide capital for development if the speculator lacked the resources himself. The speculator then had the claim developed to a depth where ore could be proven. If the claim lacked ore deposits of note, dishonest speculators perpetrated various types of fraud to convince investors that the property was, in fact, worthy of purchase. By World War I, the Las Animas district featured few claims that had not been prospected to some degree, leaving virtually no properties available for traditional speculation. Instead, the district offered numerous deep prospects, mines known to have produced in the past, and mines currently in production, which were the resources available to this new generation of speculators. By employing examining engineers, geologists, assayers, and other mining experts, the new speculators collected information to determine how much ore a property offered and the likelihood of additional discoveries. In some cases, the new speculators conducted all tasks including the actual prospecting. When they felt justified, they then acquired the properties themselves, sought investors, or joined active companies.

The last principal group included an older generation of investors, managers, and engineers who may not have ventured into the Las Animas district prior to the war, but had considerable experience in

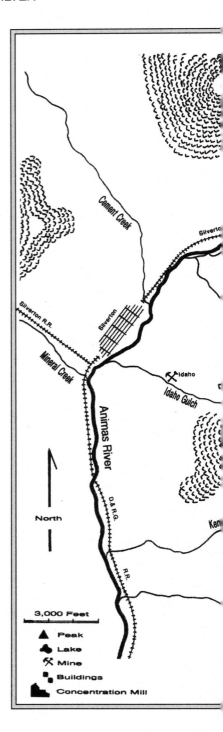

Principal places of activity, 1914 to 1922. Source: Author.

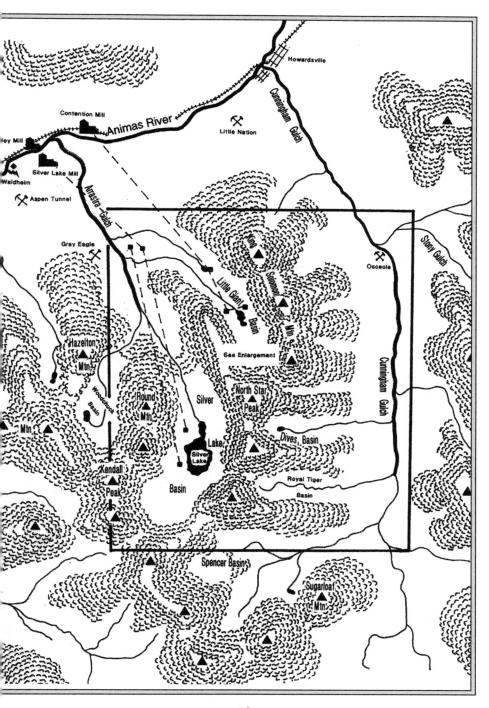

Colorado's mining industry. Like the new generation of speculators, they applied science, economics, and examination to identify and select mines that still offered potential. They tended to organize companies and lease those properties that could not be purchased outright. They shunned all but the best mines with proven records of production.

In the Las Animas district, a small party of lessees belonging to the first group took over the North Star Mine in 1916 after it had been abandoned for several years. Ultimately, they did more

Principal mines and mills in the central portion of the Las Animas Mining District, 1914 to 1922. Source: Author.

damage than good for the property because, although they managed to scrape together enough ore for several shipments, the lessees accidentally set alight the boardinghouse. Thankfully for them, the catastrophe occurred in August and the miners were able to move into the old base camp buildings in Dives Basin. With the surface plant collectively housed in the single building now gone, the North Star was even more difficult to work and became unattractive. Hence, when the lessees left after minor production in 1917, no one wanted to take their place. This important and historic mine, a cornerstone of the Las Animas district for years, would see no further activity of note.[285]

G.H. Malchus was a member of the group of experienced miners who were familiar with the most likely ore producers, which he considered his Mayflower property to be. The name is somewhat ironic since the cliffs and scree around the property were too abrupt, sheer, and unstable to support any life except for lichen and crazy miners. As early as 1913, Malchus attempted to bring the undeveloped property into production and scraped together enough capital to build a Bleichert tramway from the mine's lower tunnel down to a terminal on the floor of Arrastra Gulch, probably at the Iowa Mill. While the distance was very short, the steep, loose scree slopes made a reliable road impossible, and hence a tramway was necessary for meaningful production. Malchus hired a crew of around 15 miners who lengthened the development workings and sent out several dozen tons of ore. As the Mayflower proved itself, ASARCo examined it as a replacement for the severed Silver Lake Mine and took an option in 1914. However, they let the deal fall through.[386]

ASARCo may have felt remorseful several months later when Malchus struck an excellent ore formation and realized enough profit to pay down his debt. In 1915, Malchus entertained another party interested in buying the Mayflower as a source of ore for the Silver Lake Mill. Specifically, the American Oil Flotation Company leased the mill from ASARCo and needed a reliable producer to supplement the fluctuating custom business. The Mayflower, with all of its promise, was the logical choice because it lay almost directly on the Silver Lake tram system. American Oil took an option on the property and almost immediately lost money because clumsy workers accidentally set fire to the surface plant. By fall, the company paid Malchus $3,000 toward the purchase price and probably also as repayment for the damaged facilities. The sale failed to go through because American Oil disappeared altogether.[387]

Daniel McLean could also be lumped in with the group of experienced miners, although his history with the Las Animas district only went back around ten years. Like Martin Houk, McLean suspected that the mountain shared by the Highland Mary, Trilby, and Shenandoah mines concealed a hidden vein system that was one blast away from discovery. While this notion was not too different from Innis' lake of gold, McLean's suppositions were much more realistic and founded on geological knowledge. In 1915, McLean apparently shared his ideas with J.B. Houston, a relative newcomer who leased the Highland Mary. Houston and McLean decided to form a cooperative operation and, while each maintained their separate leases, the mine operators approached the area of undeveloped ground from different points. Based on several new strikes and existing ore in the Shenandoah, McLean easily out-produced Houston, who gave up on the Highland Mary by 1916.[388]

McLean, however, continued to search for and develop the untapped veins behind the Trilby and Shenandoah. For the most part, his miners extracted new ore as they found it and worked the older stopes, bringing out as much as four tons per day through the Shenandoah. In 1917, McLean formed the O.S. Leasing Company to drive exploratory workings in the Trilby and hopefully connect the mine with the Shenandoah. While the underground connection was not realized, he worked both mines as a single unit with great success. To McLean, the elusive veins were no longer hidden.[389]

Otto Mears and Jack Slattery were no-nonsense, hardboiled mine operators who had been cashing in on their experience and encyclopedic knowledge of the Las Animas district with their Iowa and Royal Tiger leases. The strategy that they used proved so successful that the partners decided to try operating some of the district's other important mines. The main hurdle, however, was that doing so required up-front capital for repairs, improvements, equipment, and labor in excess of what Mears and Slattery were comfortable furnishing. To obtain the necessary funding, Mears and Slattery organized a small leasing syndicate that included around five other investors.

Louis O. Bastian, formerly superintendent of the Silver Lake Mill, provided metallurgical expertise and some capital. When ASARCo

ran into trouble with the mill, he went into semi-retirement and purchased the Corner Store mercantile in Silverton during 1909, but was
easily drawn back into mining probably by Slattery. Matt Delsante
was another Silverton resident who immigrated as an Italian miner
and was familiar with the area's resources and history. King C. Gillette, a resident of Beverly Hills, California, was a major contributor
of capital. Frank Slattery, Jack's brother, was local and provided management and administrative oversight. James R. Pitcher was Mears'
right-hand man and son-in-law. Pitcher met Mears through the Mack
Brothers Motor Car Company in New York City as a mutual investor, and they were convinced that the automobile was the wave of the
future. Pitcher socialized with Mears and met Mears' daughter Cora,
and Pitcher made such a positive impression that Mears granted per-
mission for their marriage in 1904. The following year Pitcher was
appointed secretary and treasurer of the company, but he sided with
Mears during a stockholder disagreement in 1906 and walked out.
Mears brought Pitcher west out of the comfort of New York City to
gritty Silverton and offered him the position of manager over the Silverton Northern Railroad. Pitcher's business experience and family
ties made him a natural inclusion in the leasing syndicate.[390]

As a syndicate, the team of seven worked together to lease some
of the formerly most productive and largest mines in the Animas
River drainage with an emphasis on the Las Animas District. Various
combinations of two and three of the syndicate members claimed
themselves as principals in any given lease, while all seven usually
contributed some capital. As a result, when several names of the syndicate showed up on the paperwork for a lease, it was a sound bet that
all seven were actually involved to some degree.

Given the above, it comes as no surprise that the firm of Mears,
Slattery & Pitcher was the prime candidate to lease the idle Silver
Lake Mine from ASARCo in 1913. While Mears and partners asserted
that they were going to hire 100 miners, they actually employed
fewer, but when combined with their workforce in the Iowa, the total
population in the basin was enough to justify reopening the Arrastra post office and probably a commissary. Mears and Slattery put
the syndicate's capital to use rehabilitating the Stoiber Tunnel and
then producing low-grade ore through 1914. Leases at other mines
apparently distracted the syndicate during 1915, but the firm of

Slattery, Delsante & Gillette worked the Silver Lake the following year. Also known as S.D. & G. Company, the syndicate maintained a constant but limited production into 1917, when their experienced miners noticed an eight foot wide vein right in the walls of the Stoiber Tunnel. Miners, shift bosses, and engineers must have walked past the formation hundreds of times, and no one realized what it was. The vein's copper, silver, and gold content were welcomed by Mears and partners, who sent the ore along with the rest of the material that they produced to the Iowa Mill for treatment because the Silver Lake tramway was out of commission.[391]

The Mears syndicate continued its lease at the Iowa Mine with great success. While the Melville and Iowa-Tiger Leasing companies ran most of the operation, the syndicate leased additional ground in 1914 in the form of Delsante & Company. More of the syndicate's capital came under demand in 1917 when one of the tram system's most important towers caught fire and burned, stopping production. The tower stood perched on a spire that extended outward over Arrastra Gulch's headwall cliff, and a rubbing cable generated enough friction to start the blaze. The tower was one of the most difficult and dangerous to access; and how the workers maneuvered new timbers onto the foundation without toppling over the cliff remains a mystery. Fortunately, the accident happened during the summer when repairs were possible.[392]

The Mears syndicate moved quickly when the American Oil Flotation Company abandoned its efforts to purchase G.H. Malchus' Mayflower Mine. By 1916, Malchus, ASARCo, and American Oil collectively demonstrated that the Mayflower was destined to become a significant producer, which naturally attracted the syndicate. Further, the mine held the added attraction of a tramway already built to the Iowa Mill. During the year, Mears, Slattery, and Pitcher were the principals on paper behind the Mayflower Leasing Company, which found the mine almost ready for production. Two tunnels penetrated the abrupt cliff. The upper one was 800 feet long, while the lower one was an impressive 2,250 feet long and accessed a stope. The surface plant was complete and featured a motor-driven Rand Imperial Type 10 compressor capable of powering around seven rockdrills. It took little effort to develop enough ore for an excellent production run, and the crew made a big strike during the fall.[393]

The Mears syndicate was not the only entity to work the Silver Lake and Iowa mines during the first years of World War I. Small parties of lessees, mostly Italians employed by the Stoibers in years past, enjoyed ample production. In the Silver Lake Mine, Fiant leased a portion of the Whale claim, Gaski and Haffka leased the Black Diamond, Allen-Fattori leased a section of the Titusville vein, and Pete Machuni & Company worked Level No.4. Joe Tesadri & Company was one of the most profitable and worked in Level No.3, where the five miners encountered an upper extension of the same vein that S.D. & G. discovered in the Stoiber Tunnel.[394]

The Iowa Mine hosted a similar assemblage of small parties and partnerships. In 1914, Kafka & Giasi leased one of the upper levels and built a single-rope reversible tramway down to the main surface plant. The following year, the White Diamond Leasing Company accessed a block of ground through the Black Diamond Tunnel and employed a crew of seven. At the same time, Charles Voilleque & Company worked a different section of the mine with a significant workforce of 36 miners. Nearly all these parties signed subleases with the Mears syndicate and sent their ore to the Iowa Mill for treatment.[395]

The Unity Tunnel was also abuzz with parties of lessees who may have contracted directly with ASARCo. The Giono, Cunningham, Beamer, and Luckett leases worked blocks of ground above and below the tunnel level, along with other parties. The various partnerships apparently pooled their capital and modified the idle Bleichert tramway installed by the Stoibers. They apparently refitted the original tramway as a double-rope reversible system that ended near the Iowa Mill, where the lessees sent their ore.[396]

As can be surmised, the Iowa Mill, included with the Iowa lease that Mears and Slattery held since 1908, became the centerpiece for the production in and around Silver Lake Basin. Further, the mill was the king pin upon which the syndicate, the throng of sublessees, and independent customers depended for their success. To improve the recovery of metals, the company metallurgist, probably Bastian, installed flotation equipment in 1915. Seen as a panacea for rebellious and complex ore, flotation was a revolutionary technology that seemed to defy the behaviors of weight and specific gravity in separating metalliferous material from waste. Flotation relied on oil or detergent to float metalliferous material off and away from waste in rectangular cells or tanks. Mechanical sweeps or paddles shoved the metal-rich froth out of the cells and into troughs that carried the material onward to other processes. The Atlas Mill in the Sneffels district saw one of the first trials of flotation in the San Juans during 1914, and progressive metallurgists such as Bastian were quick to adopt the technology. Bastian experienced great success with flotation at the Gold King Mine in 1915, which the syndicate leased. He apparently repeated this at the Iowa Mill later in the year. With flotation, the Iowa Mill workers had a difficult time keeping up with the ore literally flowing in from all directions. In 1916 alone, the mill turned out about fifty tons of concentrates from Mayflower ore and a weighty 700 tons from Iowa ore.[397]

The Iowa, Silver Lake, and Mayflower mines were not enough for the Mears syndicate. Like earlier lessees, one of the syndicate members probably was aware that Edward Innis ignored a number of silver veins in the Highland Mary Mine during his search for the lake of gold. During the 1890s and 1900s, various parties of lessees and the Gold Tunnel & Railway Company attempted to find and mine the veins, but with limited success. A mine with such a history was the syndicate's specialty, and Mears et al. were convinced that they could make the Highland Mary pay well with proper management, ore concentration, and expert miners. In 1916, J.H. Slattery & Company, with Jack Slattery as principal, leased the property from owner Highland Mary Mining & Milling Company. Daniel Searle of Toledo, Ohio, was president, and he either reorganized or bought the Highland Mary from the Gold Tunnel & Railway outfit.[398]

Initially, Slattery's lease included the mine's upper workings and the surface plant, which was ready for action. In the past, the mine's various operators completed eight levels with the Mountaineer, the highest, as Level No.1 and the Innis Tunnel, the lowest, as Level No.8. Levels No.2 and No.3 exited the mountainside, Level No.7 was a tunnel around 2,000 feet south and up Cunningham Gulch from the main surface plant, and the other levels were strictly internal and linked via raises. The main surface plant surrounded the Innis Tunnel, and the mill erected by the Gold Tunnel & Railway outfit stood adjacent to and above the mine portal. As noted earlier, the surface plant was advanced and well-equipped, and included a large air compressor and small hydropower dynamo.[399]

Slattery's miners made use of everything but the mill because it failed to recover enough of the ore's metal content. Because concentration was necessary for profitability, Slattery put a crew to work remodeling the facility almost certainly under Louis Bastian's guidance. When finished, a jaw crusher reduced crude ore to gravel, a set of Cornish rolls and a Chilean mill ground it to sand, and a tube mill turned the material into slurry. Flotation cells and other machinery carried out the concentration. While the crew banged away refitting the Highland Mary Mill, Slattery sent the ore that the miners produced down to the Contention Mill, which Bastian remodeled for Peter Orella and his Big Giant operation. By December the workers finished the Highland Mary Mill and turned out around two tons of concentrates per day.[400]

Slattery finished one last project at the beginning of 1917 that remediated inefficiencies posed by the haphazard organization of the underground workings. According to formal mining engineering, underground levels were supposed to be linked by vertical passages that provided some degree of flow of men and materials. If this was done correctly, then ore mined in the highest levels could be easily transferred down into bins over the haulageway on the lowest level with little handling, as the Stoibers had done. The Highland Mary, by contrast, had little such organization, and instead of expending enormous sums of capital on the necessary connections, Slattery diverted the ore completely around the mess via two aerial tramways. One leg was a double-rope reversible system that descended from Level No.2 Tunnel to a station at the Level No.7 Tunnel, and the second leg followed the west side of Cunningham Gulch down to the mill. While the cost of a segmented system was high, it allowed large crews in both tunnels to produce as much ore as the buckets could carry. Miners demonstrated this to be in the dozens of tons per day when operations got underway in 1917. Between the crude ore and low-grade material that surface workers sorted from the waste rock dump at the Innis Tunnel, the mill treated around seventy tons per day. The efficiency, success, and tonnage realized by the Slattery lease confirmed the syndicate's expertise and made the mine's previous operators seem like inept amateurs.[401]

Familiarity and knowledge of the Las Animas District's historic producers did not automatically guarantee the district's experienced

Peter Orella's tram terminal at the Big Giant Mine still stands. Miners input payrock into the structure's large bin by pushing full ore cars across the trestle at left. A second tramway carried North Star Mill tailings down from Little Giant Basin and entered the double doorway in the cupola. The tram mechanism was located in the large room at the structure's bottom. Source: Author.

miners success at some of the old properties. Gustavus Anderson, Victor Nelson, Charles Vickberg, and Iowa Mill superintendent Louis Quanstrom leased the Gray Eagle Mine in 1916 after it had been abandoned for almost 30 years. Surveying the property, the men felt that the mine was a sure bet because, while the original workings offered a little ore, no one had explored below the main level where the vein was sure to continue. The assumption was not unreasonable because the veins in neighboring mines such as the Aspen held value at depth. The partners prepared a site for a haulageway on the steep scree slope far below the original workings in the cliff, which was no small amount of work. On a platform of scree so sharp that it quickly shredded boot soles, the lessees built a tunnel house for a duplex air compressor, a blacksmith shop, and the tunnel portal, and directed a small crew of miners to bore a tunnel straight toward the cliff. After penetrating 400 feet of rock, the miners finally reached the vein and drove lateral and vertical development workings, which ultimately connected with the upper stopes. The vein, however, was not as rich as assumed, and the Gray Eagle lease ended within a year.[402]

Ed Johnson belonged to the group of new speculators who contributed to the Las Animas district's World War I spike, and he took a lease on the Aspen Mine from ASARCo. Based on the mine's history and information provided by ASARCo, Johnson calculated that the mine would pay as long as the value of silver and the demand for zinc remained high. In 1916, a crew of thirteen miners brought a tonnage slightly smaller in number out of Amy Tunnel per day and sent it to the Silver Lake Mill for processing. During the next year, the Mears syndicate in the form of Mears, Slattery, & Pitcher gained control over the Aspen lease but let Johnson do the hard work of mining under a sublease.[403]

Peter Orella was another one of the new speculators, although he was in Silverton as early as 1907 when he operated the Standard Bottling Works. Based on hearsay, Orella came to the conclusion that William Keith left the Big Giant ore vein largely unexplored, and, hence, believed it still had a high potential for more payrock. As metal values and demand increased in 1914, Orella approached Theodore

Peter Orella built the tram terminal in 1914 on the framework left over from the original Big Giant Mill. The masonry foundation and lower framework for the mill are clearly evident underneath the tram terminal. Source: Author.

Grabowski, who took back the Contention assets when J.B. Lowe failed, with a deal for the Big Giant. Orella would lease the Big Giant, the Contention Mill, and the tramway at first and buy it should the property meet expectations.[404]

To round up capital for major improvements, Orella formed the modestly named Peter Orella & Company and admirably pursued an organized plan. He hired a small crew that began rehabilitating the surface plant and underground workings, and then installed a compressor. Orella wisely knew that the mill would probably not treat the complex Big Giant material, and sent a large batch to the Silver Lake Mill for testing. At the same time, a construction crew had to connect the Big Giant with the Contention tramway, which ended at the Black Prince, located about one-half mile down Little Giant Gulch. Instead of bearing the enormous cost of realigning the entire system, Orella built a double-rope reversible segment down to the Black Prince terminal. His workers then repaired the Bleichert segment that descended down to the Contention Mill on the river, and the system carried the ore that Orella mined through 1915.[405]

After more than a year of research and probably input from several mill consultants, Orella finally settled on the best treatment process for the complex Big Giant ore. In 1916, he hired Louis Bastian to install a flotation flow path almost identical to that at the Highland Mary Mill, which clearly worked for Slattery. Once Bastian was finished, the facility started treating ore not only sent down from the Big Giant, but also from independent customers. In all, Orella expended $5,500 on the Big Giant operation, most of which went into the Contention Mill. To retain the investment, he convinced Grabowski to sell him the mill.[406]

During the fall of 1916, someone, probably Orella, was struck with the bright idea of collecting the tailings left in Little Giant Basin by the 1889 North Star Mill and sending them down to the Contention Mill to be processed. The idea was novel but not original, and Orella actually followed a precedent set several years earlier by Mears and Arthur Redman Wilfley. However, instead of liquefying the tailings like Mears and Wilfley, Orella decided to ship them down on the Contention Tramway. The terminal at the Big Giant was the nearest place to load the tailings, but a deep chasm blocked easy access. To overcome this, Orella built another double-rope system 500 feet from the upper basin floor down to the Big Giant, where workers trans-ferred the material. North Star Mill tailings are currently evident at both the top and bottom terminals. The new tramway made the overall system a complex and very unusual assemblage of three separate segments. The system included the tailings segment from the upper basin down to the Big Giant, the double-rope segment down to the Black Prince, and the Bleichert tramway to the Contention Mill.[407]

It has been said that the ore in every mine was slightly differ-ent in character even when on the same geological formation, and so it was with the Big Giant. By 1917, Orella realized that despite the state-of-the-art mill designed by Bastian, the Big Giant ore was still too complex to be easily treated. As a symptom of the problem, the mill struggled to generate only one ton of concentrates for the year of 1917, forcing Orella to ship the ore as crude material. Because this was simply not economical, he closed the Big Giant by 1918 and let the property revert to Grabowski. Orella, however, held onto the mill and ran it as a custom facility, which many of the lessees and small companies in the area desperately needed to sustain production.[408]

During the World War I boom, the Lackawanna Mine saw a series of interests who fell into the first group of seasoned veteran miners and the last group of experienced but absentee investors. In 1917, John M. Wagner of Telluride, who owned and operated a number of mines in San Juan and San Miguel counties, felt confi-dent enough in the Lackawanna to purchase the group of claims. Unwilling to work the mine himself, he sought someone to lease the property. During the winter, Wagner made a deal with William A. Way, R.E.L. Townsend, and Melvin Smith to lease the main complex as the Lackawanna Mining & Reduction Company.[409]

Way and Townsend were probably the driving force behind the lease, and while Way personally never worked in a mine for an extended time, he knew potential when he saw it. A respected Sil-vertonian, Way was born in Hancock County, Illinois, in 1874 to a family of some means, attended Western Illinois Normal School, and went on to study law at the Northern Indiana Law School. He came to Silverton around 1904 and practiced law under Judge Searcy until 1913, when he established a partnership with H.E. Curran. In 1917, Way married Hazel Fletcher of Salt Lake City and went into prac-tice on his own. Townsend had slightly more direct experience with

Animas River mines than Way and had leased several properties during the mid-1910s.[410]

The Lackawanna was in poor condition when Way and partners assumed the lease, and they found that the main tunnel had caved in. After rehabilitating the entry, they hired a small crew that engaged in exploration and minor production. The Lackawanna apparently failed to meet expectations, and Way and partners dumped the lease during the year and moved on to other mines around Eureka. [411]

Before the forge in the blacksmith shop had time to grow cold, in late 1917 a group of investors from the East took a lease and prepared for business. Henry M. Kingsley served as president and C.B. Sheehan manager of the D.L. & W. Mining & Reduction Company, lessee. Since little information exists for these two individuals, they were probably late arrivals to the Animas River drainage. Sheehan and Kingsley hired a crew of 20 who disbursed across the property and attempted to ready the operation for work through the winter. One team of workers accompanied master tramway builder O.F. Sackett to the Titusville Mine, dismantled the idle Huston tramway, and rebuilt it at the Lackawanna. The upper terminal stood near the main tunnel and the lower terminal was on the Silverton Northern Railroad. A second group worked under a Mr. Gregg who erected a concentration mill at the lower tram terminal, apparently to replace the facility built earlier. They also installed an air compressor in the mill and piped the air up to the main tunnel. The third workforce consisted of miners who developed ore and engaged in minor production. Months would pass, however, before D.L. & W. finished the improvements and was truly ready to make a profit.[412]

The Lackawanna Mine was not the only product created when veteran individuals joined forces with experienced mining men who never set foot in the San Juans. Otto Mears was the veteran and Arthur Redman Wilfley was an engineer and metallurgist of great reputation who split his time between Summit County and Denver. Wilfley was born in Missouri during 1860 to a working-class family and helped his father in the family sawmills and grist mills as a boy. In 1878, the sawmill burned and, without an anchor business, Wilfley's father decided to join the Leadville rush, set up a sawmill there, and profited from the lucrative demand for lumber. The family ultimately ended up in Kokomo, just over Fremont Pass from Leadville, when that district was in boom. Young Wilfley entered the mining industry as a prospector and miner, and Victor G. Hills, an engineer and surveyor, recognized Wilfley's talent and skills and offered him a job as assistant surveyor in 1882. Wilfley learned quickly, applied his skills to become a partner with Hills, and began acquiring claims and shares of mines. In 1885, Wilfley partnered with J.B. Lovell to lease the White Quail Mine, and included Henry D. Clark, who provided the capital for a mill that Wilfley designed to concentrate the mine's low-grade ore. Under the firm of Wilfley, Clark & Company, Wilfley began his protracted career with milling and concentration.[413]

Wilfley was perpetually unsatisfied with concentration technology and tinkered with various apparatuses such as vanners and other vibrating tables to improve the treatment of low-grade ore. In 1895, he finally developed a particularly effective apparatus that he patented as the Wilfley vibrating table. He began selling a practical model in 1896. The Wilfley table featured a stationary chassis and an irregular, four-sided tabletop that vibrated rapidly. The tabletop was coated with linoleum and numerous, fine riffles and, as it oscillated, metal-rich particles settled against the riffles while a water spray washed the waste away. Sales were slow at first, but the Silver Crash climate only energized Wilfley because his device was the answer to making low-grade ore pay.[414]

The powerful and famous Eben Smith, a principal of the Mine & Smelter Supply Company, contracted with Wilfley for the rights to make and sell the table, and the device netted them a fortune as it swept the mills of the Rocky Mountain West. Smith, whose specialty was mining investment, drew Wilfley into his syndicate and provided ample opportunity for a number of lucrative ventures. Wilfley, however, was not one to rest on his laurels and continued inventing and tinkering. In 1903 he developed an odd multi-deck vibrating table specifically to treat finely ground slurry usually piped out of mills as waste.[415]

Mears, aware of Wilfley's ingenuity and skill, realized that this man could provide the technical solution to a highly unusual project he had been contemplating during the early 1910s. The project involved the sprawling dump of mill tailings that formed an artificial but inviting beach by the Silver Lake Mine's residential complex. Ironically, Edward Stoiber was concerned enough with the water quality of Silver Lake to install a sewer system for the boardinghouses but flumed at least 500,000 tons of mill tailings into the lake's north end. Supposedly, Stoiber did so to store the tailings for future reprocessing, and Samuel Hallett planned on treating them in the Silver Lake Mill after ASARCo bought the empire, but the logistics proved to be too complicated. The tailings were in essence a ready form of extremely low-grade ore, and although they had been treated once in Stoiber's original mill, the tailings still retained enough metal content to be profitable. The costly steps of crushing and grinding had already been done and the tailings only required advanced concentration, which was Wilfley's specialty.[416]

To Otto Mears, who built not one but three impossible railroads, the logistics of moving the tailings and building a concentration facility seemed daunting but reasonable. Mears already had legal access to the tailings in the form of the Silver Lake lease, and all he needed was capital, Wilfley's expertise, and a place to build a mill. In 1913, Mears explained the project to Wilfley, who was interested in its novelty, and Mears obtained the money from his leasing syndicate. Mears and Wilfley then chose a mill site and designed the mill and the means of moving the sandy tailings. The operation became nothing less than fantastic.[417]

Mears and Wilfley selected their millsite on the north side of the Animas River opposite the mouth of Arrastra Gulch, which seemed to be a highly illogical location since moving the tailings there was an engineering nightmare. The adverse climate, the propensity of water to freeze, and difficulty of access made Silver Lake Basin a poor choice. Why Mears and Wilfley did not site the mill in Arrastra Gulch remains a mystery. Perhaps it was easier to bring the tailings to the river and ship the thousands of tons of concentrates by rail rather than freight them down Arrastra Gulch in wagons.

The system that Mears and Wilfley devised for moving the tailings was quite clever if not highly unconventional. Special sand pumps mounted on a barge vacuumed up the tailings and piped them as a slurry over to the outlet of Silver Lake, whose fall was increased by a low dam. The torrent carried the suspended particles over Arrastra Gulch's cliff headwall and down to the base, where another dam diverted the current into a large wooden drain box. Excess water flowed out of the box and the tailings reverted to a slurry, which flowed into a wooden flume that descended steeply along the gulch's west side. A trestle carried the flume out beyond the mouth of the gulch and over the river to the mill.[418]

As a concentration facility, the Mears-Wilfley Mill, as it came to be known, was as unique and odd as the hydraulic tailings system. Any metallurgist visiting the Mears-Wilfley Mill would have been taken aback upon entering the 40 by 60 foot building. As has been inferred, most concentration mills featured stages of crushing, grinding, and concentration neatly arranged on a series of stairstep terraces; and given the average engineer's love of order and symmetry, multiple units of the same apparatus were usually aligned in rows or clusters. The Mears-Wilfley Mill was nothing like the normal concentration mill with which the average metallurgist was familiar. The interior was relatively level and featured only a handful of apparatuses that were radically different from anything that the concentration industry was used to. The most horizontally imposing were grossly enlarged versions of Wilfley tables around 12 feet wide and 48 feet long with two decks each, and the most vertically imposing were several twenty-four deck shaking tables. Wilfley lived up to his reputation when he designed the contraptions, which were intended to treat the tailings in economies of scale. The giant tables were for course particles and the twenty-four deck machines treated slurry that consisted of extremely fine material. The Mears-Wilfley Mill featured some additional processing machinery, although Arrastra Creek completed some of the classification and separation stages that mills usually had to carry out. In the Mears facility, a tube mill provided crushing, hydraulic classifiers segregated the tailings particles by size and weight, and special sand pumps moved the slurry between treatment stages. According to design, the custom facility was supposed to treat 600 tons of Silver Lake tailings per day.[419]

Mears' construction workers consumed nine months building the mill and flume system, while Wilfley used the time to perfect his machinery. One of the devices that he obsessed over was a sand pump capable of lasting under the performance expected for the tailings project, an obsession that Wilfley would take to the grave. The twenty-four deck shaking table, also named a slime table after the material it treated, drew Wilfley's concern and he installed a unit in the Iowa Mill for testing because the Iowa tailings were like those from the Silver Lake Mill. By late summer, Mears and Wilfley were ready to throw the mill's master switch and start the machinery after investing $22,000, which is around $407,000 today.[420]

Mears and Wilfley should not have been surprised when their curious enterprise ran into trouble early in 1915, since they had no precedent to follow. The flume presented the first problem when it developed leaks in a number of locations. When workers braved wintry conditions and grappled with the flume's ice to identify the problems, they found that the tailings slurry acted like liquid sandpaper and wore the wood rapidly. Instead of lining the existing plank trough with sheet iron, Mears opted for concrete, which was another innovation that drew the attention of engineers who became interested in the strange project. The other problem that Mears, and especially Wilfley, had to face was that Wilfley's fantastic machinery failed to perform as expected despite the results of tests that suggested otherwise. Much to Wilfley's frustration and embarrassment, Mears replaced the machinery with flotation probably installed by the expert Louis Bastian. The replacement added another $20,000 to the mill's cost, but because the machinery returned the initial investment within the first year, Mears and Wilfley had no worries.[421]

With the bugs finally worked out, Mears operated the mill around the clock because deep winter freezes reduced the working season by around three months. During the rest of the year, however, the mill recovered around $5,000 per month, which was well worth the trouble. Of this figure, Mears and Wilfley must have enjoyed high profits since the mill was relatively inexpensive and Edward Stoiber had already done the basic work of mining and crushing the tailings decades ago. From 1915 through 1918, Mears' railroad hauled off dozens of rail cars of concentrates that fetched, at the end, over $100,000. The final design for the mill was so perfect that the facility functioned smoothly and without catastrophe into 1919 when Wilfley, in ill heath, sold his interest to Mears. During the year, Mears shut the operation down probably because the richest and the most debris-free tailings were gone.[422]

While the Mears-Wilfley Mill was important for its novelty, engineering contributions, and overall concept, it was not the most significant treatment facility in the Las Animas District. The Silver Lake Mill retained the title because it provided a service vital to the wellbeing of the overall district and its workers. When the upper terminal for the Silver Lake Mine burned in 1912, ASARCo closed the mill and contemplated what to do with the facility. Rather than allow such an important asset to remain idle, ASARCo decided to remodel it for custom treatment because the Animas River drainage had few such facilities besides Peter Orella's Contention Mill. ASARCo went one step farther and used the mill as a proving ground for flotation technology, which was revolutionary at the time.

Under metallurgist R.L. Clapp, workers began refitting the massive facility in the spring of 1914. The railroad that hauled off concentrates and the tramway used to deliver ore were called into reverse use. Instead, the railroad delivered crude ore from loading stations at various points in the Animas River drainage and the tramway lifted it up to the mill's head. Some of the concentration machinery was replaced and, as noted, flotation was added to improve metals recovery from rebellious and complex ore. This was an important innovation in 1914 because the Atlas Mill was one of the only other treatment facilities in the San Juans to experiment with the technology. While the work was in progress, ASARCo aggressively solicited contracts for business, which were relatively easy to secure because a number of companies needed concentration.[423]

No sooner did ASARCo start serving the mining district than a group of investors in the form of the American Oil Flotation Company petitioned the smelting giant to lease the mill. American Oil saw the merit of custom business and needed the mill for its own mines including the Slide, Terrible, Champion, and Ben Butler. ASARCo agreed in 1915, and metallurgist D.L. Thomas and superintendent Phillip M. Collins installed additional flotation cells. By early summer, the mill was ready, and Peter Orella provided the first batch of ore from his Big Giant Mine. Afterward, trainloads of ore began arriving and the facility was highly successful. Over the course of a year the mill concentrated ore from the Little Dora, Congress, Green Mountain, Genesee, Champion, Atlantic, Detroit & Colorado, St. Paul, Barstow, and other mines. Jack Slattery's S.D. & G. Leasing Company was also a large customer.[424]

World War I lasted much longer than anyone expected or hoped for, and while no one in the Las Animas district relished the ugly conflict, they certainly welcomed what the war did for the mining industry. The prices of and demand for industrial metals remained very high, and the interest in silver was stronger than ever because of its political and economic value among foreign nations. As silver approached $.98 per ounce in early 1918, the legislature decided to lock in the price and use the foreign interest, mostly European, to leverage profits at home and support a subsidy for silver mining. Given that the Western states hosted most of the mining, it comes as no surprise that the movement started with Nevada legislators. In April, the Federal Government formalized the price program as the Pittman Act, which fixed the value of silver at $1.00 per ounce and extended the price to European nations and India.[425]

Silver mining interests gleefully rubbed their hands together because the white metal finally fetched a price not seen since the Sherman Silver Purchase Act of 1890. And, in contrast to the market trends following the silver subsidies of the past, the value of the metal actually continued to climb instead of eroding. The high price came with caveats, however, that presented great challenges to profitability. Because of the war, the prices of everything important to mining such as supplies, equipment, transportation, and smelting fees rose. This translated into higher operating costs. Skilled labor was increasingly difficult to find as fewer young men replaced the old miners who left the workforce. As a result, the existing workers were simply not as productive. To complicate matters, the ore that the workers did bring to daylight continued to decline in value and required mining companies to generate higher tonnages. Many of the companies in the Las Animas District could not, however, because most of the ore bodies, like other areas in Colorado, neared exhaustion after forty years of mining.[426]

Two other trends that developed conspired against the tantalizing, potential profitability promised by the Pittman Act. The first interfered with the transportation of ore, concentrates, and supplies, which tied the hands of the mining industry throughout Colorado. Specifically, the Railroad Administration, a federal entity, took control of all railroads as a wartime mobilization asset and operated them for two years. The administration proved incompetent at managing freight traffic, which reduced service, delayed the movement of materials, and increased freight rates by an appalling twenty percent. Congress authorized payment to railroad companies for maintenance and costs, but the values were usually under-represented, leaving some railroad companies in such a poor financial condition that they closed.[427]

The other trend struck in 1918 and was something that no one could have forecasted or even imagined. In October, the beginning of a long winter, the Spanish Influenza pandemic arrived with force. The flu spread like wildfire through Silverton and some of the large mine boardinghouses. Many individuals were struck low, and the doctors and volunteer nursing committees quarantined and attended to the sick. Most of those who contracted the illness languished for weeks then recovered, but a significant number died, which instilled fear throughout the Animas River drainage.[428]

The environmental and working conditions at the mines greatly influenced who contracted the illness, how fast the flu spread, and who died. The altitude, the extreme cold in poorly heated buildings, and air pollution contributed, and miners faced additional factors that increased their risk. From the moment a miner entered the workplace, he was exposed to a raft of biological and mineralogical respiratory offenses that put his whole system on the defensive. In addition, the underground environment was cold and damp, the work hard, and the commute from the tunnel portal to the safety of the boardinghouse frigid, especially when the miner was saturated with water and sweat. Physically taxed by a combination of these conditions, the miner was predisposed to pathogenic illnesses that were easily transmitted in crowded boardinghouses.

A second wave of flu swept through the Animas River drainage in November, and it was worse than the first. Hundreds fell ill, a high percentage died, and panic set in. Women packed their families, miners left, and mining companies closed either out of sanitary reasons or because attrition reduced their workforces to skeleton crews. The situation grew so severe that the conservative *Engineering & Mining Journal* was moved to state: "Spanish influenza caused more than 130 deaths in Silverton district in the last three weeks. Mines shut down will have difficulty in resuming normal operations owing to labor shortage, many miners having left camp. Epidemic appears under control."[429]

The epidemic, however, was nothing close to being under control. Most of the public halls and buildings became infirmaries and morgues. As the dead accumulated, the plain coffins were exhausted, forcing flu committees to bury the bodies in wooden boxes and even blankets. In January and March of 1919, two more waves of contagion swept through the region, leaving Silverton as an epicenter of despair. Of all Colorado's mountain towns, Silverton suffered the most and, like many flu survivors, the mining industry had a very difficult time recovering.[430]

While the declaration of Armistice in 1918 brought a long-awaited end to the ravages of World War I, it precipitated an irreversible decline of mining in much of Colorado, including the Las Animas District. However, the economic and political trends of 1919 belied the impending doom. As soon as the war was over, European nations began the costly and protracted process of rebuilding both physically and economically, which maintained the high demand for and value of silver and industrial metals. Much to the delight of the greater mining industry, the price of silver crept from $1.04 per ounce in 1918 to as high as $1.11 by the beginning of 1920. With metals values increasing for almost two years after the war's end and production in the Las Animas district for 1920 a record $3,617,000, how could anyone predict an industry-wide collapse across the West? Few in the Las Animas District forecasted the fall, and most pursued business as usual.[431]

Otto Mears, however, was too wise and experienced to blithely assume that mining in the Animas River drainage would continue indefinitely, and during the late 1910s he and his syndicate saw first hand the fundamental reason why in their leased mines. During 1918, the Iowa Mine was one of the best producers in the Las Animas District and the mill shipped around a dozen rail cars of concentrates per month. At first, Slattery managed three shifts of miners drilling and blasting ore around the clock, then the Influenza Epidemic put an end to such operations. The October wave of the disease swept the crew, and Slattery personally nursed the sick in the boardinghouse. When the second wave decimated the crew in November, he closed the mine and had the boardinghouse fumigated. Like most of the region's other mine operators, Slattery had a difficult time finding replacement workers at first then secured a crew by 1919. At that time, Slattery renewed the lease under the Southwestern Mining Company and the Melville Leasing Company and gradually cut the workforce to forty. The reduction was a surface manifestation of a deeper problem, which was that the Iowa group of claims was finally running out of ore and even the syndicate's expert miners were unable to find more. Under Slattery, the mine was one of the Las Animas District's best producers through 1920, and then operations utterly collapsed.[432]

The decline of production at the Silver Lake Mine was even more abrupt and apparent. The Mears syndicate began scaling back operations in 1917 and subleased blocks of ground. By 1918, the S.D. & G. Leasing Company had a mere four miners on the payroll. When the lease ended in 1919, the syndicate made a powerful statement regarding the mine's potential when the members did not renew, heralding an end to the Silver Lake as a significant source of payrock. If the Mears syndicate could not find ore, then payrock almost certainly did not exist. John Giano & Associates assumed the property and maintained operations with a meager crew of three miners and subleased blocks of ground until 1922. By the following year, a handful of independent miners brought the last few of what amounted to hundreds of thousands of tons of ore out of the Stoiber Tunnel.

The syndicate's Mayflower operation regressed in a manner similar to the Iowa. A crew of thirteen miners sent ore down to the Iowa Mill through 1918 and 1919, and they were discharged the following year. The mine remained quiet until 1922, when Slattery, John F. Barnett, and Leonard L. Aiken organized the Mayflower Mining & Milling Company to work the property with a crew of only six workers. The operation only lasted a year.[433]

The Highland Mary followed a like trend as well. Under the Highland Mary Leasing Company, Slattery not only kept the mine and mill producing through 1918, but also developed several veins. He had to suspend operations during the flu epidemic; and when Slattery resumed, he hired only around ten workers and subleased the upper levels to small parties. Slattery found that the mill was not worth operating in light of declining production, shut the facility down during 1920, and did not renew the lease when it expired.[434]

The heavy silence that filled Arrastra and Cunningham gulches when the Iowa and Highland Mary mills stopped brought to attention the fact that the Mears syndicate curtailed then abandoned its most important mining operations. The suspension of the Iowa Mill created a ripple effect because, without it, the independent lessees in Silver Lake Basin and Arrastra Gulch lacked the inexpensive concentration necessary for them to profit from the low-grade ores. As a result, they left one-by-one until the surface plants and boardinghouses, already largely vacated, became empty reminders of glory days gone. One of the reasons for the sudden implosion of large-scale mining was that Otto Mears was an admirable eighty years old and wanted to close out his business affairs. He left the railroads, including the Silverton Northern, in the hands of James Pitcher, and assumed that the rest of the syndicate would take over the mining leases. The members did not, however, because in their thoroughness, the expert miners finally exhausted most of the economical ore, leaving little to warrant renewals of the large-scale leases. A few continued to invest in or lease mines on a small scale, but most of the members turned their attention to other matters.[435]

Many of the residents in the Las Animas District saw the Mears syndicate and its activities as a bellwether for the health of the mining industry, and they did not feel comfortable with the turn of events. The sounds of mining drifting down off Kendall Mountain stopped serenading Silverton even earlier than the collapse of the Mears syndicate. The partnership of Johnson & Anderson, which leased the Aspen Mine from the Mears syndicate, worked through 1918 and probably sent the zinc-rich ore to the Silver Lake Mill for treatment. An end to profitability was at hand, however, and the following year all parties let their leases lapse. With no one interested in the venerable property any longer, the Aspen closed.[436]

The Lackawanna Mine was not far behind. In 1918, the D.L. & W. Mining & Reduction Company finished the tramway and development of the vein then began production. While the mill was under construction, the company felt that it blocked out enough ore to justify leasing the Silver Lake Mill until its own treatment facility was ready. Part of the motivation was that miners struck high-grade ore similar in content to that from the Silver Lake Mine, and the cubic lead crystals made it fantastic in appearance. But the mine was not quite what the company made it out to be. True, the property featured an impressive 5,000 feet of development workings, a 1,400 foot long main tunnel, and an electric hoist over a winze, but the mill apparently remained unfinished. Further, after miners sent 300 to 500 tons of ore to the Silver Lake Mill, little more was forthcoming. Then the compressor house caught fire and burned, and after the company collected insurance money, it rebuilt the structure then dissolved. Fraud? Perhaps. However, the company left the property in a state ready for sale, which the gathering collapse postponed.[437]

Dives Basin became a scene of quiet desolation along with the district's other mines. The passage of the Pittman Act made silver attractive enough to draw several partnerships back up to the North Star Mine and they gleaned low-grade ore over the course of several years. The lessees were limited to the upper stopes because they lacked the capital necessary to work at depth, and after exhausting a rich paystreak in 1921, the lessees found that the remaining low-grade material was no longer worth their trouble. With their departure, the North Star joined the ranks of the district's great mines that were now empty, silent, and dark.[438]

The miners employed at the nearby Shenandoah descended out of Dives Basin on the heels of the North Star lessees. In 1918, Dan McLean's Dives Leasing Company enjoyed great success in both the Shenandoah and Trilby workings and brought hundreds of tons of ore per day out through the Spotted Pup Tunnel. Because the mine was a relative late-comer in the Las Animas District, it was one of the few to possess ore rich enough to pay the cost of packing it down on mules. As one operation after another in the district closed, the Dives Leasing Company assumed the role as the most important producer by 1920, which instilled a sense of pride among the miners. However, after only nine months of operations in 1921, McLean suddenly laid off the workforce of thirty and shut down the mine. Dives Basin experienced the first quiet in decades. In 1923, McLean held enough hope for the mine that he approached Benjovsky's wife Kate and convinced her to sell the claims because he had the most history with the property. McLean then tried resuscitating operations and sent up a paltry five workers who lasted until winter then left.[439]

The Black Prince Mine was one of the few operations that seemed to respond to the high value of silver as expected. J. Robert Crouse and H.A. Tremaine of Chicago felt that the property had immense potential because the vein had never been developed to any meaningful depth. Further, the property already featured a 500 foot tunnel and an excellent surface plant ready for use on the valley floor. In 1920, the investors organized the Crouse-Tremaine Mines Company, purchased several claims from Theodore Grabowski, leased others, and assuming that ore was right around the corner, also leased the Contention tramway and mill.[440]

During the year, the company hired a full crew of workers to effect necessary repairs and began driving the haulageway. The boardinghouse was made weather-tight, a transformer and electrical system were installed, and miners lengthened the main haulageway by hand. Because this was slow, the company secured a duplex air compressor capable of powering five drills, but ran into trouble hauling the heavy machine up to the site. In a moment of creativity, the engineer struck upon an excellent idea that saved considerable backbreaking labor. Specifically, workers graded a platform for an 18 by 50 foot compressor house adjacent to the tramway's lowest point, hung the disassembled machine from the tramway, sent the pieces up, and moved them the short distance over to the compressor house platform. The workers assembled the compressor and motor on their respective foundations then erected a frame building around them.[441]

Durango residents equated prosperity with the noxious fumes that belched out of the Durango Smelter. In 1920, when this photograph was taken, the Durango Smelter continued its elemental role of underwriting the mining industry of the San Juans. Source: Denver Public Library, Western History Collection, X 61434.

Despite his creativity, the company engineer did not excel in compressed air technology, although he was somewhat progressive. Respectful of the danger posed by dynamite, he ordered workers to build an explosives magazine in the mountainside between the tunnel and the boardinghouse, and provided a separate shed for assembling blasting caps and fuse into primers. When the local mine inspector visited, he was horrified by the compressed air system and described it as the worst that he ever saw. The plumbing was poorly assembled, the valves were in awkward locations, and the air receiving tank was upside down. The inspector ordered the engineer to completely rebuild the system.[442]

By the end of 1920, the Black Prince had all the makings of a great operation, which is what the Las Animas District desperately needed to counter the decay of its industry. The staff of the *Silverton Standard* was so impressed with the progress that they claimed: "One of the largest undertakings of 1920 will be ready for production during 1921. The Black Prince Group, under development by the Crouse-Tremaine Mines Company, has been improved with sufficient buildings etc. to enable the management to carry out with the greatest speed the development of the Black Prince and other veins of the group."[443]

By the spring of 1921, miners made the long-awaited breakthrough into the main vein. In driving the haulageway, the engineer followed the proper practice of undercutting the formation at depth so miners could work the ore body from the bottom up. There was one problem, however: there was no ore. The vein was highly mineralized to be sure, but it lacked payrock of economic worth. Horrified after investing thousands of dollars, the company had to suspend operations and lay off the miners. Even though Crouse-Tremaine produced little if any ore, the loss of a promising mine was a severe blow to the psyche of the Las Animas District.[444]

The milling industry, completely dependent on the mines, finally collapsed as company after company went silent. At first, the heavy production of 1918 seemed to assure plenty of business for mine-specific mills and the handful of independent, custom facilities, and survived the slowdown following the 1907 recession. The Silverton railroad hauled so much ore down to Durango that ASARCo decided to expand its smelter. However, by 1919, ASARCo closed the Silver Lake Mill. Peter Orella tried operating the Contention Mill, but he had so much difficulty securing enough ore that he gladly leased the facility to Crouse-Tremaine in 1920. When the lease ended, Orella still could not find enough payrock and let the facility gather dust. At least one sampler may have remained in business in Silverton, but the region's ore treatment industry finally dissipated.[445]

As the Las Animas district's once mighty mining industry crumbled, residents turned to the Little Nation Mine for a ray of optimism and good news. Even though Henry Frecker's stamp mill failed in 1908, investors saw value in the Little Nation Mine because, like the Black Prince, its ore system escaped substantial development and offered potential. When the value of silver soared in 1918, a group of Kansas City investors including E.A. McNeer and H.R. Ennis realized this and leased the property for examination. Unlike the Black Prince, the Tom Trippe Tunnel, which was the lowest, proved that the vein retained value at depth. Convinced that plenty of ore existed, the investors organized the Little Nation Mining Company and conducted further exploration. By 1919, McNeer and Ennis had all the information that they needed and obtained the capital to buy the property and install a surface plant for light production.

The mine still featured the three tunnels as Frecker had left them, and it was probably superintendent J.A. Holman who renamed them for the company. The highest tunnel through which the Little Nation Vein was mined was named the Little Nation, and past operators drove it to a length of 1,000 feet. The mid-level tunnel, named the Transformer, was around 400 feet lower in elevation and 1,500 feet northeast. The Tom Trippe Tunnel, renamed the Royal Charter after the property's most important vein, lay around 200 feet downslope and ended after around 350 feet, where Frecker stopped work. Holman strategically planned to lengthen the Royal Charter Tunnel as a haulageway and, therefore, erected the mine's surface plant there.[446]

The surface plant was relatively simple, but well-engineered. Workers erected a 15 by 36 foot shed-type compressor house adjacent to and west of the tunnel portal, and the building featured two rooms. The eastern room enclosed two compressors, and the western room featured a shop plumbed with compressed air to feed the forge and to power a mechanical drill-steel sharpener. Each compressor operated independently on demand, and together they could run as many as ten small drills. Miners input crude ore from the tunnel into a 12 by 12 foot sorting house that stood on the shoulder of the waste rock dump. They deposited payrock from an ore car into a chute, and the material rolled onto a grizzly made of mine rails. The metalliferous fines dropped between the bars and the cobbles that were too large to pass through rolled down onto the floor of the room where mine workers hand-sorted through the material. They knocked off waste and dropped the recovered ore down through a port in the floor, and both the recovered ore and the fines accumulated in an ore bin below.[447]

By 1920, Holman finished the surface plant and the underground development necessary for production, which included linking the Royal Charter and Transformer tunnels with raises so ore could be sent downward. During the year, a modest crew of seven began sending payrock through the sorting house and freighting it in wagons down to the Silverton Northern Railroad for shipment. Howardsville enjoyed the business provided by the operation because the crew lived in town, the railroad station handled the ore and other freight, and the company and crew patronized local stores.[448]

The income realized from excellent ore probably paid for additional improvements and developments pursued by Holman during 1921. Miners pushed the Royal Charter Tunnel to the length of 1,300 feet to undercut the Royal Charter Vein at great depth and straightened out its crooked portal so the rail line could extend directly over the sorting house. The miners also drove the Transformer Tunnel 700 feet to serve as a mid-level platform for work on the veins. While the rest of the Las Animas District suddenly and unbelievably went into an abrupt decline, the Little Nation operation was only just getting started.[449]

The spike of prosperity fostered by World War I and the drive for normalcy in Europe came to a painful and crashing end in the Animas River drainage shortly after 1920, as it did throughout most of Colorado. The impending collapse struck the Las Animas District with full force as almost the entire hardrock industry failed and mine after mine closed, including long-term producers such as the North

Star, the Aspen, the Shenandoah, and those operated by the Mears syndicate. Conditions within and outside the district, and the greater Animas River drainage for that matter, seemed to conspire against any hope of a meaningful recovery. Within the district, nearly all the economical ore bodies had been discovered, developed, and worked to exhaustion after forty-five years of exploration and mining. With the exception of a few late-comers such as the Little Nation, the district offered little potential for anything new of note. In addition, the disappearance of the custom concentration mills ensured that the small operations had nowhere to make their low-grade ore economical for shipment to the Durango Smelter. Outside the district, as normalcy returned to the United States and Europe, the demand for and value of industrial metals threatened to collapse to their pre-war prices. As if this were not enough, a deep, post-war depression crept over the entire United States, bringing with it economic woes of all types.

While residents of the Animas River drainage faced the collapse on a personal level, outsiders merely had to consider the production figures of San Juan County to see the trouble. In 1921, the county generated a lowly $64,000 in silver, $4,000 in copper, $25,000 in lead, and no zinc, which were tiny fractions of the previous several years. Where the county's miners brought $3,617,000 out of the ground in 1920, they realized only $100,000 in 1921 and slightly double that for the following year. This was a relative paucity even when compared to the Silver Crash of 1893, the worst disaster to date.[450]

The loss of jobs, the ruined economy, and a sense of hopelessness would cast a pall over the region. Nearly half the population left. In 1910, the county was home to around 3,000 individuals, and less than 1,700 stayed behind to make a living as they could. The once-thriving basins that hosted hundreds of miners reverted to wilderness, and Howardsville lost around sixty-five percent of its people. Dozens of abandoned cabins, the idle surface plants originally designed to function for decades, and the dark and empty mines became monuments to the bust. The only sounds that the still tramways and the currentless powerlines made were moans when the wind passed through. With a decrease in business came a reduction in railroad traffic, and James Pitcher decided to close the Silverton Railroad, which served the Red Mountain District. The end seemed near, and the saving grace was the Sunnyside Mine near Eureka and a handful of mining companies that tried profiting from the still high value of silver.[451]

CHAPTER 12

Irrecoverable Decline

IF CONDITIONS WERE NOT BAD ENOUGH during the early 1920s, the value of silver took a turn for the worse. As early as 1920, the Federal Reserve began fussing about the Pittman Act, which created a sense of insecurity in the silver market, but western senators, representatives, and capitalists were unwilling to see the mining industry collapse again. They contested the anti-Pittman sentiments and saved the Act in 1922, which maintained a sense of optimism in the silver mining areas. This kept the Animas River drainage alive, and federal statisticians noted the situation from a broad perspective:

> *The situation in the Colorado metal-mining industry during the first half of 1922 was disappointing, but there was a marked improvement as the year drew to an end, particularly in November, when the prices for lead and zinc warranted hopes of a stable market. There was also an increased interest in investigation of the industry by capitalists. The price of $1 an ounce for silver derived from domestic ores under the Pittman Act was all that kept many Colorado mines in operation in 1922.*[452]

None of this was to last, however, because just as the region seemed to be on the verge of a low-level stability, the Comptroller

General forced the Pittman Act to expire in at the end of 1922. Silver reverted to its former low value of around $.65 per ounce and, like the rest of Colorado, the region's mining industry fell apart. This, coupled with a broad demographic and economic shift from precious metals mining toward finance and business investment, sealed the fate of silver mining in the Las Animas District, as well as Colorado as a whole.[453]

Between 1923 and 1929, Las Animas District residents either left or found alternative sources of income. One source, amusingly described by old-time Ouray resident Roger Henn, was distilling liquor to meet the enormous underground demand fostered by the puritanical Volstead Act, also known as Prohibition. The ethnic Slavs and Italians who originally came to mine drew upon their Old World traditions and contributed to the industry by making wine. Henn noted that Ouray was a natural center for distilling and wine-making because the town was remote and federal agents could enter only by two well-watched routes. If Ouray was a sound location, Silverton was even better and probably conducted as much business.[454]

Not everyone was adept at making liquor; and those rooted in the region who knew nothing other than mining faced a particularly difficult struggle because their skills were specialized and narrow. With no better means of financial support, many of these individuals continued to mine with the lowered expectations of mere subsistence rather than finding bonanzas. They sporadically leased blocks of ground in what had been the richest properties, secreting out small ore shoots and scraping together low-grade ore left by previous outfits. The leases tended to be short-lived, and the subsistence miners moved from claim to claim with frequency. Their production was limited to several tons per day as viable ore was difficult to find. The lessees possessed a set of resources that were opposite to organized mining companies. Specifically, they had plenty of time, very little capital, and simple needs in terms of income, which favored a business strategy that allowed for limited operations. The lessees emphasized hand labor over mechanization, which was slow, consumed time, and curtailed production; but it engendered few overhead expenses and operating costs. In an era of relatively inexpensive and readily available machinery, such methods were tantamount to reversing fifty years of technological progression, but they allowed the subsistence miners to sustain an income.

Principal places of activity,
1922 to 1929. Source: Author.

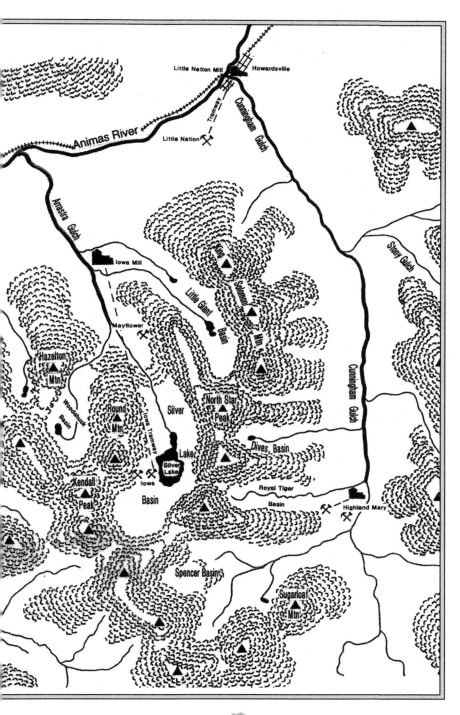

Earnest Biondi and four other miners leased the Royal Tiger Mine in 1923 and worked the mid-level stopes. Another party did likewise at the Silver Lake Mine. In 1925, P. Antonelli leased the Aspen Mine, and Cina & Hinkley continued operations through 1928. Even the Gray Eagle saw some activity. The Iowa Mine was the scene of the most substantial lease operation as the Colorado-Mexico Mining Company employed a crew of seven miners in 1926.[455]

Another strategy was to gather low-grade ore already brought to the surface and abandoned by past mining companies. While few companies willingly discarded profitable ore outright, they did eject material that was uneconomical at the time they mined it. As milling technologies improved and the railroad reduced shipping costs, the uneconomical material became profitable. All a lessee had to do to take advantage of the ore was to sort through waste rock dumps and recover the formerly unwanted payrock. Sorting through waste rock was ideal for impoverished lessees because it was readily at hand and required virtually no capital or equipment except for shovels and screens. The work was not easy, though, because the lessees had to withstand the Las Animas District's winds, storms, and brilliant sun, and, if they wished to work into late fall and early spring, frigid temperatures and snow. During the latter half of the 1920s, enough lessees were willing to brave the elements to constitute a small ore sorting industry that focused on formerly the richest mines.

To the residents of Silverton and Howardsville, every mining operation was dear, no matter how small; and they were relieved to see three ventures of substance materialize in the Last Animas district during the mid-1920s. Joseph E. Dresback organized the first, taking over the Highland Mary Mine when Slattery ended his lease. Dresback was relatively young, but was a tried and true Silvertonian involved in several businesses that helped the Animas River drainage stay afloat during the difficult times.

Dresback was born in Bellevue, Ohio, in 1891 and came with his family to Silverton as a boy. In 1909, he took a job as clerk in the First National Bank of Silverton and then worked as an agent for Otto Mears' Silverton Northern Railroad beginning in 1914. Responding to the call of duty, Dresback joined the army and went to Europe during World War I and returned in 1919 to marry Marie Gregg of Castle Rock. Once back in Silverton, Dresback revived his railroad career and replaced C.W. Montgomery as auditor of Otto Mears' Silverton and the Silverton Northern Railroads in 1920. Four years later, he was appointed manager of the Silverton Northern, which provided the service necessary for the mines around Eureka to survive.[456]

With seven levels, four tunnels, the 6,000 foot long Innis Tunnel, and thousands of feet of other workings, the Highland Mary Mine was not yet truly exhausted, so Dresback assumed. In 1923, he organized the Highland Leasing Company and put a small crew to work bringing low-grade ore out of the old stopes. The challenge to such a property was examining all 18,000 feet of passages for additional ore, which consumed a significant portion of the year. Dresback calculated that miners identified enough new and old ore to justify keeping the surface plant in operation, except for the mill. Production never attained grand proportions in part because the mine was difficult to operate; but around 10 miners kept their jobs through 1927, which was important given the regional depression.[457]

C.H. Smith, J.E. Storey, and F.P. Despain felt the same about the Lackawanna Mine as Dresback did regarding the Highland Mary. The Lackawanna, however, had a checkered history at best, although this did not seem to bother Smith and partners. In 1926, the three investors, most of whom were based in Utah, organized the Lackawanna Mining Company and hired a crew of ten to rehabilitate the surface plant. The compressed air system left by the D.L. & W. Mining & Reduction Company required little work and the tramway was still serviceable, but a new tunnel house was required. The structure that the crew built was an architectural and engineering regression compared to the mining district's boom years, consisting of little more than thin logs nailed to log posts and cross-members.[458]

Superintendent Despain found that the vein was already developed to some degree. He felt that, with a little more work, it would be ready to pay. Instead of mining, however, he waited while the company erected a concentration mill to treat the payrock. Whether the new facility was built from the ground up, or the original structure erected years before had been refitted, is uncertain, but workers hurried to prevent holding up production. When finished in 1928, the mill was a modern affair equipped to treat the Lackawanna's complex ore, or so the company thought. A jaw crusher broke the crude ore to gravel, a rod mill reduced the material to slurry, and flotation machines, filters, and tanks carried out the concentration. Because the mill stood at the base of Kendall Mountain and away from the Silverton Northern Railroad, workers built a double-rope reversible tramway to shuttle concentrates over to a station on the railroad.[459]

The company finished the mill early enough in 1928 to treat a batch of ore; and the facility apparently proved successful. The railroad carried concentrates down to the Durango Smelter but, because the region no longer offered a means to treat zinc ore, the concentrates rich with zinc had to be sent to a facility in Texas. The Lackawanna again filled Silverton with the sounds of mining and reminded despondent residents that the industry was not completely dead.[460]

The Little Nation Mine was one of the few promising operations that not only weathered the collapse of mining in the Las Animas District, but thrived and continued to grow. In 1923, even though the Pittman Act expired and the value of silver collapsed again, the Little Nation Mining Company continued with its grand plans to make the mine a sound producer. The company assembled a construction crew at Howardsville to break ground for a new mill and string an aerial tramway to the mine, all of which required an enormous amount of capital. This caused quite a stir in the region and delighted

The Lackawanna Mill still stands today at the mouth of Swansea Gulch. Source: Author.

Howardsville residents, who were honored that they should have the only mill erected in the Las Animas District in years and cater to the mine's workforce.

Completed within the year, the mill was a stately and well-built structure properly equipped to concentrate the complex Royal Charter ore with efficiency. The building was L-shaped and consisted of three components. The main part, which housed the concentration machinery, was a large and open room 48 by 53 feet in area. The second part was 21 by 36 feet in area and housed a blacksmith and machine shop. The third portion was a tower 15 by 22 feet in area and at least fifty feet high. It served as the tramway's bottom terminal. When tram buckets entered the terminal, workers dumped them into a receiving bin below and a conveyor carried the crude ore to a rod mill that ground the ore to a slurry. After screening, the material passed to four Wilfley tables and a Card table for initial concentration. Flotation cells then provided the final stage of concentration, and workers dried and stored the heavy results for shipment.[461]

The reason why the mill did not feature a jaw crusher for primary reduction like most facilities was that the upper tram terminal at the mine had the apparatus. As at the Unity Tunnel, the crusher reduced the ore to gravel so the carrying capacity of the tram buckets could be maximized. The terminal at the mine was as stout and well-built as the mill and spoke of capital and an expectation of production. The structure was 18 by 51 feet in area, two stories high, and featured a pair of sloped-floor ore bins. Each bin fed payrock into one of the two buckets on the double-rope reversible tram system, which sent the buckets back and forth between the mine and mill.[462]

With a mill now making noise in Howardsville, the tram buckets gliding back and forth, and shifts from the twenty workers coming and going, town residents had the impression that business had returned to normal by the end of 1923. The mill, however, was not recovering the ore's metal content as expected and adjustments were necessary. While the metallurgist puzzled out the problem, manager A.G. Marsh ordered the miners to drive development workings on the Royal Charter Vein. During the winter of 1924, Marsh came to the conclusion that the mill would have to be refitted. The investors, however, would part with no more capital and Marsh had to suspend operations. Howardsville became unsettlingly quiet, and the businesses panged at the loss of the miners when they packed up and left. The promising new venture seemed not so promising after all, which confirmed the growing pessimism in the Animas River drainage.[463]

In 1927, William Way, the Silverton lawyer who leased the Lackawanna, looked at the idle Little Nation from the perspective of experience. He felt that with proper management and close attention to the concentration process, the mine would probably pay. He interested F.J. Bruening and Dan Harroun in a lease, and they provided the capital necessary to resume operations. Howardsville residents tried not to get their hopes up, but they gladly welcomed the eighteen workers that Way hired to bring ore out of the main tunnel. It remains unknown whether Way tried running the mill, but he came to the same conclusion as the Little Nation Company and shut down the mine after a year.[464]

Of all the troubled mining operations in the Las Animas District that struggled through the 1920s, one did live up to its promise.

The Little Nation Mining Company built a tramway from the Little Nation Mine down to a new mill at Howardsville in 1923. The photograph illustrates the upper terminal at the mine. Miners sorted ore in the building at upper right and fed the recovered payrock through a jaw crusher below. The resultant gravel was stored in the large bin at left and loaded into tram buckets that passed underneath. Source: Author.

Experts and mining men with vast experience were convinced that the Las Animas District had little left to offer and that nearly all the significant ore bodies had been discovered and worked to exhaustion. According to Charles A. Chase, this was largely true of the high-grade

The northeast view follows the tramway's fall-line down to the mill at Howardsville. The mill stands at center. Source: Author.

The Little Nation Mill stood on the northwestern outskirts of Howardsville. The Animas River flows through the background. Source: Author.

The Little Nation Mill was a well-built, handsome structure equipped with state-of-the-art flotation. Source: Author.

ore, but the operations of the past barely scratched the surface of what he postulated were vast deposits of low-grade material. Chase, an exacting engineer, had little use for idle speculation and instead based his educated opinions on twenty-five years experience with deep mining in the San Juans.

Chase was born in Hartford, Wisconsin, in 1876 to Emma J. and Albert E. Chase, who almost seemed to impart a genetic predisposition to the mining life. Albert was a mining engineer who brought the family to Georgetown during the 1880s so he could work in the mines. Charles attended high school in Georgetown, went east to Minneapolis for more schooling, and graduated in 1893. He returned to Colorado, studied metallurgy at the University of Colorado, and finished school in 1898. Chase immediately followed his father's footsteps and sought work in the mining industry. He targeted the San Juans because of the vibrancy of the industry there. Arthur Winslow hired him as surveyor and assayer at the Liberty Bell Mine at Telluride, and Chase progressed to general manager. While at the Liberty Bell, Chase was forced to play various roles in the violent strikes that swept Telluride during the late 1890s and early 1900s. Overall, he proved responsive to reasonable union demands such as better living conditions and food, but sided with the company and the mine owners' association in the face of violence. When the industry slowed after the 1907 recession, Chase ventured out to other regions, which broadened his experience. By the 1910s, he managed the Mogul Mining Company of South Dakota and the Primos Exploration Company's operations at Empire, Colorado. Chase, well-known by this time, also became chair of the Colorado chapter of the American Institute of Mining Engineers.[465]

A consulting engineer by the 1920s, Chase secured a group of investors in Kansas City who were interested in starting a mining venture, and he apparently suggested that they focus on the San Juans. Surveying the areas with the greatest cumulative records of production, Chase paid a visit to the Las Animas District in 1925 and conducted a statistical analysis based on historical production figures and probably underground examinations. He came to the interesting conclusion that miners never actually reached the bottom of low-grade ore in the North Star Mine and quit primarily because the cost of production from depth was too great. He also noted how McLean stopped working the Shenandoah and Dives properties before the low-grade ore was gone there, and that miners in the Highland Mary never struck the bottom of its veins. The Mayflower still offered ore, and it appeared that the veins in the other properties mentioned were actually part of a large but disseminated system. Convinced that these mines accessed this grand system from different points, he felt certain that the veins extended deeper than anyone suspected, and still offered low-grade payrock. If they could be mined in economies of scale from a deep haulageway, the veins would provide returns for years.[466]

The more Chase learned and the more he concluded, the greater his excitement became. Chase contacted his Kansas City investors and explained his hypothesis, and found them to be keenly interested. Fortunately for Chase, the investors already had considerable experience with large-scale mining ventures and, in particular, James W. Oldham had organized the Wellington Mines Company which operated one of Breckenridge's largest properties since 1906. Being the pragmatic engineer, Chase recommended that Oldham and associates fund exploratory work deep in the North Star to confirm the continuation of the veins, and if the hypothesis held true, that they acquire the mines previously noted.[467]

While miners were at work in the North Star, Chase drew out a master plan for what was to be a massive mining operation. At the same time, he consulted with O.R. Whitaker, another engineer, to examine the North Star, Shenandoah, and Mayflower, and render his opinion for development. Whitaker echoed Chase's recommendations. Both men felt that the North Star group of claims could only be accessed from underneath and that the Shenandoah was not an economical location for work all year long. The Mayflower was the best location, but the tunnel portal was quite a distance from the other properties. However, if a tunnel could be driven the 5,000 feet necessary to undercut North Star Peak, the Mayflower could serve as the principal entrance, and a tramway could carry ore down to a mill on the river. The only drawback was the cost. Whitaker estimated that driving the Mayflower Tunnel would require eighteen months and a staggering $400,000, which is close to $4 million today. The investors did not flinch and instead moved forward at once. In 1926, they organized the Shenandoah-Dives Leasing Syndicate and authorized Chase to buy the North Star, Shenandoah, Dives, and Mayflower mines.[468]

Besides the location, several other qualities drew Chase to the Mayflower as the haulageway. First, the tunnel already offered a small surface plant that could support underground work from the beginning of operations. Chase, however, saw the need for improvement and hired a crew of miners who built a boardinghouse, a bunkhouse, and a shop. Second, the tunnel already accessed several veins, and one group of miners could bring ore to daylight while another crew drove the main tunnel. Third, the tramway used by the Slattery lease was serviceable and would carry ore down to the idle Iowa Mill. Last and most intriguing, who knew how many veins might be penetrated on the way to the North Star?

Because Oldham and associates were interested in the Mayflower as a long-term operation, Chase had a luxury that few managers enjoyed. Specifically, the investors understood that time and money were required before production could begin, and they granted Chase several years, an eternity in the mining industry. Chase spent 1927 managing an exploration program, where his fifteen mines drove around 2,500 feet of drifts and used diamond drills to bore 327 feet of sample holes.[469]

Like Edward Stoiber, Chase was a highly organized but conservative engineer who felt that it was best to build a gigantic mining operation—one step at a time. This probably filled Oldham and associates with confidence, which Chase only boosted when he announced that, although his miners had thousands of feet yet to go on the main tunnel, he had made arrangements for immediate production and concentration. In 1928, Chase leased the Iowa Mill with several purposes in mind. One was to concentrate the ore brought out of the Mayflower, and the second was to refit the facility as a pilot plant for a massive mill in its planning stages. Chase hired Arthur J. Weinig as metallurgist, and he supervised the concentration of an impressive 100 tons of Mayflower ore per day for a while. Later in the year, Weinig removed some of the old machinery and installed a ball mill for grinding, classifiers for segregation of particles, Wilfley tables and flotation machines for coarse concentration, and filters and thickeners for fine concentration. The new machinery worked properly from the first ton of ore treated.[470]

At the same time, Chase improved the mine's infrastructure in preparation for what he hoped would be production in economies of scale. Miners built a tunnel house that enclosed a shop and a new compressor to compliment the existing unit. They also erected another steam-heated boardinghouse, a warehouse, a snow-shed to the tram terminal, an office, and a rail line capable of accommodating an electric locomotive. Underground, miners were sinking several winzes and used electric hoists to raise skip hoisting vehicles, which, when combined with the equipment on the surface, required an advanced electrical system.[471]

Meanwhile, a portion of the Iowa Mine apparently came with the Iowa lease, and Chase figured that he may as well maximize his assets. He sent a crew of twenty-two miners to glean what ore they could from the old workings. They were not alone. The Colorado-Mexico Mining Company had been leasing the Melville workings since 1926; and, with Chase now operating the mill, the company decided to rehabilitate the tramway and send ore down to the facility.[472]

CHAPTER 13

Hard Times During the Great Depression

IN 1929, THE UNITED STATES ECONOMY destabilized again. Financial experts at first thought that market sectors were merely undergoing short-term adjustments, and as institutions such as banking and stocks continued to slide downward, they revised their opinions and forecasted a soft recession similar in scale with the one of 1907. Between September and November, however, a financial panic toppled the nation into one of its worst economic catastrophes ever, which came to be known as the Great Depression. All aspects of business and commerce imploded, thousands were thrown out of work, capital necessary for industry evaporated, and many goods and services were curtailed at best or became no longer available.

Under President Herbert Hoover, who ironically was a highly renowned mining engineer, the nation's economic climate worsened through the early 1930s and industry, including mining, ground to a halt. It was no wonder that the prices for silver and industrial metals abruptly dropped to values never seen before. During the 1920s, silver slid to around $.60 per ounce following the expiration of the Pittman Act. After the Great Depression struck, however, no one wanted the metal, and as a result it fetched a mere $.29 by 1931. At the same

Principal places of activity,
1929 to 1942. Source: Author.

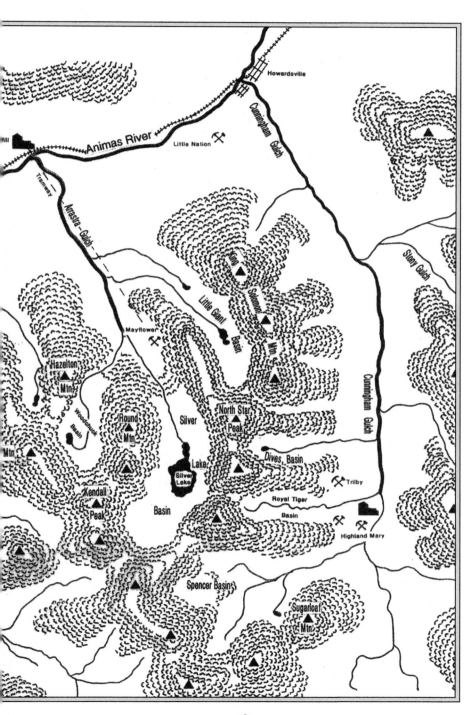

time, copper decreased from more than $.13 to $.11 per pound, lead slumped from at least $.06 to $.05 per pound, and zinc remained unchanged.[473]

The Great Depression was unlike any economic bust that the Animas River drainage had suffered through, and it tried even the most stalwart and resourceful. In such a climate, how could anyone profit from mining, let alone pay for operating costs? Most simply could not. The abrupt halt to mining caused a ripple effect that only worsened the already poor conditions. With mine after mine closing, the freight traffic handled by the railroads plummeted, and as a result, the Silverton Narrow-Gauge reduced service and James Pitcher had no choice but to mothball the Silverton Northern in 1930. Then, the unthinkable happened. ASARCo declared that it was closing the Durango Smelter because the volume of ore and concentrates coming down out of the mountains was insufficient to pay for the operating costs. By 1931, the Animas River drainage was without a smelter, which crushed the little mining that had survived. Mining companies now had to ship their concentrates by rail to distant facilities, which was just too costly.[474]

In the Las Animas District, most of the mining companies and lessees that were active when the depression began tried their best to maintain operations and wait the handful of years that everyone expected a recovery to take. In 1928, before the great crash, E.A. Hiett, president of the Highland Mary Mining & Milling Company, decided that the company would work its own mine and no longer lease the property out. Hiett's workers repaired the surface plant, ensured that the dynamo was generating power, and examined the underground workings to determine the best sources of ore. No sooner did Hiett bring the mine into production than the economy collapsed, forcing him to curtail operations. Hiett maintained a small crew through 1930, and when the depression worsened, he found that the company could no longer pay its bills and the payroll. He reluctantly let the miners go and suspended operations.[475]

In 1929, William Way and partners decided they would reopen the Little Nation Mine and try again. Way hired a small crew of miners who began production, and when the depression descended on the region, he attempted to continue on the assumption that the economy would improve. In 1930, Way even invested capital in the

By the early 1930s, the dilapidated Highland Mary Mill symbolized the general state of the Las Animas Mining District at the beginning of the Great Depression. The Gold Tunnel & Railway Company built the mill in 1902, Jack Slattery sent thousands of tons of ore through the facility during World War I, then the mill stood largely idle. The partially collapsed stone building was the original compressor house built in 1875. The workers at the lower right were employed by the Highland Mary Mining & Milling Company, which struggled during the late 1920s and closed the mine in 1930. Source: Denver Public Library, Western History Collection, X 62206.

mine's surface plant and improved the electrical system. However, when conditions worsened the following year, Way scaled back operations and focused on the highest grades of ore. At the same time, the Colorado-Mexico Mining Company struggled at the Iowa Mine, and the company was kept afloat, only because Charles Chase provided concentration at the Iowa Mill. As the depression showed no signs of abating and the value of silver slid, both outfits were unable to maintain their profitless operations and closed. Silver Lake Basin became still for the first time since the early 1880s, and chipmunks and marmots were the only signs of life there.[476]

Located high on the east side of Arrastra Gulch, the Mayflower Mine was yet another highly advanced and successful operation built in impossible conditions. By 1929, engineer Charles A. Chase had the mine in production through a tunnel that undercut the mountain above. The prominent building featured machine and blacksmith shops on the lower floors and living quarters above. To its left stands the mine's tunnel house, and below is the upper terminal for the Mayflower Tramway. Source: Denver Public Library, Western History Collection, X 62245.

The north view depicts how tightly the Mayflower Mine's surface plant clung to the mountainside. The large building was a combination shop and boardinghouse, and the tramway is to the left. A straight line for the tramway can be seen extending down through the forest to the Mayflower Mill on the Animas River. Source: Denver Public Library, Western History Collection, X 62244.

Under the management of Charles Chase, the Shenandoah-Dives Mining Company was the sole outfit in the Las Animas District capable of weathering the Great Depression. Prior to the crash, Chase contracted with Stearns-Roger to build a mill that rivaled Edward Stoiber's Silver Lake facility in size and capacity. He also hired engineer Frederick C. Carstarphen to design a tramway, and workers broke ground for both early in the year. The mill went up across the river from the Silver Lake facility and featured a flow path for ore similar to the pilot plant installed at the Iowa Mill.[477]

The tramway was a unique affair that drew the attention of the greater mining industry, which recognized it as a Carstarphen Tramway. In terms of how workers filled and emptied the tram buckets, Carstarphen's system was like the Bleichert tramways that proliferated throughout the San Juans. What made the Carstarphen system different, however, were the set of towers and the means of powering the traction cable. To save construction costs, minimize maintenance, and increase longevity, Carstarphen erected eleven steel towers instead of more numerous timber structures, which made the system rather lofty. In the upper terminal, the traction cable did not wrap around a giant sheave wheel like Bleichert tramways and, instead, made several ninety-degree bends around small pulleys powered by two motors. Approximately two miles in length, the Carstarphen Tramway was the longest operating system in the San Juans at the time, and it tugged buckets around the circuit in only forty-five minutes.[478]

When the Great Depression struck, the mill and tramway were unfinished, leaving Oldham and associates in a difficult position. Chase required more capital and time before he could produce ore in the economies of scale necessary to offset the declining value of silver. If Oldham and associates balked, they stood to lose all the work and money invested up to that point, as well as future profits. Oldham and associates gritted their teeth, provided the funds, and waited for Chase to bring his master plan to completion.

The last tasks that Chase had to attend to were a few more improvements to the mine. The traditional transportation system of single miners pushing individual cars of ore out of the mine was wholly inadequate for the level of production that the economic conditions required. Even trains of cars pulled by mules were insufficient, and Chase instead wanted nothing less than a tiny railroad. During the year, he had miners install what amounted to narrow-gauge track in the tunnel and feeder drifts for electric locomotives. Chase also sought the efficiency of crushing the ore before workers loaded it into tram buckets, as the operators of the Unity Tunnel and Little Nation Mine had done. Chase went one step farther, however, and not only had the crushing done underground, but also installed the first two stages ordinarily carried out at the mill. Miners dumped ore into the top of an old stope, it passed through a Telesmith rotary crusher for the first stage, and went through a Symons cone crusher for the second stage. By crushing the payrock in this way, the ore arrived at the Mayflower Mill already pulverized for final reduction. The only drawback was servicing the machines, which had to be done often. Machinist Louis Wyman recalls how the entire shop crew had to dismantle the heavy parts, reline the crushing plates, and replace the bearings.[479]

Because the Mayflower's workings were so vast, the company found that it was most efficient to establish stations underground for sharpening the dozens of drill-steels that miners dulled on a daily basis. In this 1930s photograph, a shop worker is using a compressed air-powered sharpening machine to process the dull steels, which are stacked at lower right. Source: Denver Public Library, Western History Collection, X 62232.

In 1930, Chase was finally ready to operate the mine and mill as a single ore production entity. A crew of at least fifty miners generated hundreds of tons of ore per day and another thirty-five workers provided support services and ran the mill. The road to profitability was a rocky one because many variables in the original calculations that Chase derived in 1925 had changed. On one hand, technology and improved methods permitted the average miner to generate several tons of ore per shift, which was a far cry from the single ton of years past. The ore trains, the tramway, and the crushing system all

The perspective provided by this southeast view taken during the late fall or early spring speaks volumes. The large structure at the left is the Mayflower Mill, also known as the Shenandoah-Dives Mill, and it was completed in 1930. A tramway ascended to the Mayflower Mine, which is buried in the snow in the background on the left side of Arrastra Gulch. In addition to treating Mayflower ore, the mill directly supported the local mining industry by accepting custom orders. The Silver Lake Mill, which played a similar role twenty years prior, stands abandoned at far right. The Silver Lake Tramway ascended from the mill through Arrastra Gulch and up and over the ice-bound headwall. The floor of the gulch was where mining began in 1860. Source: Denver Public Library, Western History Collection, X 61018.

sent massive volumes of payrock to a mill capable of treating up to 750 tons per day. However, the value of silver was half the price that Chase used for his 1925 calculations.[480]

Like the Stoibers, Chase paid close attention to all operating costs and squeezed efficiency at every turn. He personally inspected the mine and mill and constantly tried to improve operations. During one particular visit to the machine shop at the mill, Chase discovered a program where the workers used their time for matters that had little to do with the company. Specifically, the miners would often leave broken domestic items in the shop for the workers to repair when the opportunity arose. Over time, this snowballed into the sudden appearance of items such bicycles and wagons with notes and instructions written by wives and children. On one of his brisk trips through the mill, Chase happened upon shop worker Louis Wyman who was involved in repairing a leg brace for a handicapped boy. Wyman looked up to discover his terse audience. Wyman was unsure what Chase's reaction would be, but instead of firing Wyman, Chase congratulated him on such an excellent and efficient use of time. Chase obviously understood that the Mayflower Mine was more than just profits and also served as a major institution for the community.[481]

In 1932, Franklin Delano Roosevelt was elected President of the United States and immediately began developing a variety of programs to revive the nation's dismal economy. A year later, Roosevelt and advisors devised a clever program intended to simultaneously devalue the dollar while reviving metals mining on a broad scale. As part of the plan, the dollar was taken off the gold standard, and the Federal Reserve bought gold at inflated prices. The plan worked well and stimulated gold mining as expected, proven by an increase in the volume of gold that flowed into the treasury. In 1934, satisfied with the test, Roosevelt signed into law the Gold Reserve and Silver Purchase Acts in hopes that they would continue to resuscitate mining. The Gold Reserve Act raised the minimum price of gold from around $20.67 to $35.00 per ounce, and the Silver Purchase Act raised the value of silver from around $.48 to $.70 per ounce.[482]

Roosevelt's plan, combined with widespread destitution, lack of employment, and government programs, spelled a Depression-era revival for mining across the West. In general, because mineral resources offered some semblance of income, experienced miners returned to properties that were known to still possess ore, while inexperienced laborers formed a workforce necessary for operations. Adding to the growing interest in the return to the mines, advances in milling technologies rendered the production of previously uneconomical ores profitable. Overall, the revival was minor compared to mining during decades past, but the West, including Colorado, witnessed a return to the old mining districts on a scale not seen since World War I.

The nationwide movement, however, passed by the Las Animas District. The abandoned mines that had been the most productive were almost certainly examined for their potential, but few individuals with resources for meaningful development took any interest. Between 1933 and 1936, the district featured only three or four operations of note, and the Shenandoah-Dives Company was the only reliable operation. Gold became the metal of primary interest because of its relatively high value, especially compared to previous years. Because of this, some of the older miners delved deep into their memories to secret out likely sources of gold in the district. A few remembered that the Silver Lake Mill specialized in separating the gold content of ore and, in 1934, closely scratched around in search of leftover concentrates and tailings. The following year, others returned to the impoverished gold placers around Eureka and in Cunningham and Arrastra Gulches, and enough gold was gleaned to make the hard and chilly work worthwhile.[483]

The increased value of gold sparked groups of individuals into remembering the low-grade gold ore left in two hardrock mines, which became several of the Las Animas District's viable Depression-era operations. In 1933, F.R. Steelsmith and other investors organized the San Juan Mining Company to buy and operate the Mabel Mine, whose gold ore had been forgotten since around 1890. The free gold was gone, but with proper concentration, the complex material that the vein still offered could be made to pay.

Once the company had a plan, Steelsmith hired N.W. Davis as manager and sent a crew up to the property with mules that dragged in the components for a compact but highly functional surface plant. A sawmill was one of the first facilities that the workers installed, because it would turn out lumber for the rest of the mine. The crew erected a small mill, an assay shop, and a 16 by 32 foot boardinghouse set on a frame of raw logs. The mill was quite primitive and was no more than a 20 by 36 foot shed with an earthen floor; and the workers carefully arranged machinery of elfin scale. The equipment had to be small so mules could carry it through the deep forest. A tiny Blake crusher elevated on a timber frame reduced crude ore to gravel, a Chilean mill ground the material to slurry, the smallest model Wilfley table concentrated the material, and an odd amalgamating riffle bowl recovered the gold. Originally, a single-cylinder gasoline engine powered the facility, but the company replaced it with a superior six-cylinder utility engine.[484]

The mine's most important support facilities were squeezed into the already compressed mill building. A basic blacksmith shop was located in one corner and a V-cylinder compressor and drive engine stood in the other. Of note, machinery makers had just introduced V-cylinder compressors to the mining industry specifically for mining operations such as Mabel. Light and highly efficient, these compressors allowed miners working at remote properties to enjoy the luxury of rockdrills, where they would have drilled by hand otherwise. Of course, the San Juan Mining Company made great use of salvaged materials and equipment to save capital, like many Depression-era operations.[485]

During the year, J.B. Tusant replaced Davis as manager, and he put the crew of miners to work driving development workings. The operation was apparently seasonal because the mine was too deep in the forest for easy access when the snow piled high. In 1935, Tusant began production at last, and the little mill was able to recover gold—which relieved the miners because this meant that the operation would continue and keep them employed. By staying small and simple, the Mabel remained one of the few profitable mines that helped carry the Las Animas District through the Depression.[486]

Around the same time that workers prepared the Mabel for production, C. Lorimer Colburn had similar thoughts for the Trilby Mine. Dan McLean was the last to work the property, but he accessed the claims through the Spotted Pup Tunnel at the Shenandoah, leaving the Trilby Tunnel abandoned since around 1917. Colburn understood that some of the veins deep in the Trilby ground offered enough gold to support a limited operation, but he had to be careful not to stray into the adjoining claims purchased by Charles Chase. Colburn was a trained engineer who spent much of the 1910s working for the Colorado Bureau of Mines. In 1934, he was back in private industry as president of the Highland Mary Mining & Milling Company.[487]

Colburn sent S. Lawrence Martin and a small workforce up to the Trilby to begin rehabilitating the infrastructure for mining. They started with the buildings and moved underground; and, as the miners were almost ready to begin production, the company underwent a shift that changed the operation. In 1936, Joseph M. Bradley replaced Colburn as president and apparently convinced the rest of the company's investors to spend the money necessary to reopen the Highland Mary for production of substance. Colburn's skills ensured that he would retain a position with the company as engineer.[488]

Spend money the company did. Bradley hired a large crew who rehabilitated the surface plant, the upper workings, and portions of the lengthy and wandering Innis Tunnel. The company paid for a new air compressor, and some of the workers assembled a main up to the Trilby Tunnel so miners could drill and blast the ore that Colburn identified there. By 1939, Bradley brought the Highland Mary back into production and trucked the ore to the Mayflower Mill for concentration.[489]

As the company's situation improved and operations were headed in the direction of profits, Bradley convinced the directors to put up more capital. Bradley wanted a mill and direct access to the underground workings that offered the best ore, and began work on both in 1940. He had a crew of workers refit the existing mill with modern equipment, and the metallurgist proved his expertise by designing a facility that successfully recovered metals from the start. Bradley also had teams of miners bore a new tunnel westerly into Level No.3, which they previously accessed only through internal winzes and raises. Known as the Bradley Tunnel, workers located the new entry in an avalanche free area, and it became the hub of production at the Highland Mary. To accommodate this, the crew built a surface plant that included a shop, a boardinghouse, a storehouse, and barn for the draft animals used to pull trains of cars out of the tunnel. In an effort to save capital, some of the buildings were moved from the Mountaineer Tunnel, and a new tramway from the Bradley Tunnel down to the mill was assembled with materials salvaged from the old system.[490]

By the end of 1940, ore started flowing out of the Bradley Tunnel down to the mill. The company, which no longer contracted with Shenandoah-Dives, shipped its own concentrates by rail to a smelter in Leadville, and enjoyed electricity generated by the old hydropower dynamos. Thanks to Bradley and his fellow investors, the Highland Mary became a serious contributor to the Las Animas District, second only to the Shenandoah-Dives Company.

Charles Chase continued to expand operations at the Mayflower Mine during the late 1930s, and the operation became almost as extensive as Edward Stoiber's Silver Lake Mine had been, only in an inverse sense. In terms of surface facilities, few mines including the Mayflower were able to rival the old Silver Lake. But in terms of the sophistication and breadth of its underground workings, the Mayflower was one of the most significant. Chase's miners made the planned connections with the North Star workings and probably the Shenandoah as well, and drove thousands of feet of development passages. Locomotives pulled trains of cars through the mine, and the underground crushing station constantly ground ore to gravel.

Chase was heralded as nothing less than an expert as his miners proved time and again that the veins under Little Giant Basin featured more low-grade ore deeper than anyone suspected. Chase felt that the Stoiber brothers' Unity Tunnel proved the same phenomenon under Silver Lake Basin, and he was ready to test his hypothesis there by the late 1930s. In 1937 or 1938, Chase commissioned the Silver Lake Cross Cut, which was a passage 8 by 8 feet in-the-clear driven southwest toward the deepest workings in the Silver Lake Mine. Using a jumbo rig with four automatic drills, miners bored the crosscut around the clock and neared the Silver Lake Vein. This was the first of several ore formations that drew Chase's interest, but then trouble swept the Shenandoah-Dives Company.[491]

Harkening back to past decades, Chase wanted concessions from the workforce that the miners and mill workers were unwilling to concede. Both parties came to a stalemate in 1939, and the workers, who were thoroughly unionized, threatened to strike. This would have been disastrous to both sides because the Shenandoah-Dives Company was one of the most important economic contributors in the Animas River drainage. Recalcitrant, Chase figured that the threats of a strike were idle at best, and that such an action would

be short-lived because the miners had no other hope of employment. Unlike labor conflicts of the past, which were settled before
real conflict developed, the entire workforce struck in June and
completely shut the entire mine down. Although unintentional, the
action caused casualties in the form of unassociated companies that
relied on the Mayflower Mill for custom concentration. Residents in
Silverton became polarized; but because the town was built on labor,
and the miners and their sympathizers made up a major share of
the population, the strike continued through the summer. Backed by
investors with deep pockets, Chase was able to wait out the workers
who were fearful of losing their jobs, which was a serious matter in
the climate of the Great Depression. By the end of summer, the workers grew tired of reduced union compensation and voted to return
to work with no concessions. The union flexed it muscle and came
up short, and Chase was now free to resume production on a greater
scale then ever.[492]

By 1940, Chase's miners finally reached the Silver Lake Vein
after driving thousands of feet. When they made contact, samples
were collected for assay. Chase eagerly awaited the results and was
elated to find that the vein not only featured ore as he surmised, but
also some material higher in grade than expected. Since Chase had a
lease agreement with ASARCo, which still owned the ground, Chase
was more than ready to begin production in hopes of paying for the
exorbitant costs of driving the crosscut. When ASARCo realized just
how much ore came out, the company became keenly interested in
mining its own property. Adept at business as well as mining, Chase
secured a reverse lease arrangement where ASARCo paid him to use
the Mayflower as a point of access for the Silver Lake ground. The
deal was a good one for Shenandoah-Dives. ASARCo provided royal-
ties, maintained the crosscut, drove additional development workings, and assumed the financial risks should the Silver Lake and
adjacent veins not pan out as hoped. Further, the contract lasted for
eight years. Ironically, the Silver Lake Mine was technically active and
part of a massive operation again; only this time miners worked it
from the inside out.[493]

Despite hosting two significant mining operations, conditions
in the Las Animas District continued to decline during the late 1930s,
and the district needed much more than the Highland Mary and the

By the 1920s, tractors grew popular for hauling ore because they could function in most conditions. This contributed to the demise of the Silverton Northern Railroad. Source: Colorado Historical Society, CHS C-Silverton.

Shenandoah-Dives operations to maintain stability. At first, the situation brightened significantly because the Sunnyside Mine reopened in 1937, and James Pitcher felt justified in firing up the Silverton Northern locomotives and reinstituting limited traffic. The Silverton Northern's mixed trains began chuffing along the north side of the Las Animas District and through Howardsville on their way to the Sunnyside, near Eureka. For the Las Animas District, the service was more symbolic than practical, although the rail service certainly lowered the costs of shipping goods and especially ore to the Mayflower Mill for custom treatment. However, when Pitcher closed the railroad the first time in 1930, he inadvertently created conditions for competition that became too powerful to overcome. Specifically, mining companies began using trucks and Caterpillar tractors to haul ore, and the companies were unwilling to junk the machines just because the railroad resumed business. As a result, when the Sunnyside Mine closed in 1938, so did the Silverton Northern.[494]

The permanent loss of the railroad was not the only or most important sign that the Great Depression was exacting a considerable toll on the region. During the decade, around twenty-five percent of

San Juan County's population left, mostly from the small towns and hamlets directly dependent on nearby mines. In 1930 (which was a less than stellar year) around 1,900 people called the county home. By 1940, 1,400 remained, mostly in Silverton. Howardsville in particular was nearly abandoned, and the Postal Service revoked the post office in 1939. A mill was built for the Pride of the West Mine at Howardsville in the same year, but the workforce was not enough to prevent the Postal Service from its decision. At the same time, ASARCo patiently waited for ten years for mining to resume; and when the volume of ore and concentrates did not increase as everyone had hoped, the company voiced its lack of confidence in the San Juans during 1941 and dismantled the Durango Smelter. The Animas River drainage had suffered a mortal blow, which was purely psychological because the smelter had been cold and idle for years.[495]

CHAPTER 14

An End to Mining

DURING THE EARLY 1940s, a collision of domestic and international events created a social and economic environment that would grant the mining companies of the Las Animas District one last lease on life. Simultaneously, the world began to slip into a state of war while the United States showed signs of a long-awaited economic recovery. The improving economy coupled with Europe's mobilizing for yet another sweeping conflict fostered a demand for and value of industrial metals and other minerals on a scale not seen in decades. Given the potential for profits, general interest in mining grew until the fateful year of 1941, when the United States was drawn into World War II. Under President Roosevelt, the Federal Government initiated a series of programs to organize and administer to economic, material, and labor resources as part of the war mobilization effort. With domestic mineral and metal resources suddenly of supreme importance, the government naturally passed several pieces of legislation that emphasized mining.

War Production Board Ruling L-208 was among that legislation and, much to the dismay of Depression-era mine owners across the West, it mandated the suspension of gold mining by October of 1942 on grounds that it did not contribute to the war effort. Another important piece of legislation addressed the values of those metals sanctioned by the government. When the United States entered the war, the value of industrial metals and silver began to rise to record levels, much to the delight of the greater mining industry. However, given the penchant of mining companies to maximize income, the War Production Board placed price caps on the metals to prevent enervating profiteering. The last significant program was a policy where the Reconstruction Finance Corporation and the Smaller War Plants Corporation, which were federal agencies, provided low cost loans to mining companies willing to reopen idle mines and prospect for new metal deposits.[496]

The three rulings had various impacts on the Las Animas District, which were not necessarily beneficial. Ruling L-208 outlawed mining for gold, but because the Las Animas District's ores consisted mostly of silver and industrial metals, the direct impact was minimal. However, the ruling ensured that no one would be prospecting for gold. The low-cost loan program also had little impact, which is curious. Few if any companies used the program to reopen the various mines known to possess low-grade ore, such as the Lackawanna and Iowa, suggesting that the ore was so impoverished that investors knew mining would be profitless. The price caps had the greatest effect on the District, and actually discouraged mining because they took away the financial incentive to produce ore. As a result, World War II was not a time of recovery for the District, as it was for other mining regions in Colorado, and operations continued largely as they did during the Great Depression.

Charles Chase ran the Mayflower Mine like the ore factory it was. Most of the miners filled specialized positions and, in concert, brought hundreds of tons of ore out of the ground per day. Teams of miners also participated in a massive campaign to find new veins, develop the known formations, and riddle the mountains with thousands of feet of workings and diamond drill holes. Joseph Bradley pursued a similar course at the Highland Mary, only on a smaller scale. It seems interesting that Edward Innis squandered a fortune on a property that ultimately yielded over $2,000,000 to various operators who embraced whatever type of ore they encountered. In 1942, the Mermac Mining Company may have been one of the few outfits to take advantage of the low-cost loan program and reopened the Little Nation Mine. The operation, however, was short-lived.

CHAPTER 14: *An End to Mining*

The end of World War II marked a major turning point in the United States. As if by magic, the nation entered the war in a state of depression and emerged into a period of almost unrivaled prosperity. The economy soared as soldiers returning home, and persons who weathered the Great Depression, unleashed their hunger for the goods and services from which they had refrained for years. This consumerism, world-wide post-war rebuilding, and a gathering cold war with the Soviet Union fostered a demand for industrial metals on a huge scale. In theory, this should have stimulated mining, but the demand and value were only several variables in a very complex equation of incentives and disincentives.

The increase in the value of and demand for metals was certainly an incentive. While the prices for gold and silver changed little, copper almost doubled from a wartime $.11 to $.21 per pound, and lead and zinc more than doubled from around $.06 to $.13 per pound. Complimenting this, improvements in both mining and milling technology greatly reduced the cost of producing and treating ore. Taking inflation into account, the yield per ton of ore would have been at an all-time high in the Las Animas District if the region only had a local smelter, which it did not.[497]

The disincentives for mining were many, and they seemed to outweigh the incentives in the Las Animas District. In terms of economics, the values of silver and gold remained numerically static and actually declined slightly because of inflation. In 1947, foreign nations successfully lobbied the Federal Government to reduce the tariffs on their industrial metals, which were completely repealed in 1950. Eight years later, the Paley Commission actively fostered mining overseas in hopes that countries with strong economic ties to the United States would not ally with the Soviet Union. While this may have been one result of the above programs, so was the demise of mining in the West, which had an increasingly difficult time competing.[498]

Another disincentive was the dwindling labor pool. The youth of the rural West were not interested in laboring underground, and the potential for and intrigue of mineral treasure was simply not enough to command their interest. As a result, as they left, the older miners had difficulty finding skilled and dedicated individuals interested in carrying on the tradition of hardrock mining. The greatest problem, however, was the cliché but unarguable fact that the veins in the Las

Animas District, as elsewhere in Colorado, were bereft not only of high- and medium-grade ore, but also of nearly everything else.

Cumulatively, these factors were why the sun finally set on mining of significance in the Las Animas District during the 1950s. Joseph Bradley closed the Highland Mary in 1951 and Charles Chase suspended operations at the Mayflower two years later. It probably pained Chase to see a wave of regional mines dependent on the mill for custom concentration close as a result, but he had no choice. The Mermac Mining Company, which operated with great success since 1947, closed in 1954 after a last-ditch exploration campaign found nothing.[499]

The mining industry, however, did not disappear overnight and instead gradually dissipated in importance and activity. As long as miners from the older generations were able to perambulate, the Las Animas District would continue to see at least some activity. In 1957, the Marcy-Shenandoah Corporation reopened the Mayflower Mill, which fostered a short revival among independent operators, and the company reorganized itself as Standard Metals. The new outfit carried on hardrock mining at the Mayflower Mine through 1963 and at other mines into the 1970s. The Kendall Columbine Mining Company worked the old Titusville from 1964 through 1966, mostly sorting the waste rock dump and conducting underground exploration. The Osceola Mine, one of the district's late bloomers, saw limited but continuous production from 1946 through 1971; and, operations were so successful at the beginning that O.L. Larson & Associates leased the Lackawanna Mill for concentration. Ironically, the Little Giant Mine, the first hardrock enterprise in the Las Animas District, was also one of the last. From 1974 until 1976, James P. Sullivan scratched around the old property in search of something missed during the past century of examination. The Osceola saw the last activity of note in the Las Animas District when the Maverick Mining Company conducted exploration, then boarded the tunnel portal permanently in 1981, ending 140 long years of mining.[500]

Given the rich history of the San Juan Mountains and its mining fiefdoms, it seems difficult to assess whether the Las Animas District was the most important or the best, but it certainly played a pivotal role. James Baker's placer discoveries drew the first serious prospectors to the mountains; and, while the minor excitement was a bust,

By 1941, the once-costly Silver Lake Mill was already in an advanced state of decay. The mill represents the passing of an era, a culture, and an industry that will never be equaled. Source: Denver Public Library, Western History Collection, X 63057.

these adventurous wealth-seekers brought out the first gold along with descriptions of the interior of the mysterious high country. The Las Animas District became the cradle of hardrock mining in the San Juans with the development of the Little Giant Mine and Mill, and the first tramway in southwestern Colorado linked these two components. Also, in conjunction with the Little Giant and the small wave of prospecting that followed, the Las Animas District hosted the first settlers in the deep mountains. Silverton, technically located at the district's northwest corner, was the site of the first smelter in the San Juans, built in part because of the Las Animas mines and those in adjacent districts. When Edward Innis introduced rockdrills to his Highland Mary Mine in 1876, he was among the earliest in the San Juans and Colorado to employ this revolutionary technology. These machines, which sped the process of drilling and blasting, became popular twenty years later.

In addition to claiming many firsts, the Las Animas District holds a position of importance through its contributions to mining, regional economies and settlement, and the adaptation of life and heavy industry to an otherworldly environment. Some of the mines were proving grounds for the development of technologies that benefited the mining industry and modern society. Some of the longest tramways constructed served the Silver Lake and Iowa mines, and one of the best-designed ascended to the Mayflower Mine. The Stoiber brothers were principal among a handful of pioneers who developed the practice of mining and milling low-grade ores in economies of scale. Only by adopting this strategy was the greater mining industry able to rise out of the depths of the deep depression that followed the Silver Crash of 1893. As a facet of this, the Stoiber brothers' Silver Lake, Iowa, and Royal Tiger mines became examples of how to coordinate dozens of miles of underground workings, enough employees to populate a small town, and a massive infrastructure. By electrifying these mines at an early date, Edward Stoiber directly contributed to the science and engineering of AC electricity, which modern society enjoys today.

The Las Animas District was the scene of one of the kookiest mining operations in Colorado. Edward Innis paid a seeress a small fortune to tell him weekly and almost daily how to run the Highland Mary Mine and drive a meandering and confusing set of tunnels in search of a lake of gold. Connected with this property was the equally ill-conceived Gold Tunnel & Railway Company, which proposed driving a tunnel four miles long, from one side of the Las Animas District to the other!

Today, the Las Animas District possesses an exceptionally rich legacy left by an exciting history that was a microcosm of mining in the Colorado mountains. Dozens of prominent historic sites remain from the District's principal mining and milling operations, and more than one-hundred smaller ones are left from minor mines and prospects. Due to a variety of forces, the iconic buildings, engineering structures, and even pieces of machinery have disappeared. During World War II, the Las Animas District became a major source of iron in the form of abandoned machinery and equipment, which was salvaged during scrap drives. Waldheim was razed for its bricks in 1945, the Highland Mary Mill burned in 1955, and the Mayflower

Mine's surface plant suffered a like fate in the early 1970s. Avalanches smashed the buildings at the Royal Tiger, Iowa, Shenandoah, Big Giant, and Buckeye mines, while natural decay took most of the rest.

Reduced to archaeological resources, the mines and prospects of the Las Animas District still offer an incredible ambiance and a glimpse into the past for those willing to take the time and read the ruins. The archaeological evidence, as it is technically known, can tell us how miners adapted to extreme winters, what their living and working conditions were like, how engineers built functional mines and mills in the impossible wilderness, and of what these operations consisted. When reconstructed in the mind's eye, the Las Animas District was a sight to behold.

That nothing lasts forever is a cliché statement; and because mining in particular is transient, few individuals and companies intended for any of their construction to survive more than several decades. Yet, a small and powerful group of dedicated preservationists are at work in San Juan County, including the Las Animas District, to save as many historic resources as possible. They understand that the old mines and mills, even in states of archaeological ruin, are vital touchstones of an important movement in our history, one that will never be equaled or repeated. Because of the hard work of stewards of history like Bev Rich, agencies like the Bureau of Land Management, organizations like the San Juan County Historical Society, and those who tread lightly among the ruins, future generations will marvel at the legacy of the Las Animas Mining District.

BIBLIOGRAPHY

Regional History

Bauer, William H., Ozment, James L., Willard, John H., *Colorado Post Offices: 1859-1989,* The Colorado Railroad Museum, Golden, CO, 1990.

Blair, Rob, *The Western San Juan Mountains: Their Geology, Ecology, and Human History,* University Press of Colorado, Niwot, CO, 1996.

Brown, Robert L., *An Empire of Silver,* Sundance Publications, Denver, CO, 1984.

Burbank, W.S.; Eckel, E.B.; and Varnes, D.J., "The San Juan Region" *Mineral Resources of Colorado,* State of Colorado Mineral Resources Board, Denver, CO, 1947.

Collins, George E., "Metal Mining in Colorado During 1905," *Engineering & Mining Journal,* 1/6/06, p32.

Collins, George E., "Mining in the United States in 1906: Colorado" *Engineering & Mining Journal,* 1/5/07, p29.

Collins, George E. "Mining in the United States in 1907: Colorado" *Engineering & Mining Journal,* 1/4/08, p38.

Collins, George E., "Mining in the United States During 1908: Colorado," *Engineering & Mining Journal,* 1/9/09, p104-105.

Collins, George E., "Mining in the United States During 1909: Colorado," *Engineering & Mining Journal,* 1/8/10, p97-98.

Collins, George E., "Metal Mining in Colorado in 1913," *Engineering & Mining Journal,* 1/10/14, p116-117.

Collins, George E., "Mining in Colorado in 1917," *Engineering & Mining Journal,* 1/19/18, p143.

Collins, George E., "Mining in Colorado in 1918," *Engineering & Mining Journal,* 1/18/19, p152.

Collins, George E., "Mining in Colorado in 1919," *Engineering & Mining Journal,* 1/17/20, p161.

Comstock, Theodore, "The Metallurgy of the San Juan County Ores," *Engineering and Mining Journal,* 1/31/85, p69.

BIBLIOGRAPHY

Comstock, Theodore, "The Metallurgy of the San Juan County Ores," *Engineering and Mining Journal*, 2/21/85, p120.

Denver Post, Denver, CO, various articles.

Denver Republican, Denver, CO, various articles.

Denver Times, Denver, CO, various articles.

Denver Tribune, Denver, CO, various articles.

Durango Herald Democrat, Durango, CO, various articles.

"Editorial Correspondence: Denver," *Engineering & Mining Journal*, 6/4/10, p1191.

"Editorial Correspondence," *Engineering & Mining Journal*, 6/29/18, p1191.

Fossett, Frank, *Colorado Mines: 1859-1879, Boulder and Gilpin Counties* [Reprinted from *Colorado, Its Gold and Silver Mines, Farms and Stock Ranges, and Health and Pleasure Resorts – Tourist's Guide to the Rocky Mountains* 1879, by Gold Dirt Press, Colorado Springs, CO, 1999].

"Gold and Silver Stocks," *Engineering & Mining Journal*, 2/12/1876.

Henderson, Charles W., *Professional Paper 138: Mining in Colorado: A History of Discovery, Development, and Production*, U.S. Geological Survey, Government Printing Office, Washington, 1926.

Henn, Roger, *Lies, Legends & Lore of the San Juans*, Western Reflections Publishing, Montrose, CO, 1999.

Ilseng, M.C., *Mining Interests of the San Juan Region*, Colorado School of Mines Annual Report, 1885.

Kinney, W.Z. *Correspondence: Exhibit A, 1932* Colorado Historical Society, Manuscripts, Box 996.

Kaplan, Michael D., "The Toll Road Building Career of Otto Mears, 1881-1887", *The Colorado Magazine, Vol. L2, No.2*, State Historical Society of Colorado, Denver, CO, 1975.

Marshall, John and Zanoni, Zeke, *Mining the Hard Rock in the Silverton San Juans*, Simpler Way Book Co., Silverton, CO, 1996.

"Mineral Production of Colorado for 1876," *Engineering & Mining Journal*, 3/17/77, p171.

"Mines of Cement Creek: Wonderful Progress made during the past Seven Years and a Great Future planned by People of Enterprise" *Silverton Standard"* 10/19/01.

"Mining News: Colorado," *Engineering & Mining Journal,* 5/5/77, p301.

"Mining Notes from Colorado, Missouri, Montana, Nevada, and Northern Carolina," *Engineering & Mining Journal,* 7/29/76, p77.

Nossaman, Allen, *Many More Mountains: Volume 1: Silverton's Routes,* Sundance Publications, Denver, CO, 1989.

Nossaman, Allen, *Many More Mountains: Volume 2: Ruts into Silverton,* Sundance Publications, Denver, CO, 1993.

Nossaman, Allen, *Many More Mountains: Volume 3: Rails into Silverton,* Sundance Publications, Denver, CO, 1998.

Nossaman, Allen, Personal Interview, Silverton, CO, 1999. Nossaman wrote the three volume series *Many More Mountains* and served as San Juan County Justice.

Nossaman, Allen, Personal Interview, Durango, CO, 2002.

Pangborn, J.G., *The New Rocky Mountain Tourist Arkansas Valley and San Juan Guide,* Knight & Leonard, Chicago, IL, 1878.

Prosser, Warren C., "Outlook in San Juan County, Colo.," *Engineering & Mining Journal,* 4/29/11, p874.

Prosser, Warren C., "Silver Lake Basin, Colorado," *Engineering & Mining Journal,* 6/20/14, p1229.

Rickard, Thomas A., "Across the San Juan Mountains," *Engineering & Mining Journal,* July, 1903.

Rocky Mountain News, Denver, CO, various articles.

"The San Juan Mines," *Engineering & Mining Journal,* 2/11/73, p91.

"The San Juan Mines," *Engineering & Mining Journal,* 10/28/73, p284.

"The San Juan Mines," *Engineering & Mining Journal,* 12/2/73, p364.

"The San Juan Mines," *Engineering & Mining Journal,* 5/5/77, p291.

"San Juan Mining News," *Engineering & Mining Journal,* 12/20/79, p451.

"San Juan Mining News," *Engineering & Mining Journal,* 9/11/80, p170.

"San Juan Mining Notes," *Engineering & Mining Journal,* 2/28/80, p150.

"San Juan Silver Mines," *Engineering & Mining Journal,* 1/4/79, p11.

"San Juan Silver Mines - Review of the Year 1880," *Engineering & Mining Journal,* 1/8/1881, p22.

"San Juan Silver Mines - Review of the Year 1880," *Engineering & Mining Journal,* 2/5/81, p92.

Silverton Standard, Silverton, CO, various articles.

"The Silvery San Juan Has Enjoyed a Year of Unparalleled Prosperity in all Lines of Industry," *Denver Times,* 12/31/98, p18.

Sloan, Robert E., and Skowronski, Carl A., *The Rainbow Route: An Illustrated History of the Silverton Railroad, the Silverton Northern Railroad, and the Silverton, Gladstone, & Northerly Railroad,* Sundance Ltd., Denver, CO, 1975.

Smith, Duane A., "The San Juaner, A Computerized Portrait," *The Colorado Magazine, Vol. L2, No.2,* State Historical Society of Colorado, Denver, CO, 1975.

Smith, Duane A., *Song of the Hammer and Drill: The Colorado San Juans, 1860-1914,* Colorado School of Mines, Golden, CO, 1982.

Smith, Duane, *Rocky Mountain Boom Town: A History of Durango, Colorado,* University Press of Colorado, Niwot, CO, 1992 [1980].

Smith, P. David, *Mountains of Silver: The Story of Colorado's Red Mountain Mining District,* Western Reflections Publishing, Montrose, CO, 1994.

"Special Correspondence from Mining Centers: Denver," *Engineering & Mining Journal,* 11/6/09, p943.

Tucker, E.F., *Otto Mears and the San Juans,* Western Reflections Publishing, Montrose, CO, 2003.

Twitty, Eric, *The Silverton Mining District: A Selective Inventory of Principal Historic Sites, San Juan County, Colorado,* Mountain States Historical, Boulder, CO, 2002.

Twitty, Eric, *Level II Documentation of the Contention Tramway, Sites 5SA1184.1, 5SA1184.2, and 5SA1184.3,* Mountain States Historical, Boulder, CO, 2006.

Weston, W., "The San Juan Mines," *Engineering & Mining Journal,* March 2, 1878, p150-151.

Wyman, Louis, *Snowflakes and Quartz: Stories of Early Days in the San Juan Mountains,* Simpler Way Books, Silverton, CO, 1993.

Mine Histories

Bunyak, Dawn, *Frothers Bubbles and Flotation: A Survey of Flotation Milling in the Twentieth Century Metals Industry,* National Park Service, Denver, CO, 1998.

Burchard, Horatio C., *Report of the Director of the Mint,* Government Printing Office, Washington, D.C., 1881.

Burchard, Horatio C., *Report of the Director of the Mint,* Government Printing Office, Washington, D.C., 1883.

Burchard, Horatio C., *Report of the Director of the Mint,* Government Printing Office, Washington, D.C., 1884.

Chase, Charles A., *Shenandoah-Dives and North Star Mines,* 1925. On file in the Colorado Mining Engineers' Reports, Colorado State Archives, Denver, CO.

Chase, Charles A., *Shenandoah-Dives at Its Quarter Century,* Mining Year Book, 1951.

Colburn, C. Lorimer, *Information Concerning the Highland Mary Mine,* 1936. On file in the Mining Engineers' Reports, Colorado State Archives, Denver, CO.

Colorado Colorado Bureau of Mines, Manuscripts, Colorado Historical Society, MSS Box 640, v27.

Colorado Colorado Bureau of Mines, Manuscripts, Colorado Historical Society, MSS Box 640, v34.

Colorado Colorado Bureau of Mines, Manuscripts, Colorado Historical Society, MSS Box 640, v40.

"Colorado Mines," *Engineering & Mining Journal,* 10/19/78, p278.

Colorado Mine Engineers' Reports, Colorado State Archives, Denver, CO (Post 1910).
Iowa Mine
Shenandoah-Dives Group

Colorado Mine Inspectors' Reports, Division of Minerals and Geology, Denver, CO (Pre-1915).
Iowa Mine
Mayflower Mine

Colorado Mine Inspectors' Reports, Colorado State Archives, Denver, CO (Post 1910).
Aspen Mine
Big Giant Mine
Miscellaneous G
Highland Mary Mine
Iowa Mine
Laccawanna Mine
Little Giant Mine
Maybell Mine
Mayflower Mine
Mermac Mine
Osceola Mine
Shenandoah-Dives Group
Silver Lake Mine
Titusville Mine
Trilby Mine

Colorado Mine Managers' Reports, Division of Minerals and Geology, Denver, CO (Pre-1915).
Iowa Mine

Colorado Mine Managers' Reports, Colorado State Archives, Denver, CO (Post 1915).
Aspen Mine
Highland Mary Mine
Iowa Mine
Laccawanna Mine
Maybell Mine
Mayflower Mine

Mermac Mine
Mighty Monarch Mine
Osceola Mine
Shenandoah-Dives Group
Silver Lake Mine
Trilby Mine

Colorado Mining Directory, 1879, The Rocky Mountain News Printing Co., Denver, CO, 1879.

Colorado Mining Director, 1883, The Colorado Mining Directory Co., Denver, CO, 1883.

Colorado Mining Directory, 1896, Compiled by J.S. Bartow and P.A. Simmons, Colorado Mining Directory, Denver, CO, 1896.

Colorado Mining Directory, 1898, Western Mining Directory Company, Denver, CO, 1898.

Colorado Mining Directory, 1902, Wahlgreen Printing Co., Denver, CO, 1902.

"Colorado's Wealth in Water Power," *Denver Times,* 12/31/98, p10.

"Editorial Correspondence: Denver," *Engineering & Mining Journal,* 6/4/10, p1191.

"Editorial Correspondence: Denver," *Engineering & Mining Journal,* 7/30/10, p230.

"Editorial Correspondence," *Engineering & Mining Journal,* 4/4/14, p729.

"Editorial Correspondence," *Engineering & Mining Journal,* 10/17/14, p718.

"Editorial Correspondence," *Engineering & Mining Journal,* 5/15/15, p879.

Horn, Jonathon C., *Lackawanna Mill History,* Alpine Archaeological Consultants, Inc., Montrose, CO, 2005. Prepared for Bureau of Land Management, San Juan Public Lands Center, Durango, CO.

Iowa Gold Mining & Milling Company, *Stock Prospectus* Denver, CO, 1896 (on file at Denver Public Library).

Lakes, Arthur, "The Silver Lake Mine," *Mines and Minerals,* April, 1903, p389.

BIBLIOGRAPHY

Mineral Resources, U.S. Geological Survey, Government Printing Office, Washington, D.C., 1906-1931.

Minerals Yearbook, U.S. Department of the Interior, U.S. Government Printing Office, Washington, 1934-1957.

Mines Register, 1937.

"Mining News," *Engineering & Mining Journal* 1875-1920. "Mining News" is a feature in each issue where activities in prominent mining districts are documented.

"Mining News," *Mining & Scientific Press,* 1875-1920. "Mining News" is a feature in each issue where activities in prominent mining districts are documented.

"Mining News," *Mining Reporter,* 1900-1910. "Mining News" is a feature in each issue where activities in prominent mining districts are documented.

"New Mining & Metallurgical Construction in 1919," *Engineering & Mining Journal,* 1/17/20, p151

"News by Mining Districts," *Mining & Scientific Press,* 8/27/04, p145.

Niebur, Jay E., *Arthur Redman Wilfley: Miner, Inventor, and Entrepreneur,* Western Business History Research Center, Colorado Historical Society, Denver, CO, 1982.

"North Star Group," *Mining Reporter,* 10/2/02, p270.

Report of the Director of the Mint Government Printing Office, Washington, D.C., 1884-1904. "Silver Lake Mill," *Mining Reporter,* 9/25/02, p252.

"Silverton, Colorado," *Mining & Scientific Press,* 5/13/11, p672.

"Silverton, Colorado," *Mining & Scientific Press,* 1/20/12, p150.

Smith, Duane A., *San Juan Gold: A Mining Engineer's Adventures, 1879-1881,* Western Reflections, Montrose, CO, 2002.

"Special Correspondence," *Mining & Scientific Press,*.5/19/06, p331.

"Special Correspondence," *Mining & Scientific Press,* 1/20/12, p150.

Special Index to Patents: San Juan County, San Juan County Clerk, Silverton, CO.

Weed, Walter H., *The Mines Handbook: A Manual of the Mining Industry of North America,* Stevens Copper Handbook, New York, NY, 1916.

Weed, Walter H., *The Mines Handbook: A Manual of the Mining Industry of North America,* Stevens Copper Handbook, New York, NY, 1918.

Weed, Walter H., *The Mines Handbook: A Manual of the Mining Industry of North America,* Stevens Copper Handbook, New York, NY, 1920.

Weed, Walter H., *The Mines Handbook: A Manual of the Mining Industry of North America,* Stevens Copper Handbook, New York, NY, 1922.

Weed, Walter H., *The Mines Handbook: A Manual of the Mining Industry of North America,* Stevens Copper Handbook, New York, NY, 1925.

Whitaker, O.R., *Report on Shenandoah-North Star-Terrible-Mayflower Group,* 1926 (on file at the Colorado School of Mines, Golden, CO).

General History

Abbott, Carl; Leonard, Stephen; McComb, David, *Colorado: A History of the Centennial State,* University Press of Colorado, Niwot, CO, 1994 [1982].

Brown, Ronald *Hard Rock Miners: The Intermountain West, 1860-1920* Texas A&M Press, 1979.Canfield, John G., *Mines and Mining Men of Colorado,* John G. Canfield, Denver, CO, 1893.

Dallas, Sandra, *Colorado Ghost Towns and Mining Camps,* University of Oklahoma Press, Norman, 1984 [1979].

Eberhart, Perry, *Guide to the Colorado Ghost Towns and Mining Camps,* Swallow Press, Athens, OH, 1987 [1959].

"End of Pittman Silver Purchases Cut Profits Sharply" *Engineering & Mining Journal* 12/1/23 p960.

"Events and Economics of the War" *Engineering & Mining Journal* 5/18/18 p926.

Fell, James E., Jr. *Ores to Metals: The Rocky Mountain Smelting Industry* University of Nebraska Press, Lincoln, NE, 1979.

Francaviglia, Richard, *Hard Places: Reading the Landscape of America's Historic Mining Districts,* University of Iowa Press, Iowa City, IA, 1991.

BIBLIOGRAPHY

Huston, Richard C. *A Silver Camp Called Creede: A Century of Mining* Western Reflections, Montrose, CO, 2005.

"Industrial News from Washington" *Engineering & Mining Journal* 4/27/18 p804.

King, Joseph, *A Mine to Make A Mine: Financing the Colorado Mining Industry, 1859-1902*, Texas A&M University Press, 1977.

McElvaine, Robert S., *The Great Depression: America, 1929-1941*, Times Books, New York, NY, 1993 [1984].

Mumey, Nolie *Creede: The History of a Colorado Silver Mining Town* Artcraft Press, Denver, CO 1949.

"News from Washington" *Engineering & Mining Journal* 7/28/23 p165.

Noel, Thomas J., and Norgren, Barbara S, *Denver: The City Beautiful and its Architects, 1893-1941*, Historic Denver, Inc., Denver, CO, 1987.

Pritchard, Sandra F. *Men, Mining, & Machines: Hardrock Mining in Summit County, Colorado* Summit Historical Society, Summit County, CO, 1996.

Saxon, Glenn O., *Colorado and Its Mining Industry (1859-1959)*, Yale University, 1959.

Spence, Clark C., *Mining Engineers and the American West*, University of Idaho Press, Moscow, ID, 1993.

Stone, Wilbur Fisk, *History of Colorado, Vol. 1-4*, S.J. Clarke Publishing Co., Chicago, IL, 1918.

Voynick, Stephen M., *Colorado Gold: From the Pike's Peak Rush to the Present*, Mountain Press Publishing Co., Missoula, MT, 1992.

Wolle, Muriel Sibel, *Stampede to Timberline: The Ghost Towns and Mining Camps of Colorado*, Swallow Press, University of Ohio Press, 1991 [1949].

Wyman, Mark, *Hard Rock Epic: Western Mining and the Industrial Revolution, 1860-1910*, University of California Press, Berkeley, CA, 1989 [1979].

Geological History

Burbank, W.S.; Eckel, E.B.; and Varnes, D.J. "The San Juan Region" *Mineral Resources of Colorado*, State of Colorado Mineral Resources Board, Denver, CO, 1947.

Burbank, Wilbur S., and Luedke, Robert G., *USGS Professional Paper 535: Geology and Ore Deposits of the Eureka and Adjoining Districts, San Juan Mountains, Colorado,* U.S. Geological Survey, U.S. Government Printing Office, Washington, D.C., 1969.

Cross, Whitman; Howe, Earnest; and Ransome, F.L., *Geologic Atlas of the United States: Silverton Folio, Colorado,* U.S. Geological Survey, Government Printing Office, Washington, D.C., 1905.

Larsen, E.S. and Cross, Whitman, *USGS Professional Paper 258: Geology and Petrology of the San Juan Region, Southwestern Colorado,* U.S. Geological Survey, Government Printing Office, Washington, D.C., 1956.

Ransome, Frederick Leslie, *USGS Bulletin No. 182: A Report on the Economic Geology of the Silverton Quadrangle, Colorado,* U.S. Geological Survey, Government Printing Office, Washington, D.C., 1901.

Varnes, David J., *Professional Paper 378-A: Geology and Ore Deposits of the South Silverton Mining Area, San Juan County, Colorado,* U.S. Geological Survey, U.S. Government Printing Office, Washington, D.C., 1963.

Social History

Anderson, Beverly M. and Hamilton, Donna M., *The New High Altitude Cookbook,* Random House, New York, NY, 1980 [1961].

Armitage, Susan and Jameson, Elizabeth *The Women's West* University of Oklahoma Press, Norman, OK, 1987.

Baker, James H. *History of Colorado* Linderman Co., Inc., Denver, CO, 1927.

Conlin, Joseph, *Bacon, Beans, and Galantines: Food and Foodways on the Western Mining Frontier,* University of Nevada Press, Reno, NV, 1986.

History of the Arkansas Valley, O.L. Baskin, Chicago, IL, 1881.

Myres, Sandra L. *Westering Women and the Frontier Experience, 1800-1915* University of New Mexico Press, Albuquerque, NM, 1999.

Norman, Reuben O. *Who's Who of Denver 1931-1932* The Blue Book Company, Denver, CO, 1932.

BIBLIOGRAPHY

"Obituary" *Engineering & Mining Journal* 1875-1920.

"Obituary" *Mining Reporter* 1890-1920.

"Obituary" *Mining & Scientific Press* 1875-1920.

Portrait and Biographical Record of Denver and Vicinity, Colorado Chapman Publishing Co., Chicago, IL, 1898.

Portrait and Biographical Record of the State of Colorado Chapman Publishing Co., Chicago, IL, 1899.

"Prominent Men in the Mining Industry" *Engineering & Mining Journal* 5/30/91.

Reyher, Ken, *Silver & Sawdust: Life in the San Juans,* Western Reflections, Montrose, CO, 2000.

Schulze, Susanne, *A Century of the Colorado Census,* University of Northern Colorado, Greeley, CO, 1976.

Zanjani, Sally *A Mine of Her Own: Women Prospectors in the American West,* 1850-1950 University of Nebraska Press, Lincoln, NE, 2002.

Mining Technology

Horn, Jonathan C., *Cultural Resource Inventory of the Trout Lake and Lake Hope Shorelines for the Ames Hydroelectric Project (FERC No.400), San Miguel County, Colorado,* Alpine Archaeological Consultants, Inc., Montrose, CO, 2007a.

Horn, Jonathan C., *Cultural Resource Inventory of Electra Lake Shoreline, Cascade Flume, Tacoma Power Plant, and Other Areas of the Tacoma Hydroelectric Project (FERC No.12589), La Plata and San Juan Counties, Colorado,* Alpine Archaeological Consultants, Inc., Montrose, CO, 2007b.

Meyerriecks, Will, *Drills and Mills: Precious Metal Mining and Milling Methods of the Frontier West* Self Published, Tampa, FL, 2001.

Silver World, Lake City, CO, various articles.

Twitty, Eric, "From Steam Engines to Electric Motors: Electrification in the Cripple Creek Mining District," *The Mining History Journal,* 1998, p103.

Twitty, Eric, *Blown to Bits in the Mine: A History of Mining and Explosives in the United States*, Western Reflections Publishing, Montrose, CO, 2001.

Twitty, Eric, *Riches to Rust: A Guide to Mining in the Old West*, Western Reflections Publishing, Montrose, CO, 2002.

Maps

Clason, George S., *Map of the San Juan Triangle 1903*, George S. Clason, Denver, CO, 1903.

Colburn, C. Lorimer E.M., *Highland Mary Mines (Highland Mary and Trilby) Near Silverton, Colorado* Feb. 1935.

Hotchkiss Map Co., *Map of the San Juan Triangle 1935*, Hotchkiss Map Co., Denver, CO, 1935.

Iowa Gold Mining and Milling Company, *Iowa Mine Workings*, 1903.

Iowa Gold Mining and Milling Company, *Tiger Mine Workings*, 1903.

Luedke, Robert G. and Burbank, Wilbur S., *Preliminary Geologic Map of the Handies Peak Quadrangle, Colorado*, U.S. Geological Survey Open File Report, 1975.

Luedke, Robert G. and Burbank, Wilbur S., *Preliminary Geologic Map of the Howardsville Quadrangle, Colorado*, U.S. Geological Survey Open File Report, 1975.

Luedke, Robert G. and Burbank, Wilbur S. *Preliminary Geologic Map of the Silverton Quadrangle, Colorado*, U.S. Geological Survey Open File Report, 1975.

Prosser, Warren C., *Elevation of Workings on Lookout Vein, Gold Tunnel & Railway Company*, 1915.

Sanborn Map Co., *Silverton, San Juan County, Colorado, 1890*, Sanborn Map Co., Brooklyn, NY, 1890.

Sanborn Map Co., *Silverton, San Juan County, Colorado, 1902*, Sanborn Map Co., Brooklyn, NY, 1902.

Sanborn Map Co., *Silverton, San Juan County, Colorado, 1912*, Sanborn Map Co., Brooklyn, NY, 1912.

United States Geological Survey, *Silverton*, United States Geological Survey, 15 min. quad., 1897.

BIBLIOGRAPHY

United States Geological Survey, *Silverton*, United States Geological Survey, 15 min. quad., 1902.

United States Geological Survey, *Silverton*, United States Geological Survey, 15 min. quad., 1946.

FOOTNOTES

1 Brown, 1984:18; Pangborn, 1878:41; Sloan and Skowronski, 1975:14; Stone, 1918, V.1:271.
2 Brown, 1984:87; Eberhart, 1987:344; Nossaman, 1989:37, 39.
3 Nossaman, 1989:39.
4 Nossaman, 1989:39.
5 Nossaman, 1989:39; Nossaman is heavily used as a source since his research is the most accurate for the time period.
6 Nossaman, 1989:40, 51.
7 Nossaman, 1989:40.
8 Nossaman, 1989:38, 98.
9 Nossaman, 1989:38, 40.
10 Henn, 1999:56.
11 Brown, 1984:18; Nossaman, 1989:45, 50; Pangborn, 1878:41.
12 Nossaman, 1989:53.
13 Nossaman, 1989:53
14 Nossaman, 1989:56.
15 Nossaman, 1989:60
16 Brown, 1984:19; Nossaman, 1989:64; Pangborn, 1878:41; Sloan and Skowronski, 1975:14.
17 Brown, 1984:19; Nossaman, 1989:74; Pangborn, 1878:41; Sloan and Skowronski, 1975:14; Wolle, 1995:340.
18 Henn, 1999:14; Nossaman, 1989:43, 81.
19 Nossaman, 1989:82.
20 Brown, 1984:21; Nossaman, 1989:81-82; Pangborn, 1878:42; Sloan and Skowronski, 1975:15.
21 Brown, 1984:20; Nossaman, 1989:84.
22 Nossaman, 1989:86; Sloan and Skowronski, 1975:15.
23 Nossaman, 1989:89.
24 *Report of the Director of the Mint,* 1894:20; Saxon, 1959:7, 8, 14, 16.
25 Nossaman, 1989:89.
26 Nossaman, 1989:89; Ransome, 1901:19; "The San Juan Mines" *EMJ* 2/11/73; Sloan and Skowronski, 1975:15.
27 Nossaman, 1989:93.
28 Nossaman, 1989:94.
29 Nossaman, 1989:94.
30 Nossaman, 1989:95, 97.
31 Nossaman, 1989:102-103,
32 Nossaman, 1989:98.
33 Nossaman, 1989:102.
34 Henn, 1999:14; Nossaman, 1993:39, 100, 121.
35 Henn, 1999:13-14; Nossaman, 1989:100-101.
36 Nossaman, 1989:102; *Portrait and Biographical Record,* 1899:1026.
37 *History of the Arkansas Valley,* 1881:755; *Portrait and Biographical Record,* 1899:1102.
38 Nossaman, 1989:103.

FOOTNOTES

39 Brown, 1984:27; Nossaman, 1989:104, 106.

40 Nossaman, 1989:104; Dollar conversions derived from consumer price index on eh.net.

41 Brown, 1984:28; Nossaman, 1989:113; Nossaman, 1993:11; "The San Juan Mines" *EMJ* 2/11/73.

42 Nossaman, 1989:124, 220.

43 Nossaman, 1993:145-146.

44 Mumey, 1949:81-82; Nossaman, 1989:122; Nossaman, 1993:99.

45 Nossaman, 1989:109; Sloan and Skowronski, 1975:15; Dollar conversions derived from consumer price index calculator on eh.net.

46 Nossaman, 1989:122; Nossaman, 1993:99; Sloan and Skowronski, 1975:15.

47 Nossaman, 1989:126; Ransome, 1901:167; "The San Juan Mines" *EMJ* 2/11/73.

48 Nossaman, 1989:127.

49 Brown, 1984:23; Nossaman, 1989:79; Tucker, 2003:51.

50 Brown, 1984:23; Nossaman, 1989:144-145; Tucker, 2003:51, 55.

51 Brown, 1984:29, 82; Nossaman, 1989:127; Nossaman, 1993:221; Ransome, 1901:19; *Rocky Mountain News* 7/9/73 p4; Sloan and Skowronski, 1975:15.

52 Nossaman, 1989:134; Nossaman, 1998:311; Ransome, 1901:19; *Rocky Mountain News* 7/20/73 p4; Sloan and Skowronski, 1975:15.

53 Nossaman, 1989:179; "The San Juan Mines" *EMJ* 10/28/73; Dollar conversions derived from consumer price index calculator on eh.net.

54 Nossaman, 1989:147.

55 Nossaman, 1989:127, 152; Nossaman, 1993:11.

56 Nossaman, 1989:135; Ransome, 1901:19; Dollar conversions derived from consumer price index calculator on eh.net.

57 Nossaman, 1989:184, 207; Nossaman, 1993:20, 161.

58 Nossaman, 1989:162.

59 Nossaman, 1989:106, 169, 178, 261.

60 Nossaman, 1989:167, 178, 214; Ransome, 1901:20.

61 Nossaman, 1989:178.

62 Nossaman, 1989:179.

63 Nossaman, 1989:173-175.

64 Nossaman, 1989:173-175.

65 Nossaman, 1989:173-175.

66 Nossaman, 1989:173-175.

67 Twitty, 2002:79.

68 Twitty, 2002:78, 80.

69 Twitty, 2002:98.

70 Brown, 1984:29; "Mining News " *EMJ* 8/14/80 p111; Nossaman, 1993:15; Nossaman, 1989:210; Sloan & Skowronski, 1975:19, 46; Smith, 1982:26.

71 Nossaman, 1989:210.

72 Nossaman, 1989:211, 213.

73 Nossaman, 1989:175-176, 214; Ransome, 1901:19; *Rocky Mountain News* 8/26/74 p4; Sloan and Skowronski, 1975:15.

74 Nossaman, 1989:184, 187; Nossaman, 1993:11.

75 Nossaman, 1989:187.

76 Nossaman, 1989:160, 170-172; Nossaman, 1993:214-215.

77 Henn, 1999:146; Nossaman, 1989:171, 177, 185; Nossaman, 1993:279; Sloan and Skowronski, 1975:19; Wolle, 1991:401.

78 Bauer, et al, 1990:74; Henn, 1999:70; Nossaman, 1989:184; Sloan and Skowronski, 1975:19.

79 Nossaman, 1989:158; Sloan and Skowronski, 1975:17; Smith, 2002:4; Stone, 1918, V.1:198.

80 Henn, 1999:145; Nossaman, 1989:172; Nossaman, 1993:214, 279; *Rocky Mountain News*, 2/19/74 p4; Sloan and Skowronski, 1975:19.

81 Weston, 1878.

82 Henn, 1999:134; Nossaman, 1989:270; "Prominent Men in the Mining Industry" *EMJ* 9/26/91 p213; Sloan & Skowronski, 1975:46; Smith, 1992:9.

83 Nossaman, 1989:268; Sloan and Skowronski, 1975:46.

84 "Mining Notes from Colorado" *EMJ* 1876; Nossaman, 1989:267-268, 271; Nossaman, 1993:153; Sloan and Skowronski, 1975:19.

85 Nossaman, 1993:144 ; Smith, 2002:5.

86 Henn, 1999:6; Nossaman, 1989:313; Pangborn, 1878:52.

87 Fossett, 1880:524; "Mineral Production of Colorado for 1876" *EMJ* 1877; "Mining News" *EMJ* 5/12/77 p319; Nossaman, 1993:118; Nossaman, 1989:313; *Rocky Mountain News* 7/16/76 p4; Dollar conversions derived from consumer price index calculator on eh.net.

88 Nossaman, 1993:144, 252; Ransome, 1901:21; Smith, 2002:4-6.

89 *Rocky Mountain News* 10/17/77 p2.

90 Nossaman, 1993:215; A field examination by Twitty in 2002 encountered the pits.

91 Nossaman, 1993:289.

92 Nossaman, 1998:307.

93 Nossaman, 1993:35, 118; Ransome, 1901:149.

94 Henn, 1999:13; Nossaman, 1989:259.

95 *Denver Times* 7/10/01 p5; Eberhart, 1987:345; Nossaman, 1989:261; Nossaman, 1989:261; *Rocky Mountain News* 9/14/58 p65.

96 Henn, 1999:15-16; Nossaman, 1989:178, 261-262; Dollar conversions derived from consumer price index calculator on eh.net.

97 Henn, 1999:16; Nossaman, 1989:262, 319; Nossaman, 1993:120.

98 Twitty, 2002:293.

99 Nossaman, 1989:264, 266.

100 Nossaman, 1989:319; Nossaman, 1993:120.

101 Nossaman, 1993:120; Nossaman, 1998:104.

102 Nossaman, 1989:238, 283; Nossaman, 1993:12, 215, 218219; *Rocky Mountain News*, 10/17/77 p2.

103 According to Twitty, 2002:79, 83, 87, and an examination of the area.

104 Twitty, 2002:79-81, 83, 87.

105 Nossaman, 1993:127; Twitty, 2002:87.

106 Nossaman, 1993:70, 127.

107 Henn, 1999:68; Nossaman, 1993:40, 224.

108 Pangborn, 1878:54.

109 Nossaman, 1993:85.

110 Nossaman, 1993:87; Nossaman, 1993:294; Pamgborn, 1878:50, Dollar conversions derived from consumer price index calculator on eh.net.

FOOTNOTES

111 Nossaman, 1993:95, 113; Sloan & Skowronski, 1975:21.

112 Nossaman, 1993:98, 113.

113 Nossaman, 1989:250; Nossaman, 1993:13; Wolle, 1995:422.

114 Nossaman, 1989:118.

115 "Mining News" *EMJ* 7/14/77 p30, 9/11/80 p170; Nossaman, 1989:316; Nossaman, 1993:39, 116; Pangborn, 1878:52.

116 Nossaman, 1993:153.

117 Nossaman, 1989:318; Nossaman, 1993:26.

118 "The San Juan Mines" 1877.

119 Nossaman, 1993:150.

120 Nossaman, 1993:252; Nossaman, 1998:326.

121 Fossett, 1880:525; Nossaman, 1993:252; *Rocky Mountain News* 3/13/79 p4; *Rocky Mountain News* 3/20/79 p4.

122 Twitty, 2002:319-321.

123 Smith, 2002:4.

124 Nossaman, 1993:99, 252; Twitty, 2002:316.

125 Henn, 1999:16; "Mining News" *EMJ* 9/28/78 p224; Nossaman, 1993:120.

126 Bauer, et al, 1990: 72; "Colorado Mines" *EMJ* 10/19/78 p278; Nossaman, 1993:136, 252; Dollar conversions derived from consumer price index calculator on eh.net.

127 Nossaman, 1993:245.

128 King, 1977:92; *Report of the Director of the Mint,* 1894:20; Saxon, 1959:7, 8, 14, 16; Smith, 1982:92; Smith, 1994:148; Dollar conversion derived from consumer price index calculator on eh.net.

129 "Gold and Silver Stocks" *EMJ* 2/12/76; Nossaman, 1993:284.

130 Nossaman, 1993:370; Smith, 1992:6-8.

131 Henderson, 1926:11; Henn, 1999:134; "Mining News" *EMJ* 9/16/82; Nossaman, 1993:295-296; "San Juan Silver Mines" *EMJ* 2/5/81 p92; Sloan and Skowronski, 1975:47.

132 "Mining News" *EMJ* 3/27/80 p222; Nossaman, 1993:295-296; Nossaman, 1998:39, 58; Smith, 1992:18; Dollar conversion derived from consumer price index calculator on eh.net..

133 Nossaman, 1998:145; Smith, 1992:18

134 Nossaman, 1993:170; "Obituary" *EMJ* 5/13/93 p444; "Prominent Men in the Mining Industry" *EMJ* 8/22/91 p213; Spence, 1993:8.

135 "Mining News" *EMJ* 8/14/80 p111, 12/11/80 p384; Nossaman, 1998:99, 202; archaeological evidence summarized in Twitty, 2002:81-82 confirms the surface plant and residences at the Legal Tender.

136 Nossaman, 1998:18; Smith, 2002:6.

137 Nossaman, 1998: 18.

138 Smith, 2002:29; Twitty, 2002:310; Dollar conversion derived from consumer price index calculator on eh.net.

139 Smith, 2002:115; Wolle, 1991:430.

140 Smith, 2002:115.

141 Nossaman, 1998:101; Smith, 2002:118.

142 *Denver Republican* 9/24/81 p5; Twitty, 2002:252-254.

143 "Mining News" *EMJ* 2/21/80 p137, 3/13/80 p189; *Rocky Mountain News* 10/19/79 p4.

144 Nossaman, 1993:23; *Rocky Mountain News* 8/26/79 p5, 10/2/79 p2.

145 Nossaman, 1998:307.

146 "Mining News" *EMJ* 8/13/87 p119; Nossaman, 1993:38; Nossaman, 1998:44.

147 "Mining News" *EMJ* 12/30/82 p350.

148 Burchard, 1882:545; Henderson, 1926:11; "Mining News" *EMJ* 9/16/82 p151; Nossaman, 1998:215; Smith, 1992:27.

149 Burchard, 1882:545; *Colorado Mining Directory,* 1883:650; Nossaman, 1998:204, 206; *Rocky Mountain News* 5/10/82, p2 c1; Dollar conversion derived from consumer price index calculator on eh.net.

150 *Rocky Mountain News* 9/21/82, p3 c2.

151 Burchard, 1882:545; "Mining News" *EMJ* 12/30/82 p351; Nossaman, 1998:206; *Rocky Mountain News* 10/17/82, p6 c4.

152 Henderson, 1926:49; Prosser, 1914; Sanborn 1890; Sloan and Skowronski, 1975:29.

153 "Obituary" *EMJ* 8/7/15 p243; Nossaman, 1998:210; Spence, 1993:58.

154 "Mining News" *EMJ* 8/26/82 p112; Nossaman, 1998:210-213.

155 "Mining News" *EMJ* 12/30/82 p350, 12/29/83 p401; Nossaman, 1998:262.

156 Nossaman, 1998:100, 203, 307; Ransome, 1901:162.

157 Burchard, 1882:547; Burchard, 1883:409; *Rocky Mountain News* 10/17/82 p6; *Rocky Mountain News* 7/21/82 p2; *Rocky Mountain News* 8/30/83 p2.

158 Burchard, 1882:547; Nossaman, 1998:206; *Rocky Mountain News* 6/24/82 p3; *Rocky Mountain News* 8/18/82 p2.

159 "Mining News" *EMJ* 11/11/82 p259; Nossaman, 1998:308.

160 Burchard, 1882:548; Nossaman, 1998:308.

161 Ransome, 1901:157.

162 *Rocky Mountain News* 8/1/82 p3; *Rocky Mountain News* 9/19/82 p3; Twitty, 2002:180, 184, 186.

163 Burchard, 1883:409; Henderson, 1926:49; Nossaman, 1998:307; Ransome, 1901:149; *Rocky Mountain News* 8/30/83 p2.

164 Burchard, 1883:409.

165 Nossaman, 1998:325; Prosser, 1914.

166 "Mining News" *EMJ* 8/4/83 p71; Nossaman, 1998:101-104; *Rocky Mountain News* 11/3/83 p7.

167 Nossaman, 1998:38, 68, 302, 236, 304, 306.

168 Brown, 1979:45; Henn, 1999:151; Nossaman, 1998:317, 323; Sloan and Skowronski, 1975:33; West, 1996:79; Wolle, 1995:422-424.

169 Brown, 1984:44; Nossaman, 1989:322; Nossaman, 1998:250.

170 *Rocky Mountain News* 6/20/82 p2; *Rocky Mountain News* 7/18/82 p8; *Rocky Mountain News* 7/22/82 p2; *Rocky Mountain News* 9/15/82 p2.

171 Brown, 1984:53; Nossaman, 1993:166; Smith, 2002:80; Wolle, 1995:422.

172 Schulze, 1977:1880-3, 1885-1.

173 Smith, 1975:140-142.

174 Nossaman, 1989:286; Nossaman, 1993:162, 302; Nossaman, 1998:233; Schulze, 1977:1900-14; Smith, 1975:140-141

175 Twitty, 2002:453.

176 Schulze, 1977:1900-14; Twitty, 2002:452.

177 Conlin, 1986:11-16; Mehls et al, 1995:52.

178 Anderson and Hamilton, 1980:xv, 14, 171; Reyher, 2000:51; Smith, 2002:33.

FOOTNOTES

179 Anderson and Hamilton, 1980:14; Conlin, 1984:29; Reyher, 2000:54, 153; Twitty, 2002:457-458.

180 Twitty, 2002:461.

181 Brown, 1979:99; Reyher, 2000:54, 175; Pangborn, 1878:57; West, 1996:110.

182 *Rocky Mountain News* 1/7/84 p6; *Rocky Mountain News* 3/4/84 p3; *Rocky Mountain News* 5/31/84 p6; *Rocky Mountain News* 7/21/84 p6; *Rocky Mountain News* 8/13/84 p6; *Rocky Mountain News* 1/13/85 p6; *Rocky Mountain News* 5/26/85 p6; *Rocky Mountain News* 7/23/85 p6; *Rocky Mountain News* 11/12/85 p2; *Rocky Mountain News* 11/18/85; *Rocky Mountain News* 11/27/85 p6.

183 *Rocky Mountain News* 9/20/84 p2; *Rocky Mountain News* 5/18/85 p6; *Rocky Mountain News* 6/10/85 p6; *Rocky Mountain News* 9/30/85 p6.

184 *Rocky Mountain News* 1/31/85 p1.

185 *Rocky Mountain News* 1/31/85 p1.

186 "Mining News" *EMJ* 2/14/85 p112.

187 *Rocky Mountain News* 8/10/85 p6.

188 *Denver Times* 7/10/01 p5; Eberhart, 1987:345; *Rocky Mountain News* 9/14/58 p65; Dollar conversion derived from consumer price index calculator on eh.net.

189 *Rocky Mountain News* 6/10/85 p6.

190 Brown, 1984:191; "Mining News" *EMJ* 8/14/86 p119; *Report of the Director of the Mint*, 1894:20; Saxon, 1959:7-9, 14-17; Smith, 1994:184.

191 Ransome, 1901:161.

192 "Mining News", *MSP* 11/6/86 p301; Tucker, 2003:113.

193 Twitty, 2002:224, 226-228.

194 "Mining News" *EMJ* 4/30/87 p317; *Silverton Standard* 7/24/15; Twitty, 2002:344; Dollar conversion derived from consumer price index calculator on eh.net.

195 "Mining News" *EMJ* 11/22/90 p605; Ransome, 1901:161.

196 "Mining News" *MSP* 3/31/88 p205; "Mining News" *EMJ* 10/5/89 p 299; Dollar conversion derived from consumer price index calculator on eh.net.

197 "Mining News" *MSP* 5/5/88 p285; "Mining News" *EMJ* 5/12/88 p347; Ransome, 1901:162; Smith, 1982:56; Smith, 1992:27.

198 "Mining News" *MSP* 3/3/88 p141; "Mining News" *MSP* 5/12/88 p301; "Mining News" *EMJ* 9/8/88 p200; Ransome, 1901:164.

199 "Mining News" *EMJ* 6/29/89 p595; "Mining News" *EMJ* 9/21/89 p252; Ransome, 1901:23.

200 Twitty, 2002:330.

201 "Mining News" *MSP* 3/1/90 p149; Twitty, 2002:331.

202 Cross, Howe, 1905:26; Henn, 1999:134; Sloan & Skowronski, 1975:35; Smith, 1982:50; Smith, 1994:166; Tucker, 2003:91.

203 Sloan and Skowonski, 1975:98; Smith, 1994:164; Tucker, 2003:97.

204 Henn, 1999:69; Nossaman, 1998:105; Schulze, 1977:1885-1, 1890-7.

205 Brown, 1984:193; Reyher, 2000:179; Smith, 1982:92; Voynick, 1992:62.

206 "Mining News" *EMJ* 3/28/91; "Mining News" *EMJ* 9/9/93p273.

207 "Mining News" *EMJ* 11/22/90 p605; "Mining News" *MSP* 11/21/91 p331; Nossaman, 1993:180; Nossaman, 1998:123; *Silverton Standard* 12/27/90; *Silverton Standard* 1/3/91.

208 *Mining News Mining Reporter* 1/25/00 p52; *Silverton Standard* 5/24/90; *Silverton Standard* 7/4/91.

209 Colorado Colorado Bureau of Mines *Manuscripts* MSS Box 640, v27:6; "Mining News" *EMJ* 9/12/91 p314; *Special Index to Patents.*

210 "Mining News" *MSP* 11/2/89 p339; "Mining News" *MSP* 3/1/90 p140.

211 Nossaman, 1998:62.

212 Nossaman, 1989:62, 238; Nossaman, 1993:32, 60, 310.

213 "Mining News" *MSP* 11/21/91 p331; *Silverton Standard* 8/20/92.

214 Colorado Mining Engineers' Reports: Iowa Mine; *The Iowa Gold Mining & Milling Company.*

215 Colorado Colorado Bureau of Mines *Manuscripts* MSS Box 640, v27:20; Sloan and Skowronski, 1975:29.

216 Henderson, 1926:49; Nossaman, 2002; "Obituary" *EMJ* 5/5/06 p865; Prosser, 1914; Sloan and Skowronski, 1975:29.

217 Reyher, 2000:176; Sloan and Skowronski, 1975:29.

218 Colorado Colorado Bureau of Mines *Manuscripts* MSS Box 640, v27:20; Reyher, 2000:176; Rich, 2002; "Obituary" *MSP* 4/28/06 p285; Sloan and Skowronski, 1975:29.

219 Twitty, 2002:127, 130, 140-143.

220 Lakes, 1903; Ransome, 1901:156; Twitty, 2002:133-134.

221 Lakes, 1903; Ransome, 1901:156; Twitty, 2002:135.

222 *EMJ* 2/13/92.

223 Burbank, et al, 1947:396; "Mining News" *EMJ* 12/29/1888 p551; Smith, 1982:98.

224 "Mining News" *EMJ* 4/26/90 p479; "Mining News" *EMJ* 11/15/90 p581.

225 Ransome, 1901:149; Dollar conversion derived from consumer price index calculator on eh.net.

226 "Mining News" *EMJ* 9/9/93 p273; Twitty, 2002:140.

227 Sloan and Skowonski, 1975:118.

228 Henderson, 1926:216; *Silverton Standard* 5/31/90; *Silverton Standard* 10/4/90.

229 "Mining News" *EMJ* 2/6/92 p187; Nossaman, 1998:252; Ransome, 1901:23; Smith, 1982:101; Smith, 1992:28; Tucker, 2003:114.

230 Henderson, 1926:216; King, 1977:183; Saxon, 1959:7-17.

Brown, 1984:194; *Report of the Director of the Mint*, 1894:26, 30; Saxon, 1959:7, 8, 14, 16; Smith, 1982:92; Smith, 1994:184, 187; Stone, 1918, V.1:437.

232 Schulze, 1977:1890-7; Smith, 1992:68.

233 Saxon, 1959:78, 14, 16; *Silverton Standard* 6/23/94.

234 *Corporate Records, Book 37*:551; Rickard, 1903:32; Sloan and Skowonski, 1975:51, 121; Wolle, 1995:431.

235 Rickard, 1903:68; *Silverton Standard* 6/30/94.

236 "Colorado's Wealth in Water Power"; Sanborn, 1902; Twitty, 2002:165, 170-171; Dollar conversion derived from consumer price index calculator on eh.net..

237 Rickard, 1903:60; Twitty, 2002:173; Wyman, 1993:3-4.

238 *Silverton Standard* 11/9/95; *Silverton Standard* 1/28/98; Twitty, 2002:137.

239 *The Iowa Gold Mining & Milling Company* stock prospectus; "The Silvery San Juan Has Enjoyed a Year of Unparalleled Prosperity in all Lines of Industry"; *Silverton Standard* 11/9/95; Dollar conversion derived from consumer price index calculator on eh.net.

FOOTNOTES

240 "Mining News" *EMJ* 12/19/96 p 589; *The Iowa Gold Mining & Milling Company* stock prospectus; *Silverton Standard* 4/25/96; Dollar conversion derived from consumer price index calculator on eh.net.

241 *The Iowa Gold Mining & Milling Company* stock prospectus; "Iowa Mine Workings" map.

242 "Mining News" *EMJ* 12/19/96 p589; Twitty, 2002:197-198.

243 *Silverton Standard* 12/26/96.

244 "Mining News" *MSP* 12/19/96 p507.

245 "Mining News" *MSP* 12/12/96 p487; Twitty, 2002:219; Weed, 1925:730.

246 "Mining News" *EMJ* 7/27/95 p86; "Mining News" *EMJ* 8/31/95 p206; Prosser, 1914; *Silverton Standard* 5/4/95.

247 Twitty, 2002:197-198.

248 Twitty, 2002:192, 200.

249 "Mining News" *EMJ* 2/19/98 p231; "Mining News" *MSP* 9/30/99 p383; "Mining News" *MSP* 1/7/99 p7; "Mining News" *MSP* 9/30/99 p383; Schulze, 1977:1900-10; "The Silvery San Juan Has Enjoyed a Year of Unparalleled Prosperity in all Lines of Industry".

250 *Report of the Director of the Mint* 1899:94; "The Silvery San Juan Has Enjoyed a Year of Unparalleled Prosperity in all Lines of Industry".

251 *Report of the Director of the Mint* 1899:94.

252 Twitty, 2002:140-142, 144.

253 *Colorado Mining Directory*, 1898; "Mining News" *EMJ* 4/3/97 p336; "Mining News" *EMJ* 5/29/97 p549; Ransome, 1901:149; *Silverton Standard* 10/2/97.

254 "Mining News" *EMJ* 8/20/98 p226; "Obituary" *Mining Reporter* 2/18/04 p173; *Silverton Standard* 12/3/98.

255 Twitty, 2002:126-128.

256 *Silverton Standard* 2/17/94; *Silverton Standard* 12/22/94; *Silverton Standard* 4/13/95.

257 *Silverton Standard* 11/9/95; Twitty, 2002:242, 248-250.

258 *Colorado Mining Directory*, 1898:295; "Mining News" *EMJ* 4/17/97 p384; "Mining News" *EMJ* 8/17/97 p384; Twitty, 2002:250.

259 *Colorado Mining Directory*, 1896; "Mining News" *EMJ* 12/19/96 p589; Prosser, 1914; Ransome, 1901:163.

260 "Mining News" *MSP* 12/12/96 p487; *Silverton Standard* 5/23/96.

261 Emmons & Larsen, 1923:142; Huston, 2004:28; Mumey, 1947:37.

262 Brown, 1979:101, 114; "Editorial Correspondence" EMJ 4/20/12 p807.

263 *Colorado Mining Directory*, 1898; "Mining News" *MSP* 12/12/96 p487; "Mining News" *EMJ* 5/29/97 p549; "Mining News" *EMJ* 8/28/97 p255.

264 Ransome, 1901:23; Smith, 1982:101; Smith, 1992:77.

265 Henn, 1999:135; Sloan and Skowonski, 1975:127, 150.

266 Henn, 1999:134; Kaplan, 1975:168; Sloan and Skowonski, 1975:34, 127, 129; Tucker, 2003:91, 104.

267 Henderson, 1926:216.

268 Schulze, 1977:1920-13; Sloan & Skowronski, 1975:321.

269 Henderson, 1926:216.

270 Henderson, 1926:49; MSS 640 Colorado Bureau of Mines V.27 p79; "Obituary" EMJ 5/5/06 p865; Ransome, 1901:23; *Silverton Standard* 1/8/10.

271 *Silverton Standard* 1/11/02.

272 "Mining News" *EMJ* 4/30/98 p531; "Mining News" *EMJ* 8/20/98 p225; Prosser, 1914; Ransome, 1901:156; "The Silvery San Juan Has Enjoyed a Year of Unparalleled Prosperity in all Lines of Industry"; *Silverton Standard* 1/28/98; Twitty, 2002:155.

273 "Mining News" *EMJ* 8/20/98 p225; "Mining News" *EMJ* 8/27/98 p256; "The Silvery San Juan Has Enjoyed a Year of Unparalleled Prosperity in all Lines of Industry".

274 "Mining News" *EMJ* 2/19/98 p231; "Mining News" *EMJ* 8/20/98 p226; Ransome, 1901:156.

275 Lakes, 1903; Ransome, 1901:156.

276 "Mining News" *EMJ* 1/28/99 p 128.

277 Lakes, 1903; Ransome, 1901:156.

278 Colorado Colorado Bureau of Mines, *Manuscripts* MSS 640 V.27:19 1901; "Mining News" *EMJ* 12/1/1900 p648; "Mining News" *EMJ* 5/11/01 p600; *Mining News Mining Reporter* 12/4/00 p361; Ransome, 1901:156.

279 "Mining News" *EMJ* 5/11/01 p600; Sanborn, 1902; "Silver Lake Mill" *Mining Reporter* 9/25/02 p252.

280 Lakes, 1903; "Mining News" *EMJ* 8/4/1900 p137; Sanborn, 1902; *Silverton Standard* 3/30/01; Twitty, 155; Wyman, 1993:2.

281 "Mining News" *EMJ* 2/19/98 p231 ; "Mining News" *EMJ* 3/11/98 p301; "Mining News" *MSP* 5/14/98 p519; Dollar conversion derived from consumer price index calculator on eh.net.

282 *Colorado Mining Directory*, 1898;

283 Iowa Gold Mining and Milling Company *Tiger Mine Workings* 1903; "Mining News" *MSP* 5/14/98 p519.

284 *Colorado Mining Directory*, 1898; Twitty, 2002:220.

285 "Mining News" *EMJ* 8/27/98 p256; "Mining News" *MSP* 5/14/98 p519; Ransome, 1901:160.

286 "Mining News" *EMJ* 7/14/00 p48; *Mining News Mining Reporter* 1/25/00 p52; *Silverton Standard* 1/26/00.

287 *Denver Times* 12/4/00 p11; "Mining News" *EMJ* 2/17/1900 p208; "Mining News" *EMJ* 12/22/00 p788; *Mining News Mining Reporter* 12/4/00 p360; *Mining News Mining Reporter* 12/31/00 p6; *Silverton Standard* 5/26/00.

288 Lakes, 1903; "Mining News" *EMJ* 12/8/00 p677; Twitty, 2002:147-150.

289 Twitty, 2002:150.

290 Ransome, 1901:160; Twitty, 2002:229.

291 *Colorado Mining Directory*, 1898:295-296 ; "Mining News" *EMJ* 1/27/1900 p118; "Mining News" *EMJ* 9/29/1900 p377; Ransome, 1901:167.

292 "Mining News" *EMJ* 7/16/98 p76; "Mining News" *EMJ* 3/18/99 p328; "Mining News" *EMJ* 11/17/1900 p588; "Mining News" *MSP* 1/21/99 p68.

293 "Mining News" *EMJ* 2/25/99 p243; "Mining News" *EMJ* 10/21/99 p496; "Mining News" *EMJ* 7/14/1900 p48; "Mining News" *EMJ* 10/27/1900 p497; *Silverton Standard* 10/8/98; *Silverton Standard* 4/15/99.

294 "Mining News" *EMJ* 7/3/97 p16.

295 *Silverton Standard* 10/8/98.

296 Fell, 1979:223, Ransome, 1901:23; Smith, 1982:101; Smith, 1992:78.

297 Fell, 1979:227; Smith, 1992:78-79.

298 *Denver Times* 6/7/99 p2; Fell, 1979:230; Smith, 1982:128.

FOOTNOTES

299 "Mining News" *EMJ* 7/14/00 p48; "Mining News" *EMJ* 5/15/09 p1019; "Mining News" *EMJ* 1/26/01p128; "Mining News" *MSP* 5/22/09 p708; *Silverton Standard* 1/8/10; Sloan and Skowonski, 1975:121, 142.

300 "Mining News" *MSP* 9/30/99 p383; Schulze, 1977:1900-10.

301 *Denver Times* 12/31/98; *Denver Times* 12/13/99 p4; *Denver Times* 3/16/00 p8; *Denver Times* 11/19/00 p11; *Denver Times* 12/30/00; *Denver Times* 12/29/01 p6; *Denver Times* 2/23/02 p14.

302 Armitage and Jameson, 1987:150, 181; Conlin, 1984:158; Myres, 1999:243; Reyher, 2000:51; Schulze, 1977:1900-14; Zanjani, 1997:29, 72, 108, 264, 306.

303 Armitage and Jameson, 1987:172; Myres, 1999:149, 159, 242, 244-245.

304 Schulze, 1977:1900-14; Twitty, 2002:454.

305 ""Mining News" " EMJ 8/23/1902 p257.

306 *Silverton Standard* 5/21/98.

307 *Silverton Standard* 10/31/01; *Silverton Standard* 12/13/02.

308 *Silverton Standard* 7/13/07.

309 *Silverton Standard* 11/27/97.

310 *Silverton Standard* 3/20/09; *Silverton Standard* 7/10/09; *Silverton Standard* 8/25/17.

311 *Silverton Standard* 2/21/91; *Silverton Standard* 9/28/18; *Silverton Standard* 4/7/06.

312 *Silverton Standard* 2/17/00; *Silverton Standard* 12/24/04.

313 *Silverton Standard* 2/27/97; *Silverton Standard* 1/29/98.

314 Twitty, 2002:461.

315 Twitty, 2002:455.

316 Colorado Colorado Bureau of Mines *Manuscripts* MSS 640 V.27:16, 18, 27, 59 1901; "Mining News" *EMJ* 7/20/01 p77; *Mining News Mining Reporter* 1/9/02 p30; *Mining News Mining Reporter* 1/30/02 p146; Dollar conversion derived from consumer price index calculator on eh.net.

317 *Silverton Standard* 7/18/03; Twitty, 2002:242.

318 Colorado Colorado Bureau of Mines *Manuscripts* MSS 640 V.27:59 1901; *Mining News Mining Reporter* 11/7/01 p369; "North Star Group" *Mining Reporter* 10/2/02 p270; Prosser, 1914; Twitty, 2006:9.

319 Colorado Colorado Bureau of Mines *Manuscripts* MSS 640 V.27:58, 59 1901; "Mining News" *EMJ* 1/25/02 p149; *Mining News Mining Reporter* 7/14/01 p391; *Mining News Mining Reporter* 11/7/01 p369; *Mining News Mining Reporter* 1/30/02p147; "North Star Group" *Mining Reporter* 10/2/02 p270.

320 Colorado Mining Engineers' Reports: Shenandoah-Dives Group; Prosser, 1914; *Silverton Standard* 1/2/04.

321 *Mining News Mining Reporter* 12/3/03 p548; *Mining News Mining Reporter* 5/12/04 p489; *Silverton Standard* 8/22/03.

322 Colorado Colorado Bureau of Mines *Manuscripts* MSS 640 V.27:72 1901; *Silverton Standard* 7/18/03; Twitty, 2002:337, 240.

323 "Mining News" *EMJ* 5/23/03 p797; *Mining News Mining Reporter* 12/3/03 p548; *Mining News Mining Reporter* 10/27/04 p446; "Mining News" *MSP* 10/21/05 p282; *Silverton Standard* 11/11/05; *Silverton Standard* 12/9/05.

324 Collins, 1907; "Mining News" *MSP* 3/24/06 p209; *Silverton Standard* 9/18/09; Sloan and Skowonski, 1975:219; Wolle, 1991:426.

325 "Mining News" *EMJ* 2/23/01 p253; *Mining News Mining Reporter* 7/11/01 p29; *Silverton Standard* 10/26/01, 1/4/02.

326 Colorado Bureau of Mines *Manuscripts* MSS 640 V.27:6, 34; "Mining News" *EMJ* 11/16/01 p645; *Mining News Mining Reporter* 7/11/01 p29; *Silverton Standard* 10/26/01, 1/4/02.

327 "Mining News" *EMJ* 3/19/02 p563; "Mining News" *EMJ* 4/19/02 p563; "Mining News" *EMJ* 12/13/02 p795; *Mining News Mining Reporter* 2/12/03 p159; *Silverton Standard* 2/22/02.

328 *Mineral Resources*, 1906:232; "Mining News" *MSP* 8/27/04 p145; "Mining News" *MSP* 7/15/05 p49; "Mining News" *MSP* 1/13/06 p30; *Silverton Standard* 1/30/04; *Silverton Standard* 8/27/04, 10/8/04; Sloan and Skowonski, 1975:150.

329 Colorado Mining Engineers' Reports: Shenandoah-Dives Group; *Mining News Mining Reporter* 11/20/02.

330 "Mining News" *EMJ* 12/13/02 p795.

331 Twitty, 2006:10.

332 Twitty, 2002:233, 239.

333 Colorado Bureau of Mines *Manuscripts* MSS 640, V.27 p20; *Denver Times* 5/2/01 p4; *Denver Times* 12/29/01 p6; Henderson, 1926:13; "Mining News" *EMJ* 5/11/01 p600; "Mining News" *EMJ* 8/27 01 p539; *Mining News Mining Reporter* 1/9/02 p30; Prosser, 1914; *Silverton Standard* 6/7/02; Wolle, 1991:428; Dollar conversion derived from consumer price index calculator on eh.net.

334 "Mining News" *EMJ* 10/11/02 p494; *Mining News Mining Reporter* 9/25/02 p258; *Mining News Mining Reporter* 10/30/02 p363.

335 Wolle, 1991:428.

336 *Denver Times* 11/23/01 p9; "Mining News" *EMJ* 3/14/03 p423; "Mining News" *EMJ* 6/20/03 p945; *Mining News Mining Reporter* 5/1/02 p437; *Mining News Mining Reporter* 6/11/03 p549; Prosser, 1914.

337 "Mining News" *EMJ* 12/13/02 p795; *Mining News Mining Reporter* 11/20/02 p428; Twitty, 2002:49.

338 Colorado Bureau of Mines *Manuscripts* MSS 640 V.27:98 1902; "Mining News" *EMJ* 5/2/03 p684; Twitty, 2002:47.

339 "Mining News" *EMJ* 5/2/03 p684; "Mining News" *EMJ* 8/15/03 p251; *Silverton Standard* 7/18/03.

340 *Mining News Mining Reporter* 10/15/03 p366; "Obituary" *Mining Reporter* 2/18/04 p173; *Silverton Standard* 2/14/04.

341 "Mining News" *MSP* 2/4/05 p77; *Silverton Standard* 10/24/04; *Silverton Standard* 12/17/04.

342 "Mining News" *MSP* 5/6/05 p291; "Mining News" *MSP* 1/13/06 p30; *Silverton Standard* 7/21/06.

343 *Mineral Resources*, 1906:232; "Mining News" *MSP* 5/5/06 p301.

344 "Obituary" EMJ 5/5/06 p865; "Obituary" *MSP* 4/28/06 p285; Noel and Norgren, 1987:56.

345 *Silverton Standard* 1/18/02; *Silverton Standard* 2/22/02.

346 Colorado Mine Inspectors' Reports: Iowa Mine; "Mining News" *EMJ* 8/15/03 p251; *Mining News Mining Reporter* 10/29/03 p419; *Silverton Standard* 1/18/02; *Silverton Standard* 2/22/02.

FOOTNOTES

347 "Mining News" *MSP* 8/12/05 p116; "Obituary" *Mining Reporter* 1/13/03 p61; Sloan and Skowonski, 1975:163.

348 Colorado Bureau of Mines *Manuscripts* MSS 640 V.27:98 1902; "Mining News" *EMJ* 2/8/02 p223; "Mining News" *EMJ* 7/19/02 p93; *Mining News Mining Reporter* 3/12/03 p249; *Silverton Standard* 1/25/02.

349 Colorado Bureau of Mines *Manuscripts* MSS 640 V.27:11 1901; "Mining News" *EMJ* 9/6/02 p321; *Mining News Mining Reporter* 11/5/03 p445.

350 Colorado Bureau of Mines *Manuscripts* MSS 640 V.27:43 1901; Colorado Bureau of Mines *Manuscripts* MSS 640 V.27:83 1902; "Mining News" *MSP* 1/21/05 p45; "Mining News" *MSP* 11/18/05 p350; *Silverton Standard* 8/17/01; *Silverton Standard* 8/26/05; Twitty, 2002:255.

351 "Mining News" *EMJ* 6/27/03p982; *Silverton Standard* 1/3/03; *Silverton Standard* 5/16/03; Sloan and Skowonski, 1975:147.

352 "Obituary" *Mining Reporter* 6/2/04 p563.

353 Horn, 2007b.

354 Horn, 2007b; "Mining News" *MSP* 8/12/05 p114; *Silverton Standard* 8/26/05; *Silverton Standard* 11/25/05;

355 *Silverton Standard* 7/1/05; *Silverton Standard* 9/22/06; Sloan and Skowonski, 1975:222; "Special Correspondence" EMJ 1/20/06 p151.

356 Collins, 1909; Collins, 1910; Cross, Howe, 1905:26; Henderson, 1926:216; *Mineral Resources*, 1908:395; Saxon, 1959:7, 8, 14, 16.

357 Brown, 1984:71; Kinney, 1932; "Mines of Cement Creek"; Sloan and Skowronski, 1975:49.

358 "Special Correspondence from Mining Centers" EMJ 7/20/07 p133; "Special Correspondence from Mining Centers" EMJ 7/27/07 p180.

359 Collins, 1908; *Mineral Resources*, 1906:232; *Mineral Resources*, 1908:396; *Mineral Resources*, 1910:432; "Mining News" *MSP* 3/9/07 p293; *Silverton Standard* 7/21/06; *Silverton Standard* 8/4/06; *Silverton Standard* 5/11/07; "Special Correspondence" *MSP* .5/19/06 p331.

360 Collins, 1908; *Mineral Resources*, 1907:271; *Mineral Resources*, 1908:396; "Mining News" *MSP* 1/30/08 p172; Prosser, 1914.

361 "Mining News" *EMJ* 3/20/09 p625; "Mining News" *MSP* 2/5/10 p239; *Silverton Standard* 2/13/09; Sloan and Skowronski, 1975:257.

362 "Editorial Correspondence: Denver" EMJ 6/4/10 p1191; *Mineral Resources*, 1910:432; "Mining News" *EMJ* 10/16/09 p799; "Mining News" *EMJ* 10/30/09 p893; Prosser, 1911; Dollar conversion derived from consumer price index calculator on eh.net.

363 "Mining News" *EMJ* 4/4/11 p487.

364 Bauer, et al, 1990:13; *Mineral Resources*, 1912:694; "Mining News" *MSP* 7/8/11 p59; "Silverton, Colorado" *MSP* 1/20/12 p150; *Silverton Standard* 7/15/11.

365 "Mining News" *MSP* 7/27/12 p126.

366 "Mining News" *EMJ* 12/7/12 p1098; "Mining News" *MSP* 7/20/12 p96.

367 *Silverton Standard* 8/10/12.

368 *Mineral Resources*, 1908:396; "Mining News" *MSP* 8/2/08; Sloan and Skowonski, 1975:285; Tucker, 2003:114; Weed, 1925:730.

369 Sloan and Skowronski, 1975:285; *Silverton Standard* 4/29/99.

370 Colorado Mine Inspectors' Reports: Iowa; "Mining News" *EMJ* 10/30/09 p893.

371 Twitty, 2002:194, 200.

372 "Editorial Correspondence: Denver" EMJ 7/30/10 p230; "Mining News" *MSP* 7/23/10 p130; Sloan and Skowronski, 1975; Dollar conversion derived from consumer price index calculator on eh.net.

373 "Mining News" *MSP* 1/21/11 p153; "Mining News" *EMJ* 4/4/11 p487; "Silverton, Colorado" *MSP* 5/13/11 p672; *Silverton Standard* 1/20/12.

374 "Mining News" *EMJ* 12/20/13 p1192.

375 "Mining News" *EMJ* 5/23/08 p1073; "Mining News" *EMJ* 8/29/08 p441; "Mining News" *MSP* 7/10/09 p43; "Mining News" *MSP* 12/12/08 p796.

376 *Mineral Resources*, 1911:558; *Mineral Resources*, 1912:694; "Mining News" *EMJ* 1/1/10 p38; "Mining News" *EMJ* 10/1/10 p687; "Mining News" *MSP* 6/11/10 p879; Prosser, 1915.

377 "Mining News" *MSP* 7/12/13 p72.

378 "Mining News" *EMJ* 5/2/08 p925; "Mining News" *MSP* 2/23/07 p231; *Silverton Standard* 4/18/08.

379 Schulze, 1977:1910-18; Sloan and Skowonski, 1975:134.

380 "Mining News" *EMJ* 5/16/08 p1025; "Mining News" *MSP* 5/2/08 p580; "Mining News" *MSP* 7/4/08 p6; *Silverton Standard* 4/18/08.

381 "Mining News" *EMJ* 4/18/08 p832.

382 "Mining News" *EMJ* 5/15/09 p1019; "Mining News" *MSP* 5/22/09 p708.

383 *Silverton Standard* 9/9/05; *Silverton Standard* 5/26/06; *Silverton Standard* 12/29/06; *Silverton Standard* 2/23/07; Sloan and Skowonski, 1975:223.

384 "Mining News" *EMJ* 5/15/09 p1019; "Mining News" *MSP* 5/22/09 p708.

385 Henderson, 1926:216; King, 1977:183; Saxon, 1959:7-17.

386 *Mineral Resources*, 1916:374; "Mining News" *EMJ* 8/19/16 p365; "Mining News" *EMJ* 10/27/17 p777.

387 Colorado Mine Inspectors' Reports: Mayflower; "Mining News" *EMJ* 12/20/13 p1192.

388 "Mining News" *EMJ* 4/18/14 p833; "Mining News" *EMJ* 6/17/15 p123; "Mining News" *EMJ* 10/2/15 p577; *Silverton Standard* 7/18/14; *Silverton Standard* 7/17/15.

389 "Mining News" *EMJ* 7/17/15 p123; "Mining News" *EMJ* 9/18/15 p497; Whitaker, 1926.

390 Colorado Mine Inspectors' Reports: Shenandoah-Dives , Trilby; "Mining News" *EMJ* 1/20/17 p167; "Mining News" *EMJ* 9/15/17 p499; *Silverton Standard* 3/31/17.

391 Baker, 1927, V.5:153; *Silverton Standard* 4/17/09; *Silverton Standard* 7/3/09; *Silverton Standard* 9/24/10; Sloan and Skowonski, 1975:51, 242, 333; Tucker, 2003:115.

392 Bauer, et al, 1990:13; Colorado Mine Inspectors' Reports: Silver Lake; *Mineral Resources*, 1916:374; "Mining News" *MSP* 10/18/13 p628; Prosser, 1914.

393 "Mining News" *EMJ* 10/24/14 p763; "Mining News" *EMJ* 7/21/17 p149; *Silverton Standard* 10/10/14; Weed, 1916:631.

394 Colorado Mine Inspectors' Reports: Mayflower; "Mining News" *EMJ* 8/5/16 p280; "Mining News" *EMJ* 11/4/16 p845; *Silverton Standard* 7/28/17; Tucker, 2003:117.

395 Colorado Mine Inspectors' Reports: Silver Lake; *Silverton Standard* 1/2/15.

396 Colorado Mine Inspectors' Reports: Iowa ; "Mining News" *EMJ* 10/24/14 p763; *Silverton Standard* 10/10/14.

FOOTNOTES

397 "Mining News" *EMJ* 2/28/14 p495; "Mining News" *EMJ* 1/16/15 p171; *Silverton Standard* 12/12/14; *Silverton Standard* 6/3/16.

398 "Editorial Correspondence" EMJ 10/17/14 p718; "Mining News" *EMJ* 9/4/15 p412; "Mining News" *EMJ* 5/27/16 p962; "Mining News" *EMJ* 8/19/16 p365; "Mining News" *EMJ* 12/16/16 p1078.

399 Colorado Mine Inspectors' Reports: Highland Mary.

400 Colorado Mine Inspectors' Reports: Highland Mary; "Mining News" *EMJ* 8/9/16 p365; Prosser, 1915.

401 Colorado Mine Inspectors' Reports: Highland Mary; "Mining News" *EMJ* 10/7/16 p688; "Mining News" *EMJ* 11/4/16 p845; "Mining News" *EMJ* 12/16/16 p1078; "Mining News" *EMJ* 12/23/16 p1117.

402 Colorado Mine Inspectors' Reports: Highland Mary; "Mining News" *EMJ* 9/29/17 p579; "Mining News" *MSP* 3/17/17 p389.

403 Colorado Mine Inspectors' Reports: Misc. G; Twitty, 2002:98.

404 Colorado Mine Inspectors' Reports: Aspen; *Mineral Resources*, 1916:374; *Mineral Resources*, 1917:840; "Mining News" *EMJ* 10/6/17 p622; Weed, 1918:697.

405 *Silverton Standard* 10/17/04.

406 Colorado Mine Inspectors' Reports: Big Giant; "Mining News" *EMJ* 11/28/14 p980; "Mining News" *MSP* 4/3/15 p534; *Silverton Standard* 10/17/04; *Silverton Standard* 1/2/15, 11/13/15.

407 Colorado Mine Inspectors' Reports: Big Giant; "Mining News" *EMJ* 11/4/16 p845; "Mining News" *EMJ* 4/7/17 p647.

408 "Mining News" *EMJ* 10/21/16 p769; Twitty, 2006:16.

409 *Mineral Resources*, 1917:840; "Mining News" *EMJ* 10/13/17 p663; "Mining News" *EMJ* 10/27/17 p777.

410 Colorado Mine Inspectors' Reports: Lackawanna; Horn, 2004; Weed, 1918:700.

411 "Mining News" *EMJ* 7/10/17 p37; *Who's Who*, 1938:1033.

412 Colorado Mine Inspectors' Reports: Lackawanna; "Mining News" *EMJ* 6/2/17 p1001; Weed, 1918:700.

413 "Mining News" *EMJ* 4/13/18 p703;"Mining News"*MSP* 12/8/17 p841; "Mining News" *MSP* 5/25/18 p733; *Silverton Standard* 10/27/17; *Silverton Standard* 11/3/17; *Silverton Standard* 11/10/17;

414 Niebur, 1982:12-23, 30; Pritchard, 1996:37.

415 Niebur, 1982:73-75; Spence, 1993:369.

416 Niebur, 1982:82, 84-88, 132-134.

417 "Mining News" *EMJ* 9/6/13 p475; "Mining News"*MSP* 10/12/01 p157.

418 "Mining News" *EMJ* 11/22/13; Niebur, 1982:144; Tucker, 2003:116-117.

419 "Editorial Correspondence" EMJ 4/4/14 p729; Niebur, 1982:162; Prosser, 1914; *Silverton Standard* 8/28/15; Tucker, 2003:117.

420 "Mining News" *EMJ* 5/16/14 p1027; Niebur, 1982:159; Prosser, 1914; *Silverton Standard* 8/22/14.

421 Niebur, 1982:164; Prosser, 1914; Dollar conversion derived from consumer price index calculator on eh.net.

422 *Mineral Resources*, 1915:468; "Mining News" *MSP* 5/22/15 p813; "Mining News" *EMJ* 5/29/15 p967; "Mining News" *EMJ* 8/14/15 p123; Niebur, 1982:164; *Silverton Standard* 8/28/15.

423 *Mineral Resources*, 1917:840; "Mining News" *EMJ* 10/7/16 p688; "Mining News" *EMJ* 10/6/17 p622; "Mining News" *EMJ* 7/27/18 p195; Niebur, 1982:166.

424 *Mineral Resources,* 1914:299; "Mining News" *MSP* 5/23/14 p867; *Silverton Standard* 10/10/140.

425 "Editorial Correspondence" EMJ 5/15/15 p879; "Mining News" *EMJ* 5/29/15 p967; "Mining News" *EMJ* 6/12/15 p1056; "Mining News" *EMJ* 6/17/15 p123; "Mining News" *EMJ* 9/30/16 p607; "Mining News" *MSP* 5/15/15 p775.

426 "Events and Economics of the War" EMJ 5/18/18 p926; "Industrial News from Washington" EMJ 4/27/18 p804; Saxon, 1959:8.

427 Collins,1919.

428 "Editorial Correspondence" EMJ 6/29/18 p1191; Sloan and Skowonski, 1975:319.

429

430 "Mining News" *EMJ* 11/23/18 p932.

431 *Denver Times* 10/23/18 p4; *Denver Times* 12/6/18 p17; Smith, 1992:103; Wyman, 1993:54.

432 Henderson, 1926:216; Saxon, 1959:8.

433 Colorado Mine Inspectors' Reports: Iowa; "Mining News" *EMJ* 11/23/18 p932; *Silverton Standard* 7/20/18; *Silverton Standard* 11/2/18; Weed, 1922:635, 676.

434 Colorado Mine Inspectors' Reports: Mayflower; "Mining News" *EMJ* 7/27/18 p195; *Silverton Standard* 8/16/19.

435 Colorado Mine Inspectors' Reports: Highland Mary; *Mineral Resources,* 1918:861; "Mining News" *EMJ* 7/27/18 p195; Weed, 1925:724.

436 Sloan & Skowronski, 1975:285; Tucker, 2003:118-119.

437 "Mining News" *EMJ* 1/19/18 p176.

438 "Mining News" *EMJ* 2/9/18 p307; "Mining News" *EMJ* 6/15/18 p1109; "Mining News" *EMJ* 4/12/19 p678; "Mining News" *MSP* 7/20/18 p96; "Mining News" *MSP* 5/3/19 p614; "New Mining & Metallurgical Construction in 1919" EMJ 1/17/20 p151; *Silverton Standard* 4/27/18; *Silverton Standard* 1/18/19; Weed, 1920:523; Weed, 1922:586.

439 *Silverton Standard* 10/22/21.

440 Colorado Mine Inspectors' Reports: Shenandoah-Dives; *Mineral Resources,* 1920:588; *Mineral Resources,* 1921:503; "Mining News" *MSP* 2/24/20 p135; *Silverton Standard* 12/28/18; Weed, 1922:586.

441 Colorado Mine Inspectors' Reports: Black Prince.

442 Twitty, 2002:234.

443 Colorado Mine Inspectors' Reports: Black Prince; Twitty, 2002:238.

444 *Silverton Standard* 1/1/21.

445 Colorado Mine Inspectors' Reports: Black Prince.

446 "Mining News" *MSP* 2/2/18 p175.

447 Colorado Mine Inspectors' Reports: Mermac.

448 Colorado Mine Inspectors' Reports: Mermac; Twitty, 2002:260.

449 Colorado Mine Inspectors' Reports: Mermac; *Mineral Resources,* 1920:588; *Mineral Resources,* 1921:503.

450 Colorado Mine Inspectors' Reports: Mermac.

451 Henderson, 1926:216; King, 1977:183; Saxon, 1959:7-17.

452 Schulze, 1977:1920-13; Sloan & Skowronski, 1975:321.

453 *Mineral Resources,* 1922, V.1:527.

454 "End of Pittman Silver Purchases Cut Profits Sharply" EMJ 12/1/23 p960; "News from Washington" EMJ 7/28/23 p165.

FOOTNOTES

455 Henn, 1999:50-52.

456 Colorado Mine Inspectors' Reports: Aspen, Iowa ; *Mineral Resources*, 1923:637; *Mineral Resources*, 1924:566; *Mineral Resources*, 1926:761; *Mineral Resources*, 1927:559; *Mineral Resources*, 1928:856.

457 Sloan and Skowonski, 1975:320; *Who's Who*, 1938:1032.

458 Colorado Mine Inspectors' Reports: Highland Mary; *Mineral Resources*, 1923:637; *Mineral Resources*, 1924:566; *Mineral Resources*, 1926:761; *Mines Register*, 1937:409.

459 Colorado Mine Inspectors' Reports: Lackawanna; Horn, 2004; *Silverton Standard* 10/2/26; Twitty, 2002:42, 43.

460 Colorado Mine Inspectors' Reports: Lackawanna; Horn, 2004; *Mineral Resources*, 1928:856.

461 Horn, 2004.

462 *Mineral Resources*, 1923:637; Twitty, 2002:361.

463 Twitty, 2002:262.

464 Colorado Mine Inspectors' Reports: Mermac; *Mineral Resources*, 1924:566.

465 Colorado Mine Inspectors' Reports: Mermac Mine; *Mines Register*, 1937:810; *Mineral Resources*, 1927:559.

466 Stone, 1918, V.2:91; Norman, 1932:47.

467 Chase, 1925.

468 Chase, 1925; "Mining News" *EMJ* 10/30/20 p885; Weed, 1918:711.

469 Chase, 1925; Colorado Mine Inspectors' Reports: Mayflower; Whitaker, 1926; Dollar conversion derived from consumer price index calculator on eh.net..

470 Colorado Mine Inspectors' Reports: Mayflower; *Mineral Resources*, 1927:559.

471 Colorado Mine Inspectors' Reports: Iowa, Mayflower; *Mineral Resources*, 1928:855.

472 Colorado Mine Inspectors' Reports: Iowa, Mayflower; *Mineral Resources*, 1928:855.

473 Colorado Mine Inspectors' Reports: Iowa.

474 *Minerals Yearbook*, 1937:115; Saxon, 1959:7-9, 14-17.

475 Sloan and Skowonski, 1975:335; Smith, 1992:114.

476 Colorado Mine Inspectors' Reports: Highland Mary; *Mineral Resources*, 1929:954.

477 Colorado Mine Inspectors' Reports: Iowa, Mermac; *Mineral Resources*, 1929:855; *Mineral Resources*, 1930:1072

478 Bunyak, 1998:59, 63; Colorado Mine Inspectors' Reports: Mayflower; *Mineral Resources*, 1929:954; *Mineral Resources*, 1930:1072

479 Bunyak, 1998:60-62; Colorado Mine Inspectors' Reports: Mayflower; Twitty, 2002:109.

480 Bunyak, 1998:59; Colorado Mine Inspectors' Reports: Mayflower; *Mineral Resources*, 1930:1072; Wyman, 1993:74.

481 Colorado Mine Inspectors' Reports: Mayflower; *Mineral Resources*, 1929:954; *Mineral Resources*, 1930:1072.

482 Wyman, 1993:71.

483 McElvaine, 1993:164; Saxon, 1959:7, 8, 12, 14, 16.

484 *Minerals Yearbook*, 1935:229; *Minerals Yearbook*, 1936:268.

485 Colorado Mine Inspectors' Reports: Maybell; Twitty, 2002:348.

486 Colorado Mine Inspectors' Reports: Maybell; Twitty, 2002:348.

487 Colorado Mine Inspectors' Reports: Maybell; *Mines Register*, 1937:830.

488 Spence, 1993:246.

489 Colburn, 1936; Colorado Mine Inspectors' Reports: Highland Mary; *Mines Register*, 1937:409.

490 Colorado Mine Inspectors' Reports: Highland Mary.

491 Colorado Mine Inspectors' Reports: Highland Mary; *Minerals Yearbook*, 1941:311; Twitty, 2002:290.

492 Colorado Mine Inspectors' Reports: File: Mayflower.

493 *Durango Herald Democrat* 6/29/39; *Minerals Yearbook*, 1940:277; *Silverton Standard* 7/14/39.

494 Colorado Mine Inspectors' Reports: Silver Lake; *Minerals Yearbook*, 1942:340.

495 Sloan and Skowonski, 1975:338, 341.

496 Bauer, et al, 1990:74; Schulze, 1977:1940-15; Smith, 1992:118.

497 *Minerals Yearbook*, 1942:80; Saxon, 1959:17.

498 Saxon, 1959:9, 14, 16, 17, 37.

499 Bunyak, 1998:79; Saxon, 1959:37, 39.

500 Colorado Mine Inspectors' Reports: Highland Mary, Mermac, Shenandoah-Dives.

501 Bunyak, 1998:80; Colorado Mine Inspectors' Reports: Little Giant, Mayflower, Osceola, Titusville; *Minerals Yearbook*, 1947:1371; *Minerals Yearbook*, 1960, V.3:246.

INDEX

Gibbs, Charles W. 143
Gill & Fischer Brewery 76
Gill, Henry P. 75
Gillette, King C. 277-278
Gladstone 87, 99, 108, 254
Gold King Consolidated Mining
    Company 218, 246, 251, 254,
    280
Gold Reserve Act of 1934 329
Gold Tunnel & Railway Company
    219, 235, 236, 280, 323, 342
Goodwin, John N. 39, 89-90
Gordon, James 234
Grant, James B. 220
Gray Eagle Mine 51, 53, 55, 57, 58,
    68, 88, 115, 125, 134, 137, 282,
    308
Green Mountain claim 38, 52, 118,
    291
Green Mountain Mill 118, 237
Greene & Company 57-60, 65-68,
    87
Greene, Eberhart & Company 64
Greene, Edward 58, 64-67, 71, 86,
    88, 99
Greene, George 46-47, 64, 67, 71,
    86, 88, 99
Greene Smelter 57-59, 65-66, 71,
    85, 98, 100, 104-107
Guess, H.A. 245-246, 254-255
Guggenheims 239, 241-242, 244,
    247
Guillette, Henry 123
Guiterman, Frank 220
Gunsolus brothers 75

H is for Highland Mary

Hackett, F.B. 60
Hackett, Thomas 119
Hallett, Samuel I. 242-244, 288
Hallett table 242
Hamilton, Emery 41-42, 54-55, 59,
    73-74

Hancock claim 145
Hanson, O.C. 219
Hazelton Mountain 52-54, 67, 75,
    76, 85, 88, 106, 141, 247
Hiett, E.A. 322
Higgins, Thomas P. 44, 52-53, 67-
    68, 77, 106, 113, 119, 243
Highland Leasing Company 309
Highland Mary claim 34, 50, 52,
    72, 73
Highland Mary Gold Mining &
    Railway Company 235
Highland Mary Leasing Company
    295
Highland Mary Mill (built in 1882)
    123
Highland Mary Mill (built in 1902)
    236-237, 280-281, 309, 323, 332
Highland Mary Mine 73-75, 94,
    95-96, 123, 136, 235-237, 265,
    276, 280-281, 295, 308-309, 316,
    322, 323, 332-333, 338, 340, 341,
    342
Highland Mary Mine, avalanche 96
Highland Mary Mine site, archaeo-
    logical analysis 74
Highland Mary Mining & Milling
    Company 280, 322, 323, 332
Hine, Lemon G. 115
Hines, Rogert 243
Hinsdale County 63
Holman, J.A. 300-301
Hook, Robert 112-113
Houk, Martin 249-250, 264-265
Howard, George W. 16-17, 33-34,
    37, 38, 60-61
Howardsville 61-62, 63, 74, 75-76,
    84-86, 118, 125-128, 131, 143,
    144, 145, 184, 203, 221, 223,
    266-267, 301-302, 310-312, 314,
    335, 336
Hughes, Charles J. 166

INDEX